BRITAIN'S CENTURY

A Political and Social History 1815–1905

W.D. Rubinstein

Professor of History, University of Wales, Aberystwyth

A member of the Hodder Headline Group
LONDON · NEW YORK · SYDNEY · AUCKLAND

First published in Great Britain in 1998 by
Arnold, a member of the Hodder Headline Group
338 Euston Road, London NW1 3BH

http://www.arnoldpublishers.com

Co-published in the United States of America by
Oxford University Press Inc.
198 Madison Avenue, New York, NY 10016

The advice and information in this book are believed to be true and
accurate at the date of going to press, but neither the author nor the
publisher can accept any legal responsibility or liability for any errors or
omissions.

British Library Cataloguing in Publication Data
A catalogue record for this book is available from the British Library

Library of Congress Cataloging-in-Publication Data
Rubinstein, W.D.
   Britain's century: a political and social history, 1815–1905 /
W.D. Rubinstein.
      p.   cm.   -- (The Arnold history of Britain)
   Includes bibliographical references and index.
   ISBN 0-340-57533-6. -- ISBN 0-340-57534-4 (pbk.)
   1. Great Britain--Politics and government--19th century.   2. Great
Britain--Social conditions--19th century.   I. Title.   II. Series.
DA530.R77   1998
941.081--dc21   98-8219
                                                                          CIP

ISBN 0 340 57533 6 (hb)
ISBN 0 340 57534 4 (pb)

1 2 3 4 5 6 7 8 9 10

Production Editor: Julie Delf
Production Controller: Priya Gohil
Cover Design: T. Griffiths

Typeset in 10/12 Sabon by Photoprint, Torquay
Printed and bound in Great Britain by MPG Books Ltd., Bodmin, Cornwall

What do you think about this book? Or any other Arnold title?
Please send your comments to feedback.arnold@hodder.co.uk

Contents

Preface

The nineteenth century was Britain's century, the period when the United Kingdom more closely approached the status of world hegemonic power than before or, of course, since. Yet this position of international supremacy was accomplished in unusual ways. Except on the rarest of occasions, Britain never directly intervened militarily in European affairs. The one occasion on which it did so, the Crimean War of the 1850s, began ineptly and concluded successfully only after a hard struggle. In general, Britain did everything possible to woo its former colonies in North America, then in the process of emergence as a world super-power of unlimited potential. Britain reserved its military resources for small, remote colonial wars at which (contrary to popular belief) it was very good and very successful. The international hegemony of Great Britain came chiefly through its economic position as both the 'workshop of the world' and the 'clearing-house of the world'. Until 1870, Britain was the unchallenged industrial and manufacturing leading power of the world, while until 1914 (and possibly beyond) the City of London was the world's financial centre and arbiter. All of the world's liberal intelligentsia looked to Britain as their 'homeland of the mind', the nation whose evolution proved that modernization, freedom and tolerance, and national power were not mutually contradictory possibilities, and Britain offered refuge to those fleeing their homeland of every conceivable ideological and political position from King Charles X of France to Karl Marx. London was the world's largest, in many respects the world's greatest, city. Whatever its faults, in the nineteenth century the British Empire brought Western values and knowledge-systems, and the rule of British law, to much of the Third World, and democratic self-government to Britain's white colonies. Britain's global hegemony in the century after Waterloo gave the Western world its longest continuous era of peace, and a hundred years of progress and advance in virtually every field of knowledge.

Of course, there was another side to this coin. Britain's class system, and the near-impossibility of three-quarters of the population escaping from poverty, the exploitation of the working classes, the degradation of the cities, and the failure to grant women equal political rights, are – to us, at any rate – obvious and manifest failings. Yet on balance, and by any reasonable criteria, the century of British hegemony was a good one, a period which, post-Cold War and with international economic global-isation and development, we will be fortunate indeed if we can recreate in modern form over the decades to come. To understand this success, and why the successes so strikingly outweighed the failures, it is surely neces-sary to understand the historical evolution of Britain's central political institutions, and of the social milieu surrounding them, which is the aim of this work.

The arrangement of this textbook is perhaps somewhat unusual. The first two-thirds of the book consist of a general political history of Britain from 1815 until 1905, divided by prime ministerial government. Rather oddly, this arrangement is very uncommon and may indeed be unique among nineteenth-century British history textbooks with which I am familiar (although many textbooks of twentieth-century British history are structured in this way). Almost invariably, the former employ such broad divisions as 'The Age of Reform, 1827–35', 'The Mid-Victorian Period of Equipoise, 1851–67', and the like. There is nothing wrong with this arrangement, which obviously has heuristic value to both the author and the student. Nevertheless, I feel rather strongly that what is most required is a textbook which will set out the main British political events between 1815 and 1905 in a coherent way, informing today's students from the ground up. I currently teach at the University of Wales-Aberystwyth, a good, upper-middle ranked university and the oldest in Wales, with a copyright library, the National Library of Wales, situated a few hundred yards away. I suppose that we attract over a hundred new first-year students reading history each year. Most if not all were among the better students in their secondary schools (two-thirds of whom, I might note, come from England rather than Wales). There is no reason to suppose that they are in any way unrepresentative of any group of new first-year students reading history at almost any British university, or indeed any-where else in the English-speaking world. Now, suppose I were to give an unannounced test to one hundred of these first-year students in history, asking ten easy and straightforward questions about nineteenth-century political history along the lines of 'Who were Cobden and Bright?', 'Who were the Liberal Unionists?', 'Against whom was the Crimean War fought, and why?', I would be genuinely surprised if more than five or six students could answer all of them correctly, or, indeed, if more than say forty per cent of these students could answer *any* of them correctly. Even twenty-five or thirty years ago, when most university students attended a grammar school, and when history was defined in the old-fashioned way as meaning public events, especially governmental events, which occurred in the past, the number of first-year university students in history who would know the answers to a quiz of this kind as a matter of course would certainly have been much higher. Today, however, one would be more accurate to assume that ignorance about the basic political facts of nineteenth-century British history, rather than knowledge, is the norm among even budding historians. Primarily for this reason, I have tried to write a textbook about nineteenth-century British history which explains, in a clear and hopefully interesting manner, the basic facts of the subject, in an assimilable way. I make no apologies for writing this textbook in this fashion, or for concentrating heavily on what is now known as 'high politics' and political leaders. My guess is that those students who are likely to read or purchase this book will be more grateful for this format than for many others. One can only discuss and debate history after one knows and has internalised its basic facts; until this is done, anything further is useless. I myself (who was born and educated in the United States) recall that perhaps the two most useful books I read about British history and current events when I was an undergraduate were Ivor Bulmer-Thomas's *The Growth of the British Party System* (1967) and Anthony Sampson's *Anatomy of Britain Today* (1965), both of which are especially notable for stating the facts clearly and lucidly, and in the case of Sampson's book, explaining to this outsider the precise nature of the British Cabinet and its main ministries and of the House of Lords (a great mystery to most non-British students). I am rather confident that most sixth formers and first and second-year undergraduates, as well as foreign students studying nineteenth-century Britain for the first time, will find the approach taken here more useful than those found elsewhere, especially in works expressed in the clap-trap of post-modernism, or in more valuable and straightforward political histories which are written in an arch and allusive style, assuming that the student will understand the subtle nuances of nineteenth-century British politics, whereas the need of the student is for something much more basic.

While the chapters of this book on political history are fairly straightforward, the portion on social history is almost the precise opposite: openended as to broad and particular subjects, and with a literature now so vast, and written from so many different perspectives, as to be virtually impossible to master or even to keep up with. It is difficult to believe that there is any single scholar who can accurately claim to have a comprehensive knowledge (to take two examples which immediately occur) of *both* nineteenth-century women's history and nineteenth-century business history. (And many scholars who feel an affinity with one of these are likely to be unsympathetic to the subject-matter and ideological underpinnings of the other.) Given that few if any scholars can possibly present the whole range of topics now firmly in place as 'British social history' of the nineteenth century, let alone in a textbook of this type, I have treated the four topics which strike me as most significant and useful to the student:

population and demographic history; the role of religion in nineteenth-century British society; social class; and gender. Each of these chapters attempts to present a broad overview of their subject, incorporating an up-to-date perspective, although surely no two historians can fully agree on where the boundaries now lie. The viewpoint and methodology of these chapters are broadly similar to those found in the historical chapters. Bifurcating the two components of this work, the political and the social, so sharply may strike some as odd, but I am convinced that it is the most effective way to teach students whose knowledge of either is limited, and who prefer to be taught in the least confusing way.

I am happy to acknowledge the help and support of Deakin University in Victoria, Australia, and of the University of Wales-Aberystwyth, whose libraries and other facilities allowed me to complete this work, and of my typist, Margaret Moulton, for her unfailing efforts. I must certainly thank my wife, Dr Hilary L. Rubinstein, for her continuous support, knowledge, and skills, and Christopher Wheeler, of Arnold, for his encouragement, humour and patience.

W.D. Rubinstein

Introduction: Britain in 1815

The year 1815 saw the end of a long period of conflict. Virtually the whole of the period from 1793 until 1815 found Britain at war with France. For Britain during the eighteenth century, wars were not unusual; indeed they were normal. During the period from 1750 alone, Britain found itself at war with France between 1755 and 1763 (known as the 'Seven Years War', although it lasted nearly eight years) and with the North American colonies between 1775 and 1783, the only war which Britain has ever lost. This period comprised such celebrated events as the killings at the 'Black Hole of Calcutta' (1756) and the Battle of the Plains of Abraham in Quebec (1759), which helped to add Canada to the British Empire. As well, there were numerous smaller colonial wars, especially in India, where British power was being firmly asserted at this time. Nevertheless, nothing in Britain's recent past prepared it for the epochal wars with France which were fought between 1793 and 1815. Britain and France were continuously at war for the whole of this period, with the exception of a brief interregnum of peace between March 1802 and May 1803. Britain was thus at war with the French Revolutionary government and later with Napoleon and his empire for 21 years. Although not a 'total war' in the twentieth-century sense, as many as 500 000 Britons are believed to have served in the war at some point between 1793 and 1815, when the population of the United Kingdom (including Ireland) was only 16 million. The war with revolutionary and Napoleonic France also introduced strong ideological elements into the traditional dynastic struggle between Britain and France. Nevertheless, at base the wars remained Britain's attempt to deny France hegemony throughout Europe, and thus emphasised a long-standing element in British policy.

The French Revolutionary and Napoleonic Wars affected British politics and society in many ways; four stand out in particular. Most obviously, the French Revolution itself and the wars with France acted to stifle for a generation any realistic chances of political reform to bring about greater democracy. As soon as the French Revolutionary leaders turned to violent radicalism and terror, the British Establishment responded by turning against all political reform at home, regardless of how moderate or necessary it might seem. For 25 years the French experience became an object-lesson, endlessly reiterated throughout the British nation, of the horrors which awaited sudden, radical reform: the anarchy and mass murders of the Reign of Terror giving rise, almost by necessity, to the Napoleonic dictatorship, the two regimes united only by the propensity of each to foreign conquest and warfare. Men who had previously been moderate reformers, like Edmund Burke and William Pitt, now became profound conservatives. Indeed, conservatism as an ideology began as a response to the French Revolution, with Burke's *Reflections on the Revolution in France* (1790) normally regarded as its Bible and seminal work. At the same time, extreme radicals like Thomas Paine (1737–1809) and William Cobbett (1762–1835) were effectively ostracised from British society, both of these men leaving Britain during this period. Closely associated with the ascendancy of conservatism was the Romantic movement in literature and the arts, which appeared to ally itself with political conservatism during these years by fundamentally questioning the possibilities of progress and the deliberate construction of utopian societies, notions which animated the theorists and practitioners of the French Revolution. Owing largely to Burke and to the Romantics, societies came to be seen as 'organisations' which grew slowly and in complex ways; radicals and political theorists tampered with the complexities of society at their peril. The marginalisation of political radicalism as a result of the Napoleonic Wars meant that far-reaching measures of reform would not be seriously considered until the late 1820s when, really quite suddenly, the reform of Parliament and other measures like Catholic emancipation became central political preoccupations after the lapse of nearly 40 years.

The French wars' heightening of political conservatism and diminution of politically significant radicalism also engendered positive effects for British national unity and British patriotism. Britain was almost alone among European states in that the French wars brought about no fundamental or drastic changes in the country's formal constitution, the ending of the separate Irish Parliament being the only exception. Britain's political institutions in 1815 were, for the most part, identical to what they had been in 1785. This successful continuity in itself was often highlighted by conservatives as proof that Britain's constitution was superior to those found elsewhere. In contrast, virtually every European country had experienced profound political change as a result of the French wars, and especially because of Napoleon's conquests throughout Europe. Time-honoured institutions like the Venetian Republic and the so-called Holy Roman Empire (the very loose German Confederation) vanished and boundaries changed significantly. As a general rule, the French brought a large measure of modernity and reform in their wake, although Napoleon had a habit of placing his relatives and associates on the thrones of Europe. Napoleon's three brothers were made Kings of Naples and Spain, Holland, and Westphalia; a brother-in-law, Joachim Murat, was made King of Naples.[1] In 1815 the Congress of Vienna attempted to restore the pre-1789 order throughout continental Europe. It could indeed restore monarchs to their thrones, but could not make anyone forget what had occurred, and other waves of European revolutions followed in 1830 and 1848.

The necessity for Britain to raise what, by the standards of the day, was a mass army was also in itself a powerful force for national unity. Recruitment was made throughout Britain, and soldiers were assigned throughout the country (and world-wide). Irish and Scottish officers commanded English troops and vice versa. In 1801 the separate Irish Parliament was abolished and a legislative union between Great Britain and Ireland was established. This Act provided that Ireland was to send 100 MPs to the Westminster Parliament, as well as 20 Irish peers, elected for life from among the Irish aristocracy, to the House of Lords. Additionally, four Church of Ireland (Anglican) bishops were also given the right to sit in the Lords, and the Churches of England and Ireland were administratively united. While Irish Catholics were given some important concessions in this period, including the right to vote on the same basis as Protestants in 1793, the 1801 Act of Union cemented the rule of the Anglo-Irish ascendancy. The Napoleonic Wars also produced two of the greatest war heroes in British history, Nelson and Wellington, potent and universal symbols of British patriotism and national greatness. Lord Nelson, in particular, cut down in the very moment of his supreme triumph, became a nationally admired, indeed revered, figure, even among liberals normally cool to symbols of martial glory. During the war, George III's madness, and the rule of his eldest son as Prince Regent, made the King into a national figure who aroused considerable pity as well as some admiration owing to his high standards (high by the standards of the aristocracy) of morality and family life. In 1807, by coincidence, the last Jacobite pretender, Henry, Cardinal York (b.1725), grandson of James II, died without children. British Jacobites, a group quite possibly stronger in the eighteenth century than many would credit, now had no choice but to recognise the reigning House of Hanover as legitimate. York was the the son of James Francis Edward Stuart, the 'Old Pretender' (d.1766), who invaded Scotland in 1715–16, and the younger brother of Charles Edward Stuart, the 'Young Pretender' (d.1788), who invaded Scotland in 1745–46. He lived in Italy and was Cardinal and Archbishop of Corinth and Bishop of Tusculum. In his last years he received gifts of charity from George III and left the Jacobite Crown Jewels to George IV in his will. Thus, although many historians see

---

1 In 1810 Sweden's parliament chose one of Napoleon's French generals, Marshal Bernadotte, as Crown Prince of that country. In 1818 he ascended the Swedish throne as King Charles XIV, ruling until 1844. His descendants are still the Kings of Sweden, the only remaining Bonapartist dynasty on a European throne.

the period of the French wars as one in which radicalism grew in Britain and was firmly suppressed, it was also the case that both the substance and symbolism of the British 'Establishment' increased markedly in these years, an era in which strong dissent could readily be labelled as treasonous.

The third important effect of the period of the French wars was economic. The European continent was largely cut off from British trade. By Napoleon's Berlin Decree, promulgated in November 1806, France closed Europe to British economic penetration, inaugurating the so-called 'Continental System'. As a result, Britain attempted to increase its trade with South America and other remote areas which, in general, it did very successfully, assisted crucially by Britain's control of the seas after Trafalgar. The French wars directly stimulated demand in such areas as iron manufacturing and shipbuilding, while Britain's extension (and enhancement) of its extra-European markets allowed the classical components of the industrial revolution to continue to grow. The import of cotton (chiefly from India and Egypt), for instance, rose from 32.5 million pounds in 1789 to 62 million pounds in 1804 to 132.4 million pounds in 1810. It is, indeed, difficult to identify any significant area of British manufacturing which languished because of the French wars, and relative British prosperity during the conflict itself contributed greatly to consumer demand. The Napoleonic period was also the zenith of canal-building, providing one of the chief means of the transport of goods prior to the railway age. The effects of the end of the French wars in 1815 was paradoxical. On one hand, the stimulus given to industry by wartime demand was lost, and tens of thousands of soldiers returned to an uncertain civilian future. On the other hand, Britain had built up an enormous industrial lead during the quarter-century of European conflict, especially in mass-produced manufactured goods, and was now free to sell its products in Europe. The lead built up during these years was in fact sufficient to better any European competition for another two generations. In the 1780s it was not entirely clear that France would be overtaken by Britain as a modern industrial power. By 1815, however, France trailed behind Britain by a vast distance. For over half a century after 1815, Britain was the world's industrial superpower and hegemon, a fact which owed much, perhaps nearly all, to the experience of the Napoleonic Wars. In addition, the City of London remained as the world's most important financial entrepôt, a role it continued to hold until the First World War. As peace returned in 1815, Britain was poised for unchallenged economic supremacy.

The final area in which the wars affected Britain involved its standing as a great power. Britain had always, since the sixteenth century, been recognised as an important international force, but in the eighteenth century it was certainly not seen as a more formidable power than France, although it was generally ranked slightly ahead of Austria, Prussia and Russia, the other major European nation-states. The Napoleonic Wars marked the second serious attempt by France at achieving European hegemony, occurring a century after the efforts of Louis XIV, and came exceedingly close to complete success: Napoleon could (and should) have consolidated his astonishing conquests rather than invade Russia. There is no reason to suppose that a consolidation of French power on the Continent after 1810 could not have lasted indefinitely, perhaps permanently, with incalculable consequences for the whole future history of Europe. Instead, following Waterloo, France was no longer able to attempt to dominate the European continent. By the end of the nineteenth century France's population had declined considerably relative to the other European powers, while German military prowess became evident during the Franco-Prussian War. Britain's naval and military victories in the Napoleonic Wars marked it out, for most of the nineteenth century, as the first among equals of European powers, although a power which steadfastly declined to intervene militarily in European power politics. Britain's overriding desideratum in Europe, maintenance of the balance of power so that no continental hegemon could emerge, was a successful consequence of the Napoleonic Wars. As an outcome of the Treaty of Paris (1814) and the Congress of Vienna (1815), which concluded the Napoleonic Wars, Britain also increased its colonial holdings, extending its rule to Malta, Tobago, Mauritius, the Ionian Islands, and various other places around the globe useful for trade or as naval stations. At the Congress of Vienna Britain – rather remarkably, in view of the firmly Tory nature of its government – assumed the role of the liberal opponent of Absolutism and the champion, at least to a certain extent, of human rights and the rights of small nations. Throughout the nineteenth century it retained this reputation, and often acted in the interests of liberalism against autocracy. This greatly enhanced Britain's standing in the eyes of liberals and intellectuals throughout Europe.

PART

I

POLITICAL HISTORY

1

The Liverpool government: victory abroad, unrest at home, 1815–1822

When the Battle of Waterloo was fought and won on 18 June 1815, Great Britain was governed by a Tory Cabinet of 13. Nine members of the Cabinet sat in the House of Lords but only four in the House of Commons. Apart from a handful of extreme radicals, few thought this odd, and, indeed, as late as 1895, eight of 18 members of the Cabinet still sat in the House of Lords. At the head of the government was the Prime Minister, Robert Banks Jenkinson, second Earl of Liverpool (1770–1828). Despite his grandiose title, Lord Liverpool was only a second-generation aristocrat. His father, Charles Jenkinson (1727–1808), a Tory country gentleman, MP, and influential Cabinet minister for over 30 years, was created Baron Hawkesbury in 1786 and Earl of Liverpool a decade later. The Prime Minister's mother was the daughter of a naval captain. Rather than attending the prestigious Eton or Westminster, the Prime Minister was a student at Charterhouse, a middle-ranking London public school. On the other hand, at Oxford he became a close friend of George Canning and other men of future influence. He was also present in Paris in 1789 at the capture of the Bastille. Meanwhile, the first Earl had continued to play the game of patronage and advancement extremely well. Apart from his elevation in the peerage, he had managed to find his son a seat in Parliament at the age of only 20, had married him to the daughter of a nobleman who was simultaneously Earl of Bristol and Bishop of Derry, and had secured for him the sinecure office of Master of the Mint, which paid its holder £3000 a year essentially for doing nothing. Even by the standards of the day, the second Lord Liverpool's rise was extraordinarily rapid. He became Foreign Minister at the age of only 30, proving to be almost too ready to compromise with Napoleon. He had also served as Home Secretary and Secretary for War and the Colonies in May 1812 when Spencer Perceval, the Prime Minister, was shot and killed in the lobby of Parliament by a bankrupt, insane merchant with a long-standing grievance against the British government.[1] Liverpool had been offered the premiership before, when Pitt died in 1806, but had declined it. In 1812, however, he accepted it after a good record as Secretary for War, giving unquestioned support to Wellington in Spain. He remained Prime Minister for 15 years, retiring only through ill-health. His term of office was longer than that served by anyone since. Liverpool's Cabinets contained six other men who had held or would hold the Prime Ministership (Addington, Canning, Goderich, Wellington, Peel and Palmerston) as well as personalities as diverse as Lord Eldon and W. J. Huskisson. Liverpool also fought and won four general elections, in 1812, 1818, 1820 and 1826. Although pre-Reform general elections can hardly be compared with those contested by parties and their machines much later, this, too, remains a record. Under Lord Liverpool, Napoleon was defeated at Waterloo, the map of Europe was redrawn at Vienna, Britain passed successfully through perhaps its most troubled period of social unrest in modern times, and the first railways were built. Despite all of this, Liverpool remains virtually unknown as either a political leader or as a human personality. Disraeli, in his novel *Coningsby* (1844), referred to Liverpool as 'the Arch-Mediocrity, who presided, rather than ruled, over a Cabinet of Mediocrities'. Most radicals of the time regarded him, and his government, with detestation. Yet all of his later biographers agree on his considerable merits: tact, intelligence, fairness, freedom from bias in appointments and patronage, great practical experience of office, and an excellent judgement of the potential abilities of his ministers (Palmerston, Liverpool's Secretary at War during the entire 15-year period of his government, still held office as Prime Minister, and certainly remained the most popular politician in Britain, when he died in 1865). Liverpool's unquestioning firmness, even ruthlessness, in suppressing widespread social unrest and popular disturbances was one side of the coin; on the other side were the very considerable reforms, in such areas as crime and economic life, that he achieved in the 1820s.

Between 1812 and his suicide in 1822, Britain's Foreign Minister was Robert Stewart, Viscount Castlereagh (1769–1822; he succeeded as the second Marquess of Londonderry in 1821). Although he is known by his courtesy title of 'Lord Castlereagh', the Foreign Minister sat in the House of Commons and was Leader of the House during this period. Castlereagh had led an adventurous life, and had once fought a duel with George Canning. His greatest achievement was his success in leading the victorious coalition against Napoleon, especially in preventing the allies from dealing separately with the French ruler. Castlereagh was Britain's chief representa-

1 This was the only successful assassination of a British Prime Minister, and a contrast to the United States, where four Presidents have been assassinated. Perceval's killer, John Bellingham, (as extraordinary as this sounds), was tried and convicted *four days* after the assassination and was executed precisely one week after the killing. A surprising number of political assassins are lone-wolf malcontents with private grudges, rather than politically motivated extremists.

tive at the Congress of Vienna of 1814, and a year later secured Napoleon's banishment to St Helena. He personified the relative moderateness of Britain's foreign policy goals, preventing a harsh peace treaty with France and leading the anti-Absolutist claims of Metternich and other rulers who wished to crush revolutionary movements in Europe. At Vienna, however, Britain managed to gain numerous colonies around the world, among them Ceylon, Trinidad, Malta, the Cape of Good Hope, Mauritius, and Heligoland in the North Sea.

Castlereagh's main aim after 1815 was to preserve the balance of power. Despite Britain's strength and prestige, this was more difficult than it seemed, for Britain had no permanent forces on the Continent and could, essentially, prevent a major European power from gaining territory only by forming an alliance with another power and intervening. No British government would have agreed to do this except in the most extreme circumstances such as the rise of a Napoleon. Britain backed the notion of a 'Concert of Europe' (cooperation among the major European powers to ensure stability), and wished for regular meetings of the powers. On the other hand, the Absolutist powers, especially Austria and Russia, wanted any such alliance to suppress all revolutionary movements, which Britain consistently opposed. During this period, and for many decades afterwards, Britain was at least mildly liberal in its attitude to reformist and revolutionary movements in Europe and elsewhere which did not threaten Britain's interests. At the Congress of Aix-la-Chapelle of 1818, France (now ruled by the Bourbons) was readmitted to the 'Concert of Europe' and foreign troops were withdrawn. The proposal by Russia's Czar Alexander I that all European states permanently guarantee both the frontiers and the rule of the monarchs throughout Europe (thus committing Britain and all other powers to suppressing all European revolutions, without exception) was rejected, thanks mainly to strong pressure by Britain. The responses of the powers to revolutionary movements were put to the test in 1820, when troops revolted in Spain, forcing its King to grant a democratic constitution.[2] Revolutions then broke out in Portugal and several Italian states. Castlereagh vigorously and pointedly refused to allow Britain to intervene, although he did acquiesce in permitting Austrian troops to suppress the revolutions in Italy. Castlereagh's policies pleased nobody. Radicals and Whigs in Britain blamed him for restoring Absolutism to the Continent and for his important role, as Leader of the House of Commons, in suppressing movements for social reform and other measures. In contrast, most European rulers regarded him as little better than a Jacobin. Castlereagh began to crack under the strain, and became convinced that he was being blackmailed because of a scandal involving alleged homosexuality. In

2 These troops had been gathered at Cadiz in readiness to crush the independence movements in Spanish America, where many Latin American states, including Argentina, Chile and Mexico, had just declared independence.

August 1822 he committed suicide.[3] Castlereagh left a permanent legacy to his successor George Canning, and, indeed, to his successors throughout the nineteenth century. He was chiefly responsible for the far-sighted policy of compromise and pacific intent with the United States, following the inconclusive War of 1812 (actually fought between June 1812 and January 1815), during which British troops captured Washington DC and burned the White House, but were defeated on Lake Eire by Commander Oliver Perry and at New Orleans by Andrew Jackson.[4] In 1818 Britain and America settled most of their outstanding border disputes concerning Canada, and thereafter came into serious disagreement with each other only at infrequent intervals. Castlereagh also initiated the continuing favouring, by Britain, of the sovereignty of Turkey against encroachments by Russia and other European powers, a policy which remained one of the cornerstones of British foreign affairs throughout the nineteenth century. Perhaps more importantly still, the Liverpool government was instrumental in acquiescing in the independence of Latin America. Such a policy was strongly supported by British manufacturers and merchants, and Latin America became one of Britain's most important, and loyal, overseas markets for more than a century. Shortly after Castlereagh's death, in 1823 the United States proclaimed, with British knowledge and *de facto* support, the 'Monroe Doctrine' warning the European powers that any interference by them in Latin American affairs, especially any attempt at conquest, would lead to American retaliation. This effectively kept Latin America independent, but allowed Britain to gain a strong economic position there without alienating the United States.

It cannot be emphasised too strongly that after 1815 Britain was the most important country in the world, its leading position somewhat similar to that of the United States after 1945. Supreme on the seas, and on land the victor at Waterloo and the protector of European peace, Britain's acknowledged supremacy was itself a potent defining factor in the national consciousness of its people for another 150 years. Although Waterloo was celebrated by virtually all as a great event, one of the greatest in Britain's history, closer to the hearts of the people lay Nelson's victory at Trafalgar in 1805, and especially his death in the very hour of his supreme triumph. The potency of Waterloo and, particularly, Trafalgar as national myths and symbols cannot be overestimated and should not be underestimated by today's historians. This potency was universally shared by all British people, even those on the radical left, and the victories at Trafalgar and Waterloo defined the self-perception of the British people towards military

3 A number of other prominent English political figures of this time also committed suicide (for unrelated reasons), among them Sir Samuel Romilly (1757–1818), the law reformer and MP, and Samuel Whitbread (1758–1815), the Whig politician.

4 Britain's attack on Baltimore, about 50 miles from Washington, was also repulsed. It was during the bombardment of Baltimore that Francis Scott Key wrote the poem which was later set to music and, in 1931, became America's National Anthem, 'The Star-Spangled Banner'.

affairs for many generations. On the other hand, Britain's hegemony in foreign policy during the century after 1815 was of a peculiar and limited kind, based wholly upon the domination of the oceans of the world by the Royal Navy. Britain deliberately and wisely refrained from military interference on the European continent, Crimea being the only significant exception between 1815 and 1914. Indeed, Britain restricted its military operations to limited, small-scale colonial operations at which, by and large, it was rather good. Britain's hegemony was thus based, as much as anything else, on 'masterly inaction', except in the Empire and a handful of other engagements. It was clearly very different from America's world-wide hegemony after 1945, and the notion of Britain as 'the world's policeman', while it is to some degree an accurate description, always needed much heavier qualification than the analogous role of the United States after the Second World War. An element of the moral fervour and purpose of modern American foreign policy did animate some British leaders like Canning and Gladstone, but it was always more ambiguous than the conduct of American foreign policy and disappeared almost entirely from the conduct of foreign affairs under most Conservative governments.

In 1815 Britain faced an economic situation of great, perhaps unprecedented, difficulty. Paradoxically, these great difficulties were largely short-term in nature; in the long term, Britain's economic prospects were very bright. Owing to the Napoleonic Wars, the national debt had reached £861 million, nearly three times the British gross national income of about £300 million. Gross government expenditure had nearly doubled during the course of those wars, from £66 million in 1802 to £113 million in 1815. Of the latter sum, £30 million was used to pay the charges on the national debt, and £73 million to pay for the military costs of the wars. For the British economy, however, the abrupt ending of hostilities was a very mixed blessing. Military expenditure declined from £73 million in 1815 to only £17 million in 1819. Considerable unemployment resulted directly from the decrease in the post-war size of Britain's forces, the army's manpower declining from 236 000 in 1814 to 81 000 in 1819 and the navy's from 147 000 to only 23 000 in the same period. The war had also greatly inflated the price of wheat, as sources of foreign imports had been cut off. Although high prices hurt the consumer, they also created demand for agricultural labourers and gave bountiful profits to farmers and land-owners, further fuelling the economy. As well, both Britain's import and export trades were harmed in the short term by the ending of the war, adding to unemployment and to the unrest it generated. Once Britain had recovered itself, the future, naturally, was bright. The war had allowed Britain to obtain a lead in the technological innovation and business organisation of its manufacturing industries which lasted for over half a century. The average annual value of British exports increased from £25 million during the decade 1800–09 to £35 million in 1810–19 to £47 million in 1820–29, although most prices were lower. Nevertheless, factory industrialisation had not really begun by the time the war ended. Only 114 000 persons were employed as factory workers in the cotton industry in 1815, compared with 220 000 handloom weavers. (Thirty years later the respective figures were 273 000 and 60 000.) The use of steam power in the great industrial cities was as yet in its infancy, while of course the first railway was 10 years in the future. The end of the war thus created an enormous problem of readjustment which in the short term had no obvious solution.

The Tory governments of the post-war years grappled with these problems as best they could. Economic theory was in its infancy, and economic thinkers were bitterly divided over many key issues. For example, Thomas Malthus and David Ricardo, the two most important economists of the day, held diametrically opposed views regarding the Corn Laws (the tax on importing wheat), with Ricardo advocating free trade and Malthus the maintenance of a tariff. There were at this time virtually no modern statistics of economic productivity and none of the modern economic concepts such as gross national product (statistics for this period were calculated by recent historians, not contemporaneously). In 1815 the government and its Chancellor of the Exchequer, Nicholas Vansittart (1766–1851; later first Baron Bexley), were defeated in the House of Commons on a vote of fundamental importance, the House voting narrowly, against the wishes of the government, to abolish the income tax.[5] Income tax, levied at the rate of 10 per cent, had been introduced as a wartime measure by William Pitt in 1798. The government greatly needed the revenues it raised, but also came under enormous pressure from the City of London and the business community to abolish it as soon as the war ended. Parliament proceeded to do this, and no income tax existed in Britain from 1815 to 1842. Vansittart also came under great pressure from brewers to abolish the malt tax, which he was also forced to do early in 1815. As a result, the government lost £10 million in revenues which (despite the decline in government expenditure) it was forced to make good by a series of ill-conceived loans. Vansittart's policies to set the economy on a sounder course in the long term were better conceived. In 1815 the Corn Laws were modified so that the free export of corn (wheat) was permitted whenever its price rose above 80 shillings per quarter, but was absolutely prohibited below this price. This draconian law probably protected the agricultural workers of Britain after the war, although it was obviously contrary to the economic theory of free trade. The gold standard, and the stability of the currency, was restored in stages from 1820 to 1823, while, slightly later, country banking was liberalised by the Bank Charter Act of 1825. The aim of these measures was to produce price deflation, and the years after the war indeed saw the price of most goods drop. By the 1820s Britain's economy was growing strongly, its industrial revolution in full

5 Vansittart was Chancellor of the Exchequer from 1812 to 1823.

swing. Steam power came to the great manufacturing towns and, in 1825, the railway age was born.

If the first five or ten years after Waterloo are remembered for anything, however, they are recalled for the marked increase in social unrest and popular agitation to levels unknown for many decades. Popular unrest sprang from several sources. The end of the war took out of cold storage the eighteenth-century tradition of popular and democratic agitation, associated in the post-Napoleonic years with Major John Cartwright (1740–1824) and William Cobbett, and added to it a newer variety of reform agitation, more closely linked with the rise of an urban proletariat, associated with radicals like Henry 'Orator' Hunt (1773–1835) and Francis Place (1771–1854). Much about these radicals does not sit easily with our common conception of left-wing ideologues and ideologies as they emerged later in the nineteenth century. Cobbett (1763–1835), for example, was opposed to big cities, above all to London, as well as to financial manipulators. He was a vicious anti-Semite, one of few in a country where virulent anti-Semitism has been virtually unknown, and he also detested Scots and Quakers. Jews, Scots and Quakers were renowned for their abilities as financial and commercial capitalists. Cobbett consistently linked these groups with the 'parasites' of the British aristocracy, especially those who benefited from 'Old Corruption' (the gaining of lucrative government sinecures and perquisites), and the financial magnates of the City of London, who were engaged, via manipulation of the national debt, in a great conspiracy to rob and impoverish the mass of honest English tradesmen and farmers. This conspiracy stemmed from London, which Cobbett also detested and named 'the great wen [wart]'. Cobbett's doctrines were not merely peculiar, but seemingly were also profoundly reactionary, looking backwards to a golden age before urbanisation and finance capitalism had destroyed the traditional English virtues. Yet Cobbett was a consistent radical and democrat, greatly admiring the democratic constitution of the United States (where he lived for some years). He enjoyed enormous popularity, and was elected the Radical MP for Oldham (a cotton manufacturing town near Manchester) in 1832.

Many historians, like E. P. Thompson and Harold Perkin (normally far-removed from one another on most issues), have also pointed to this period as the time when the British 'working classes' were born, and probably the years 1815–25 were those when the term the 'working class' was first commonly used in its modern sense.[6] Trade unionism in the modern sense began in this period, and the undisciplined mob and riot, so common during the eighteenth century, gave way to the disciplined demonstration and organised mass political movement. Reform of Parliament and many other reforms came during this period. Yet one can insist too strongly on the 'birth' of the British working classes during this period. Factory

6 Although the term was used in its modern sense during the mid-eighteenth century.

capitalism, and the growth of a proletariat at work in mines and railways, came only several decades later, and still comprised only a fraction of all British capitalist enterprises until mid-century or later, by which time Britain's industrial ascendancy made revolution unlikely. The ideas of the radical movements of the post-war years were, by and large, democratic and reformist, and hence clearly linked with the older radicalism of the eighteenth century. They did not, except at the fringes, embrace any drive towards socialism or even social reform (as opposed to political democracy).[7] Radicals could and did work with the Whig aristocracy and others in the 'Establishment' who wished for reform.

Rioting over wages and shortages was common during the decade before the end of the war, but reached a crescendo during the first post-war years, especially 1816–20. This heightened unrest was clearly related to the economic and social dislocations caused by the end of the war, and fanned by the arguments of Cobbett (through his newspaper the *Weekly Register*) and others, that with the end of the war the movement for democratic reform, in abeyance since just after the start of the French Revolution, could now resume. While food riots, disturbances, strikes, machine-breaking and assorted 'risings' marked the post-war years, several incidents of unrest have become universally known.

In December 1816 a group of extreme radicals and early socialists (the 'Spencians', named after Thomas Spence (1750–1814), a Newcastle schoolmaster who advocated the equal division of land among the whole population) announced a meeting to be held at Spa Fields, Bermondsey, to be addressed by Hunt, Cartwright, the 'Spencian' Arthur Thistlewood, and many other well-known radicals. Its aim was to promote parliamentary reform[8] and protest the contemptuous treatment by the authorities of petitioners advocating such reform. The crowd, stirred up by one speaker, Dr John Watson, marched on the Tower of London, carrying a French tricolour flag, the symbol of the 1789 French Revolution. Looting *en route*, the crowd briefly caused great anxiety but was quickly dispersed by the Lord Mayor of London and some constables at the Royal Exchange. The Spa Fields affair greatly frightened the government and led directly to the 1817 Coercion Acts (discussed below).

1819 saw the era's most famous incident of radical demonstration accompanied by violence, perhaps the most celebrated such occurrence in modern British history, the so-called 'Peterloo Riots'. A series of rallies and demonstrations advocating parliamentary reform had been held in Manchester during the summer of 1819, in an atmosphere of strikes and unrest. These culminated in a mammoth meeting held at St Peter's Fields in that city on 16 August 1819, attended by thousands, and presided over by 'Orator' Hunt. Policing of this crowd was in the hands of the Lancashire

---

7 Nor did they, except at the fringes, include any notion of women's rights whatever.
8 This was actually the second radical meeting held at Spa Fields, the first being held a month earlier.

justices of the peace, who handled the occasion with foolishness and inconsistency. They allowed the great crowd to gather, but also had a considerable body of soldiers, including yeomanry, infantry, hussars and special constables, standing by. The chief constable of the county pointlessly attempted to arrest Hunt; a riot ensued when four troops of hussars charged into the crowd. Six people were killed and hundreds were injured. 'Peterloo' entered the consciousness of British radicalism and has remained there as one of the greatest acts of injustice ever perpetrated by the British 'ruling class' against ordinary people demanding their rights.

In 1819–20 occurred the so-called 'Cato Street Conspiracy'. In 1819 Arthur Thistlewood (1770–1820), a 'Spencian' socialist who had been imprisoned after taking part in the Spa Fields riots of 1816, led a group of extreme radicals who planned to assassinate members of the Cabinet as they attended a dinner at a house in Grosvenor Square in late February 1820. The Home Office had planted a spy among the group. Eighteen were arrested as they assembled at a loft in Cato Street, Marylebone, where the government had drawn up a detachment of Coldstream Guards to apprehend them. Six of the ringleaders, including Thistlewood, were hanged for treason and five transported overseas.

These were only the most famous of many incidents of popular political violence and unrest at this time. To all such disturbances the government responded with unremitting firmness, enacting several pieces of new legislation designed to suppress unrest and cracking down hard on anything which smacked of revolutionary violence. It was this unremitting firmness which, to this day, has earned the Liverpool government a reputation on the left for mindless repression. The government's tough approach continued a lengthy tradition, after 1789, of Tory activism in suppressing anything which hinted at civil unrest, viewing virtually all such incidents as traitorous conspiracies. For the British right, and indeed most of the centre, the spectre of the French Revolution remained a real one: the anarchy and mass murder of the Reign of Terror, followed by a dictatorship under Bonaparte. Britain's Tories, and others, genuinely believed that centuries of British liberty and parliamentary rule were threatened by radical conspiracies.

The government's policy of consistent repression is particularly associated with several ministers, above all with Henry Addington, first Viscount Sidmouth (1757–1844), formerly Prime Minister 1801–04 and Home Secretary 1812–22, and John Scott, first Earl of Eldon (1751–1838), Lord Chancellor for most of the period from 1801 to 1827. As Home Secretary, Addington was primarily responsible for framing the government's legislation to suppress disorder. Consequently, he was detested by most radicals and indeed by most Whigs, Lord John Russell describing him as 'the incarnation of prejudice and intolerance'. Lord Eldon, the Tory Lord Chancellor for a generation, was a self-made man who had amassed a fortune at the Bar; he was the personification of judicial conservatism and legal delay of the kind pilloried by Dickens in *Bleak House*. Fervent advocates of the repression of dangerous radicals, Eldon and Addington (together with Castlereagh, the Foreign Minister) were the constant butts of satire and opprobrium from the pens of radical writers like Byron.

Addington piloted through two important pieces of legislation to control radicalism, the Coercion Acts of 1817 and the so-called Six Acts of 1819. The Coercion Acts (sometimes known as the 'Gag Acts') became law a few months after the Spa Fields riots, while the Six Acts were passed in response to Peterloo. The former laws temporarily suspended habeas corpus for the first time in English history; they extended a 1798 law making seditious meetings illegal; they made illegal the 'seduction' of soldiers and sailors from their allegiance to the Crown; and they extended to the Prince Regent all the safeguards against treasonable activities normally granted to the King. The Six Acts prevented delays in trials for misdemeanours. They authorised the seizure of arms in disturbed districts, increased the penalties for blasphemous and seditious libels, imposed newspaper stamp duty on all periodical publications containing news (thus curtailing the radical press), prevented meetings for the training of persons in the use of arms, and made illegal 'seditious assemblies' of more than 50 persons. As was the case during the Napoleonic Wars, the Home Office also organised a national network of spies and *agents provocateurs* within Britain's radical groups. There is also some evidence that the implementation of justice became more severe. Crime apparently rose sharply in the post-war period, with total committals in England and Wales increasing from 5337 in 1811 to 14 254 in 1819, and convictions rising from 3163 to 9510 in the same period. The death sentence was imposed more frequently (despite the fact that some offences previously carrying the death penalty had been moderated), with 359 death sentences imposed in 1811 and 1206 in 1819. Actual executions rose as well, from 45 in 1811 to 108 in 1819.

The government took some positive steps to ameliorate the unrest, although they could do virtually nothing to correct the economic dislocations caused by the end of the war. The relatively generous provisions of the post-Speenhamland Poor Law (explained below) were allowed to continue, with poor relief rising from £4.1 million in 1803 to £5.7 million in 1815–16, and then peaking at £7.9 million in 1817–18 before slowly declining (although not by much). The cost of poor relief fell chiefly on the landed classes. Some attempts were made to tighten up the Poor Laws, especially to reduce discretionary powers by JPs to grant special relief, but the system remained essentially the same until the New Poor Law of 1834.[9] In 1817, most remarkably, Parliament authorised the expenditure of £750 000 for the employment of the labouring poor on public works, an act foreshadowing Keynesian approaches to unemployment 120 years

9 The tightening up was carried out by the so-called Sturges Bourne Acts of 1819, named for Sturges Bourne MP, who carried them through Parliament.

ahead of its time. In 1819 the government carried through its only significant piece of social legislation during this period, the Cotton Factory Act, which forbade the employment of children under 9 in cotton factories and limited the hours of work for minors aged 9–18 to 12 hours per day. The government also relied more heavily on the likely effects of the spread of the Established Church on the working classes. In 1818 the government induced Parliament to vote £1 million for the erection of Anglican churches in the most populous parishes. Another £50 000 was raised privately. Tories firmly believed that the message of the Established Church would quell revolutionary unrest, and that the lack of churches in the largest urban areas was itself a potent cause of popular unsettlement, which would therefore decline if more churches were built. They pointed out that in Manchester's parish church there were 40–50 christenings on every Sunday afternoon, a total which rose to upwards of 200 at Christmas and Easter. There were, typically, 120–200 banns of marriages published there each Sunday. The Liverpool government regarded Anglican church building as crucially important, Lord Liverpool stating that it was 'the most important' measure he had ever introduced. Evangelical Anglicanism, in the ascendant at this time, invariably stressed the duty of obligation of the government of the day. So, too, did most Nonconformists, although they were frequently depicted by Tories as fomenters of revolution and breeders of radicalism. Methodism and other forms of the 'New Dissent' grew rapidly during this period, with the official totals of all branches of Methodism rising from 92 000 in 1801 to 195 000 in 1819, with thousands more present at revivalist meetings. The great French historian Elie Halévy attributed the fact that no English revolution occurred during the years between 1789 and 1832 chiefly to the influence of Methodism. This may well be an exaggeration, but certainly the influence of Wesley and his followers was profound. These years also saw the beginnings of many voluntary societies concerned with the education and welfare of the poor, including the British and Foreign Bible Society (1804), the National Society For Promoting Education (1809), the Association for the Relief of the Manufacturing and Labouring Poor (1811), and the British and Foreign School Society (1814). Education, at least to the most basic level, also increased markedly, from a mixture of endowed schools, unendowed schools and Sunday schools, so that by 1819 1 152 000 out of a total of about 2 509 000 children aged 5–14 were attending one (or more) of the remarkable number of 24 693 schools of all types which existed in England and Wales.[10] It is likely that, by 1820, the majority, perhaps the great majority, of British children attended some school for some part of their childhood, and the great majority of the British population was, by this time, certainly basically literate, including even women and the very poor.

10 In Scotland at the same time, a total of 229 974 children were attending one of the 4440 schools which existed there, of a total of 471 000 children aged 5–14.

The increased radicalism and unrest which took place during these years found one of their most curious and unexpected, but most celebrated, targets in the so-called Trial of Queen Caroline in 1820, an event which deeply divided both the 'Establishment' and ordinary people. In 1795 George, Prince of Wales, had married Princess Caroline of Brunswick-Wolfenbüttel, an unattractive German aristocrat of possibly dubious morals whom he detested and treated very badly.[11] They were separated soon after the birth of their only child, Princess Charlotte (1796–1817), briefly the wife of Prince Leopold of Saxe-Coburg-Saalfeld. In 1806 George actually initiated an inquiry into Caroline's allegedly scandalous lifestyle, which acquitted her of wrongdoing. After 1814 she lived abroad, and in 1818 the Prince Regent began to collect evidence for divorce proceedings against her, with results described below.

The life and behaviour of George, Prince of Wales, later Prince Regent and still later King George IV (1762–1830) was also unusual, to say the least. A fat man (dubbed 'the Prince of Whales') of exotic but well-informed taste, he won over most persons from the world of art and literature who met him, built the celebrated Royal Pavilion in Brighton, and lived extravagantly. As is not unusual in the Royal Family, he set out to be the opposite of his father, George III, a clean-living patriotic Tory, and thus in his early years was a Whig who moved in Whig circles. In February 1811, as George III showed increasing signs of madness, his son was declared to be Prince Regent, that is, the heir-apparent to the throne who, owing to the incapacity of the monarch, is allowed to exercise all the normal powers of the Sovereign. George III had been born as long ago as 1738; his end could not be far off and he died on 29 January 1820. During his time as Prince Regent, George IV (as he now became) had moved from supporting the Whigs to strongly supporting the Tory government of Lord Liverpool. As a result, he was mocked and denigrated by his former Whig allies and by most radicals.

George IV was determined to divorce Queen Caroline, and the government was keen to oblige him. From June 1820 until the Queen's death in August 1821 there ensued one of the most squalid episodes in the history of the British monarchy, but one which had strong political implications. Upon his official accession to the throne in January 1820, George IV had the name of Queen Caroline omitted from Anglican prayer books. The Queen took great offence and returned to England from the Continent with the aim of winning popular support. She was indeed received at Dover, and on the way to London, with acclamation from immense crowds (reminiscent of Charles II's reception upon his Restoration). The government supported the King in his wish for an inquiry into the Queen's conduct, while Whig leaders, especially Henry Brougham (1778–1868, later first

11 George had in the 1780s contracted an illegal marriage with Mrs Fitzherbert, a Roman Catholic, with whom he lived for many years.

Baron Brougham and Vaux), the great radical barrister, strongly supported the Queen. After she refused a compromise offered to her by the House of Commons, in July 1820 Liverpool introduced a bill to deprive her of her titles and end her marriage. The matter was debated at length in the House of Lords, Brougham making a famous speech in her defence in October. The second reading of the bill was carried by 28 votes, but the third reading by only nine votes, at which point, knowing that the House of Commons supported the Queen, the government decided not to proceed with the bill. Three days of popular celebrations took place in London. It would be interesting to know why: was this popular radicalism in action, or, perhaps, some early demonstration of feminist assertiveness for a woman traduced? The House of Commons voted her an annuity of £50 000. Queen Caroline, however, persisted in her efforts to be recognised as the Queen of England in fact and in name. On the day of George IV's Coronation, 19 July 1821, she attempted to force an entrance to Westminster Abbey and was turned away, apparently having lost the sympathy of the populace. She was taken ill two weeks later and, pathetically, died on 7 August 1821. Paradoxically, the King appears to have become more popular, rather than less.[12] As monarch, over the next nine years George proved to be surprisingly and enormously popular, and he is often said by historians to have been the first 'modern' British King, deeply conscious of making a positive popular impression and combining majesty with the common touch. His visits to Ireland in 1821 and Scotland in 1822 were triumphs, the first popular tours of these countries by the Sovereign. George IV interfered little with the Tory government until its last years, and he exercised his powers of interference with Cabinet government only over Catholic emancipation and a few other issues at the end of his reign.

---

12 The many parallels between this affair and the ill-fated marriage of Prince Charles and Princess Diana 170 years later are quite uncanny.

2

The decline of Tory rule, 1822–1830

Historians normally make a distinction between the first half of the years of Tory government headed by Lord Liverpool and his successors and the second half, with the dividing line being drawn around the time of George IV's Coronation in 1821. While the earlier phase of the Liverpool government is normally characterised (fairly or unfairly) by the government's firm repression of radicals in the context of widespread post-war unrest, during the latter phase the Liverpool administration showed considerably more liberalism, making important reforms in criminal justice, the economy, and over Catholic emancipation. Such ministers as Sir Robert Peel and William Huskisson who entered the Cabinet at this time brought a new sense of responsibility and intelligence to the proceedings of the government, giving it, indeed, a stamp prefiguring the high-mindedness of the Victorian era and its governments. As with all common images, there are significant areas where one might reasonably dissent from this description, but it also contains a strong element of accuracy.

Three ministerial changes in particular marked the alteration in the Tory government's mood. In January 1822 Robert Peel, second Baronet (1788–1850), became Home Secretary in place of Lord Sidmouth. In September of the same year, after the suicide of Lord Londonderry (formerly Lord Castlereagh), George Canning (1770–1827) became Foreign Secretary and Leader of the House of Commons. In October 1823 William Huskisson entered the Board of Trade as President of Trade and Treasurer of the Navy. These three men put their stamp most firmly on the era. There were other changes in Liverpool's government, too. For instance, in 1818 Frederick John Robinson (1782–1859; later first Viscount Goderich and then first Earl of Ripon) became President of the Board of Trade and in 1823 became Chancellor of the Exchequer, while in 1819 the great Duke of Wellington (Arthur Wellesley, 1769–1852) entered the Cabinet as Master-

General of the Ordnance.[1] By the later 1820s only a few Cabinet ministers remained from the formation of the government in 1812, chiefly Liverpool himself, the seemingly immortal Lord Eldon, the Earl of Harrowby as Lord President of the Council, and Viscount Melville at the Admiralty. Only Eldon belonged to the group known as the 'Ultra-Tories', wholly resistant to change.

George Canning was something like Disraeli in his brilliance, wayward-ness, unusual origins, and in the respect and admiration he eventually achieved. Like Disraeli, Canning had a father who was a writer, in this case of Irish origin. The elder Canning died young and poor and his widow, born in Ireland as Mary Anne Costello, was forced to become an actress. She had several illegitimate children by two lovers. A more improbable Tory Prime Minister (as Canning became in 1827) was not seen before Disraeli came along. Canning was, however, rescued from poverty by a rich uncle, Stratford Canning, who paid for his aristocratic education at Eton and Oxford. There, Canning developed his brilliance at phrase-making and his Tory political views. At Oxford, he contributed to a periodical called *The Anti-Jacobin* (where he penned such verses as 'A steady patriot of the world alone/A friend to every country but his own'). He married an heiress, may have had an affair with Princess Caroline, and held a variety of government positions while retaining a well-deserved reputation for both flippancy and brilliance. (On one famous occasion, he sent a coded message to the British Ambassador in the Netherlands which read 'In matters of commerce/the fault of the Dutch/is offering too little/and asking too much'.) In 1822 he was about to go out to India in the lucrative position of Governor-General, when, on Castlereagh's suicide, he was offered the Foreign Office. King George IV – who had learned that Canning might well have been Queen Caroline's lover – at first refused to sanction Canning's appointment to the Foreign Office, giving way only after pressure from Wellington.

Canning is generally viewed as a strong and independent Foreign Minister who definitely oriented Britain's foreign policy away from the Absolutist assumptions of the Concert of Europe to an independent stance which was predisposed to support liberalism and nationalism. As was noted in the discussion of Castlereagh, this is not wholly fair to his predecessor, who, despite his reputation for reaction, had already moved to a fairly similar position. Nonetheless, Canning moved even further to align Britain with liberalism. At the Congress of Verona of 1822, the British delegation, headed by Wellington, made it clear that it would not side with the other European powers in any intervention to restore Absolutism to Spain (although this did in fact take place). Canning was also instrumental, in 1824–25, in recognising the independence of the Latin American republics

1 Wellington (then Sir Arthur Wellesley) had previously served in a government, though not at the Cabinet level, in 1807–09 as Chief Secretary for Ireland.

which had successfully revolted from Spain. (It was during the parliamentary debate over Latin American independence that Canning made his celebrated claim that 'I called the New World into existence, to redress the balance of the Old'.) A major crisis also erupted in Greece, where Britain's response was more balanced and complex. Greece had, for centuries, been a province of Turkey, and newly aroused nationalist feeling was bent on achieving Greek independence. The struggle for Greece had remarkable and widespread support throughout Britain, derived from the grounding of British secondary and tertiary education in the Greek Classics, and from sympathy for Greece as a small nation oppressed by the barbaric Turks. The poet Byron gave his life for Greek independence; even Lord Eldon donated £100 to the London committee of Greek nationalists. Yet Britain could not give the full-hearted support to Greek independence that so many wished. Weakening Turkey and establishing an independent Orthodox Christian state in the Mediterranean would necessarily strengthen Russia and possibly other European powers. Canning was unwilling to go the whole way with the Greek rebels, urging a semi-independent status for the country. In October 1827, just after Canning died, the British fleet under Vice-Admiral Edward Codrington, with French allies, was forced to destroy the Turkish and Egyptian fleets at the Battle of Navarino, the last great sea fight of the age of sail. In the meantime, war broke out between Russia and Turkey which ended, in 1829, with a Russian victory. In 1830 Greek independence was recognised internationally, although the boundaries of the state were, initially, very small. In both Latin America and Greece, Britain – somewhat unwillingly in the latter case – found itself supporting movements of national liberation.

In domestic affairs, the changes associated with the latter phase of the Liverpool government are strongly linked with Peel and Huskisson. It is commonly believed that economic liberalism, and the drive to free trade and *laissez-faire*, began in earnest in this period, propelled especially by William Huskisson, President of the Board of Trade, although the role of F. J. Robinson (later Prime Minister, when known as Lord Goderich), the Chancellor of the Exchequer, was also very significant. It is difficult to imagine that the move to freer trade would have gone as far as it did unless Britain had recovered completely from the post-war years of economic dislocation: the vested interests opposed to free trade would probably have proved too strong. In the early 1820s, however, nearly all of the indices of economic output turned sharply upwards, with, for instance, raw cotton consumption for textiles increasing from £109 million in 1819 to £167 million in 1825. As well, prices declined significantly during the years after Waterloo, decreasing by about 29 per cent in the 11 years between 1815 and 1826. During the 1820s Britain was moving decisively into the urban, factory, steam-powered phase of industrialisation, with Manchester's population growing from 96 000 in 1811 to 135 000 in 1821 to 194 000 in 1831, Birmingham's from 83 000 to 144 000, and Leeds's from 63 000 to

123 000 in the same years. British mass-produced exports now conquered the world, entering decisively into markets in North and South America and continental Europe before any other country had industrialised. Since many British finished products depended upon the importing of raw materials from abroad (cotton is the most obvious example), a movement naturally grew up to remove tariff barriers and other outmoded restrictions on their free importation. The drive to free trade was given intellectual impetus through the writings of David Ricardo and his contemporaries. Ricardo (1772–1823), a wealthy stockbroker who published seminal works on economic theory advocating *laissez-faire*, became an MP and achieved extraordinary influence in Parliament before his premature death. With some exceptions, the generation of economic theorists writing at this time also advocated free trade and *laissez-faire*. Their viewpoint also appeared to enjoy the support of Utilitarians like Jeremy Bentham (1748–1832), who argued for systematic rationality in government.

On the other hand, it is still somewhat surprising that the Liverpool government embraced the free trade measures it enacted as enthusiastically as it did. Protection, rather than free trade, was in many respects more consistent with the animating philosophy of early nineteenth-century Toryism, with its emphasis on patriotism, order and tradition, and its hostility to liberalism and cosmopolitanism. The final instalment of the free trade philosophy, in 1846, meant the abolition of the Corn Laws, which, of course, split the Conservative party of the day and alienated most Conservative landowners. Although no one contemplated 'repeal' in the 1820s, any move to *laissez-faire* faced continuing hostility from significant economic interests which benefited from protection. Apart from the new-found prosperity of the British economy and the intellectual climate, the move to *laissez-faire* was strengthened by the fact that the Liverpool Tory government was consensual in its nature, enjoying support from all sections of the propertied classes, including manufacturers who had excellent access to government ministers and the sympathies of many in the Cabinet. Because the British political elite had not yet fully split into the recognisable segments of nineteenth-century British politics, with most businessmen, especially self-made manufacturers, supporting the Liberals, the Tory government of the 1820s was more responsive to the needs of Britain's modern industrialists than one might have expected.

Huskisson's first significant move towards greater *laissez-faire* came in 1823 with the reform of the Navigation Acts. These Acts, dating from the mid-seventeenth century, provided that British ships alone were to carry virtually all goods imported into Britain.[2] After many European protests, the right to import goods into Britain in European vessels was conceded by

2 As a concession to the United States, this requirement was eliminated from trade with America in the treaty ending the War of 1812. This removed a subject of dispute with the greatest potential to fuel continuing conflict between the two countries, and helped to spark America's great age of 'clipper ships'.

the 1823 Reciprocity of Duties Act to countries which extended this right to Britain. While British shipowners suffered in the short run, the greatly expanded volume of trade vastly increased their earnings in the long term. Huskisson also reduced duties on a wide variety of other imported goods, establishing a general rule that the import duty on manufactured goods, unless otherwise specified, should be 20 per cent rather than 50 per cent. Another area of reform in the interests of freer trade undertaken by Huskisson was the removal of restrictions on the right of Britain's colonies to trade directly with foreign countries, eliminating the hamfisted requirement that all goods had first to pass through Britain. This change was significant in building up Britain's white colonies, in Canada, Australia and elsewhere, as growing and viable economic units in their own right, incidentally having the effect of increasing their importance as 'safety valves' for emigration from Britain's overcrowded cities and of downtrodden industrial and agricultural workers. Lastly, in 1828 Huskisson modified (though he did not eliminate) the 1815 Corn Law, introducing a sliding scale of duties with steep falls in the level of duty on corn (wheat) after its price rose over 66 shillings per quarter, so that when the price reached 73 shillings the duty was only 1 shilling. Remarkably, Huskisson was able to pilot this change through Parliament without the fierce controversy generated by Sir Robert Peel's government 18 years later. Huskisson enjoyed the support of the entire government, including especially F. J. Robinson, the Chancellor of the Exchequer, who became known as 'Prosperity' Robinson for the booming state of the British economy during the period from 1823, when he took office, until an economic recession took hold in 1826.

That there were distinct limits to the radicalism of the Tory government is illustrated by its actions regarding the Combination Laws. Trades unions had been illegal since the Combination Act of 1799, which forbade workers from 'combining' with other workers to improve conditions or raise wages, to induce a strike, or to attend a meeting whose purpose was to improve wages or conditions. Some of these provisions were modified by the Combination Act of 1800 which, among other things, forbade owners from combining to reduce wages, increase hours, or worsen conditions.[3] The Combination Act had, in other words, made both trades unions and strikes illegal. The Act certainly did not prevent strikes from occurring, nor attempts to form trades unions. By the 1820s, a campaign to repeal the unduly harsh and unrealistic Combination Acts was launched, headed by Francis Place, the celebrated radical tailor of Charing Cross who was almost continuously active in a variety of radical movements from the 1790s till the 1840s. Rather surprisingly, Place had a number of influential supporters in Parliament, for instance Sir Francis Burdett (1770–1844), the radical MP and activist who married the daughter of the founder of Coutts

3 There were no reported cases of this happening (which is difficult to believe reflected reality).

Bank, and Joseph Hume (1777–1855), a physician and radical MP who was renowned for his frequent predictions of national disaster. Place's supporters argued that the Combination Acts were unworkable and counter-productive, actually preventing cooperation between owners and workers and hence the rational amelioration of just grievances. Trades unions in any case already existed *de facto* as friendly societies, which were encouraged by the government. Hume succeeded, in 1824, in the setting up of a parliamentary committee of inquiry, and Hume and Place so success-fully stage-managed the workers who gave evidence that the Tory govern-ment, through Huskisson, agreed most remarkably to the repeal of the 1799 Act, a step literally inconceivable a few years earlier.

As a result, the government passed the Combination Act of 1824, which repealed the 1799 and 1800 Acts. Under the new law, trades unions or strikes were no longer liable to prosecution, although threats of violence to persons or property by workers to coerce an agreement was made illegal. This new Act led to a wave of strikes and the government responded to pressure from manufacturers by setting up, in 1825, a parliamentary committee to inquire into the 1824 Act. Although Joseph Hume was again on the committee, the terms of the 1824 Act were severely tightened up by its replacement, the Combination Act 1825. This new Act exempted from prosecution only those combinations of workmen (or masters) which met together solely to agree what wages or hours of employment to require or demand. 'Combinations' for any other purpose were made unlawful. Trades unions remained legal, but they were not allowed to 'intimidate', 'molest' or 'obstruct' in carrying out their aims. Trades unions were thus guaranteed continued legality, but within tightly prescribed boundaries.

Just as the economic reforms of the 1820s are associated with Huskisson, so the penal reforms of this era are associated with Robert Peel, the Home Secretary. In particular, we associate Peel's name with the abolition of the death penalty for virtually all crimes except murder and treason. In 1800 there were about 200 crimes on the statute books whose conviction carried the death penalty. Many were quite trivial, where the death penalty could not be justified by any conceivable consideration of natural justice. Until 1868, executions were carried out in public, with a large crowd looking on, cheering and jeering. (It was widely noted that when pickpockets and thieves were hanged, thieves and pickpockets were often at work in the crowds!) Since the system of policing for the apprehension of criminals was inefficient and primitive, it has often been observed that the underlying philosophy of English justice at this time was that few criminals would be caught and convicted, but those who were would meet with truly savage punishment as a deterrent to others. This philosophy is very different from that which prevailed later in the nineteenth century (or today), wherein an efficient police should aim at apprehending all serious criminals, whose punishment would fit the crime.

Some amelioration of the number of capital offences had taken place before Peel became Home Secretary in January 1822, with, for instance, the death penalty abolished for larceny from the person by an Act of 1808. Peel's first measure, the Judgment of Death Act 1823, gave discretionary powers to a judge to abstain from imposing the death penalty on a person convicted of any crime, except murder, if the judge felt that the offender was fit to be recommended for mercy. This, in effect, virtually abolished the death penalty for all but the most heinous crimes. In 1827 came a series of five measures, known as 'Peel's Acts', which consolidated and collated most existing criminal law. The most important of these bills, the Criminal Justice Act 1827, reversed the previous position on the punishment of felonies, restricting the imposition of the death penalty, even in theory, to the most serious crimes. Imprisonment or transportation (usually to the Australian colonies) remained the punishment for non-capital felonies. As a result of Peel's Acts, although the number of criminal convictions in England and Wales rose sharply, from 9500 in 1819 to 12 800 in 1830, the number of executions declined, from 108 to only 46 in the same years, despite a considerable increase in the population.

Peel was also responsible for other very basic penal reforms. The use of spies and *agents provocateurs* to report on domestic radicals was abolished. Peel's Gaols Act of 1823 was one of the first attempts to introduce prison reform, requiring, among other things, that prisons had to be inspected regularly, that women gaolers were to supervise women prisoners (one of the earliest uses of women employees by the government), and that all prisoners had to receive some education and medical care. While applying only to gaols in the large cities, it marked a major reform. Peel's best-known reform, which became law in the last year before the Whigs came to power, was the famous Metropolitan Police Act 1829, which first introduced police in the modern sense to London. Under the Act, 1000 uniformed police (quickly known as 'bobbies' or 'Peelers' after their originator), with their headquarters at Scotland Yard, paid for by the local rates, replaced *ad hoc* and small-scale local and private police forces. London's 'bobbies' carried no guns and no weapons stronger than a truncheon, an amazing state of affairs for the time. Other large cities, and then the counties, in Britain followed suit with their own forces, although there was no national coordination of local police forces until 1856. By the 1860s there was general agreement that the crime rate had fallen significantly, and it then kept falling until the Edwardian period or even later. Unfortunately there were no national crime statistics until 1857, but it appears that the number of indictable offences known to the police per 100 000 of the population in England and Wales declined from 448 on average in 1857–61 to only 249 in 1897–1901, steadily falling during the whole late Victorian period. By the end of the nineteenth century the streets of London, Manchester, Bristol and Glasgow were probably the safest in the world among cities of their size and extent of primary poverty.

In February 1827 Lord Liverpool suffered a stroke and he retired two months later (he died, at the age of only 58, in 1828). There now ensued one of the most confused and crucial periods in modern British political history. Within a year of Liverpool's retirement two other Prime Ministers had come and gone and a third was in office; by November 1830 the Whigs were in power and in 1832 the Reform Act had transformed the basis of British political life. Apart from the individual personalities within the Tory party, this period revolved around the two crucial questions of Catholic emancipation and parliamentary reform, and centred as well on the nature of the Whig opposition which, after many years in the wilderness, came triumphantly to power in 1830.

Especially after 1822, Liverpool had maintained the unity of the Tory party by espousing popular change but avoiding the most difficult questions, particularly Catholic emancipation and parliamentary reform, and by moving to enact progressive measures during the 1820s without loosening the government's firmness or its constitutional moorings. His retirement in 1827 fundamentally altered the balanced nature of the Tory government, forcing a choice between moving left or right, splitting the Tory coalition whatever choice was made.

The first of the great challenges to the Tory hegemony concerned Catholic emancipation. The term 'Catholic emancipation' (like 'Jewish emancipation' 30 years later) was something of a misnomer. Until 'Catholic emancipation', Roman Catholics could not sit in Parliament or occupy public offices, being barred solely because upon taking office one was required to swear allegiance to the Thirty-Nine Articles of the Church of England. In all other respects, Catholics (and Protestant Dissenters, who suffered from somewhat similar disabilities until 1828, as well as Jews) could do anything that Anglicans could do. They could vote, own property, and, of course, freely practise their religion. The issue of 'Catholic emancipation' might have continued to be a minor one rather than one central to British politics, except for the fact that it was intimately connected with the question of Ireland. In 1800 Ireland's population of about 4 500 000 consisted of 3 150 000 Catholics (70 per cent of the population), 450 000 adherents of the Church of Ireland (the Anglican Church in Ireland) (10 per cent), and 900 000 (20 per cent) Presbyterians, chiefly in Ulster. Although Catholics could vote, they could not serve in Parliament or hold most local offices, and were also compelled to pay over £500 000 in tithes to the Church of Ireland. A campaign for the removal of their grievances had begun in 1811, and took active shape in 1821 when a motion for Catholic 'emancipation' (the right to serve in Parliament) passed the Commons but was defeated in the Lords. In 1823 the Catholic Association was formed in Dublin to put pressure on Parliament for Catholic emancipation. It was one of the first, and one of the most successful, extra-parliamentary pressure groups in the modern sense, and also the ancestor of all the Irish nationalist and quasi-nationalist groups which followed it. The founder and head of the Catholic Association was Daniel O'Connell (1775–1847), a Catholic barrister from Dublin, known as 'the Liberator', who, while viewed by many Irishmen as the first great modern Irish leader, is also widely viewed as an unscrupulous demagogue. The Catholic Association collected funds from ordinary Irish Catholics, often using priests as collectors. Fearful of its power, the government dissolved it, but it quickly reappeared as the New Catholic Association. At the 1826 general election, Catholic candidates supported by the Association were returned throughout Ireland. The Liverpool government realised that addressing the issue of the rights of Catholics could not be put off indefinitely. However, it faced enormous pressure from right-wing Tories (as well as from many ordinary Anglicans and some Nonconformists), for whom the Catholic Church remained anathema, and any breach in the wall of the Anglican ascendancy virtually a treasonable act. The King and his brother, the Duke of York (who died in 1827), were known to view Catholic emancipation as inconsistent with the solemn royal oath taken at the Coronation to act as 'Defender of the Faith' and head of the Churches of England and Ireland. Opponents of Catholic emancipation, and of other seemingly radical reforms undertaken in the 1820s, became known as 'Ultra Tories', and proved to be a powerful source of division within the Tory government.

When Liverpool retired, the obvious candidate to succeed him was George Canning, by far the most talented man in the Cabinet. The choice lay with the King. 'Ultra-Tory' peers lobbied hard for the King to choose the Duke of Wellington. They detested Canning, fearful above all that he was sympathetic to Catholic emancipation. Canning lobbied vigorously for himself, and on 10 April 1827 George IV invited him to form a government. Here, great difficulties were encountered. Wellington, Peel, Eldon and other right-wing Tories refused to serve under him.[4] Canning was compelled to form a Cabinet of 12 with some curious expedients. Canning himself served as Chancellor of the Exchequer, and several leading Whigs, among them the Marquess of Lansdowne and the Duke of Devonshire, were given Cabinet positions. The Canning government lasted less than four months. In that period, it managed to conclude a treaty with Turkey, but was narrowly defeated on Catholic emancipation and on an attempt to liberalise the Corn Laws. On 8 August 1827, however, Canning, who had been continuously ill during his premiership, unexpectedly died at the age of only 57. It is possible, perhaps probable, that, had Canning lived, he would have enacted Catholic emancipation and even parliamentary reform. (Canning, it should be noted, enjoyed the strong support of the King during his brief administration.) With his death, the liberal wing of the Tory party lost its greatest leader.

The question of who was to succeed him was resolved by the King, still all-important in choosing a Prime Minister, especially in these circum-

---

4 Peel, although a progressive Home Secretary, was at this stage an adamant opponent of Catholic emancipation.

stances. The choice fell on 'Prosperity' Robinson, who had been ennobled earlier in 1827 as Viscount Goderich. Goderich was well-respected, with roughly the same range of virtues as Liverpool – integrity, sound judgement, acceptability to all factions in the party. He was well-liked by liberal Tories for his adept handling of the economy as Chancellor of the Exchequer in 1823–27, but was recalled by right-wingers as a close friend of Lord Castlereagh. On paper, there was nothing wrong with the choice of Goderich, who formed his Cabinet of 15 on 31 August 1827. While Peel and Wellington still declined to join the Cabinet, an anti-Catholic Tory, J. C. Herries, became Chancellor of the Exchequer. Most of the moderate Whigs remained. The King was especially influential in suggesting several key appointments.

Despite this, the Goderich government was under severe strain from the first, with splits and quarrels developing almost at once. A major dispute arose between Herries and Huskisson (Secretary for War and the Colonies) over an appointment. Goderich was prevented by the King from making several new Cabinet appointments, and both the liberal and 'Ultra Tory' wings of the party were fearful of the strength of each other. In addition, Goderich was deeply anxious about the health of his wife. He had also made the mistake of writing to the King in December 1827 to explain his feelings of inadequacy as Prime Minister, a communication the King chose to regard as a letter of resignation. More bitterness and intrigues followed, with Huskisson being approached by George IV to form a government and declining. Political paralysis ensued, and when visiting the King on 8 January 1828 Goderich was informed that His Majesty regarded the government as having come to an end: George used Goderich's letter of the previous month as a pretext. Thus ended, after less than five months, one of the most unsuccessful governments in British history.

The King now turned to the 'Iron Duke', the Duke of Wellington himself, to form a government. Wellington became Prime Minister on 22 January 1828, appointing a Cabinet of 13. The King had stipulated that Wellington was to have a free hand, but that Lord Grey, the leader of the Whigs, be excluded, that 'the Roman Catholic question was not to be made a Cabinet question', and that Catholics be debarred from key Irish positions.

Although the appointment of Wellington broke with tradition in many respects, it was not as foolish as it subsequently seemed. Wellington enjoyed unrivalled and unequalled prestige not merely in Britain, but throughout Europe. Few would openly oppose him on any issue without excusing their actions. Wellington's prestige meant that he was in a strong position (like Charles de Gaulle in France 130 years later) to initiate and carry out major reforms if he wished. While Wellington was universally renowned as a general, he was also a politician, having sat in Parliament since 1806 and serving in the Liverpool Cabinet between 1819 and 1827. Strongly associated with the anti-Catholic right wing of the Tory party (and, by origin, an Anglo-Irish aristocrat), Wellington was nevertheless not an 'Ultra' and was a close confidant of Peel and other sophisticated, flexible men. Yet Wellington's appointment also carried many risks. He notably lacked the common touch, was used to commanding rather than to persuading, and held an exaggerated view of the 'perfection' of the British Constitution, and of the role of the Prime Minister in heading the King's government. He was unable to head a government of reform equal to the very difficult problems he faced.

Wellington began successfully enough by reuniting in his Cabinet the elements of the Liverpool Tory party who had remained outside of the two previous governments. Five 'Canningites' (including the long-serving Huskisson and also Lord Palmerston, a Cabinet minister since 1809 and yet destined to sit in Cabinets until 1865) were appointed, and Robert Peel (who inherited the title of Sir Robert upon the death of his father in 1830) rejoined the Cabinet as Home Secretary. Henry Goulburn (1784–1856), a West Indies planter and merchant who had held a variety of junior ministerial positions since 1810, most recently as Chief Secretary for Ireland in 1821–27, became Chancellor of the Exchequer. Lord Eldon, aged 79, was left out of the ministry, as were the Whigs who had served under Canning and Goderich.

This period also saw the revival of a viable Whig opposition. A characteristic ideology of the Whig party now took shape, based around the demand for retrenchment (economy) in the running of the government, especially in the elimination of 'Old Corruption' (lavish sinecures, government places, and emoluments for the relatives and minions of the aristocracy), religious freedom and equality, and a movement towards accepting the necessity of parliamentary reform. The 1820s saw the emergence of younger Whig leaders, normally scions of the great aristocratic Whig houses, who embraced a wider notion of the aims of Whig governance than had existed for many decades. One of the most notable of these younger Whig leaders, though by no means the only one, was Lord John Russell (1792–1878; later first Earl Russell), a younger son of the Duke of Bedford. In 1828 Russell very cleverly moved a motion, passed by the House of Commons, to repeal the Test and Corporation Acts, under which Protestant Dissenters were debarred from holding public offices. By 1828, these legal disabilities were no longer fully enforced, an Indemnity Act being passed each year to allow them to hold office. Russell's motion was staunchly opposed by most right-wing Tories as marking a fundamental breach in the Anglican nature of the English state. Nevertheless, it was passed by 44 votes in the Commons and was also passed by the House of Lords once it was agreed to insert a clause requiring all office-holders to do nothing hostile to the Church of England.[5] By fundamentally breaching

5 The House of Lords also inserted a clause requiring all office-holders to take an oath, upon assuming office, swearing loyalty 'upon the true faith of a Christian'. It was this clause which led to the struggle over 'Jewish emancipation' until 1858, when Jews elected to the House of Commons were finally allowed to take their seats.

the long-standing connection between Anglicanism and governance, Russell's bill made it illogical to resist the demands of Roman Catholics for legal equality. It also further highlighted the deep divisions which existed in the Tory government, and demonstrated the independence of the House of Commons.

In May 1828 Wellington's government was further shaken by the resignation of Huskisson, Palmerston and three other 'Canningite' ministers over the disenfranchisement of two particularly corrupt 'rotten boroughs' (see below). Thus Wellington's government, only five months after taking office, lost any pretence to being a broadly based coalition of the type Liverpool had headed. Worse was to follow. In July 1828 Daniel O'Connell was elected MP for County Clare. He defeated Vesey Fitzgerald, an Irish landlord who had been appointed President of the Board of Trade in place of Charles Grant, a 'Canningite' minister who had resigned with Huskisson and Palmerston.[6] O'Connell had the overwhelming support of the poorer Catholic electors, while Fitzgerald was supported by Protestants and conservatives. O'Connell was triumphantly elected, despite the fact that, as a Catholic, he was ineligible to sit in the Commons. For the next ten months the issue of 'Catholic emancipation' dominated British politics. The government understood that the election of O'Connell was, certainly, only the first in which aroused Irish Catholics would elect Catholics to Parliament, making Ireland ungovernable. It seems clear that Peel, a strong realist, and greatly influential in the Cabinet, changed his mind on 'Catholic emancipation' shortly after the Clare election. On the other hand the King remained adamant in his opposition to change, as did most peers and, possibly, most Englishmen. In February 1829 the King's speech foreshadowed that Catholic emancipation would soon be granted. Peel resigned his parliamentary seat at Oxford University, and lost the ensuing by-election to Sir Robert Inglis, an extreme opponent of the Catholics, by 755 votes to 609.[7] Re-entering Parliament, Peel then changed decisively in favour of Catholic emancipation, moving the relevant bill in Parliament in March 1829. Under this bill, Catholics were free to hold any public office in the United Kingdom. Nevertheless, they were still obliged to disclaim any intention of subverting Britain's Protestant government, and were debarred from holding the positions of Lord Chancellor of England or Ireland, or Lord-Lieutenant of Ireland. No Catholic could become Sovereign or Regent, hold any university position, or exercise ecclesiastical patronage. No Jesuit could openly migrate to Britain.[8] In order to ensure

6 Until the early twentieth century, any MP appointed to a new ministerial position had to stand for re-election before his appointment became official.
7 Peel was chosen to represent Oxford University over Canning as he was felt to be more strongly anti-Catholic, and felt that he was duty-bound to stand for re-election when he changed his mind. Following his defeat, he was elected for Westbury. Until 1950, Britain's universities elected MPs to Parliament, with university graduates being entitled to vote.
8 The bar on a Catholic holding the office of Lord Chancellor was only repealed in the 1980s.

that Catholics did not dominate the Irish political scene, the minimum requirement to vote in Irish county elections was increased from the possession of a 40 shilling freehold to one worth £10. Clearly, this was far from religious toleration in the modern sense. The bill passed its second reading in the Commons in March 1829 by a vote of 353 to 180. Wellington's support ensured its passage in the Lords by a large majority, and the bill became law in April 1829. Nevertheless, Wellington and Peel had alienated an influential body of anti-Catholic right-wing Tories, normally the backbone of their support.[9] Since the Canningite left of the party had also been alienated, the government appeared hopelessly weak and divided, notwithstanding its strong stand over the Catholic question.

In this atmosphere, the all-important question of the reform of Parliament now made its appearance as the central political issue of the day. The movement for parliamentary reform was an old one, which enjoyed a strong following just before the French Revolution. In abeyance with most other reform questions during the years of the French Revolution and Napoleon, it re-entered the radical agenda just after the Napoleonic Wars. The case made by radical reformers was that the methods of electing the House of Commons, and the distribution of seats, was hopelessly antiquated and irrational. The vote ought to be given to a much wider number of adult males (many believed to all adult males), selected by rational criteria, and seats in Parliament ought to be divided to reflect the changes in Britain's population in recent decades. In particular the scandalous situation wherein huge cities like Birmingham, Leeds and Manchester returned no MPs at all, while dozens of insignificant villages returned two MPs, needed to be reformed. These tiny borough seats were almost invariably 'pocket boroughs' of a wealthy patron who, in effect, owned the right to elect MPs to the national Parliament. Another point made by the reformers was that the length of time between parliamentary elections, up to seven years, was far too long.

The case presented by the reformers is obviously easy to understand and it must seem to us that no rational person could make an intelligent case against reform. Yet it must be appreciated that many people in the mainstream, among them the whole of the Tory party and many intellectuals, opposed reform. Britain's parliamentary system, the opponents of reform argued vociferously, was an extraordinarily successful mechanism, the envy of Europe, which had, for centuries, prevented both revolution and tyranny. While it was perfectly true that its basis was neither democratic nor consistent, its very variety ensured that all parts of the community were represented and their voices heard. Burke, Pitt, Canning and other luminaries had sat for the much-despised 'nomination boroughs', whose very nature made it possible for unusual men of distinction to gain

9 So intense did feelings run over the Catholic question that, in March 1829, Wellington fought a duel with Lord Winchilsea over insulting correspondence, initiated by Winchilsea, on this issue. Both men deliberately fired their pistols wide.

election to Parliament instead of demagogues. Short of manhood suffrage, which no one in the political mainstream wanted, there would always be some limitations on the right to vote, so why substitute an untried, theoretical system for one whose success was proven? Some conservatives conceded that a degree of change to Parliament might be necessary, for instance by giving seats to the rapidly growing industrial cities, but none wished to see wholesale change or regarded it as anything but potentially disastrous.

Extra-parliamentary movements to bring about parliamentary reform, and attempts by reformers within Parliament to achieve a vote for change in the House of Commons, occurred for decades prior to 1830, and greatly increased after 1815. A Union for Parliamentary Reform was founded in 1811 by leading radicals, and, from 1816 onwards, Cobbett's enormously popular *Weekly Register* drew continuing attention to the absurdities and injustices of the unreformed system. In 1817 Sir Frances Burdett's motion in Parliament to form a select committee on reform was defeated by 265 votes to 77. The following year, Sir Robert Heron's motion for triennial parliaments was defeated by 117 to 42, while Burdett's extremely radical motion for manhood suffrage, annually elected Parliaments, the secret ballot, and equal electoral districts was defeated by 106 votes to zero.[10] In 1820 Lord John Russell moved a proposal to disenfranchise four of the most corrupt 'pocket boroughs': Grampound, Penryn, Barnstaple and Camelford. His motion was carried in the Commons but defeated in the Lords. In 1822 Russell's motion to remove 100 members from the smallest boroughs and redistribute them to counties and unenfranchised large towns was defeated by 269 votes to 169, indicating that a substantial constituency for reform had already come into being in the unreformed House of Commons. Russell tried again, in 1826; his second resolution was defeated by 247 to 124. Other reform measures were proposed at the time, and defeated by similar margins.

In the course of the 1820s, it became increasingly clear that the reform of Parliament would soon emerge as the central political issue of the time, overshadowing Catholic emancipation and every other question. In 1822 a number of Whig leaders resolved that parliamentary reform was a pressing necessity, giving the stamp of the Opposition to the emerging movement. The government's response remained that of unyielding hostility to wholesale change. It was, nonetheless, ready to make some minor concessions. In 1821 Grampound, a notoriously corrupt 'pocket borough' in Yorkshire, was disenfranchised, its two MPs transferred to the Yorkshire county constituency. (Russell, who moved the motion, wanted its two MPs to be transferred to the then-unrepresented city of Leeds, but his proposal was defeated.) Voting in borough constituencies was reformed in 1828 so that

10 Until 1882, voting was done in public, the voter stating his choice aloud. It was widely believed that this was more consistent with independent 'manliness' than was the secret ballot.

elections took place over an eight-day period and several polling places were provided in larger boroughs, instead of just one. Nevertheless, there were always clear and very wide limits beyond which the Tory government was not prepared to go. In 1827 bills to disenfranchise Penryn and East Retford, two very corrupt 'rotten boroughs', were proposed; the Penryn bill was carried by the Commons, the East Retford bill would probably have been had not the session ended. The Cabinet's attitude was crucial. It was agreed that Penryn should be merged with the surrounding county, but Huskisson's demand that East Retford's MPs should be given to un-represented Birmingham was rejected.

This was the situation as the Wellington government was in the process of self-destruction over Catholic emancipation and other issues. Once the Catholic issue was settled, the question of parliamentary reform, touching on the future of the whole country rather than on a relatively small section, took its place as the centre of radical concern. In December 1829 the Birmingham Political Union was founded by Thomas Attwood (1783–1856), a wealthy Birmingham banker, and 15 others. It quickly came to play a leading part in the agitation for reform, and was one of the earliest extra-parliamentary movements led by business and professional men of the middle classes in the new towns, the predecessor to the Anti-Corn Law League and other later bodies of middle-class reform. On 26 June 1830 King George IV died, and was succeeded by his brother William IV. As the Duke of Clarence, the new King had held government office (although outside the Cabinet) as Lord High Admiral in 1827–28, a most unusual arrangement in the nineteenth century. Nevertheless, he was known to be a man of rough common sense, having served as a naval officer many years before. His private life was somewhat unusual. By his long-time mistress, Mrs Dorothy Jordan (1762–1816), he had ten children (one of whom, George Fitzclarence, was created Earl of Munster) without attracting much criticism. In 1818 he married Princess Adelaide of Saxe-Meiningen, by whom he had two daughters, both dying in infancy. In politics (and rather oddly) the new King was believed to be a decided Whig, who had initiated debates in the House of Lords, hostile to the Tory government, on state prosecutions for libel and on colonial slavery. His succession to the throne was thus one more portent disturbing to the continuation of the long Tory hegemony, and an extremely important one. A number of other events favourable to reform also took place at this time. In July 1830 France erupted in revolution, the constitutional monarch Louis-Philippe taking the place of the absolutist Louis XVIII after a comparatively bloodless struggle. Many historians have long seen this as instrumental in assisting the growth of the reform movement in Britain, but other historians have questioned whether news of the revolution reached Britain in time for it to have had any effect. A more relevant political event overseas might be found in the triumphant election to the American presidency in 1828 of Andrew Jackson, an arch-democrat whose election is seen as marking one of the turning-points to mass democracy in the United States. Jackson's inauguration, in March 1829, witnessed a virtual invasion of the White House by thousands of his supporters. Given the strong social and psychological links between America and Britain, it is quite possible that Jackson's victory changed the climate to a degree in Britain.

The death of George IV necessitated a general election: under the law as it stood then (and until the twentieth century), a general election had to be held whenever the Sovereign died. This election, held in July–August 1830, could clearly not have come at a worse time for Wellington and the government. The Whigs appeared to reflect popular opinion, and the government had alienated both the left and the right of its own party. In the case of the 'Ultra Tories' on the right (consisting of about 40 MPs), hostility to Catholic emancipation was often combined with a sense of betrayal over the government's agricultural and economic policies, especially its attempts to relax the Corn Laws. Agricultural distress and disturbances were now rife in Britain, especially in southern England, where the 'Captain Swing' epidemic of machine-breaking and arson broke out in April 1830. Led by local radicals and agricultural labourers, landowners and local clerics were threatened, and 'Swing' was suppressed with the usual firmness.[11] Their opposition to the deflationary economic policies of the government in the wake of the 1826 Banking Act was, in fact, not far-removed from the economic criticism of the government voiced by middle-class radicals. As well, many 'Ultra Tories' were now grudgingly coming to the view that parliamentary reform might well provide government closer to, and more sensitive to, the wishes of local landowners and farmers, rather than to self-made, wealthy borough-mongers.

That the general election of 1830 was likely to be a vote of no confidence in the government was clear enough. Nevertheless, there were also distinct limits on the extent to which any general election could have resulted in a resounding defeat for the government. Given that there was no popular electoral constituency in the modern sense, and several hundred seats were controlled by patrons and borough-mongers, normally friendly to the government, any 'political earthquake' could be felt only in the county seats and in the relatively independent boroughs. This is what happened in 1830: it is estimated that about 50 seats changed hands, more than at any previous election.[12] The Tories could now carry on only with difficulty. On 5 September 1830, shortly before Parliament was scheduled to convene, came another portent: William Huskisson was killed by a train at the opening of the Manchester–Liverpool Railway, the first man to be killed in

11 'Captain Swing' was the name of the imaginary leader of the outbreak, who 'signed' its manifestos. 'Swing' apparently denoted the swing of the flail.
12 Some sources give the government's losses as 30. No precise figures can be given. On one calculation, of the 236 MPs returned in constituencies with a relatively open franchise, 141 supported the opposition, 79 the Tory government, and 16 were neutral.

a railway accident. Wellington and Peel were present and, indeed, Huskisson was walking to shake hands with the Duke when he was struck by the train.[13]

There was still hope that Wellington would embrace a moderate scheme of reform, disenfranchising the worst of the 'rotten boroughs' and enfranchising the larger industrial towns, which might have saved his government. Unfortunately, the King's speech, delivered in early November 1830, failed to mention parliamentary reform. Addressing the House of Lords on the same day, Wellington made a celebrated speech declaring that the unreformed parliamentary system could not be improved upon, and absolutely ruling out any reform bill, even a moderate one. It seems clear that Wellington made this speech before consulting his Cabinet colleagues, who might well have agreed to carry a moderate reform bill. More trouble ensued: the Cabinet decided to cancel an engagement of the King and Queen with the Lord Mayor-elect of London at the Mansion House when it received word that a riot would ensue. The stock market fell sharply, and some disturbances broke out in London. On 15 November Sir Henry Parnell, a Whig MP, moved a minor resolution on the Civil List which Wellington and Peel interpreted as a vote of confidence for the government. The government lost by a vote of 233 to 204. Twenty-nine 'Ultra' Tories had voted with the Opposition. The following day, 16 November 1830, Wellington resigned, and the Tory coalition which had dominated British politics for several generations went with it. It would be 56 years before the Conservatives again became the 'natural' governing party of Britain, and longer before they again included most of the British 'Establishment'. A new day had genuinely dawned in British politics.

---

13 Huskisson had never seen a train before (nor had many people) and apparently imagined that, like a stagecoach, it could move to one side to avoid striking someone. Unfortunately, he failed to appreciate that trains cannot leave their tracks.

3

The Whig government and the Great Reform Act, 1830–1834

The first important act of William IV as King, and among the most important acts he ever undertook, was to invite Lord Grey, the leader of the Whigs, to form the new government when Wellington resigned. Charles Grey, second Earl Grey (1764–1845), was the scion of a landed family from Northumberland. His father, General Charles Grey, had been given an earldom for his military services; an uncle was a baronet. Lord Grey, the Prime Minister, married into the Ponsonby family and was related by marriage to Samuel Whitbread, the wealthy radical brewer. Nevertheless, he was not really sufficiently high-born to count as a *bona fide* member of the inner Whig aristocracy. He was educated conventionally enough at Eton and Cambridge, made the Grand Tour, and entered Parliament as the MP for Northumberland in 1786, aged 22. A good deal about his background suggests that he should have been a fairly conventional Tory. Nevertheless, he became a friend and devotee of Charles James Fox, the celebrated Whig politician, and became, and remained, a lifelong Whig radical. The reform views Grey held in 1832 were, essentially, those he had formed 50 years earlier. In the 1780s he had been an associate of Fox, Burke and Sheridan in the impeachment of Warren Hastings. In 1791 he opposed war with revolutionary France, and, a year later, helped to found the Society of the Friends of the People to bring about moderate reform. Somewhat more circumspect in his outlook as the years progressed, he served as First Lord of the Admiralty and then Foreign Minister in the so-called 'Ministry of All the Talents' in 1806–07.[1] Remarkably, this was his only experience of government prior to becoming Prime Minister in 1830, although he was recognised as leader of the Foxite Whigs in 1807 and of the Whig party as a whole in 1821 when the more moderate supporters of Lord Grenville gave their support to the Liverpool government. Never-theless, he refused all blandishments to joining any broadly based Tory

1 Grey was known by his courtesy title of Viscount Howick until his father died in 1807.

government, helping to maintain the image of a 'pure' Whig party. Part of this image was to foster the impression that, as in 1688, the Whig aristocracy would lead the nation in a moment of supreme peril or national chaos. The chaotic state of the Tory government, and the rising demands for parliamentary reform, meant that the image of the Whigs as leaders in a time of peril became a prophecy fulfilled in 1830, when William IV sent for Grey to form a government.

The Whigs and their followers certainly did not hold a majority of seats in the House of Commons in 1830, and it was necessary for Grey to form a broadly based coalition government, one indeed not too different from what might perhaps have emerged had Canning or Huskisson lived and headed a government determined to enact parliamentary reform. Grey's Cabinet was thus distinguished from virtually any other in modern times which was not an explicit coalition by including very considerable numbers of opposition Canningite Tories, among them (extraordinarily) the former Prime Minister Lord Goderich, who served as Secretary for War and the Colonies from 1830 to 1833; Lord Palmerston, who had served in all Tory Cabinets from 1809 till 1828, Charles Grant, and Lord Melbourne, the future Prime Minister, who had served as Chief Secretary for Ireland in 1827–28. It also included one 'Ultra Tory', the Duke of Richmond, who served as Postmaster-General in 1830–34. Most members of the Cabinet were Whigs, either moderate Whigs of Grey's own generation like the third Marquess of Lansdowne, who had held the position of Home Secretary under Goderich, or younger, more radical Whigs like Lord John Russell, Edward Stanley (later fourteenth Earl of Derby), Viscount Althorp,[2] and Sir James Graham. By and large, these younger Whigs set the pace and direction of the Grey government, especially over parliamentary reform. It also included a number of men regarded as radicals, especially 'Radical' Jack Lambton (later first Earl of Durham, 1792–1840) and Henry Brougham (first Baron Brougham and Vaux, 1778–1868), who became Lord Chancellor. The diversity of the new government might best be illustrated by the fact that, apart from Grey, it contained five other men who became Prime Minister: three as Whigs or Liberals (Melbourne, Russell and Palmerston) but also two as Tories (Goderich and Stanley). Few Cabinets ever had more talent, and few governments which lacked both the diversity and talent of Grey's Cabinet could have carried a measure as sweeping as the Reform Act. It was also a Cabinet of large landowners like Durham, Lansdowne, Stanley (later Lord Derby) and Althorp (later Lord Spencer), and Grey claimed that its members owned more acres than did those of any previous British Cabinet.

The inner core of the government consisted of Whigs, and it might be as well to offer a working definition of what the term means. It is an

---

2 Viscount Althorp (1782–1845) was known by his courtesy title, borne as heir to the earldom of Spencer. Since he was not a nobleman he could sit in the House of Commons. Later in 1834 he inherited the title, becoming the third Earl Spencer.

ambiguous one. During the late eighteenth and early nineteenth centuries the term was generally used to refer to the largely aristocratic group of opponents of the Tory governments of Pitt and Liverpool who stood for reform and liberty. After 1832, and especially after 1867 or so, the term was often used to refer to right-wing Liberals, generally aristocrats, most of whom left the Liberal party during the 1886 Home Rule crisis. For the period around 1832 historians generally use the term to mean an inter-related, interconnected group of enormously wealthy aristocratic families, centring around the Dukes of Bedford and Marlborough, who stood for the liberal values which animated the 1688 revolution. This inner core of Whigs was, thus, paradoxically at one and the same time incredibly exclusive and wealthy and also championed liberalism and reform. Around this central core were other groups and individuals who were regarded as Whigs – reformist and liberal intellectuals like Macaulay, less grand landed aristocrats like the Greys, newer wealthy families like the Barings and Labouchères. Early nineteenth-century Whiggery had also been seminally influenced by Charles James Fox (1749–1806), the great Whig politician who once offered a toast (in 1798) to 'Our Sovereign, the people', causing his name to be erased from the Privy Council. It is probably not possible to be more precise about the definition of a 'Whig' than this.

Against the Whigs stood the Tories, who were in power for almost all of the period from 1783 until 1830. As a group Tories were even more diverse than Whigs, sharing in common little beyond a desire to carry on the King's government with as little disturbance or reform as possible. Tories repre-sented the political 'right', Whigs the political 'left', but the differences were not as clear as they later became. One paradoxical feature of early nineteenth-century Toryism is that many of its leaders were the sons or grandsons of self-made men, and fewer were *bona fide* aristocrats than among the inner circle of Whigs. The father of Lord Eldon, the arch-conservative Lord Chancellor, owned a coal barge in Newcastle upon Tyne; Addington's was a doctor; Canning's widowed mother was forced to go on the stage as an actress. Many benefited directly or indirectly from 'Old Corruption', the system of government sinecures and payments to holders of offices and positions with no duties. While all Prime Ministers since Pitt modified and diminished the lavishness of 'Old Corruption', most radicals felt that, through the 1830s, vast amounts of unearned incomes were still being distributed to the aristocracy and government favourites. John Wade's *Extraordinary Black Book*, which appeared in several editions from the mid-1810s onwards, proved to be an immensely popular compendium of the names and incomes of thousands of government 'placemen'. 'Old Corruption' and its evils were also a central theme of William Cobbett's attack on the Tory governments of the period. In the 1820s the Whigs became committed to reforming 'Old Corruption' comprehensively. This became a part of the Whig programme of 'retrenchment and reform', which bridged the gap between Whig aristocrats and middle-class radicals who increasingly sided with the Whigs.

The long success of the Tories was, however, in part a product of the fact that they represented most of the British 'Establishment' of the time in a consensual way, comprising most landed aristocrats (apart from the Whigs) and landowners, a surprisingly large portion of the business middle classes, the older professions, the Church of England, and the universities. What the Whigs did in 1832 was, essentially, to split the consensual Tory 'Establishment' by building a new coalition of Whig aristocrats, newer sections of the middle classes, especially industrialists in the northern cities, and Dissenters. The 1832 electoral system gave this coalition a normal majority, especially after the 1846 split in the Conservative party, although the electoral system also gave the Tories a significant number of MPs. Not until the Liberal Unionist split of 1886 was the old Conservative-dominated 'Establishment' reformed as the normal majority group in Parliament, and then under very different circumstances.

Lord Grey's first speech to Parliament, in November 1830, disclosed that he had received the King's permission to introduce a reform bill. Grey appointed a committee of four – Lord Durham, Lord John Russell, Sir James Graham and Lord Duncannon (later the fourth Earl of Bessborough) – to draft a reform bill, with instructions that it should be based essentially on property and preserve existing territorial divisions and accepted forms, yet be sweeping enough to forestall demands for further reform for an indefinite time. Grey's chief role in the reform struggle was to keep the King on side, and to keep the Cabinet united, despite its very disparate elements. He did this with great skill. He handled the King with tact, cleverly warning that if William IV rejected the moderate reforms proposed by the Cabinet, more radical rather than less radical measures would become inevitable. Lord Durham and Lord John Russell (who held the office of Paymaster-General, outside the Cabinet, until June 1831, when he was promoted to Cabinet rank) were the most influential members of the committee which drafted the Reform Act, and Russell has ever since been remembered as the man who introduced the Reform Bill into Parliament and was chiefly responsible for carrying it through successfully.[3]

The aims of the Whig government in proposing reform were varied. Among the most important was the elimination of most 'pocket boroughs', controlled, in effect, by wealthy proprietors. On one estimate, 276 out of 489 English MPs in the 1820s were elected from seats controlled by an owner or patron. Most of these MPs were Tories, and many were wealthy businessmen, often self-made. A charge raised against the Whigs and the Reform Bill was that the Reform Bill, as it was enacted, ended most Tory

3 Russell sat in the House of Commons until 1861, when he received a peerage. 'Lord' John Russell was a courtesy title, that is, one borne by Russell as the younger son of a duke but not conferring true aristocratic status: he was thus eligible to sit in the House of Commons.

'rotten boroughs', but left the Whig-controlled boroughs alone. In fact, the Whigs were perfectly happy to retain 'legitimate' as opposed to 'illegitimate' influence in the boroughs, by which they seemingly meant control by local landowners with a stake in the local community rather than by absentee borough-mongers from afar, often London merchants who wanted a political career (and, possibly, a title) to crown their careers. Secondly, the Whigs wanted to rationalise the constituencies sending MPs to Parliament, so that the worst 'rotten boroughs', those with insignificant numbers of voters (like Old Sarum, which had precisely seven voters, yet returned two MPs to Parliament), were disenfranchised and their places taken by great cities like Manchester and Birmingham, which hitherto had returned no MPs. Thirdly, the Whigs wished to see the right to vote rationalised and extended to the entire middle class, instead of the strange and *ad hoc* variety of qualifications for voting, varying from seat to seat, which ranged from boroughs where only members of the town corporation could vote to some boroughs with virtual manhood suffrage.

The 1832 Reform Act accomplished these aims in a fairly comprehensive way, but only after an enormous struggle which has itself become one of the most famous parliamentary sagas in modern history. Lord John Russell initially introduced the government's bill into the House of Commons on 1 March 1831. Both the government and the Tory opposition expected a much more moderate proposal than the one actually announced. When Russell read out a list of 60 'rotten boroughs' to be totally disenfranchised under Schedule A of the proposed bill, the Tory benches reacted with insane laughter. The bill's second reading, eight weeks later, saw its passage by only one vote, 302:301. Shortly afterwards, an amendment by General Gascoyne, the Tory MP for Liverpool, moved that the overall representation for England and Wales not be diminished. On 19 April 1831 Gascoyne's motion was carried by 299 votes to 291. The opposition then successfully defeated a motion for the grant of supplies, tantamount to a vote of no confidence in the government, and Grey persuaded the King to grant a dissolution.

A near-riot had occurred on the arrival of the King at Parliament formally to dissolve it and call another general election. This presaged the mood of the country during the campaign for the general election held in May–June 1831, when Apsley House, Wellington's London mansion, had its windows broken, and the cry went up for 'the bill, the whole bill, and nothing but the bill'. Although the elections themselves were orderly, there was widespread fear of heightened unrest.

The general election of 1831 resulted in a considerable victory for the forces of reform. Some 76 out of 82 English county members elected in 1831, and the four members returned by the City of London, were avowed reformers. Since it was the Parliament of 1831–32 which passed the great Reform Act, in a real sense the 'unreformed' Parliament reformed itself, showing that, in very extreme circumstances, when public opinion was fully aroused, it was capable of taking very radical action. Paradoxically, in some measure this justified the belief of the opponents of reform that the unreformed House of Commons still represented the will of the nation. A new Reform Act, introduced into Parliament in June 1831, and nearly identical with the old, was passed on its second reading by a margin of 136 votes on 8 July 1831 and by a margin of 345 to 236 on its third reading. The tactic of the Tories was to delay the passage of the bill for as long as possible and it was at this stage that the famous 'Chandos clause' (named for Lord Chandos, MP, the son of the Duke of Buckingham, who introduced it) was added to the bill, extending the right to vote to most tenant farmers. The bill next went to the Lords, and here everything almost came unstuck. On 8 October 1831 the Lords rejected the Reform Bill by a vote of 199 to 158. Twenty-one bishops had voted against it, making the crucial difference in the outcome. Window-breaking struck London and rioting occurred in a number of provincial cities. At Bristol, troops called out to suppress angry rioters acted weakly (presumably out of sympathy with the bill), and many public buildings in Bristol were burned and looted. The Home Secretary, Lord Melbourne, acted firmly, but there was a strong sense that a near-revolutionary situation was emerging throughout Britain, fanned by radical Political Unions which grew up throughout the country.

In December 1831, a new Reform Bill was introduced and passed. It differed slightly from the earlier versions in disenfranchising somewhat fewer seats, but giving more to unenfranchised towns. It finally passed its third reading on 23 March 1832 by 355 votes to 239. King William IV was finally persuaded to a course long recommended by Grey, the creation of enough new peers to carry the bill in the Lords. Grey also successfully lobbied members of the Lords, especially the bishops, to change sides, and on 14 April 1832 the Act was passed in the Lords by a vote of 184 to 175.

Yet again, however, everything almost came unstuck, when Lord Lyndhurst, the Tory Lord Chancellor in 1827–30, moved a resolution, adopted by the Lords by 151 to 116, delaying consideration of Schedule A of the Act which abolished the 'rotten boroughs'.[4] The King now demurred from his promise to create a large number of peers. The Whig government resigned, and from 8 to 15 May 1832 occurred the so-called 'May days' when something approaching anarchy reigned in the British government. Wellington was approached by the King to form a government which would carry a moderate Reform Act acceptable to the Lords. He was willing to do this, despite his previous proclamations about the perfection of the existing Constitution, but was met by the adamant refusal of Peel to participate in any such government. Despite his liberalism, Peel feared that his previous about-face over Catholic emancipation would, combined with

4 Lord Lyndhurst (born John Singleton Copley, 1772–1863) was born in Boston, Massachusetts, the son of the famous American portrait painter John Singleton Copley who was opposed to the American Revolution and settled in London in 1775.

any about-face over parliamentary reform, ruin his reputation. As well, many right-wing peers feared a Tory reform bill and refused to support Wellington. On 10 May the House of Commons passed a vote of confidence in Grey by a majority of 80. The mood of the country was very ugly, and Francis Place and other radicals were planning a campaign to create an economic crisis by having depositers at the Bank of England withdraw their holdings in the form of gold: 'To stop the duke, go for gold!' was Place's plan.

On 14 May 1832 Wellington became convinced that he could not form a government and advised the King to recall Grey, which he did on 15 May 1832. Wellington also decided to acquiesce in reform by abstaining, and advising Tory peers to abstain from voting on the passage of the amended bill in the Lords. Grey had also now received definite and clear assurances from the King about the creation of new peers, and the great Reform Bill finally passed its third reading in the Lords on 4 June 1832 by a vote of 106 to 22, the 'die-hard' opponents of reform now shrunk to a tiny minority. The new Act received the Royal Assent on 7 June 1832, modernising the House of Commons in a way which all knew was highly significant if not, perhaps, as radical as either its supporters or opponents imagined. Grey also decided on yet another general election, the first to be held under the new order of things. Parliament was dissolved in December 1832, and a general election was held the same month. Throughout the reform crisis Grey and his ministers acted with great skill and unswerving resolution.

The Great Reform Act of 1832 affected the British political system in two distinct ways: first, it changed the representation in the House of Commons of many seats, disenfranchising, or reducing the number of members returned by, no fewer than 143 boroughs which had elected members of Parliament before 1832, and, in turn, adding precisely the same number of seats to rapidly growing boroughs while increasing the representation of 38 counties. Second (and only indirectly related to the first point), it rationalised and extended the qualifications for voting in all seats, increasing the size of the electorate, it is generally believed, by about 49 per cent between 1831 and 1833. Together, these changes in Britain's formal political structure brought about a far-reaching and permanent change in Britain's political system and its outcomes, although the continuities with the pre-1832 political system were also important and should not be overlooked.

The Reform Act totally disenfranchised 56 boroughs in England, each of which had previously returned two members to Parliament.[5] All of these were found, in the 1821 Census, to contain fewer than 2000 inhabitants; these were, by and large, the classical 'rotten boroughs' like Old Sarum, Corfe Castle, Ludgershall and Saltash, which had – so its champions

5 One disenfranchised seat, Highamferrers in Northamptonshire, had returned one member to Parliament.

argued – returned statesmen and wealthy businessmen to the Commons. Of these 56 disenfranchised boroughs, 33 were in the agricultural and coastal counties of south and south-west England (13 in Cornwall) which had been largely untouched by economic advance. (On the other hand, seven were in the Home Counties, three in Yorkshire, and one, Newton, in Lancashire.) A further 30 English boroughs, those whose populations in 1821 were found to have been between 2000 and 4000, lost one of two members they had been entitled to send, while the representation of Weymouth and Melcombe Regis, which had returned four MPs before the Act, was reduced to two.

The Act thus ended, abruptly and comprehensively, the most dramatic examples of unworthy parliamentary representation under the old system. To balance this reduction, it added 125 new seats under a variety of guises. Twenty-six English counties were each divided into two divisions, with each new division now returning two members, an addition of 52 seats. These 26 counties whose representation doubled were spread throughout England, and included remote rural districts like Cornwall, Cumberland and Shropshire, as well as Lancashire, Warwickshire and some of the Home Counties. In addition to these 26 counties, seven other counties (Berkshire, Buckinghamshire, Cambridgeshire, Dorset, Herefordshire, Hertfordshire and Oxfordshire) were to return three members instead of two, while the Isle of Wight (part of Hampshire) was given its own MP. Each of the three Ridings of Yorkshire, the very large county in the north of England, was to return two MPs, instead of the whole county electing four.

Apart from the disenfranchisement of the 'rotten boroughs', the most dramatic change in the representation of England was the enfranchisement of 41 boroughs which had, prior to 1832, no parliamentary representation at all. Twenty-two large boroughs were each henceforth to return two members of Parliament. In this category were most of the great cities, previously unrepresented, which had grown enormously during the previous half-century, among them Manchester, Birmingham, Bradford, Leeds and Sheffield, as well as a range of middle-sized industrial towns like Blackburn, Bolton, Halifax, Oldham, Stoke-on-Trent and Wolverhampton. Five unrepresented boroughs in London also received two MPs each (Finsbury, Greenwich, Lambeth, Marylebone and Tower Hamlets), while a variety of other significant non-industrial towns were now to elect two MPs, among them Brighton, Devonport and Stroud. In addition to these 22 boroughs now electing two MPs, a further 19 boroughs, also unrepresented in Parliament before 1832, were now to return one MP each. The mixture here was fairly similar to the other enfranchised towns, including industrial towns like Bury, Gateshead, Huddersfield, Rochdale, Salford and Walsall, as well as non-industrial local centres like Cheltenham, Frome, Kendal, Whitby and Whitehaven, but notably did not include a single borough in London, with only the naval port of Chatham being in the Home Counties, and only the fashionable resort of Brighton within reasonable travelling distance of the capital. In all, 125 new seats were created in England to balance the 143 which had been disenfranchised. The total number of English MPs was actually reduced by the Great Reform Act, with 471 English constituencies instead of the previous 489.

Changes in Wales, Scotland and Ireland were more minimal. Five additional Welsh constituencies were created, with three Welsh counties (Carmarthenshire, Glamorganshire and Denbighshire) each returning two members instead of one. Two new Welsh boroughs, Swansea and Merthyr Tydfil, were also created. In all, Wales's contingent in the House of Commons rose from 24 to 29. Scottish representation was also increased, from 45 to 53. Before 1832, several Scottish constituencies most bizarrely returned members to alternate parliaments; these seats were thus also unrepresented in alternate parliaments. The Reform Act ended this peculiarity, by uniting Clackmannan and Kinross shires, by giving separate representation to Bute and Caithness shires, and by uniting Cromarty with Ross-shire and Nairn with Elgin, all of which had previously taken turns at electing a member. Edinburgh was given an additional member, and new seats were created at Paisley, Leith Burghs and Greenock. Other adjustments were made in the former grouping together of Scottish boroughs. For instance, before 1832 Glasgow, Dumbarton, Renfrew and Rutherglen voted together to elect one member. After 1832, Glasgow elected two members, while Dumbarton, Renfrew and Rutherglen were grouped together with Kilmarnock and Port Glasgow jointly to elect one member.

Changes in Ireland were also fairly minimal, with Ireland's representation at Westminster increasing from 100 to 105 by the addition of one extra member elected by Dublin University, Belfast, Galway, Limerick and Waterford.

There are several ways in which to view the impact of the Great Reform Act upon parliamentary representation. On one hand, unquestionably the Act was far-reaching in giving representation to many of the new urban areas and in ending, at a stroke, most of the grosser abuses of the rotten boroughs. No contemporary observer saw the Reform Act as anything but far-reaching – indeed epochal – and our common perception of one world, now frequently termed the British *ancien régime*, having ended in 1832 and another era begun is not hyperbole. As well as the actual specifics of the changes in representation brought about by the Great Reform Act, a world and its ambience, the world of what was then and is now often called 'Old Corruption' also ended. On the other hand, the redistribution of seats brought about by the 1832 Act should not be exaggerated. Most parliamentary seats were actually unaffected by the Act, among them dozens of small boroughs only slightly larger than the 'rotten boroughs'. For the most part, the Act respected and almost invariably built upon pre-existing local boundaries, with the old counties and boroughs continuing to be the geographical units of representation. Most importantly, the number of new industrial urban seats created was relatively small, no more than 50 or 60 in a House of Commons of 658. London in particular continued to be grossly underrepresented, all of the metropolis returning only 16 MPs including four elected by the City of London. Manchester, Liverpool and Birmingham together comprised about 2 per cent of the population of the United Kingdom (and probably generated a higher percentage of the national income) but returned only six MPs, less than 1 per cent of the total number of members. This bias against urban and industrial Britain was deliberate, and had important political consequences for the nature of politics in Britain during the whole of the 35-year period (1832–67) during which the constituencies created by the Reform Act existed. Under the Reform Act settlement, urban and industrial Britain was simply too underrepresented, too minor a part of the parliamentary nation, ever to dream of comprising more than a small and unimportant portion of the House of Commons, let alone aspire to form the central part of the parliamentary nation. Conversely, rural and small-town Britain was just as important and central to the representation of the House of Commons as it had been before 1832, perhaps more so. Moreover, the constituencies created by the Reform Act were intended by the Whigs to remain in place for at least 50 years, if not forever: the Reform Bill contained no method of changing or modifying parliamentary boundaries (such as by periodical redistribution) as population shifted and changed, and in fact the representation created by the Reform Act remained virtually unaltered until 1867 with the Second Reform Act. Since Britain's industrialising cities were obviously growing ever-larger with each passing year, both in absolute and relative terms, the underrepresentation of the larger cities became even more acute as time passed.

Apart from changing the constituencies of the House of Commons in significant ways, the Great Reform Act had a second, unrelated aim which was probably even more important, namely to widen the number of men entitled to vote in parliamentary elections by broadening the basis of the franchise. In place of the jumble of types of franchises which existed, essentially without rhyme or reason, in the pre-1832 parliaments, the Reform Act extended the franchise in England and Wales by creating a new basic qualification for the franchise in the boroughs, a £10 householder qualification, and by supplementing the pre-existing 40 shilling freeholder qualification in the counties by a large number of new franchises. (In Scotland and Ireland the basis for the revised franchise was slightly different.)

In the English boroughs, occupiers (owners or tenants) of any building with an annual rateable value of £10 or more were to be entitled to vote, provided they had been in possession of that building for a year and had paid their taxes. Certain types of lodgers were also enfranchised, while virtually all franchise-holders before 1832 were allowed to retain their vote for life. The vote in the English counties was vastly more complicated, with no less than 17 different categories of persons being enfranchised. Basically,

40 shilling freeholders (i.e. men whose property had a rateable annual value of £2 or more) were to be entitled to vote, plus £10 freeholders and copyholders (possessors of a type of land tenure), tenants whose rent totalled £50 or more, and most leaseholders. The clause enfranchising tenants whose rent totalled £50 or more is known as the 'Chandos Clause'. It was introduced against the wishes and objections of the Whig government by the Marquess of Chandos (heir to the Duke of Buckingham) with the intention of enfranchising most tenant farmers, who would (he believed) be likely to vote the way their landlords wished. It will be seen that while the qualifications to vote in boroughs became simpler, the franchise in the English counties actually became much more complex.

The changes to the franchise in Scotland and Ireland were somewhat different, and less complex. In the Scottish and Irish boroughs, occupiers of houses with a rateable value of £10 or more were enfranchised, together with 40 shilling freeholders and many tenants and leaseholders in the counties.

While the increase in the number of men entitled to vote was large, it was, rather surprisingly, not truly enormous (except in Scotland), and in England and Wales the legislation of 1832 actually brought about a *lower* percentage increase in the proportion of the population entitled to vote than did any subsequent Reform Act. It is generally believed that the number of men entitled to vote in England and Wales grew from about 435 000 in 1831 to about 653 000 in 1833, an increase of 219 000 or about 49 per cent. It is usually estimated by modern scholars that about one adult male in five was entitled to vote in 1833 in England and Wales. The obverse of this fact is, of course, that four-fifths of the adult men in England and Wales (and all women) lacked the vote. Since at the time some American states had virtually universal male suffrage, the Act's effects hardly seem revolutionary, and it is obvious that Britain did not become a democracy in 1832. Moreover, even fewer men would have had the right to vote after 1832 had not many tenant farmers been enfranchised by the 'Chandos Clause' and existing franchise-holders retained their right to vote for life even if (as with some borough freemen) they would not have been qualified to vote under a franchise based purely on property ownership.

In Scotland, however, the growth in the electorate was vastly greater than in England and Wales. Because so few Scotsmen had the vote before 1831, with borough corporations and a tiny group of landowners virtually alone choosing Scotland's MPs, the new property-based franchise was bound to extend the right to vote far more dramatically than in England and Wales. In 1831 it was believed that only 4579 men had the right to vote in all of Scotland, of whom just 1303 lived in the Scottish borough seats. By 1833, after the Reform Act, this figure had risen to 64 447, an increase of 59 868 or over 1300 per cent. Even so, in relative terms a far lower percentage of adult Scottish males could vote than was the case in England, as both the minimal borough and county property qualifications brought fewer men into the franchise net north of the border. It is generally estimated by modern scholars that about one adult male Scotsman in eight could vote in 1833, a considerably lower proportion than in England and Wales. In Ireland – in contrast to Scotland – the Reform Act added many fewer new voters than anywhere else, with the number of men entitled to vote estimated to have risen from 75 960 in 1831 to 92 152 in 1833, an increase of only 21 per cent. Moreover, the percentage of males in Ireland entitled to vote was very much lower than in England or even Scotland: Ireland was a country of impoverished smallholders, and accordingly fewer men met the property qualifications which conferred the suffrage. Hence in 1833 only about one Irishman in 20 was entitled to vote. The Reform Act changed only marginally the £10 freeholder qualification imposed at the time of Catholic emancipation, and did not bring Ireland in line with the 40 shilling freeholder minimum in England.

The new electorate which was created by the Reform Act had certain distinctive characteristics. The right to vote was now based upon rational criteria, applied impartially and equally throughout all borough and county constituencies. While individual constituencies still varied enormously in size in a haphazard way, the qualifications for voting no longer included any particularistic anomalies wherein wholly different criteria for voting applied in one borough in contrast to another a few miles away. This criteria of rationality was very much in keeping with most of the Whig-engendered improvements of the 'age of reform', but wholly at variance with the Tory, Burkean notion of the preciousness of historically derived anomalies. Owing to its basis in property ownership, the 'political nation' created in 1832 was largely if not wholly upper-middle-class, with the proviso that it included many tenant farmers and 'ancient right' voters from before 1832. Because it rested chiefly upon two types of property-ownership, £10 occupiers in the boroughs and 40 shilling freeholders in the counties, it was biased in favour of the south of England and the Home Counties, where real estate values were higher and a much larger per-centage of the adult male population owned or occupied property exceed-ing the minimal rateable value.

Perhaps the most important single change brought about by the altera-tions in the qualification for voting in the Great Reform Act, however, was the type of man who was likely to become an MP. Before 1832, the existence of so many 'pocket boroughs' meant that significant numbers of rich businessmen and professionals could indeed secure election to Parlia-ment. These were often merchants, bankers, and men who had made a fortune overseas, or wealthy lawyers and army officers, who normally secured election from a 'pocket borough' where they personally did not live, and which they may never have set eyes upon before their election. After 1832, it became harder for this type of business or professional man to enter Parliament, at least via the old kind of 'pocket boroughs' which had now largely vanished. In place of these men, however, came a new type of middle-class MP, the businessman, often a manufacturer, who was firmly rooted in the seat which returned him to Parliament (or one nearby). These men were often seen as indeed their town's 'representative' in Parliament, being closely associated with local prosperity and often being major employers of labour in their constituencies. As we have seen, very few manufacturers entered Parliament before 1832. After 1832 their number grew consistently, although one should not exaggerate their impact: it would be many decades indeed before more than a small minority of Parliament consisted of manufacturers or representatives of the post-industrial revolution forms of wealth and income. However, the older type of wealthy MP, especially the Indian 'nabob', the West Indian planter, and government contractors, declined in number fairly consistently after 1832. Certainly the total number of businessmen in the House of Commons, contrary to what one might have expected, did not rise astronomically. In the Parliament elected in 1826, there were apparently about 179 business-men; in 1830, 186; in 1831, 185. In 1832, the first election after the Reform Bill, there were about 215 (168 among the Whig-Liberals and 47 from the Conservatives). These estimates are derived from the research of two different historians, Gerrit P. Judd and J. A. Thomas, and are both subject to margins of error, but it seems clear that the number of businessmen-MPs rose only marginally as a result of the Reform Act, with the newer type of manufacturers barely making up for the older type of merchants in 'pocket boroughs'.

Instead, the House of Commons continued to be overwhelmingly domi-nated by the traditional landed elite, with (on J. A. Thomas's estimate) no fewer than 434 landowners or their close relatives (321 Whig-Liberals and 123 Tories) in the House elected in 1832. Given that there were 253 county seats in the new House (65 *more* than before the Reform Act) plus dozens of small boroughs where the landowners continued to exert a predominant influence, this could hardly be otherwise, and it would be decades – perhaps, indeed, over half a century – before this would change in a decisive way.

It was, nevertheless, clear that the Reform Act would benefit the Whigs and their associates and harm the Tories. That this was the immediate outcome of reform was indeed shown by the results of the 1832 general election. It is generally believed that the Whigs and their supporters won 479 seats, the Tories (increasingly known as Conservatives) only 179. The Whigs were predominant in every part of the country, even in the English counties, where they won 104 seats to the Tories' 40. In the English boroughs the Liberals were ahead by 244 seats to 83. Some of the long-term geographical trends in British politics now emerged clearly: the Whigs gained 43 seats in Scotland to only 10 for the Tories, and were ahead in Ireland by 72 to 33. In Wales, however, the Conservatives emerged slightly ahead, 16 to 13, and Wales remained surprisingly competitive between the two parties until 1868. The number of uncontested seats, where only one candidate stood, was at 124 relatively low for an election at this time. The Whig benches now contained a great many radicals, among them William Cobbett, elected for the manufacturing town of Oldham, and such 'philosophical radicals' as George Grote and Sir William Molesworth. The first practising Quaker, Joseph Pease, was elected for South Durham, attending the House in the sober black clothes worn at the time by most members of the Society of Friends. Joseph Gully, a famous prize-fighter who became the proprietor of a coal mine in Sunderland, was elected for Pontefract. On the Tory benches, there was much less new blood, the most notable fresh recruit being William Ewart Gladstone, elected for Newark and at this stage of his career an extreme right-wing intellectual, deeply concerned for the welfare of the Church of England in the new regime, who quickly became tagged by Thomas Babington Macaulay, the famous essayist and Whig MP, as 'the rising hope of those stern and unbending Tories'. Wellington, looking down on the new House from the peers' gallery, stated that he had never seen so many bad hats worn on a public occasion, an appropriate judgement on the number of newcomers in Parliament.[6] On the other hand, it was also widely noted that the intellectual level of debate, and the seriousness with which MPs attended to business, had also risen. As well, the 'golden age' of the 'Blue Book' (official reports and annual returns about a specific topic or of a government department) and of the Royal Commission now ensued, with all manner of statistics being officially collected and published, and serious, wide-ranging commissions of inquiry being made on many topics. (Karl Marx is said to have written *Das Kapital* using chiefly the parliamentary 'blue books'.) Reporting of Parliament became much more accurate, and long extracts from *Hansard* (the verbatim record of parliamentary debates) became a staple of quality newspapers like *The Times*. Hundreds of well-educated middle-class readers now poured over every *Hansard* in detail, a hobby that has become largely obsolete!

Both parties faced considerable problems in their self-definition and outlook after the passage of the Reform Act. These problems were particularly acute within the Conservative party: indeed, the political bases of the old Tory party vanished in considerable part with Reform. There could, of course, be no question of repealing the Reform Act, and Tories would have to come to terms with the new situation. In general, this took the form of adamant opposition to any further, especially very radical, reforms in church or state, and regrouping as a largely agricultural and Anglican party but with a surprisingly large middle-class base of support as well. In the years immediately after 1832, Sir Robert Peel emerged as the foremost spokesman for coming to terms with the new situation as directly as possible. Peel's most famous enunciation of the new, moderate Tory response to Reform was made in the celebrated 'Tamworth Manifesto' at

6 At this time, MPs often kept their hats on while sitting in Parliament.

the end of 1834, when he briefly formed a Tory government. Taking the form of an address to the electors of Peel's constituency of Tamworth, Staffordshire, the 'Manifesto' set out Peel's wider views on the situation in the wake of Reform. Noting that he had always supported 'judicious reforms' such as the law reforms he made as Home Secretary in the 1820s, Peel announced that he accepted the Reform Act as 'a final and irrevocable settlement of a great constitutional question' which could not then be questioned. He went even further, announcing that he approved of making 'a careful review of institutions, civil and ecclesiastical, undertaken in a friendly temper' in order to facilitate 'the correction of proved abuses, and the redress of real grievances', and giving a list of potential reforms, affecting for instance borough corporations, church rates, and the redistribution of Church revenues and the commutation of tithes providing that no Church property was to be diverted to secular uses. These were sweeping concessions indeed, and did not sit easily with unreconstructed old-fashioned Tories of the Eldon school, nor with younger Conservative intellectuals like Gladstone and Newman who feared that Reform inevitably entailed harming the Anglican Church and other traditional institutions.

Nevertheless, the post-1832 Conservative party continued to enjoy a surprising measure of support throughout the country, and over the next few general elections it recovered much (though not all) of the electoral ground it had forfeited in 1830–32. The continuing strength of Conservatism was not lost on shrewd observers of the day, who knew that the Tories still had considerable reservoirs of support, while the Reform Act was not really as sweeping as it seemed. For example, John Stuart Mill (a radical and Utilitarian who once termed the Conservatives 'the stupid party') produced a very perceptive account of the sources of political strength a few years after Reform, in his 'Reorganisation of the Reform Party', published in the *London and Westminster Review* in 1839. Mill believed that the Conservative party could count on the support of virtually the whole of the landed classes, 'nearly the whole class of very rich men', most of the old professions (among them the army and navy, and the law), the clergy of the Church of England, and those businessmen in 'protected trades' who benefited by the legal exclusion of competition, a category which Mill thought included 'the shipping interest, the timber interest, [and] the West India interest', trades where foreign competition was partially or wholly prohibited. This is a formidable list, and Mill was well aware that, as the Conservative party adapted itself to the new political realities, this combination of forces was likely to prove stronger than the forces of the 'Reform party'. To Mill, in the late 1830s the 'Reform party' comprised (besides a few Whig aristocrats) smaller landowners and prosperous farmers and yeomen, 'the bulk of the manufacturing and mercantile classes', the 'bulk of the middle classes of the towns', most English Dissenters, and 'nearly all Scotland and Ireland'. Mill also included 'the whole effective political strength of the working classes', who were, of course, still 'disqualified' from direct participation in parliamentary affairs.

Mill thus saw the chief political divisions in Britain, shortly after the Reform Act, as *already* drawn along the familiar lines which have persisted, arguably, to this day, with the rich, especially 'old money', supporting the Conservatives, the aspiring classes and the poor supporting the Radicals, while the chief non-economic division in British political life was the religious/ethnic divide between Anglican England on one side and Dissenters, Scotland and Ireland on the other. Mill also believed, most perceptively, that the Corn Laws were likely to prove to be a major line of political conflict and division, and that these, and other tariff barriers and restrictions, were a substantial prop of the Conservative party and its allied interests. Most of all, he believed that the two parties were almost evenly matched, and any potential numerical advantage enjoyed by the 'Reform party' was balanced by the fact that most of the poor were still excluded from the political process. The balance of forces he discerned, which was characterised by a growing Conservative strength leading to a Conservative majority in Parliament, did indeed persist into the mid-1840s when it was shattered by a bitter conflict over the Corn Laws. The ensuing split in the Conservative party, with free trade Tories led by Sir Robert Peel breaking ranks with the majority of the party, led to a 40-year span during which the Whig-Liberal party, and the coalition of forces it represented, indeed held a near-permanent majority in the House of Commons. Nevertheless, one must appreciate that the new political system created in 1832 was a highly competitive one, where the Conservative party quickly made up the ground it had lost by opposing Reform. On the other hand, after 1832 but before 1846 the Conservatives were no longer a consensual party of the established classes, as they had arguably been under Pitt and Liverpool, having lost most industrialists and the growing large towns to the Whigs.

The Whig government also had problems of self-identity after 1832. Coming to office as a remarkably broad coalition whose chief aim was to enact Reform, it was bound to lose some of its supporters once Reform was enacted. In particular, any extension of a radical agenda into other areas beyond parliamentary reform was, sooner or later, very likely to drive former Tory adherents, and even some moderate Whigs, into the arms of the Tories. Nevertheless, the record of the Whig government in the brief period between the enactment of Reform in 1832 and Grey's retirement in July 1834 was remarkable.

The most pressing problem facing the government concerned Ireland, and here all the potentially divisive tendencies within the Whig government revealed themselves. Little had been done about Ireland owing to the central question of parliamentary reform. Despite the granting of political rights to Catholics, Ireland had, in the early 1830s, fallen into a state approaching anarchy, with dozens of murders or attempted murders, widespread boycotting of the tithe collection and the formation of new secret societies. The response of the government was twofold. First, in 1833 it passed an Irish Coercion Bill (foreshadowing many subsequently passed during the nineteenth century) giving the Lord-Lieutenant of Ireland sweeping powers to suppress subversive meetings, declare curfews, and, remarkably, carry out trials for disorder under military rather than civilian law. Radicals in the Cabinet, especially Lord Althorp, attempted to delay or modify this bill, which was passed, against the furious opposition of O'Connell and his followers, chiefly because of the strong support of Edward Stanley, the former Tory who served in the Cabinet as Chief Secretary for Ireland.

At about the same time, the government passed an even more controversial bill, the Irish Church Temporalities Bill, a radical measure designed to win friends among the Irish Catholics alienated by the Coercion Act. As noted, the Church of Ireland included only about 10 per cent of the Irish population, and this Act was designed to reform it and make it more acceptable to the Catholic majority. Two out of the four Church of Ireland archbishoprics and eight of 18 bishoprics were abolished, and there was widespread consolidation of dioceses in underpopulated areas. A graduated tax was imposed on clerical incomes of £200 or more, to be used for church repairs and the like, and as a result Irish ratepayers (many Catholic or Presbyterian) were relieved from paying a tax known as the 'vestry cess' which was obnoxious to non-Anglicans.

At once, the Church Temporalities Bill attracted a remarkable degree of hostility and, indeed, emerged as one of the most controversial proposals of the nineteenth century, to some as controversial as the Reform Act. Although the proposed law seems moderate enough, to many conservatives it represented sacrilegious meddling, by a Parliament composed of radicals and non-Anglicans, with a divinely appointed institution (as Anglicans believed the Church of Ireland to be), confirming the worst fears of opponents of Reform as to what post-Reform parliaments were likely to do. The Irish Church Temporalities Act was one of the leading causes of the foundation of the Oxford Movement among young clerical conservative intellectuals like Newman and E. B. Pusey. Since the Whig government pointedly refused to use any of the money saved by the Irish church reforms for the Catholic Church or community, the bill also deeply offended O'Connell and the Irish Catholics. It had a stormy passage in the Lords, but was finally passed in August 1833 because Wellington and Peel gave it grudging support. Ireland continued to fester as an issue, with right-wing members of the government increasingly fearing any further concessions to the Irish Catholics or any reduction in the privileges of the Church of Ireland. In May 1834 the majority of the Cabinet approved the principle of the 'appropriation' of superfluous Church of Ireland funds for other purposes. This triggered the simultaneous resignation of four Cabinet ministers, Edward Stanley, Sir James Graham, the Duke of Richmond and the Earl of Ripon (formerly Lord Goderich), with Stanley and Ripon serving in Peel's 1841–46 Cabinet and Stanley (as Lord Derby) serving as Tory Prime Minister three times between 1852 and 1868.

Other genuinely momentous laws were passed by the Grey government. The most important of these was the abolition of slavery throughout the British Empire, passed by Parliament in 1833. The slave trade (the kidnapping of negroes from Africa and their sale to plantation owners or their subsequent sale) had been prohibited in 1807 to British subjects and to ships carrying British flags. Between then and 1833 a great campaign for the abolition of slavery throughout the Empire grew up, headed by William Wilberforce, Sir Thomas Fowell Buxton (1786–1845) and, in particular, many Quakers like Elizabeth Fry. All proposals to ameliorate the condition of slaves (most of whom lived in the West Indies) met with the adamant opposition of the well-organised West India planters' lobby, which was usually represented in Parliament by between 25 and 40 MPs in all Parliaments elected between 1807 and 1831. In 1833 the emancipation of the slaves was finally carried by Parliament chiefly owing to the efforts of Edward Stanley, who had become Colonial Secretary in 1833. A total of £20 million was given to the planters in compensation; in exchange, all slaves received their freedom within a year, although with mandatory apprenticeship to their former masters until 1838 or 1840 (this provision was abolished in 1838). Nevertheless, emancipation did little to improve the condition of the negroes of the West Indies, who remained largely uneducated and powerless. In any case, intense international competition in the sugar trade, and the abolition of sugar duties between 1846 and 1851, meant virtual impoverishment for both many plantation owners and negro workers. Improvement of the living standards of the black population of the West Indies did not come with freedom, while that region languished as a forgotten backwater of the Empire until the twentieth century. Nevertheless, the peaceful emancipation of the Empire's slaves should not be underestimated as a great moral and political achievement, correcting an obviously odious situation by peaceful means. The drive to abolish slavery was one of the noblest movements of reform in British history. However, the abolition of slavery had its critics, those at the time contrasting the government's support for the welfare of slaves in the West Indies with its lack of interest in the welfare of the poor and exploited in Britain. Some recent historians have also noted that both slavery and the sugar trade were uneconomical and declining, suggesting that not such a great sacrifice of British wealth was involved as a result of this reform.

Not without considerable difficulties, the government also passed one of the first important Factory Acts in 1833. This followed a Royal Commission of 1832, which produced evidence of the exploitation of children in factories, and which had been led by Michael Sadler MP, a Tory radical who denounced *laissez-faire* capitalism, and Lord Ashley (later the seventh Earl of Shaftesbury, 1801–85), the famous Evangelical social reformer. The bill, which applied to most textile factories, forbade the employment of children under nine, limited to 48 per week the hours of work of children aged nine to 13, and to 12 per day the hours of work of any person under 18. It also required children under 13 to attend school for at least two hours per day. Finally, it created a factory inspectorate to police the enforcement of these regulations, among the first government inspectorates in Britain. This last provision was chiefly the work of Edwin Chadwick (later Sir Edwin, 1800–90), Bentham's devoted follower who became, over the next 20 years, the most important member of commissions dealing with questions of social reform and government administration. The 1833 Factory Act passed the House owing to an alliance of landowners and radicals, against great opposition from manufacturers and *laissez-faire* economists who argued that factory costs would rise as a result of the Act and Britain would lose its international competitiveness. Since Britain's industrial growth continued in spectacular fashion for another 30 or 40 years, this argument evidently had little merit.

The Whig government also introduced two other very significant pieces of economic legislation. In 1833 the charter of the East India Company came up for renewal, and the government made very substantial changes in its nature. It provided for completely free trade with China (which came under the Company's domain) and restricted the Company's role to administering British India, subject to the ultimate rule of the Crown through the Governor-General in Bengal. It also opened all offices in the government of India to Indian natives and made British law universal throughout India. This reformed role for the East India Company was far from satisfactory, giving a private monopoly the power to administer a government, and came crashing down with the Indian Mutiny of 1857.

The other important economic measure was the Bank Charter Act of 1833, which slightly modified the Bank's privileges as issuer of its own banknotes, giving country banks (i.e. those situated outside of London) the right to use Bank of England paper banknotes worth over £5 as legal tender rather than pay its depositors in gold. Critics predicted the over-issuance of paper banknotes, leading to potential panics and depressions, but this did not occur.

Both because economic conditions were good during this period, and because so much centred on the Reform Act, radicalism, and certainly popular unrest, were less in evidence than before. Radical movements, however, now became better organised, increasingly on a national basis. In 1834 an attempt was made to form a Grand National Consolidated Trades Union, heavily influenced by the theories of Robert Owen (1771–1858), a Welshman who had run a cotton mill in Manchester. Deeply concerned with improving the condition of factory hands and their families, and concluding that personal character was largely formed by one's environment, Owen formed at New Lanark, near Manchester, and New Harmony, Indiana in the United States, the first cooperative communities, hallmarked by education and social welfare schemes for the workers. Owen, who apparently coined the term 'socialism', wished, in the long term, for cooperative ownership and production to take the place of capitalism, though by peaceful means. The aim of the Grand National Union was to obtain for workers control of their industries, reorganising them into cooperative ventures. Owen was rich, and devoted considerable funds to his scheme, which quickly gained over half a million members, although it collapsed after staging a wave of strikes, but before it could reorganise any industries.

Although the government did not crack down directly on the activities of the Grand National Union, it was alarmed at the wave of strikes and unrest that unionism brought about, and decided to make an example of one group of agricultural labourers in Tolpuddle, Dorset. In 1833 George Loveless, an agricultural labourer who was also a Methodist lay preacher, formed a 'Friendly Society of Agricultural Labourers' to fight the reduction of wages. While other rural, unskilled trades unions had been formed, this one had had help from trades unions elsewhere, including the Grand National Union. A local JP, James Frampton, had six of its leaders arrested for violating the 1797 Act against Unlawful Oaths. Frampton had direct assistance from Lord Melbourne, the Home Secretary, and the grand jury which tried the men was chaired by Melbourne's brother-in-law. After a hurried mock trial, the six were sentenced to be transported to Australia for seven years. Their case, however, was taken up by many prominent radicals, including Hume and O'Connell, and they became known as the 'Tolpuddle Martyrs'. In 1836 Lord John Russell, a more liberal Home Secretary than Melbourne (although serving under him as Prime Minister), granted them a free pardon. All returned to Britain by 1839, but, ironically, soon afterwards all re-emigrated to Australia.

Foreign affairs were largely quiet during Grey's term of office. The most important source of European disturbance occurred in the Low Countries, where, in August 1830, a revolution broke out in Belgium, then a part of the Kingdom of the Netherlands. The British were anxious to check France's ambitions towards annexing this country, while France's new king, Louis-Philippe, was forced to respond to internal liberal pressures. As a result, the independence of Belgium was recognised by Britain and France. Belgian independence was not recognised by the Netherlands, and a period of conflict ensued. The upshot was that Belgium became an independent kingdom. Its throne was offered to Prince Leopold of Saxe-Coburg (King Leopold I, who reigned from 1831 until 1865), Queen Victoria's uncle and a favourite of the British Royal Family. In 1839 a general international settlement of the Belgian question was achieved at London. Article VII of the Twenty-Four Articles, as they were known, guaranteed the 'independent and perpetually neutral state' of Belgium. (Seventy-five years later, this clause was not merely remembered by the British Cabinet, but led directly to Britain's declaration of war on Germany in August 1914, in response to the invasion of Belgium by German armies marching into France.) Britain's Foreign Minister, Lord Palmerston, was broadly sympathetic to Belgium's liberal demands for independence. He did, however, draw the line at anything more than a protest at Russia's suppression of a revolt in Poland, which broke out in November 1830 and led to Poland declaring its independence. As with the earlier revolt in Greece, this uprising had widespread popular support among liberals and intellectuals throughout Europe, especially in France, but no country could realistically come to the assistance of the rebels. Poland would have to wait nearly 80 years for its independence.

The end of Grey's government came suddenly and rather murkily. After the resignations of Stanley and three other ministers in May 1834, Grey attempted to patch up his government, promoting a number of unusual ministers, among them three businessmen, Edward Ellice (Secretary at War) and C. Poulett Thomson (subsequently first Baron Sydenham; President of the Board of Trade) to the Cabinet, and Sir Francis Baring of the great merchant banking family (later first Baron Northbrook) to the post of Financial Secretary of the Treasury outside of the Cabinet. However, a complex set of negotiations over the proposed renewal of the Irish Coercion Bill led to the resignation of Lord Althorp, the popular and influential Chancellor of the Exchequer and Leader of the House of Commons. A few days later, on 9 July 1834, convinced that he could not carry on without Althorp, Grey also resigned. There was no real reason for him to have done so, although his broadly based government had been weakened by the resignations earlier in the year. Grey had, in fact, wished to resign in January 1834 over another minor matter, but had been persuaded by the King and Cabinet to continue. It appears that Grey, 66 when he resigned, had simply had enough of turbulence during the previous four years and wanted peace and quiet. He never held office again. When lists are made of the greatest of British Prime Ministers, perhaps six or eight names are invariably suggested: but not Lord Grey's. This is, surely, unfair; indeed, a good case can be made that Grey was the very greatest British Prime Minister, at least in peacetime, ever to serve. It is doubtful whether any other leader at that time could have successfully headed a broadly based government which would have persisted in passing the Reform Act with the skill that Grey demonstrated, thus averting a British revolution; to this must be added the successful measures of reform in other areas passed by his government. It was an impressive achievement.

4

Lord Melbourne and the Whig governments of 1834–1841

Following the resignation of Lord Grey in July 1834, a period of considerable political confusion ensued, lasting until April 1835, when Lord Melbourne formed a Whig government which lasted for six years. The King turned to Lord Melbourne, the Home Secretary, expecting him to form a coalition of moderate Whigs and Tories; Peel and Wellington declined to join, and Melbourne carried on with much the same government as Grey had just headed. Melbourne became Prime Minister on 16 July 1834. Wavering as to whether or not to form a government, he was advised by a friend to accept: 'if it only lasts three months, it will be worthwhile to have been Prime Minister of England'. This apparently turned the balance in favour of accepting. Melbourne convinced Althorp to withdraw his resignation, and made a few other changes, for instance appointing Viscount Duncannon Home Secretary in place of himself. In general it was much the same Whig government (now without its right wing after the departure of Stanley and his allies) as Grey had led. It contained seven peers and nine Commoners, two of whom (Althorp and Russell) were the sons of peers, one of whom (Palmerston) was an Irish peer, and one of whom (Sir John Hobhouse, 1786–1869, later first Baron Broughton) was a baronet. Few had expected Melbourne ever to have become Prime Minister: 'he is certainly a queer fellow to be Prime Minister' was Greville's view, and a common one.

Although the first Melbourne government lasted only four months, it had a few measures to its credit. Althorp abolished the house tax, an unpopular measure which was widely opposed in the cities. It passed a milder Irish Coercion Bill, to take effect for only one year. The government wrestled again with the Irish tithe question but its proposals, which strongly bore the stamp of O'Connell, were defeated in the Lords. This was the situation when Parliament went into recess in August 1834. Over the next few months a series of curious and unusual events occurred. Lord Brougham, the influential radical Lord Chancellor, went on a triumphant tour of his native

Scotland, where he was enthusiastically received as the virtual saviour of his country. This went to Brougham's head, and he boasted more and more about his influence with all and sundry, including the King, whom he deeply alienated by his remarks.[1] Some historians, indeed, see this as tipping the balance against the Whig government. At this very time, on 16 October 1834, the old Houses of Parliament burned down, when orders were given to destroy the old-fashioned wooden tallies which had been used, until 1826, to keep track of Court of Exchequer accounts. The job was incompetently handled, and most of the building was destroyed within a few hours. Enough survived, however, for the Commons to use the House of Lords and the Lords to use the Painted Chamber (a smaller room in Parliament) until Sir Charles Barry's magnificent Houses of Parliament in Gothic style were built between 1837 and 1847. ('Big Ben', Parliament's clock tower, was not completed until 1858.)

On 10 November 1834 Althorp's father, the second Earl Spencer, died, and Althorp succeeded to the peerage. Melbourne offered to resign, since he had made Althorp's support a condition of becoming Prime Minister. As a peer, Althorp could not serve as Chancellor of the Exchequer, and the King would not accept Lord John Russell, Melbourne's choice as a replacement. King William accepted Melbourne's rather half-hearted offer of resignation and sent for the Tories to form a government. This was the last time in British history that any Sovereign interfered in the choice of a Prime Minister in this way: although the leaders of minority opposition parties sometimes formed minority governments (as Campbell-Bannerman's Liberals did in 1905–06 and, indeed, as Ramsay MacDonald's Labour party did in 1924), this was always on the recommendation of the outgoing Prime Minister rather than of the Sovereign. At the time (and for many years afterwards) it was believed that the King had 'dismissed' Melbourne and the Whigs, but Melbourne made the first move by offering to resign. By this time, in the last years of his reign, William IV, the former Whig, had moved far to the right and preferred the Tories, egged on by his brother Ernest Augustus, Duke of Cumberland (1771–1851), who toyed with the idea of staging a military *coup d'état* against a radical government.[2] The King was also very concerned at the possibility of further Whig interference with the Irish Church.

1 Brougham held a rather curious and facetious attitude towards his position, once scandalising the King by using the Great Seal of the Realm (which is held by the Lord Chancellor, and is a large silver object weighing over eight pounds, used to authenticate state documents by a wax impression) to make pancakes! Brougham was also the first Briton to spend his holidays at Cannes, on the French Riviera, and did more than anyone else to popularise holidays on the Riviera among wealthy British tourists.

2 On the death of King William IV in 1837, Cumberland succeeded as King of Hanover. The four King Georges and William IV had also been kings of Hanover (their ancestral home) as well as of Great Britain. When Victoria became Queen of Britain in 1837, however, Cumberland (Victoria's uncle) succeeded as King of Hanover, as women were debarred, under the so-called 'Salic Law' of continental monarchies, from succeeding as sovereigns in their own rights if any male heir existed.

William IV sent for Sir Robert Peel to form a government. Peel was in Rome at the time, and so the Duke of Wellington formed an interim or provisional government which lasted from 17 November until 9 December 1834, when Peel returned from abroad. The 'government' consisted of Wellington and Lord Lyndhurst as Lord Chancellor, with a group of six Lord Commissioners delegated to carry out the office of the Lord High Treasurer, i.e. to carry on the necessary financial business of the government. At the same time, a general election was called for January 1835, shortly after Peel's return. Peel formed his Tory government on 10 December 1834. His Cabinet consisted of 12 men. Peel held both the premiership and the Chancellorship of the Exchequer, an arrangement undertaken before by Canning and later by Gladstone. Wellington became Foreign Minister, and Henry Goulburn, Wellington's Chancellor of the Exchequer in 1828–30, Home Secretary. Seven of the 12 Cabinet ministers sat in the Lords and five in the Commons. Lord Aberdeen, Secretary for War and the Colonies, later followed Peel during the Corn Law split, and in 1852–55 headed a coalition government of Liberals and Peelites which conducted the Crimean War. The Cabinet also contained a businessman as President of the Board of Trade, Alexander Baring (1774–1848; later first Baron Ashburton), of the merchant banking family, and an uncle of the Francis Baring who held office in the previous Whig government. Many future Tory notables were, however, missing: Stanley and Gladstone were absent, as was Lord Ripon (Goderich), again a Tory fixture after 1841, but his elder brother, Earl de Grey, sat in Peel's first Cabinet as First Lord of the Admiralty. It contained, in fact, few men of ability.

The government clearly did not enjoy a majority in the House and in any case faced the imminent prospect of a general election a month after its formation. (It was in the course of this general election that Peel issued the 'Tamworth Manifesto'.) This election took place in January 1835 and was the first which occurred under what might be termed normal conditions after the dust had begun to settle on the Reform Act. While the Conservatives certainly made gains, the results demonstrated just how far the electoral geography of Britain had shifted since 1831, and how, in the reformed electoral system, the Tories were no longer the consensual party of government as they had been before the Act. The Whigs, Liberals and Irish together won 383 seats compared with the Tories' 275, a majority of about 108, certainly enough to keep the Whigs in office, barring some surprising event, for a full Parliament. The Whigs and their allies secured a majority of seats in virtually all types of constituencies. In England, the Whigs were ahead 266:205; in Scotland 38:15; in Ireland 67:38. Only, rather oddly, in Wales did the Conservatives elect a majority of MPs, 17:12. Among the English county seats – the very backbone of the Conservative party's strength – the Whigs still elected a narrow majority of MPs, 74:70. In the English borough seats, the Tories had made strong gains, increasing their number from 83 in the Parliament elected in 1832 to 135 in 1835, but were still outnumbered by the Whigs and their allies, who elected 192 MPs to these seats. The spirit of reform, which had triumphed in 1832, was still very much to the fore. On the other hand, it was clear that the Conservatives were by no means an anachronism, and still enjoyed considerable sources of electoral strength. They had managed to survive 1832.

The weakness of Peel's government became evident at once. As soon as Parliament convened, an election was held for the post of Speaker of the House. The incumbent, Sir Charles Manners-Sutton (1780–1845; later first Viscount Canterbury), a Tory who had held the post since 1817, was opposed by a Whig, James Abercromby (1776–1858; later first Viscount Dunfermline), who had served in the Cabinet as Master of the Mint under Melbourne in the closing stages of the previous Whig government. Despite Manners-Sutton's incumbency, Abercromby won narrowly by 316 votes to 306. The government was defeated on various amendments to the Royal Address, despite Peel's assurances that moderate measures of reform would be introduced. Peel in fact attempted to introduce rather far-reaching clerical reforms, introducing an Act to allow civil marriages, something long sought by Dissenters, and another wide-ranging measure of tithe reform. He also appointed a commission to examine comprehensively the distribution of church revenues. Nevertheless, the Whigs and Radicals held the upper hand, carrying, against the wishes of the government, a motion declaring Parliament in favour of establishing the University of London. Daniel O'Connell had formed an alliance with the Whigs (whom he mistrusted and repeatedly denounced) known as the 'Lichfield House compact', ensuring cooperation between the Whigs and the Irish. Realising his position was hopeless, Peel resigned on 8 April 1835.

The King was now forced to turn again to Lord Melbourne, who formed a purely Whig government with Lord John Russell in the Cabinet as Home Secretary. Melbourne became Prime Minister in April 1835, and remained in that office (with the exception of three days in May 1839, when the government temporarily resigned) until 30 August 1841. William Lamb, second Viscount Melbourne (1779–1848), is one of the more difficult nineteenth-century Prime Ministers for the historian to assess. Most accounts of Melbourne's life note his curiously negative qualities, especially his failure to give strong leadership or to play a central role in the events of his time. Yet they have also pointed out that Melbourne is one of the better-known political leaders of that era, much more famous than Goderich, Sidmouth, or perhaps even Grey. Part of this lasting fame has been due to Lord David Cecil's sparkling biography *Melbourne* (published in two parts in 1939 and 1954), while some comes courtesy of Melbourne's notorious wife Lady Caroline Lamb (née Ponsonby, 1785–1828), whose tempestuous affair with the poet Lord Byron scandalised Regency society, used as it was to aristocratic sexual immorality. (Lady Caroline Lamb was also the author of three novels published between 1816 and 1823; she became mentally disturbed in 1824 when she encountered Byron's funeral procession.)

Melbourne was educated, like so many of his aristocratic contemporaries, at Eton and Cambridge, and, like so many of them, was returned as a Whig for a 'pocket borough' at the age of 27. Largely because he was a lifelong Whig, but also owing to a diffident streak, he held no office until he became Chief Secretary for Ireland, without a seat in the Cabinet, under Canning in 1827 when he was already 48. Succeeding to the family title and a seat in the Lords in 1828, his rise thereafter was rapid: he served as a right-wing Home Secretary under Lord Grey in 1830–34. Melbourne was, in fact, one of the most conservative of Whig ministers, a fact which made him more acceptable to the King (who effectively chose the Prime Minister) than any other leading Whig. Although Melbourne believed deeply in the traditional hierarchal ordering of society, and particularly in the efficacy of aristocratic government, he accepted the need for a considerable measure of reform, and his period as Prime Minister contained almost as much in the way of important reform legislation as did that of Lord Grey's administration. While most of the impetus for these reforms came from other ministers (or from influential figures outside Parliament like Edwin Chadwick), Melbourne must take much of the credit for successfully passing them.

Lord Melbourne formed a Whig Cabinet of 12. Lord John Russell, as Home Secretary, and Lord Palmerston, as Foreign Secretary, were its leading figures. Rather oddly, Spencer (Althorp) was omitted, as was Brougham as Lord Chancellor. No Lord Chancellor was, in fact, appointed until January 1836, when Lord Cotenham (Sir Charles Pepys, 1781–1835) was finally given the position; for the previous nine months the position was, curiously, held 'in commission' without an appointee, Brougham being regarded as impossible to work with. Thomas Spring-Rice (1790–1866; later first Baron Monteagle), who had held office under Canning, became Chancellor of the Exchequer, but many of the ministers were hold-overs from Melbourne's previous government. The Cabinet originally consisted of six peers and six Commoners. Some of the subsequent appointments to Melbourne's Cabinet are noteworthy: in 1839 Thomas Babington Macaulay (1800–59; later first Baron Macaulay), the celebrated historian and essayist, became Secretary at War. In the same year Sir Frances Baring succeeded Spring-Rice as Chancellor of the Exchequer, a position he had held before, while Henry Labouchère (1798–1869, later first Baron Taunton), who had married into the Baring family and was also connected with Baring's Bank, became President of the Board of Trade.

The first great piece of reform legislation of this period, actually reaching the statute book in August 1834, during Melbourne's first, brief period as Prime Minister, was the New Poor Law (the Poor Law Amendment Act), one of the most famous pieces of social legislation of the nineteenth century. The story of the Old and New Poor Laws is well-known, and can only be summarised here. Historically, from the 1601 Poor Law Act, the relief of poverty was the responsibility of each parish, which raised a special 'poor laws rate' to deal with paupers. It drew a sharp distinction between able-bodied poor and those (the 'impotent' poor) whose poverty was due to circumstances beyond their control, such as old age. In the eighteenth century, many parishes established workhouses, to which the poor were increasingly sent. In 1795, amidst growing rural poverty, came the famous Speenhamland system, devised by justices of the peace in the Berkshire parish of that name. There, those justices (who were responsible for matters of poor relief) decided upon a more generous method, supplementing low wages by parish relief payments to each labourer based upon the size of his family and the price of bread. Well-meant – indeed, incredibly generous – the system spread throughout southern England, probably assisting in diminishing economically based social unrest. Yet it had many faults. Relief is meant to assist those who cannot reasonably help themselves: yet the 'Speenhamland' payments were made to able-bodied men actually in employment. Worse still, the system actually encouraged farmers and others to cut the wages of their workers, safe in the knowledge that the parish as a whole would foot the bill. Indeed, 'Speenhamland' may be seen as a kind of rort by farmers and landowners at the expense of other ratepayers. 'Speenhamland' obviously deterred the geographical mobility of labour, many workers naturally being reluctant to leave a parish where their wages were supplemented for an unknown fate elsewhere. Total payments made by all of England's 15 000 parishes for poor relief escalated open-endedly, from £2 million in the mid-1790s to £7 million at the time of the formation of the Poor Law Commission of 1832.

That 'Speenhamland', despite its generosity, failed to end unrest by the rural poor was evidenced by the 'Swing' riots of 1830–31, which broke out primarily in rural areas in the south of England where 'Speenhamland' was most commonly found. At this time, too, widespread disquiet and criticism of the existing system of poor relief was expressed by liberal intellectuals, especially the Utilitarians, and by middle-class taxpayers. As a result, the Whig government was happy, in 1832, to create a commission to examine the whole question. Given an extremely wide brief, it was chaired (remarkably) by C. J. Blomfield, the Bishop of London, and included, among its seven members, the Bishop of Chester. As is well-known, however, its leading and most influential member was Edwin Chadwick, the great Utilitarian social investigator. It seems reasonably clear that the commission, and especially Chadwick, was biased against the existing Poor Law, and prepared a case to prove its point. For instance, the commission did not investigate poverty in the northern industrial towns (which was highly cyclical in nature, linked to the 'boom-and-bust' nature of factory production). The conclusions of the commission about the evil effects of 'Speenhamland' shocked middle-class opinion. It was shown, apparently with clarity, that in parishes where 'outdoor relief' was limited to those in genuine need, wages rose and productivity increased. The commission recommended changes of the most sweeping kind. 'Outdoor relief' (i.e. the payment of an income to the poor by the parish) was to be virtually abolished for all of the able-bodied poor. Instead, the workhouse system was to be expanded to become the central mechanism for the relief of poverty. Virtually all relief of the poor was to be carried out in local workhouses. By the famous 'principle of less eligibility' advocated by the Poor Law Commission, conditions in the workhouse were deliberately to be worse than anything known outside, in order to discourage people from using them except as a last resort. During the nineteenth century, an extensive system of workhouses was maintained throughout Britain. Anyone could enter, the only requirement being that he or she had to remain overnight. In a workhouse, one could be sure of finding meals sufficient to keep body and soul together and a bed (men and women were rigorously separated), but little else. The commission also recommended the grouping of parishes into Poor Law Unions for the maintenance of workhouses, and a system of paid officials to oversee the system. Except in limited and specific cases, no other state-granted welfare was to exist: there was *no* state-provided unemployment or sickness insurance, nor any old-age pension of any kind.

As draconian as they seem to us, the recommendations of the commission had widespread support, especially by the Cabinet, and the bill for the New Poor Law passed its second reading in May 1834 by a vote of 200 to 20. Some radicals like Cobbett bitterly opposed the bill, as did *The Times* newspaper, but virtually all Whigs and Tories in Parliament supported it, and it passed its third reading in July 1834 by a vote of 157 to 50.

Opinion about the New Poor Law has been bitterly divided. During the nineteenth century it was normal to praise the Act, pointing to the fact that government expenditure on poor relief in England and Wales declined from £7.0 million in 1832 to £4.0 million in 1837, and never reached £7 million again until 1868, when the English population was 57 per cent higher than in 1832. It probably contributed to the willingness of labourers to move to the industrial north, where labour was required. It unquestionably assisted the growth of friendly societies (voluntary societies to which one contributed on a weekly basis and which paid out sickness, unemployment, and old-age payments) among the skilled working classes and the lower middle classes. It unquestionably encouraged prudence, savings and thrift among those who were able to provide for themselves. The fact that fear of 'ending up in the workhouse' was both real and proverbial certainly placed provision for one's old age high up on the agendas of anyone with a steady income. On the other hand, most modern historians have severely condemned the New Poor Law, pointing especially to the fact that it was based upon a superficial and erroneous theory of the causes of poverty. The New Poor Law took no account of the cyclical nature of industrial poverty nor of its 'life cycle' chronology, with the wages of working-class males typically peaking among workers aged 20–35, and with most working-class males older than that gradually losing their ability to carry out hard physical work. It took no account whatever of the position of women in nineteenth-century society, or of the lack of any career paths for most women. The workhouses (or 'poorhouses') became universally detested as symbols of failure. While most were maintained in a reasonably humane way, frequently the lack of facilities meant that children were housed together with alcoholics, criminals and the mentally ill. Many scandals occurred, especially one at the Andover workhouse in which inmates, engaged in crushing the bones of animals, were forced to eat the rotting carcases because they were so hungry. As a general rule, conditions in workhouses gradually improved in the late nineteenth century, although there was no state provision of any kind for old-age pensions until 1909 and workhouses were not abolished until 1929. One possible unintended consequence of the New Poor Law was an increase in emigration overseas, to countries like America, Canada and Australia with higher living standards (at least in theory), although the growth of safer, cheaper ocean-going steamships from about the same time was also clearly a factor.

The second major piece of legislation passed by Melbourne's government was the Municipal Corporations Act of 1835, the most far-reaching reform of local government of the nineteenth century. A very typical Act of the 'age of reform', it followed from the report of a commission of the House of Commons appointed in 1833, and was aimed at altering the age-old, oligarchical closed corporations in the boroughs, which allowed local power to be concentrated in the hands of a small, self-appointed group. Under the 1835 Act, all boroughs with the exception of the City of London were to have one constitutional form of government, identical everywhere.[3] Every borough was to have a mayor, aldermen and councillors, together comprising the town council, with councillors elected by male ratepayers. Councillors were to hold office for three years, aldermen for six, mayors for one year only. Many other surviving anomalies were swept away, for instance the right of boroughs to grant exclusive trading privileges. Despite extraordinarily intense attempts by right-wing Tories to stymie the bill, it became law in September 1835.

In 1836 Melbourne's government enacted the civil registration of births, marriages and deaths, ending the old system, based largely on Anglican clergymen providing this service in each parish. Apart from the obvious benefits to statisticians in knowing, for the first time, Britain's major demographic trends, this Act brought with it several other important changes.[4] Marriages conducted by non-Anglican clergymen were now made fully legal, including, most particularly, marriages conducted by Dissenting ministers in Nonconformist chapels. This change was warmly

3 The City of London (the historical square mile containing Britain's financial institutions) was exempted from the Act, but London's other boroughs (Westminster, Marylebone, etc.) were subject to it. The Act, however, did not unify the many boroughs of London or create a government for the whole of London: this would have to wait until 1889.

4 There had, of course, been a Census, taken at 10-yearly intervals, from 1801. Strictly speaking, owing to the lack of legal penalties, the registration of births, marriages and deaths would not become truly mandatory until the 1870s.

sought by Nonconformists, and ended what they long regarded as the humiliation of requiring banns (an announcement of the intention to marry) read out in the local Anglican church, even for non-Anglican couples. (Quakers and Jews were accorded further autonomy in this area, with the Board of Deputies of British Jews, the representative body of the Anglo-Jewish community, given the right to register all Jewish marriage celebrants.) Secondly, death certificates, which became mandatory in the case of every death in Britain, had to contain information about the cause of death, provided by a physician or medical officer. It is believed that this provision greatly reduced the number of murders and attempted murders in Britain, and also brought physicians into contact with the working classes for the first time.

Further steps were also taken in the reform of justice, extending the trends of the previous 20 years. A series of seven Acts passed in 1837 abolished the death penalty for almost all cases of burglary, robbery, forgery, arson (except where a serious danger to life occurred), and all non-violent crimes except treason. In 1841 the Substitution of Punishments for Death Act further reduced the number of crimes (including rape and rioting) punishable by death. In practice, after 1836 executions were carried out only for murder and attempted murder, and, after 1841, only for murder. In 1835 power was given to the Home Secretary to appoint inspectors for local prisons. The following year, the Prisoner's Counsel Act corrected one of the strangest anomalies that hitherto existed in English law. Before the passage of this Act, as bizarre as this may seem, barristers were not allowed to defend persons indicted for a felony nor to address a jury on their behalf, and had to be given this power by the 1836 Act. Another reform introduced by the Melbourne government was the lowering of the stamp duty on newspapers from 4d to 1d, thus greatly increasing the market for daily newspapers. Until the abolition of stamp duty on newspapers, proprietors of newspapers were required to pay a variety of duties on their journals, making them prohibitively expensive for the poor, and even for many middle-class persons. In the early 1820s an issue of *The Times* cost 7d; by the early 1860s, after these duties were abolished, an issue cost only 3d. Criticised as 'taxes on knowledge' by radicals, their abolition led to a vast expansion in both the London and provincial press. Of similar intent was the introduction of adhesive postage stamps, which, as everyone knows, first went on sale on 1 May 1840 in the form of the celebrated 'penny black', bearing a picture of the young Queen Victoria, and valid for standard postage throughout the United Kingdom. Mail had, of course, been carried since ancient times, and in Britain from the late sixteenth century. In 1837 Rowland Hill (later Sir Rowland, 1795–1879), a schoolmaster from Kidderminster, published a pamphlet advocating a single rate of postage throughout the United Kingdom, to be prepaid by the sender rather than paid for, as was the case before 1840, by the recipient. In his pamphlet, Hill suggested 'using a bit of paper just large enough to bear the [cancellation] stamp and covered at the back with a glutinous wash'.[5] The Melbourne government accepted Hill's proposals in 1839, while Hill's own design for the 'penny black' was also accepted.[6] Originally, postage stamps were not perforated, and had to be cut apart from others in their roll with scissors; perforated stamps, easily separated from one another, were not introduced until 1854. Hill's idea spread around the world within a generation: by the late 1850s virtually every government in Europe and America was issuing stamps. Stamp collecting as a hobby soon followed (Stanley Gibbons, the oldest philatelic dealer in Britain, was founded in 1864). Pillar boxes (suggested by Anthony Trollope, the novelist, who was then employed as a Post Office surveyor) were first introduced in 1852–53. The introduction of postage stamps was chiefly responsible for the phenomenal increase in the volume of postage carried in the Victorian period, via an unbelievably efficient system of postal deliveries.[7] Letter-writing became even more common than before, comprising a remarkable parallel with the railway in narrowing distances and increasing access and communications.

Yet another important innovation of these years was the official granting of a charter to London University in 1836, enabling it to act as an examining body for the awarding of degrees. Until the 1820s there had, of course, been only two universities in England and Wales, Oxford and Cambridge. At both universities non-Anglicans were debarred from taking degrees (non-Anglicans could matriculate at Cambridge, but not graduate; at Oxford they could not matriculate). Both universities taught a curriculum centring round the Classics, theology and mathematics, eschewing other subjects, especially the sciences. The four Scottish universities were generally acknowledged to be more modern and more 'practical' than Oxford or Cambridge. In 1827 the first university college in England or Wales outside of Oxbridge was founded, remarkably at Lampeter, a small, utterly remote town in west Wales. St David's College, Lampeter, came into

---

5 There is a famous saying that success has a hundred fathers (while failure is an orphan), well-illustrated by the claims made by many other men to have suggested postage stamps before Rowland Hill. The most persistent such claims were made by James Chalmers (1782–1853), a Dundee bookseller who may have advocated the use of stamps some years before Hill's pamphlet. Between 1879 and 1940, the descendants of Chalmers and Hill published at least 50 pamphlets on behalf of their respective ancestors, refuting the claims of the others! Claims of advocacy prior to Hill have also been made on behalf of at least six other men. Adhesive postage stamps, not dissimilar to today's, were definitely used briefly in Paris in the 1650s, although no examples have survived.

6 No person, apart from the Sovereign and members of the Royal Family, was ever depicted on a British postage stamp prior to William Shakespeare in 1964.

7 There is a well-known story, which is probably apocryphal but may be true, that a fire was reported in mid-nineteenth-century London by a man who *posted a letter* with this news to the local fire station! So efficient was the Victorian postal system that the letter reached the fire station in time for the fire trucks to come and put the fire out! It is a fact that there were, typically, *eight or nine* deliveries of mail per weekday to commercial addresses in most cities, with two or three on Sundays, during the later half of the nineteenth century.

existence purely to train candidates for the Anglican clergy in Wales. At the same time, from the mid-1820s, a much more significant movement, led by intellectuals and 'Philosophical Radicals' like Macaulay, Grote and Hume, grew up to establish a modern, secular university in London. 'London University', as it was known, opened in 1828 to teach the arts, law and medicine, on a non-denominational basis, and pointedly declined to teach divinity. It was founded as a joint-stock company, since incorporation was successfully resisted by Oxbridge. In 1831 a rival institution, King's College, London, was founded, with support from the Duke of Wellington and other Anglicans, as an Anglican-based university college in London. By a compromise reached in 1835–36, the older 'London University' was to become University College, London, while a 'University of London' was created as the examining body for University College and King's College, giving to London University the fractured, semi-independent organisation it still retains. Another new university, the University of Durham, the first in the north of England, was also established in 1833 by the Anglican dean and chapter of Durham, as a new Anglican university. No further new developments in higher education took place in Great Britain until the establishment of Bedford College, London, the first for women, in 1848, and of Owen's College, Manchester, in 1851.

As with the Grey government, the Melbourne administration resisted all demands for more far-reaching reforms to facilitate political democracy as were advocated by most radicals. Radical MPs like George Grote and Joseph Hume put forward motions for annually elected parliaments and household suffrage, which the Whig government notably opposed and which attracted virtually no support in the Commons. By 1836 or so many Radicals had become thoroughly disillusioned with the Whig government, despite its strong record of reform in many areas of government and administration. J. A. Roebuck, a 'Philosophical Radical' and MP, attacked the government as 'aristocratic in principle, democratic in pretence', and left-wing members of the Whig government like Lord John Russell readily admitted that they could never fully satisfy the demands of Britain's radical movement. As a result of this disillusionment (and, again, despite the government's notable record of reform in many areas) there emerged perhaps the best-known movement of political radicalism to be formed after the Reform Act, the Chartist movement, or Chartism. 'Chartism' was named for the so-called 'People's Charter' which comprised the basic demands of the group. The beginnings of the Chartist movement are usually seen in the establishment of the London Working Men's Association in 1836, founded by William Lovett, a cabinet-maker, and Francis Place, the ubiquitous radical tailor. Unlike most other radical movements of the time, the leaders of Chartism were primarily drawn from the working classes: middle-class radicals like Thomas Attwood largely abandoned the movement once it flirted with radicalism. The Charter, conveying the specific demands of the movement, was drawn up in 1837 and contained six planks: universal adult male suffrage; the secret ballot; parliamentary constituencies of equal size; the abolition of property qualifications for MPs (who were, at this time, required to own a certain amount of land or have an independent income); the payment of MPs, so that working men could serve in Parliament; and annual elections for Parliament. It will be seen that all of these demands were political in nature, aimed at achieving political democracy more progressive than the system produced by the Great Reform Act. None, however, was economic or social in nature, and the lack of explicit economic goals distinguished Chartism from radical working-class movements which emerged later in the century. Some radical groups at this time had, among their goals, such aims as the achievement of an eight-hour day for all factory workers and the abolition of slavery, but Chartism's aims remained purely political, to extend the achievements of 1832.

While the original leaders of the Chartists were moderates who rejected the use of force or violence, Chartism quickly attracted its share of advocates of violence whose presence divided the movement. Among these were Feargus O'Connor (1796–1855), an Irish Protestant barrister and MP who founded the London Democratic Association in 1837 as a radical rival to the London Working Men's Association. He then purchased a radical Leeds newspaper, the *Northern Star*, transforming it into the main journalistic organ of Chartism. O'Connor advocated a general strike of workers and seemed to flirt with, but never directly advocate, revolutionary force. To O'Connor's left were the even more radical Bronterre O'Brien (1805–65), another Irish lawyer, and Julian Horney, who initially advocated a British revolution, but who became more circumspect after John Frost, a radical draper of Newport, Monmouthshire, attempted to lead an armed rebellion against the government in that county. Fourteen of Frost's followers were killed by troops, and Frost was sentenced to death, later commuted to transportation for life.[8] The existence of the so-called 'physical force' Chartists (as opposed to the 'moral force' moderates) split the movement.

The Chartist movement unquestionably became immensely popular during the decade after its foundation, and was arguably the first organised mass movement of British radicalism in the modern sense. It has been noted that Chartism won many adherents from areas of declining industry, especially from handloom weavers in the north and areas like the south-west which had been bypassed by factory capitalism. Nevertheless, it was temporarily strong everywhere, and in 1838 staged enormous rallies in Glasgow, Manchester and other large cities. In February 1839 a National Chartist Convention was held in London. Here the moderates gained control, the presentation of a petition to Parliament their central aim,

---

8 Feargus O'Connor was asked by Frost to lead a simultaneous uprising in northern England, but decided instead to visit Ireland, 'my unfortunate country'.

although the Convention went on record as supporting a general strike if Parliament rejected the petition. A petition, advocating the Six Points, and containing an estimated one million signatures, was prepared and brought to Parliament in a cart, where it was introduced by Thomas Attwood, the wealthy radical banker who sat for Birmingham. It was debated and attacked by the Whig government before being rejected by the Commons by a vote of 235 to 46. The petition's rejection split the movement, with the Whig government becoming increasingly alarmed at the possibility of insurrection, and increasingly willing to use force to counter the Chartist threat. The government did have the good sense to appoint General Sir Charles Napier (1782–1853), a distinguished and intelligent soldier, to command the northern district against the Chartists. Napier (who was himself something of a radical and had been offered commands in the Greek army) was actually sympathetic to many of the Chartist demands. Rather cleverly, he invited Chartist leaders to view a demonstration of the military's artillery fire, from which they drew the pointed inference that they would be annihilated if they attempted violence. Rioting did break out in Birmingham in July, while in November came the uprising in Newport led by John Frost. By 1840, many Chartist leaders were in gaol, and with a revival of the economy the Chartist impetus died down until 1842, when another National Chartist Convention drew up a second petition, also presented to Parliament, allegedly containing over three million signatures. Similar to the earlier one, this petition also denounced the New Poor Law. It experienced the same fate as its predecessor, being rejected by 287 to 49 votes, and being attacked in the House by many liberals like Macaulay and Roebuck. Violence again broke out throughout the industrial areas of northern Britain, in particular the so-called 'Plug Riots' in Lancashire (so called because striking workers hammered out the plugs from factory boilers). Rioting and looting occurred in many northern industrial cities, always met by draconian punishment. Again, trade revived, and by 1843 Chartism had declined again, only to revive for the last time in the later 1840s.

Chartism was unquestionably a success at channelling the discontent which existed in industrial Britain, and was one of the most significant movements of political protest in modern British history. Yet it failed to achieve any of its aims, which took generations to succeed, when they eventually did (MPs were not paid a salary until 1908, for example; the annual election of Parliament has never been achieved and is never likely to be). Why Chartism failed is no mystery: divided aims and leadership; the advocacy of violence by some of its leaders; the failure to attract a large middle-class following; a firm but not brutal response by the government. Most importantly of all, perhaps, was the irrelevance of its political aims to the economic motives which attracted most of its working-class followers, and its inability to formulate a coherent, economic programme, something which was probably impossible at that time, before effective left-wing critiques of capitalism had been enunciated, and while *laissez-faire* was itself a radical goal, not a target for radical criticism. Chartism showed both that the potentiality for revolutionary violence existed and also that such a movement lacked a base among the British majority.

On 20 June 1837 King William IV died, leaving no legitimate children: none of his 10 illegitimate children by Mrs Jordan could, of course, succeed to the throne. William's successor as Sovereign was his young niece, Alexandrina Victoria, daughter of Edward, Duke of Kent (1767–1820) and Princess Victoria of Saxe-Saalfeld-Coburg (1786–1861). Born on 24 May 1819 in Kensington Palace, she was thus barely 18 years old when she succeeded to the throne. We are so used to thinking of Queen Victoria as an old woman, immensely experienced, and whose personality and traits are known to all, that it is somewhat startling to realise that she was a naive teenage girl when she first became Queen. She had few friends, and none of her own age; she detested her widowed mother's principal adviser, Sir John Conroy, and knew virtually nothing of politics. Lord Melbourne therefore acted as her chief adviser and confidant during the first crucial years of her reign, in preference to Baron Stockmar, the private secretary to Prince Leopold of Belgium, Victoria's uncle by marriage, whom Victoria's mother would have preferred. Melbourne proved charming, successfully combining the avuncular with the didactic, and for many years Queen Victoria was probably a Whig in politics, although, after the 1870s, attracted by Disraeli and repelled by Gladstone, she was certainly a Tory. Queen Victoria's coronation took place in June 1838; in February 1840 she married her cousin Albert of Saxe-Coburg-Gotha (1819–61), who, unusually for royals of the time, was reasonably well-educated at the University of Bonn. Prince Albert was interested in philosophy and improvement. He was, rather surprisingly, a political liberal, and on the whole (and despite what many historians have said) fitted in rather well with the ethos of early and mid-Victorian Britain. His early death was a great tragedy for the Queen, who had borne him nine children.

One immediate political effect of the death of William IV and the accession of Queen Victoria was the necessity to call a general election, then mandatory on the accession of a new Sovereign. Parliament was dissolved in July 1837, and an election held shortly afterwards. The general election of 1837 produced broadly similar results to that held two years previously, but another gain in strength for the revivified Tories. After the 1837 election, there were 349 Whig and Liberal MPs and their supporters, compared with 309 Conservatives. The Tories now, for the first time since Reform, had a majority among English MPs, 239:232, and a clear majority in the counties, 97:47. They were also ahead in Wales, 18:11. The Whig-Liberal majority was based on the English boroughs, where they outnumbered the Tories by 185:142, and on majorities in Scotland (33:20) and Ireland (73:32). The British electoral system was already beginning to be recognisably modern in main features. The reliance of the Whig government on the votes of the Irish MPs made it potentially more unstable than it appeared, and foreshadowed a situation which would reappear again down to 1914, with a left-of-centre government heavily dependent upon the Irish contingent to survive.

Melbourne made no changes at all in his government as a result of the 1837 election, but found its majority constantly slipping further. In May 1839 it survived a vote of confidence over its handling of a crisis in Jamaica by a majority of only four, and Melbourne actually resigned, much to Victoria's chagrin. The Queen was forced to send for Sir Robert Peel, the leader of the Opposition, whom she found insufferably cold and officious. Peel's attempts to form a minority government foundered in one of the most curious political crises in British history. He suggested making changes in the composition of the Ladies of the Bedchamber (women who attend upon the Queen on public occasions and often become private confidantes as well; normally they are the wives of leading peers), replacing Whig Ladies with Tories. Victoria, at this stage an ardent Whig, refused, and both sides dug in their heels. As a result of the 'Bedchamber Crisis', as it was known, Peel declined to form a government, and Melbourne resumed office on 10 May 1839, three days after resigning. One result of the 'Bedchamber Crisis' was that appointments of most Ladies of the Bedchamber became non-political, although the leading Lady, the Mistress of the Robes, remained a political appointment – uniquely and almost incredibly, an official government position held by a woman, and appointed on a party political basis.[9]

Melbourne remained Prime Minister until his government was defeated by a margin of one on a vote of confidence in June 1841. Parliament was dissolved on 23 June 1841, and a general election called. When the new Parliament reassembled on 19 August, Melbourne was still Prime Minister, but resigned, yielding to Peel, on 30 August 1841. Peel became Prime Minister, with a substantial Conservative majority, the same day.

Apart from the important legislation of the years 1835–41, this was also a time of enormous social and economic change, perhaps the time when Britain altered most decisively. Railways open in Britain in 1835 totalled just 338 miles; by 1841 this had risen to 1775 miles, and most of the chief trunk routes were planned or being built. Raw cotton consumption rose from 318 million pounds in 1835 to 459 million in 1840, and while the number of cotton factory hands increased from 220 000 to 264 000

9 There was no Mistress of the Robes between the Duchess of Sutherland, who served in 1835–37, and the Duchess of Buccleuch, appointed by Peel in 1841, who served until 1846. The position of Mistress of the Robes is included in many complete lists of government ministers as an official appointment. What made the identities of the Ladies of the Bedchamber important was the confidential access they had to the Queen, who was young and impressionable. If Britain had had a King during this period, the Mistress of the Bedchamber would have attended the Queen Consort, and thus been of little or no influence.

between 1835 and 1840, the total of handloom weavers declined from 188 000 to 110 000 in the same years. The deep recession of the later 1830s and early 1840s was perhaps the first in the modern capitalist sense which struck much of the whole economy, a periodic economic crisis of the kind familiar down to 1929 and beyond at roughly decadal intervals. The later 1830s were also years when the ambience of the Regency had definitely passed away, and the Evangelical earnestness of the early Victorian period had nearly replaced it: from Byron to Tennyson.

While foreign affairs were fairly quiet in the years of the Melbourne government, there were a few notable events. The settlement of New Zealand, the remotest significant British colony, began in earnest with the foundation, in 1837, of the New Zealand Association by Edward Gibbon Wakefield (1796–1862), who began his studies of British colonisation schemes in the 1820s from prison, where he was serving a sentence of three years for eloping with an heiress under false pretences. Wakefield's New Zealand Company (formed in 1839) sold land to prospective colonists at £1 per acre, ensuring their enthusiasm. Colonists under his scheme first landed in New Zealand in 1840, and concluded an agreement with the Maori natives of that country at the Treaty of Waitangi in February 1840. Although wars with the Maoris followed a few years later, in general New Zealand was spared the slaughter of natives common elsewhere, for instance in Australia. There, across the Tasman, Wakefield was instrumental in founding the colony of South Australia in 1834, under the same general principles as in New Zealand, while the immensely fertile lands of Victoria were first settled at the same time. Melbourne was founded as a village in 1835; within 50 years, owing in part to the Gold Rush of the early 1850s, its population had increased to over 600 000.

These were also crucial years in Canada. In 1837 a rebellion broke out in the two regions which now comprise Canada – Upper Canada (the English-speaking areas) and Lower Canada (French Quebec) – between traditional interests around the legislative council and popular leaders; in Lower Canada this largely took the form of French hostility to the British governing minority. Fighting and rebellion broke out around Toronto and Montreal, with rebels being actively supported by American sympathisers. In May 1837 the Earl of Durham (John George Lambton, 1792–1840), the radical son-in-law of Lord Grey and one of the Whig MPs who drew up the Reform Bill, but had been given the position of Ambassador to Russia rather than a Cabinet position by Melbourne, was sent to Canada as Governor-General. His lenient treatment of the rebels led to disavowal by the British government and Durham's resignation in October. In February 1839 Durham produced his famous *Report on the Affairs of British North America*, in response to his experiences there. He proposed the union of Upper and Lower Canada and the grant of responsible government to the colonies, Britain retaining control only over Canada's foreign relations, regulation of trade, and the determination of public lands. The government accepted most of Durham's suggestions, and in July 1840 passed the Union Act, which united Upper and Lower Canada into one government, and created an appointed legislative council and a popularly elected assembly, in which the two former provinces had equal representation. (Lord Durham died prematurely in the same year.) Over the next decade, boundary disputes with the United States were settled and the Navigation Acts, restricting foreign shipping with Canada, were repealed, but self-government had to await the famous British North America Act of 1867. In South Africa, British territory was extended from 1835 onwards, leading, in 1835–37, to the celebrated 'Great Trek' of about 10 000 Boer cattlemen and farmers to the north and east of the Orange River, in response to British interference and expansion. Coming into constant conflict with the Zulus, and engaged in a losing war with the British in 1842–43, the farmers of the Trek created the central myths of Boer nationalism which survived as a dominant political force in South Africa until the 1990s. All of these changes in the temperate parts of the British Empire eased the way to much increased settlement by Britain's ever-growing population, and the sympathy of the British government to these developments was in part due to its realisation that the relatively uninhabited white Empire served as a potent 'safety valve' for radicals and malcontents. As well, it was testimony to the dominant liberalism of the period, with the white Empire viewed as ripe for democracy.

The end of the East India Company's monopoly over trade with China in 1833 produced tragic results. British merchants, determined to control and expand the enormously wealthy opium trade from the treaty port of Canton, ran into the hostility of Chinese imperial officials. In 1840 Britain occupied Chusan and the Canton River forts and engaged, in 1841–42, in the first British-Chinese war. Britain seized Hong Kong, several more coastal ports and the city of Chinkiang; at the Treaty of Nanking (29 August 1842) which ended the War, China formally ceded Hong Kong to Britain, and opened Canton, Shanghai and three other ports to trade, established a uniform tariff of 5 per cent on British goods, and agreed to pay Britain an indemnity of £21 million. The first Anglo-Chinese war began a period of decay, chaos and bloodshed in the world's most populous nation and oldest continuous civilisation which, in a sense, ended only with the Communist takeover in 1949, or even perhaps with the death of Mao Tse-tung in 1975. In 1850–64 came the incredibly murderous Taiping Rebellion, and for the 110 years following the 1841–42 war China was at the mercy of Europe and Japan.

|5|

Sir Robert Peel and repeal,
1841–1846

Sir Robert Peel (1788–1850) briefly held office as Prime Minister for four months between December 1834 and 1835, but his great moment came in the period, just less than five years, between August 1841 and June 1846, when (unlike his previous term as premier) he headed a Conservative government with a strong majority in the House of Commons. Of all the leading nineteenth-century British statesmen, Peel is one of the most difficult men for the historian to understand or to come to terms with: perhaps only Gladstone, his disciple, is more enigmatic. Peel's social origins were curious and remarkable. His father, the first Sir Robert Peel (1750–1830), from whom he inherited his title, was the first authentic cotton manufacturing millionaire of Britain's industrial revolution.[1] Although this fact is itself fairly well known, virtually no biographer of Peel has ever drawn attention to it as a possible factor in his readiness to support the manufacturing interest's wishes by repealing the Corn Laws in 1846. One might contrast this, for instance, with the extreme readiness of biographers of Disraeli, Gladstone and many other nineteenth-century political leaders to link their political stances to their fathers' social and economic position. In the case of Peel, his manufacturing origins are invariably regarded as less significant than other salient facts about his social origins: his education at Harrow (where he was a contemporary of Byron and Palmerston) and at Christ Church, Oxford, where he took one of the earliest recorded double firsts (in Classics and Mathematics). Unlike most industrialists in politics, he became a politician early rather than late – an invaluable advantage for anyone seeking to rise high in political life – entering Parliament at the age of 21 for the unlikely pocket borough of Cashel in County Tipperary. As noted, Peel's father had already acquired a baronetcy and a large landed estate; Peel apparently had no direct business

1 Peel's father was created a baronet in 1800, and was himself a Tory MP for many years. A baronetcy is a hereditary knighthood, which passes to the eldest son upon its holder's death.

links of any kind and may never have seen the inside of a cotton factory. (Peel's father was a cotton manufacturer in Blackburn, Bury and other parts of what was semi-rural Lancashire; he made his cotton fortune before steam power was widely applied to cotton manufacturing and certainly before the industry was centred in Manchester and other great industrial cities.) It is also worth emphasising that Peel and his family were, of course, loyal Anglicans rather than Protestant Dissenters, in contrast to so many radical manufacturers. This both eased his ascent into political leadership and helps to explain his Toryism.

In everything but the source of his wealth, Peel was thus a fairly typical member of the traditional British upper classes. Indeed, to understand Peel one must realise that he embodied a continuation, in the best sense, into the post-1832 political world of the old Pittite Conservative consensual national tradition whose leaders sought to govern Britain in the national interest regardless of what prescriptions were necessary. Ideology mattered much less to Peel than governing well, and doing what was necessary to advance Britain's best interests. Peel's downfall in 1846 came from precisely the same cause, an inability to grasp the fact that in the new post-Reform Act political world, ideology and broad sectional interest could not only not be ignored, but were central to the semi-democratic political process which now existed: most of all, one should not ignore one's most ardent supporters, but should begin by building a coalition around them. Peel never understood this: he never understood that in post-1832 Britain the Conservative party was not the consensual party of governance it claimed to be under Pitt and Liverpool, but was centrally a party of the landed interest and of the old pre-industrial elites like the Church, old-fashioned merchants, and the Bar. Even if a portion, perhaps an ever-growing portion, of the business class were ready to join the Conservatives, the radical manufacturing and industrial elite of the north of England and the Celtic areas would not yet, in the 1840s, do so, and it was folly to alienate one's bedrock supporters in order to engage in a quixotic attempt to achieve the impossible. By then, as Gladstone put it in 1841, 'The principle of party has long predominated in this country; it now has a sway almost unlimited'.

It will be seen, too, that Peel's vision of serving the national interest was quite different from Disraeli's 'One Nation' Conservatism, at any rate as it is normally understood. Disraeli attempted, at least in theory, to identify and win over the 'Tory working man' and sought an alliance between the latter and the traditional supporters of the Conservative party in the landed elite. Peel, in contrast, sought to win over the manufacturing elite (and, in the process, to quell working-class unrest) in the manner of the pre-1832 consensual Tory party. He pursued this aim regardless of political cost and, as a result, split and weakened the Conservatives for nearly 30 years, incidentally leaving the way open for Disraeli, the hitherto little-known and bizarre 'man of mystery', to become perhaps the dominant figure in the Conservative party's history.

In May 1841 the Whig government of Lord Melbourne was defeated by one vote in the House of Commons on a vote of confidence over the Corn Laws. A general election was held in the summer of 1841, which the Conservatives won handily. While after the 1837 general election the Whig-Liberals were generally seen as having 349 MPs to the Tories' 309, in 1841 the Conservatives won 368 seats to the Whig-Liberals' 290. This was the largest number of seats which the Conservative party would win until Disraeli's great victory in 1874, 35 years later. In 1841, the Tories swept the English county seats, winning 124 to the Whigs' 20, and came close to gaining a majority in the English borough seats, winning 160 to the Whigs' 167. Overall, the Tories won 284 seats in England, compared with the Liberals' 187, and also gained a majority of seats (19:10) in Wales. In Scotland (22:31) and in Ireland (43:62) they were in a minority, but overall the Conservatives won a famous victory. The Whigs and Liberals were dispirited, disunited and unpopular; it has been widely noted by historians that the later 1830s saw an increasing drift of Whig MPs to the Conservative camp. Peel made great (and sincere) efforts to appear genuinely moderate, for instance by supporting the re-election of a Whig Speaker when Parliament reconvened. His election victory has often been seen as a personal triumph for him, a man who had successfully gained the confidence of much of the middle classes. Queen Victoria, who disliked Peel because of the 1838 Ladies of the Bedchamber affair and for his notoriously wooden and officious manner, was of course compelled to appoint him to the premiership, and he kissed hands at the end of August 1841. His government was a relatively strong one. It included, apart from the usual number of great aristocrats and territorial magnates, one past and three future Prime Ministers (Wellington, the Minister Without Portfolio; Aberdeen, Derby, and Gladstone, who officially joined the Cabinet in May 1843; it is curious to think that Wellington and Gladstone once sat in the same Cabinet). It also included such luminaries as Sir James Graham, a mainstay of the 1830–34 Whig government, Sidney Herbert, and Lord Lyndhurst. This Cabinet, however, most notably did not include Benjamin Disraeli, by then a well-known novelist and philosopher/organiser of 'Young England', but at the time a backbench MP for only four years. Disraeli believed himself to have been entitled to a ministerial position, and had an unpleasant exchange of correspondence with the unyielding Peel over an appointment. It is, of course, interesting to speculate, if Disraeli had been offered, say, the Parliamentary Secretaryship of the Colonial Office in 1841, whether the whole course of British political history would have been altered.

Peel's term as Prime Minister was dominated by two great issues, fundamental improvements to the British economy and Ireland. Peel was, before anything else, a great creative statesman, perpetually searching for constructive solutions to the problems and questions before him. In the 1820s as Home Secretary Peel reformed the criminal law and the police (facts of which he boasted in the Tamworth Manifesto), and, in an age when the governance of Britain was in the hands of aristocratic amateurs, Peel was a thorough professional who treated every issue with seriousness, objectivity and intelligence. Among the serious-minded and the discerning, Peel was a political leader without equal. Gladstone, Peel's most prominent disciple, thought Peel to be the greatest man he had ever met, and 'taken all around the best man of business who was ever Prime Minister', and Peel has continued to have hero-worshipping partisans among academic historians to this day. Yet he was almost entirely lacking in warmth or the human touch.[2] That his smile resembled the silver lid on a coffin has become proverbial; even well-wishers strongly noted that he was 'cold', 'reserved', 'peppery', and, above all, surprisingly shy, a product, perhaps, of his ambiguous social origins.

Peel addressed both of the great issues he faced with remarkable energy and initiative. The period when he was Prime Minister is often known as the 'hungry forties'.[3] Historians have often debated whether they were 'hungrier' than any other decade. Certainly, by such quantitative economic indicators as exist, this label may well be an exaggeration. Raw cotton consumption in Britain, for instance, rose steadily every year from 1840 to 1846, declined sharply in 1847–48 (after Peel left office, of course), then rose again. Total employment in the cotton industry rose from 259 000 in 1838 to 331 000 in 1850. British shipping tonnage rose from 2 768 000 in 1840 to 3 565 000 in 1850. The 'railway mania' reached its zenith in the mid-1840s. British gross national product, on the best-known estimate, rose from £452 million to £523 million between 1841 and 1851. Yet there was also a sense that something had gone terribly wrong. The population of Great Britain (England, Wales and Scotland) rose from 16 517 000 in 1841 to 20 817 000 in 1851. It is problematical that the growth of the British economy was sufficient to keep these 4.3 million extra mouths to feed in even a meagre level of comfort. Apart from the 'railway mania', the 1840s were the decade of the irresistible decline of the handloom weavers, whose number dropped from 123 000 in 1840 to 43 000 in 1850, of Engel's *Manchester in 1844*, Carlyle's *Chartism* (1840), and of Dickens's *Hard Times*. Above all it was the decade of the Irish potato famine, the greatest demographic catastrophe in Europe in the nineteenth century. The British economy had, perhaps, reached a climacteric in the 1840s, still being dominated by a pre-steam transport and communications network, unable as yet to link the world by steamships and telegraphs as it would a decade or two later, yet burdened by an ever-growing population and a restless working class, as well as turmoil over religion, foreign policy and Ireland.

2 In both sides of his character Peel appears closely to resemble Sir Edward Heath, Conservative Prime Minister 130 years later.
3 The phrase itself was only coined in 1903 and was not used by anyone during the 1840s.

Peel came to office at a time when it was widely believed that a major economic depression, which had begun around 1836, had reached its climax. Unemployment markedly increased in much of northern England. Chartism emerged as a mass working-class movement, producing its famous 'Six Points of the Charter' in 1838 and splitting into 'physical force' and 'moral force' factions the following year. In 1839, too, the so-called 'Newport Rising' occurred in the town on the Welsh border, led by John Frost, a local radical who had been made a justice of the peace by Lord John Russell. Chartism again grew in strength in 1842, fanned by strikes and unrest in the coal-mining towns of Staffordshire. 1842 has been termed (by Professor Norman Gash) 'the worst year of distress and disorder that Britain experienced in the nineteenth century', and there was ample room for a constructive policy to put side-by-side with the tough policy of suppressing violence which any government would have pursued.

The Peel government dealt with this situation in a variety of ways. When Chartist and other radicals broke the law and stirred up violence, they were dealt with firmly but not harshly. Peel, however, had as well a wide-ranging economic policy whose aim was to improve the British standard of living, especially for the working classes, and stabilising the long-term future of the British economy. In 1842 Peel reintroduced the income tax, which had previously been levied during the Napoleonic Wars but had been abolished in 1815. This was an extremely courageous step, which significantly raised revenues available to the government and also paved the way for the loss of revenues which followed from the repeal of the Corn Laws and other measures aimed at diminishing tariff protection. By the time Peel left office in 1846, income tax was raising nearly 10 per cent of all central government expenditure, an invaluable source of income when other forms of revenue available to the government – stamp duty, customs and excise, land taxes – hardly rose at all. Income tax was, however, not a straightforward tax on incomes over a certain level, but was levied on types of income according to a complex series of Schedules. Business and professional incomes were assessed under one schedule, and it was the levying of this new tax on industry and commerce which may have convinced Peel that it was not unfair to remove the protection accorded to landowners and farmers. Unfortunately, however, landowners and farmers were also taxed under other Schedules of the income tax, and in a way which they considered unfairly harsh, especially farmers. Only incomes over about £150 per annum were taxed, exempting the working classes, but this lower limit was varied from time to time, sometimes being as low as £100 during the nineteenth century. It should also be noted that there was one percentage level of tax for all incomes assessed under each Schedule; very high incomes paid the same percentage in taxation as much smaller ones. The notion that higher marginal rates of taxation should be paid on very high incomes did not enter British taxation law until just before the First World

War. The income tax was envisioned by Peel as a 'temporary' measure, but it has (needless to say) outlived its architect by 150 years.

Peel also introduced major reforms into the banking system. These built upon the reforms pioneered by the Liverpool government of the 1820s (when Peel was Home Secretary) and aimed at stabilising the banking system. By its Bank Charter Act of 1844, the Peel government reorganised the functions of the Bank of England. The Bank, founded in 1694, was not (as its name might suggest) a British national bank, and in fact remained a purely privately-owned bank until the Labour government of the 1940s. It was a normal clearing bank to which were increasingly added the duties and powers of a national bank, especially the power to control credit and the interest rate. Peel strengthened these powers, especially by forbidding any further issuance of paper bank notes by any other bank. (Prior to 1844, strangely enough, a private bank could issue its own paper currency.) The issuance of bank notes by the Bank of England was to vary with the gold reserves it held, thus linking Britain more firmly to an objective inter-national standard of value. This legal limitation on the issuance of bank notes, though wise in the long term, also restricted the expansion of credit during periods of economic growth (as during the Railway Booms of the 1840s) and actually increased, rather than decreased, economic instability in the short term, necessitating special government authorisation for the issuance of excess bank notes in 1847, 1857 and 1866. Nevertheless, a powerful weapon in the interests of Britain's economic hegemony, not merely within the United Kingdom, but throughout the world, had been forged.

The Peel government also attempted, perhaps with less success, to intervene in the construction and direction of Britain's railways, then in the process of expanding enormously. William E. Gladstone, the President of the Board of Trade, attempted in 1844 to introduce a bill which would have allowed the government to buy out any railway 15 years after the date of its charter. Peel regarded this as much too sweeping, and, working with the already powerful 'railway lobby', successfully put through legislation requiring that every company run at least one third-class train each day, in closed carriages, at a fare of a penny a mile; these were known as 'parliamentary' trains.[4] By the 1844 Railway Act, however, Parliament gained the right to purchase any railway company after 21 years. This power was never used. Another Act passed by Peel's government in 1844 greatly simplified the process of incorporation by a company, although sweeping reforms in the interest of creating limited liability companies did not come until the years 1856–62.

4 During the nineteenth century, there were three classes of train carriages, first, second, and third. Third-class travel, chiefly for the working classes, was of course the cheapest. Railway companies often attempted to provide as poor a third-class service as they could, normally in open carriages at the most inconvenient times. Peel's act required that closed carriages be provided in 'parliamentary' trains.

Peel's most famous legislative measures, and those which will forever be linked with his name, came, of course, in the area of free trade, especially the celebrated repeal of the Corn Laws in 1846. At the time, the tariff on corn (wheat) was governed by the Corn Laws of 1828, which authorised a sliding scale of duties. Under this Act, wheat was admitted virtually free of duty if its price rose above 73 shillings per quarter, but was to carry a very stiff tariff of 20 shillings per quarter whenever the domestic price fell to 54 shillings or less; in between there was a sliding scale of duties which decreased whenever the price of wheat rose in Britain. The 1828 Act had been introduced by the Wellington government (of which Peel had been a prominent member); thus a Conservative government had gone a long way towards free trade in wheat in a previous decade.

Peel first attempted to reform the Corn Laws in his earliest budget of 1842. (The Chancellor of the Exchequer at the time, Henry Goulburn, was a senior Tory minister who had first entered Parliament in 1808 and served in the Commons for the next 48 years.) Under this measure, the 20 shilling maximum tariff on wheat became operative when the price reached 50 shillings. As well, Peel's first budget reduced duties on no less than 700 dutiable items, cut tariffs sharply on raw materials, and enacted the provision that no import was to be entirely prohibited.

In the meantime, one of the greatest mass movements of reform in British history had grown up, whose aim was to eliminate the tariff on wheat altogether, and, implicitly if not explicitly, to remove all British tariffs. This was the Anti-Corn Law League, founded in 1839 as an extension of an Anti-Corn Law Association of Manchester radicals established the previous year. The League had many leaders, but is permanently linked with two men in particular, John Bright (1811–89) and Richard Cobden (1804–65). Bright, a Quaker manufacturer in Rochdale and later closely associated with Birmingham, and Cobden, an Anglican warehouseman and local political leader in Manchester, were both Radical MPs and articulate orators. Both were unquenchable optimists about the capacity of manufacturing and free trade to bring peace and prosperity to the world and both were radical opponents of the landed aristocracy and of 'monopoly'.

It is often remarked that the Anti-Corn Law League was more a religious movement than an ordinary political agitation, and its leaders brought to it a missionary zeal seldom found in British political debate. Emanating especially from Dissenting and Anglican Evangelical sources in the manufacturing areas, it had a close association with meetings of Protestant Nonconformist sects and ministers, and managed to commit Dissenting conferences to supporting free trade. The Anti-Corn Law League was also seen as a counterweight to the working-class agitation of the Chartist movement. Its central point was that repeal of the Corn Laws would benefit both the middle and working classes. For the middle-class manufacturers it would lower costs (and quell working-class unrest); for the working classes it would directly lower the price of bread and indirectly lower the price of all other commodities, as well as ensuring a constant supply of grain in times of domestic scarcity. Repeal of the Corn Laws thus united the two classes, while Chartism divided them. It also presaged the long period of international amity which most advocates of free trade believed that unhindered world-wide commerce would herald.

A great campaign to repeal the Corn Laws was waged by the League from about 1843 onwards. Its weapons included a newspaper, mass rallies, trained speakers, and endless published propaganda. The League erected the Free Trade Hall in Manchester, the main venue for public meetings in the northern metropolis. This was a campaign without equal since the Reform Bill agitation, but more to be feared, perhaps, than the Chartist agitation since it came from a prosperous section of the business community. While Peel had been moving to a position favourable to ending the Corn Laws for some time, the Conservative party in Parliament and in the Cabinet, consisting of the great majority of landowners and heavily dependent upon the landed interest, made a complete volte-face in policy impossible. Indeed, the success of the Anti-Corn Law League sparked the establishment of a great counter-movement of rural protectionist societies, often known as the 'Anti-League', which began as early as 1843 and swept through the farming counties of rural England. This movement secured the loyalty of most Conservative MPs, especially those in rural seats, so that only 112 Tory members of the House of Commons (out of 368 elected in 1841) followed Peel in the crucial vote over repeal of the Corn Laws. While many of Peel's Cabinet colleagues followed him in supporting repeal, Peel also succeeded in alienating many Tories whose numbers and abilities would be sufficient to comprise a successful protectionist opposition, especially Derby and Disraeli, and leaders of the agricultural interest like Lord George Bentinck.

Peel did not foresee going all the way to abolishing the Corn Laws until the middle of 1845, when the Irish potato famine first manifested itself. At this point, Peel was converted to the repeal of the Corn Laws chiefly as a means of helping Ireland. Unable to convince the Protectionist majority in his Cabinet, he temporarily resigned as Prime Minister in December 1845, but soon returned when Lord John Russell and the Whigs were unable to form a government. In February 1846 he announced the momentous measures his government was now prepared to take, known officially as the Corn and Customs Bill. He abolished or greatly diminished tariffs on a wide variety of manufactured goods. Most foodstuffs were henceforth to be allowed into Britain free of duties. Maize (American corn) was allowed in free of duties at once; tariffs on all other grains were to be reduced until 1849, when they, too, could enter freely subject to the payment of a 1 shilling duty. To compensate the landed interest, Peel abolished the requirement that paupers from manufacturing districts had to be returned to their place of birth (often in rural areas); he reduced the local costs of other parts of poor relief, rural road maintenance, the police, and criminal prosecutions, which were henceforth to be borne by the central government.

Peel's proposals were ingenious and far-reaching. Yet they also contained several problematical features. It has often been pointed out by historians that, though they were designed to help Ireland's starving peasants, Peel's proposals would have had virtually no effect upon Ireland's rural millions, who were too poor to afford grain at any price; in any case, the tariff on grain did not fully disappear until 1849, when the Irish rural poor would be dead, or have migrated abroad, or recovered. More centrally, while Peel admitted an intellectual conversion to free trade 'due to the progress of reason and truth', as he put it, it is by no means absolutely clear that free trade either engendered or maintained Britain's economic superiority. Britain's commercial and industrial revolutions took place while it still had innumerable tariffs and a Corn Law. After 1870, Britain was challenged for industrial supremacy by Germany and the United States, two powers whose economies grew strong behind high tariff walls, deliberately kept high to encourage domestic industry. By the 1880s a movement to re-erect a British tariff wall took shape; by 1903, with Joseph Chamberlain's proposals for Imperial Preference, it became a central political issue. By that time, however, the primary legacy of over half a century of British free trade was that Britain, increasingly vulnerable to foreign competition, lagged behind its main competitors. Free trade clearly benefited Britain for no more than about 25 years, that is, until Germany, America and other rival countries were industrialised. And while we think of the Victorian business middle classes as inextricably linked with support for free trade, there were, in the 1840s and 1850s, a surprising number of middle-class men who were Protectionists, including 'Railway' Hudson and Thomas Baring, of the merchant banking family, a prominent Conservative MP who was repeatedly offered a place in a Protectionist Cabinet. Lord Derby was toying with the idea of an imperial tariff (allowing Canadian grain in free of duties while taxing non-Empire grain), and the Central Protection Society (as the Anti-League had become) explicitly stood in 1845 for 'the Protection of Native Industry' and not merely agricultural protection. Yet nothing came of this, and mid-Victorian Britain became synonymous with free trade. To most contemporaries, it seemed absolutely certain that Britain's role as the 'workshop of the world' had its foundation in free trade, yet this was a palpable historical error and inconsistent with the experience of Britain's most successful rivals.

The crucial vote over repeal of the Corn Laws came in February 1846 and lasted for 12 parliamentary sittings, one of the longest periods ever given over by Parliament to discussing a single topic. (It was on the occasion of his House of Commons speech on the Corn Laws that Disraeli coined the phrase 'the Manchester School' to describe *laissez-faire* liberals; the phrase entered the language, as so many of Disraeli's did.) In the end, the Corn Laws were repealed by a majority of 97 votes. At a time when party labels were sometimes imprecise, it is generally agreed that 227 Whigs, Liberals and Radicals voted for repeal, together with 112 of Peel's Tory supporters. But 242 Tories voted against the bill, following Lord George Bentinck and Disraeli, who had emerged as the leaders of the Protectionist cause. Rather surprisingly, the repeal bill passed the House of Lords without much difficulty, in large part because the Duke of Wellington, although himself a firm Protectionist, remained entirely loyal to Peel and managed to secure enough proxy votes of absent peers to carry the measure. It might also be reiterated that Peel's bill was a gradualist one; a motion for immediate and total repeal of the Corn Laws was rejected by the Commons in March 1846 by a vote of 265 to only 78.

Peel unquestionably viewed repeal as a component of a much wider attempt to treat the 'Condition of England question' and ameliorate the condition of the working classes. By engendering cheap and plentiful grain, Peel hoped to increase the standard of living of the working classes, in addition to improving employment opportunities for workers by cutting costs to manufacturers. It must not be forgotten that Peel was Prime Minister 90 years before the notion gained currency that the state, through deficit spending and work-creation schemes, could decrease unemployment during a depression. There were few other cogent measures available to Peel to deal with poverty and unemployment. The government was sympathetic to legal restrictions on the hours which women and children could work in coal mines, and in 1842, after great publicity on this subject, it passed the Mines Act, prohibiting girls, women, and boys under 10 from working underground. In 1844 it secured the limitation of hours of work for children (aged between 8 and 13) and women in factories, and a rule was laid down (to discourage evasion) that the hours of all workers should begin at the same time each day, the first time that the hours of work of adult males were regulated by Parliament. Some safety improvements in machinery fencing were introduced, and in 1845 calico printing works were subject to safety legislation for the first time. Most of this legislation is closely associated with the name of Lord Ashley (later the seventh Earl of Shaftesbury), the great social reformer and a Protectionist MP.

Protectionist MPs were often far more likely to support such legislation than were Liberals and Radicals. Tories were even then evolving an ideology of what later became known as 'Tory socialism', in which, led by the landed aristocracy, the rights of factory workers would be enhanced and protected. Radicals like John Bright regularly opposed such legislation because it represented the improper interference by the state between voluntary contracting partners. As well, they argued that state-imposed limitations on the hours of work in a factory, by adding to the cost of manufacturing, injured the export potential and profits of British industry. A widespread notion grew up at this time, expressed most pithily by the economist Nassau Senior, that manufacturing firms made their profits in the last hour of work, and employees therefore had to work for long hours for a factory to be profitable. For all his evolution into something like a Liberal, Sir Robert Peel generally supported the position of Lord Ashley and rejected the extreme *laissez-faire* views of a Bright, as befitted a leader who considered himself the head of a 'national' government.

Nevertheless, in the battle over repeal of the Corn Laws the Tory Protectionists felt that they had a strong case. To many, agriculture rather than manufacturing or commerce remained the most fundamental of all industries, the landowners and farmers the backbone of the nation. Many pointed out that agriculture still employed far more workers than any other part of the economy. In 1841, for instance, 1 434 000 males were employed in agriculture compared with only 525 000 in textiles and 218 000 in mining. Agriculture was in employment terms still Britain's largest industry by far. To remove protection from agriculture thus threatened to create unemployment on a vast scale, and would do the most harm to the agricultural labourers of Britain and Ireland, the poorest and worst-paid workers in the whole economy. (Peel's reply to this was that an efficient British agriculture, able to stand on its own feet, was the best guarantee of continued rural employment.) To the Protectionists, even worse than the economic dangers of repeal was the political betrayal it represented. Here was a radical, indeed revolutionary, measure, threatening the most loyal of Peel's supporters in the Conservative party, for which no political mandate of any kind existed: Peel had made no mention of moving towards total repeal in 1841, and had necessarily to rely on the parliamentary votes of 227 assorted Whigs, Liberals and Radicals to secure its passage. It is almost impossible to exaggerate the sense of shock and betrayal felt by many Protectionist Tories; the only parallel to this sense of outrage in modern British political history is to be found, perhaps, in the feelings of the Labour party towards Ramsay MacDonald after he formed the National government in 1931. There are instances of members of aristocratic families, divided over repeal, never speaking again until the older man was on his deathbed. Bentinck, Disraeli and Peel nearly fought duels over accusations of betrayal. So bitter was the split that reconciliation became almost impossible, and talented younger Tory free traders, headed by Gladstone, never returned to the mainstream of the Conservative party and were lost to it.

While Peel's conversion to free trade may thus have benefited the British nation, it demonstrated a woeful political ineptness for a man of his experience and reputation. It is normal to attribute this ineptness to two factors. Only once in his career did Peel face a truly contested election; after 1830 he sat for Tamworth, a small proprietary in Staffordshire which the Peel family itself controlled. He was thus virtually unfamiliar with the rough-and-tumble of electoral politics as it developed after 1832. Secondly, Peel still conceptualised British politics in its pre-1832 dimensions. He thought it possible to head a 'national' government of the type which Pitt and Liverpool headed, and failed to grasp that it had evolved into a party system based in broad social and ideological divisions. It was said of repeal that Peel 'had caught the Whigs bathing and walked away with their clothes', but the majority of Tories wanted him to dress as he had always done. By alienating his most loyal supporters he accentuated the process of semi-democratic party government, making the formation of a 'national' government of the pre-1832 type even more difficult than it would have been.

Entirely apart from economic and trade issues, Peel faced another area of intractable difficulty, namely Ireland. Ireland surfaced as a central matter for Peel's attention in the latter part of his term as Prime Minister, from 1843 on. Peel's policies towards Ireland, and the balance of forces ranged for and against them, were somewhat similar to those which existed over the Corn Laws. In Ireland, Daniel O'Connell (1775–1847), the first of the great nineteenth-century Irish nationalist leaders, led a campaign to repeal the 1801 Union with Great Britain. Peel banned a great meeting O'Connell planned at Clontarf, and prosecuted its extreme leaders. But Peel also explicitly condemned 'mere force' as a solution to Ireland's 'social evils', and determined on a series of reforms aimed at improving relations between the British government and the Irish people. Peel and his Cabinet were determined upon timely concessions to the Catholic Irish majority, more necessary now than ever given the electoral force of Catholic Ireland and the growth of nascent Irish nationalism. To this end, the Peel government gave much sympathetic consideration to the problem of Irish tenant farmers and was equally sympathetic to the possibility of an Irish national university which would offer places to Catholics. It facilitated the private endowment of the Irish Catholic clergy and, most controversially, planned to increase the annual grant paid to Maynooth College, a training college for Catholic clergymen in Ireland, from £9000 to £26 000 and to make it permanent rather than subject to annual renewal by Parliament.

It is hardly an exaggeration to say that Peel's Maynooth proposals, introduced in the spring of 1845, were nearly as controversial as his plans for repeal. Evangelical Anglicanism and Protestant Nonconformity were both enormously powerful and perhaps at their zenith of zeal in the 1840s, while traditional Protestant hostility towards Catholicism, never far from the surface, was now also rising and determined to check what it increasingly viewed as deliberate Catholic attempts to increase that Church's influence throughout Britain. As with repeal of the Corn Laws, increasing the grant to Maynooth College was also seen by very many Tories as pointless undermining of the Protestant Church of Ireland, the Established Church in that country, and as a precedent for a wider attack upon the Church of England itself. And while Protestant Dissenters in Great Britain were known for their strong support of free trade, they were also likely to be, if anything, even more hostile to Catholicism than were many Anglicans and also strongly disapproved of state aid for religion *per se*. During four months in 1845 the government received hostile petitions, from Anglican and Dissenting sources, containing nearly 1.3 million names in contrast to favourable petitions with only 17 482 names. Peel's Maynooth grant proposal split the Conservative party, with fully one-half of Tory MPs voting against the grant, which passed through Parliament on the strength of the Whig, Liberal and Irish members' votes. One consequence of the Maynooth controversy was that Gladstone, then President of the Board of Trade, resigned from the Cabinet in February 1845 and remained outside of the Peel Cabinet until he was reappointed Secretary for War and the Colonies in December of that year. Gladstone's stance appeared to be thoroughly confused, strongly opposing the measure in Cabinet yet voting for it in Parliament. Later in 1845 came the Irish potato famine, which convinced Peel of the necessity of free trade, and the majority of his Tory supporters of his duplicity and lack of fixed principles.

Peel's fall was, however, delayed until sometime after the repeal of the Corn Laws: when it came, it was triggered by Ireland rather than by free trade. To deal with unrest in Ireland, Peel attempted to pass a Protection of Life (Ireland) Bill. Normally this would have had the support of virtually all Tories. Unfortunately it came up for a crucial vote in the Commons on the very day that the Lords approved the bill repealing the Corn Laws. A vengeful minority of Protectionist MPs combined with Whigs and Liberals to defeat Peel's Irish bill by 73 votes. Peel resigned a few days later, without calling a general election. In a memorable resignation speech, he praised Richard Cobden (with whom he had previously quarrelled and whose reconciliation with Peel was arranged by Harriet Martineau, the writer) and attacked 'every monopolist who . . . clamours for protection because it conduces to his own individual benefit', remembering those 'whose lot it is to labour, and to earn their daily bread by the sweat of their brow' who now could restore 'their exhausted strength with abundant and untaxed food, the sweeter because it is no longer leavened by a sense of injustice'. Peel's resignation led to the appointment of Lord John Russell, the Whig leader, as head of a minority Whig-Liberal government three days later.

Peel's legacy is thus a mixed one. To his supporters, he was arguably the greatest man of principle and courage ever to hold the premiership during the nineteenth century, and his legacy lived on, in the form of an unvarying basic commitment by successive British governments to free trade, until the 1930s. Peel became a virtual folk-hero to a section of the radical working classes, and received many semi-literate letters from workingmen when he resigned, praising him in extravagant terms. To his opponents he was a man of no principles and no political sense. In terms of the structure of elites and interest groups discussed throughout this book, Peel's unsuccessful attempt to recreate the 'national' elite consensual system as it existed before 1832, when it was headed by Conservative governments, merely exposed the impossibility of maintaining a unified elite structure in the post-Reform era: manufacturers and landowners could simply not be accommodated in the same party, or the same ruling group, at that time, and the reforms with which Peel is associated could not have been made by an old-style Tory Prime Minister. Given the surprising strength of the residual Protectionist Conservatives in Parliament and in the country, Peel also hastened the period of unstable and relatively weak government which marked the next 22 years of British politics and may be seen as having persisted in a real sense until the Liberal Unionist split of 1886. More concretely, Peel's fall had profound effects for the key personalities of British politics over the next 40 years. Had Peel remained Prime Minister and the Conservative party remained intact, Disraeli's rise to Tory ascendancy is virtually inconceivable, Derby and Palmerston were perhaps unlikely ever to have become Prime Ministers, and Gladstone, if he ever became Prime Minister at all, would probably have done so as a Peel-inspired Conservative rather than as the greatest figure of Liberalism.

Although Peel was repeatedly urged to head a government consisting of Whigs, Liberals and Peelite Tories, he always declined, and remained out of office and aloof from politics until his tragic death in 1850 when, at the age of 62, he was thrown from his horse and trampled by it while riding in a London park, dying four days later. His death was an occasion for universal grief, even among his opponents.

6

The mid-Victorian Whig ascendancy, 1846–1852

The 20-year period between the downfall of Peel and the last of the three minority Conservative governments, which took office in 1866, was dominated by the Whig party and its Liberal allies and supporters in Parliament. During this long period, the Protectionist Tories held office for less than two and a half years, in 1852 and 1858–59; for the remaining 17 years, Whigs formed the government or dominated it, producing two of the three Prime Ministers at the head of these governments, Lord John Russell (later Earl Russell) and Lord Palmerston. (The third Prime Minister at the head of a largely Whig government, Lord Aberdeen, had been a member of Peel's Conservative Cabinet who brought the Peelite Tories into coalition with the Whigs and Liberals.) This long period, 1846–66, marked the high point of Britain's industrial greatness and, following the collapse of Chartism, is seen as a period of national peace, unity and relative prosperity, whose apogee was the Great Exhibition of 1851. Yet it also saw a destructive war in Crimea which lasted for nearly two years, the Indian Mutiny of 1857, the effects of the 'cotton famine', produced by the American Civil War, upon Lancashire, and the publication in 1859 of the most momentous and disturbing book of the nineteenth century, Charles Darwin's *Origin of Species*. The Whig party, or rather the faction of the Whig-Liberal-Radical coalition known as the Whigs, was increasingly marginalised within that coalition, with Radicals increasingly in the ascendancy.

Nor was this coalition as firmly based as it might seem. To be sure, the split in the Conservative party over repeal of the Corn Laws meant that there was an overwhelming parliamentary majority for free trade, with the Protectionists reduced to no more than 225 MPs in 1847–52 compared with about 431 Whigs, Liberals and Peelite Tories. Nevertheless, the Whig-led coalition which governed Britain during this 20-year period was itself divided into several recognisable factions, often founded in deep-seated social and sociological causes. Most of the inner circle of governance of the coalition, men who comprised the great majority of all of its Cabinets, were

Whigs. The term 'Whig' is even harder to define in this period than at other times. At the core of Whig identity were a small number of immensely wealthy, higher aristocratic families, such as Russell (Dukes of Bedford), Cavendish (Dukes of Devonshire), Leveson Gower (Dukes of Sutherland), and Grosvenor (Earls, later Dukes of Westminster).[1] These families were intermarried and are sometimes said to have been defined by a 'sacred circle of great-grandmotherhood', as all were descended from, or closely related to, the great Duke of Marlborough and a number of other great seventeenth-century aristocrats such as William, Lord Russell (the 'martyr', who was executed in 1683). Other, slightly lesser aristocratic Whig families like the Greys and Pagets were also regarded as being within this inner grouping, and outsiders were occasionally admitted by marriage, such as some members of the Baring dynasty of merchant bankers. With their supporters, these families continued to dominate the inner circles of the Whig party until the 1860s or even later. They supported religious and intellectual freedom, limited government, liberal rule, and regarded the 'Glorious Revolution' of 1688 as the defining moment of modern British history.

The Liberal and Radical factions of the Whig-Liberal coalition were, however, very different. For the most part, their MPs were middle-class, often self-made businessmen and professional men. Many were Non-conformists; most sat for urban industrial seats in the north of England and the Celtic areas or for London and the Home Counties. Most endorsed the radical programme of limited government, free trade, religious freedom and equality, and a decrease in the power and influence of the Tory 'Establishment' as they understood it. A growing number, however, were themselves moving to the political right, keen to see their children enter the gentry class and glorying in Britain's power and might. Additionally, the coalition in Parliament continued to include a handful of Chartist extreme radicals and, more importantly, 60 or more Irish Liberal members, mainly Catholics, only loosely affiliated to the rest of the coalition. This coalition could and did cooperate for purposes on which they agreed, especially the maintenance of free trade and of 'retrenchment', that is, of continuing economies in the cost of central government, but was, as well, almost always riven by an underlying sense of disquiet with one another. Many (certainly not all) Radicals resented the seemingly perpetual rule of Whigs in the Cabinet, while Whigs generally feared any growth in democratic (or working-class) agitation which might disturb their rule or lead to demands for full-blooded democracy. Militant Protestant Nonconformists disliked both the established Anglican Church and Roman Catholics; Evangelical Anglicans often sought an accommodation with Nonconformists but were also deeply suspicious of Catholics. Most Irish disliked British rule *per se*. Many right-wing Whigs and a growing number of middle-class Liberals

---

1 Leveson Gower is pronounced 'Looson Gore', while Grosvenor is, of course, pronounced 'Grovenor'.

should, naturally, have seen the Protectionist Tories as more natural allies than Radicals and Irish semi-Fenians; many Radicals increasingly questioned a party led by the landed aristocracy. There was, as well, the entirely separate question of the relationship between the Peelites and the Whig-Liberals. These inner divisions and tensions were almost always greater in the Whig-Liberal party than among the remaining Protectionist Tories, who were sociologically and ideologically more unified.

During the years between 1846 and 1866 these divisions never centrally threatened the hegemony of the Whig-Liberal coalition; indeed, there was growing official unity between the elements of the coalition as the modern Liberal party took shape. Nevertheless, this unity was caused just as much by good luck as by deliberation: the prosperity of all sectors of the British economy – industry, commerce and agriculture – most of the time; the moderate nature of the coalition's leadership, especially under Palmerston; the failure of post-Chartist British radicalism; the numerical weakness of the Protectionist opposition. When Britain became much more like a modern democracy with the 1867 Reform Bill, the fragility of the coalition became more evident and was responsible for its demise in the 1880s.

The first of the Whig Prime Ministers in this period was Lord John Russell (1792–1878; created first Earl Russell in 1861); he was also the last, serving briefly as Prime Minister again in 1865–66. Russell became Prime Minister for the first time in June 1846 when Peel was defeated on a parliamentary vote, and served until February 1852. Russell, a Whig of Whigs, was the scion of one of Britain's greatest aristocratic houses; he was a younger son of the sixth Duke of Bedford. In 1846 Russell had been an MP for over 30 years and was best known for introducing the Great Reform Act into Parliament in 1831–32 and in successfully piloting it through Parliament in the face of adamant hostility from the Tories. Russell had served as Home Secretary and Leader of the House of Commons under Melbourne, and his conversion to free trade and repeal of the Corn Laws in the early 1840s eased Peel's task very considerably.[2]

Russell was a somewhat difficult, curious and contradictory man. He was only 5 feet 5 inches in height, weighed only 8 stone, and was often caricatured as a midget or a small boy. As a young man, Russell had written a novel and a five-act play, which Disraeli – not the most objective source, of course – described as 'the feeblest in our literature' in their respective genres. Russell had visited Napoleon in late 1814 when the Emperor was in exile on Elba. Various accounts survive of what was said; according to one, Russell enlarged at length to the ex-Emperor on the history of the Russell family; Napoleon made no reply but 'went to a corner of the room and relieved himself'.

2 Although known as 'Lord John Russell', he was not a peer or a member of the House of Lords until he received an earldom in 1861. The younger sons of dukes are known as 'Lord' (plus their names), a 'courtesy title' which has no legal status. Russell was thus able to be elected to the House of Commons until he was ennobled.

While no one doubted Russell's capacity for hard work or his intelligence (which he presumably passed to his offspring: Bertrand Russell, the famous philosopher, was his grandson), there were many doubts about his political abilities and aspects of his character. Russell was notoriously touchy about criticism or any perceived slight; he had little time for the social graces or for social contacts. His political views, too, were somewhat inconsistent and hard to pin down. Although Russell was the principal author of the Great Reform Act, in 1835 he mortified the radical tail of the Whig-Liberal coalition by proclaiming himself against any further measure of parliamentary reform, becoming widely known as 'Finality Jack' as a result. One of the most consistent strands in Russell's outlook was his unvarying belief in religious liberty and tolerance; he was a notable supporter of equal rights for Protestant Dissenters and Jews and was widely accused by conservative Anglicans of wishing to undermine the Churches of England and of Ireland. Yet in 1850, for no particularly strong reason, he issued a notorious denunciation of 'Papal Aggression' which might have come from a lifelong Protestant religious extremist. The aura of captaining the Great Reform Act, amidst great difficulties, through Parliament gave to Russell the status of a national hero, and a popular man, for the rest of his life, but he was much more at home in the small, closely knit world of the great Whig families than in the democratic nation which was emerging. Yet Russell, despite his exalted lineage, was not a rich man, scraping along on the relatively meagre allowance of a ducal younger son. From 1847 he lived most of the time in a country house near Richmond, then in the country south-west of London, given to him for life by Queen Victoria: he could not afford to buy his own.

Russell was asked to form a government when Peel fell in June 1846, but before a new general election (held the following year) took place. Russell thus depended upon the split between Peelite and Protectionist Tories not being healed; if it were, the Conservative MPs elected at the 1841 general election would have outnumbered Russell's supporters by 70 seats. Russell formed a purely Whig government: of the 16 ministers in his first Cabinet, eight sat in the House of Lords, one (Palmerston) held an Irish peerage, another (Lord Morpeth) was the heir to the Earl of Carlisle, Russell was the younger son of a duke, and three were well-connected Whig baronets. Russell's Cabinet included only two unadorned Commoners, Henry Labouchère, a wealthy banker of Huguenot descent who had married a daughter of the Earl of Carlisle, and – most anomalously – Thomas Babington Macaulay (1800–59), the great historian and intellectual champion of Whig Liberalism whom Russell appointed Paymaster-General. Macaulay, the unmarried son of a famous Evangelical colonial governor, has been described as 'probably the only man who, being born outside [the Whig elite], ever penetrated to its heart and assimilated its spirit'. Russell's Cabinet pointedly contained no businessmen (although Sir Francis Baring, later Lord Northbrook, of the great merchant banking family, joined the

Cabinet in 1849), let alone manufacturers. Richard Cobden might have been appointed, a move which Russell seriously considered, but Cobden nearly bankrupted himself during the Corn Laws campaign and was in poor health. Russell also wished to appoint some prominent Peelites (although not Peel himself) to the Cabinet, but they declined. After this, Russell showed little enthusiasm for an alliance with the Peelites, and many historians believe that he regarded them as a much greater threat to the ascendancy of the Whigs than the Protectionists, especially an alliance of Peelites and Radicals, something just possible realistically to imagine.

In contrast to the remarkably far-reaching programme of reforms offered by Peel, the Russell government's legislative achievements, though considerable, were moderate and reformist rather than radical. In the economic sphere, Russell helped to complete the free trade revolution begun by Peel by virtually abolishing the Navigation Acts in 1849. Though very complex, in a nutshell, the Navigation Acts had made it mandatory for British ships to carry many types of non-British goods and, in other cases, required that foreign goods be carried to Britain either in British ships or in ships of that nation: the intent of this point was to restrict, for example, American ships from carrying wine from Spain to Britain. The British shipping interest of course opposed this reform, but quickly found that the growing volume of world trade ensured that British shipping tonnage continued to expand rapidly. Indeed, Britain now moved into the iron shipbuilding age ahead of its rivals, spearheaded by Brunel and the other great mid-Victorian shipping innovators, and actually reclaimed some of the ground lost to America and France during the last stages of the age of sail.

Nevertheless, the economic situation facing the Russell government during its first few years of office was far from rosy. In Ireland, conditions went from bad to worse as the Great Famine became even more severe in 1846–47. Government intervention was meagre, although soup kitchens, initially established by Quaker philanthropists, became financed on a limited basis by the British government. The British pinned their hopes for long-term relief of Irish starvation on the consolidation and elimination of tiny, poverty-stricken peasant-like plots of land of the type found in great numbers in Ireland but virtually unknown in Britain. To this end, the government passed the Encumbered Estates Act of 1849, with the aim of making the purchase of small estates by the owners of outside capital possible, and actively encouraged the sale of the land of the impoverished Irish rural poor (and, implicitly, their emigration to America). The British government in fact had no real solution to the Irish famine, and looked to long-term structural, social and legal changes to rural Ireland as the only realistic means of amelioration. The famine, with its unequalled suffering and emigration, created a lasting mood of bitterness and resentment among nationalist-minded Irish persons which persists to this day, building on a previous legacy of deep hostility to Britain by Catholic Ireland. Nevertheless, to term this a deliberate policy of genocide, as some extremist Irish voices have done (in New York state in 1996 a law was enacted requiring that the Irish Famine be taught in all schools as an act of British genocide), is pernicious nonsense. It is simply unclear, given the technology which existed in the 1840s, how any measures of relief were possible on the vast scale and in the limited time to save many of the hundreds of thousands of rural Irishmen who tragically perished. The Irish Famine occurred because Ireland was, indeed, largely a one-crop economy with a backward, counter-productive system of land tenure. Most notably, there was no equivalent famine in any other part of the United Kingdom (including *northern* Ireland), where a more progressive regime of land tenure and land use prevailed. There was no famine in the heartland of industrial England, despite the ever-increasing size of its factory towns and the dire poverty there, nor in Celtic Scotland or Wales.

In 1846, too, Great Britain as a whole experienced a severe but temporary economic downturn, exacerbated by a poor harvest, the sudden end of the first wave of the great 'Railway Mania' and a country banking system unable to deal with a severe industrial depression. A run on the amount of gold (i.e. species, preferred by many to bank notes) held by the Bank of England ensued; interest rates rose, first slowly, then abruptly. Bank failures ensued, and a general panic was averted only by skilful intervention by the Bank of England in October 1847 by suspending the norm of operations of the Bank Charter Act. Given the underlying strength of the British economy, however, a strong rebound occurred in 1848: the Index of Industrial Production, a statistical measurement used by modern economic historians, rose from 164 in 1847 to 180 in 1848 (1831 = 100) and raw cotton consumption increased from 441 million pounds to 577 million in the same span.

The Russell government also made an attempt to deal with the perennial question of the relief of distress and poverty, building on previous reforms. In 1847 further changes were made in the Factory Acts reducing the length of time that women and young persons could work in a factory to 10 hours. The 1847 Factory Act specifically did not apply to adult male operatives, although in effect Saturdays became a factory half-holiday. Nevertheless, through evasion and loopholes in the law, many operatives, even women and young persons, continued to work for much longer hours than the Act envisioned. Opposition to the 1847 Act from factory owners had considerably diminished in only a few years, but this legislation was, in general, supported by Protectionist Tories and most Radicals, with the Whigs divided and many Peelites, staunch advocates of *laissez-faire*, generally opposed. Its champion in Parliament, the great Lord Ashley (1801–85, later the seventh Earl of Shaftesbury), a devout Evangelical Anglican, was a Protectionist Tory.

The Whig government also enacted significant changes to the Poor Laws of 1834. In 1847 the Poor Law Commission, with its headquarters at Somerset House and its much-disliked 'pashas' (allegedly arbitrary heads, like middle eastern potentates) was abolished and a Poor Law Board established, headed by a President who was always an MP and was included in most governments. In practice, there was little change in the administration of the Poor Laws, although poor law schools – inhuman, barracks-like structures – were established on a large scale. The New Poor Law was also extended in a modified form to Ireland, although (unlike other parts of Britain) it was specifically permitted to give 'outdoor relief' to the able-bodied poor if the workhouses were full. The Whig government also renewed the income tax otherwise scheduled to expire, to obvious disapproval from the well-off.

In 1848 the Russell government established a central Board of Health. The Board was the product of agitation by social investigators like Sir Edwin Chadwick, appalled at the sanitary and medical conditions in Britain's slum cities, and also of widespread public anxiety caused by a serious cholera epidemic in 1847, widely seen as the product of inadequate sanitation and drainage. The central Board had the power to create local boards of health in some circumstances (for instance, in places where the death rate exceeded 23 per 1000). Nevertheless, despite the creation of these local boards in areas with over two million people, the Act had less effect than its proponents hoped. Originally foreseen as establishing a body with very wide compulsory powers, it was watered down in Parliament so that towns had the option of agreeing to its functions or not. Many towns created their own local committees to look after such matters as improved drainage, street-lighting, and pollution caused by factories, but there was no national direction.

The Whig government called a general election in the middle of 1847, a year after it took office. A confused affair given the split in the Conservative ranks, it would seem that the Whig-Liberal coalition gained about 39 seats (Russell thought the figure was 52), with the Liberals electing about 329 MPs and the two wings of the Tories about 327 MPs. The Conservatives were, of course, hopelessly divided between about 225 Protectionists and perhaps 100 (some sources say 85–90) Peelites. The Whig-Liberal coalition itself contained many waverers, while the Irish contingent was even more deeply divided and almost impossible to classify. As usual, England elected a majority of Tory MPs, although the central division within the party made that figure meaningless. In any case, unless the two wings of the Conservative party reunited, which they never did, the Whig government appeared reasonably safe.

The Whig government was faced, a year after the election, with the effects of the great wave of revolutions that swept Europe in 1848, temporarily producing liberal governments and regimes throughout the Continent until crushed by the forces of the old order. In France, the Orléans dynasty, headed by King Louis-Philippe, was overthrown, the King going into exile in England and thus, as it were, trading places with his successor who had been in exile in England. His successor was Louis-

Napoleon Bonaparte, nephew of the great Emperor, who was most unexpectedly elected President of the second French Republic by a huge
majority, put into office, it is often said, by the votes of France's peasants
who could recognise no other name on the ballot. Another political exile in
1848, virtually unknown at the time but eventually of momentous import,
was Karl Marx (1818–83), a German revolutionary who had just urged a
Communist revolution in *The Communist Manifesto*, but who lived for the
next 35 years in London. Marx produced *Das Kapital* from his researches
in the British Museum, and was financially and politically supported by his
German-born collaborator and fellow-Communist Friedrich Engels
(1820–95), despite his politics a wealthy umbrella cloth manufacturer in
Manchester.

The great historian Sir Lewis Namier described the European revolutions
of 1848 as 'a turning point at which history failed to turn'. By this he
meant that, by the expected course of historical evolution, popular middle-
class liberalism 'should' have triumphed in 1848 in France, Germany, Italy
and elsewhere. Instead, the forces of the old regime regained control
everywhere except in France, where Louis-Napoleon Bonaparte established
a 'Second Empire' several years later.

The 1848 revolutions passed Britain by with relatively little impact. This
is, in itself, at least mildly surprising and it was certainly not a foregone
conclusion that the Continent's unrest would fail to spread to Britain. On
the contrary, the economic depression of 1847, the great famine in Ireland,
and, above all, the very recent occurrence of the Chartist agitation, with the
nation-wide infrastructure of organised Chartist radicalism, made it likely
that at least some echoes of revolutionary Europe would be felt in Britain.
To be sure, there was also much to make for stability, especially the fact
that, unlike continental Europe, Britain already possessed a long-
established constitutional government enjoying wide legitimacy which had
at least partially integrated its middle classes into the country's governance.
Some serious rioting did indeed take place in the spring of 1848, beginning
at Glasgow. In April a monster rally of Chartists, a crowd numbering at
least 25 000, assembled at Kennington Common in south London. (Remarkable photographs of the rally, one of the earliest historical 'events'
ever to be photographed, survive.) They were forbidden to march from
Kennington to Westminster and obeyed, Feargus O'Connor carrying the
rally's petition in favour of the Charter to Parliament in a cab. Mindful of
events on the Continent, the authorities were taking absolutely no chances,
and swore in nearly 200 000 special constables to deal with any trouble. In
addition, the aged Duke of Wellington, still Commander-in-Chief, stationed
regular troops throughout the capital. As a result of this show of force,
virtually no violence was experienced in Britain during the revolutionary
year.

Trouble did come to Russell's government from somewhat unexpected
quarters. Religion was one. The early and mid-Victorian years represented

perhaps the apogee of the period when religious issues were virtually paramount in politics. In 1845 John Henry Newman and some of his followers in the Oxford Movement left the Church of England to join the Roman Catholics, a renowned event which shook Britain's intelligentsia to its core. The question of what constituted orthodoxy within the Church of England itself was now profoundly important. The Church was still widely, perhaps generally, regarded as the soul of the English nation, the arbiter of its moral life, and an institution possibly more important than Parliament. Yet it was wracked by factions and had already been affected by the so-called 'Higher Criticism' emanating from Germany which questioned the literal truth of the Bible. In matters relating to the Church of England, Russell was a liberal who preferred the so-called Low Churchmen, Evangelical and quasi-Protestant, to the High Churchmen, who were objects of deep suspicion to many because of their alleged sympathies with Rome, which Newman's spectacular defection obviously did nothing to allay. Russell, of confirmed anti-High Church views, became involved in several notable theological conflicts. In 1847 he appointed Renn Hampden, Professor of Divinity at Oxford, to the bishopric of Hereford.[3] Hampden had long been the object of hostility by High Churchmen and others because of his unorthodox views, which had actually been officially censured by Oxford University. When Hampden's appointment was announced, 13 bishops sent Russell a strong protest, while Samuel Wilberforce, Bishop of Oxford, instituted heresy proceedings against Hampden in the Court of Arches, the ecclesiastical court which tries such cases. Russell stood firm, despite an enormous national uproar.

At the same time as Hampden's appointment created a national dispute, another controversy raged in the Church of England. The doctrine of infant baptism had long vexed the Church: should infants be baptised, that is long before they consciously knew what baptism was or voluntarily assented to it? Many Protestants argued that infants should not be. Low Church Anglicans viewed that infant baptism was 'conditional' to salvation and had to be merited by faith in later life, while High Church Anglicans argued that the Church had the authority to grant salvation to infants through their baptism. (This was more than an arcane debate for the thousands of Anglican parents who each year witnessed the deaths of their infant children. For them the question of whether or not they would be saved in the next life was an intensely real one.) In 1847 an enormous controversy arose when Bishop Phillpotts of Exeter, a pugnacious High Churchman, refused to institute (that is, confirm the appointment to a living of) a clergyman named George Gorham, who held deviating Low Church views on this question. A famous controversy ensued, attracting nation-wide publicity and a lengthy series of trials in both the ecclesiastical and civil

3 Until very recently, the Prime Minister (including non-Anglican Prime Ministers) appointed all bishops (and the archbishops) of the Church of England, based upon any criteria he saw fit.

courts. In the end, Phillpotts's decision not to institute Gorham was quashed by the Judicial Committee of the Privy Council, a body consisting wholly of lay barristers and judges, unversed in Anglican canon law; they need not themselves even have been Anglicans.[4] Thenceforth, it became virtually impossible for bishops of the Anglican Church to enforce conformity in religious outlook upon their clergymen. The Gorham verdict outraged High Church opinion in particular, and caused some to compare the laxity of belief in Anglicanism with the mandatory orthodoxy of Roman Catholicism. On the other hand, it ensured that Anglicanism would accommodate an enormously wide body of beliefs and interpretations and almost certainly made impossible destructive 'heresy-hunting' which could easily have produced major splits and divisions within the Church of England. In 1850 Nonconformity appeared to many to be gaining the upper hand over Anglicanism; by 1900, however, it seemed to many objective observers that Anglicanism had been relatively more successful than Nonconformity during the past half-century, and that much of the enthusiasm and vigour of Dissent had waned. The fact that the Church of England increasingly accommodated a variety of theological interpretations within itself probably enhanced its position considerably.

As important as both of these matters seemed at the time, they were less dramatic than an incident directly involving Lord John Russell which occurred in 1850, the so-called matter of 'Papal Aggression'. As a result of the Reformation, the Catholic Church no longer maintained a hierarchy of bishops in England; even after the growth of religious toleration and a very considerable increase in the size of England's Roman Catholic population caused by Irish migration and conversions, the Catholic Church in Britain was headed by vicars-apostolic, offices normally held in the Church by its missionary leaders in heathen countries. In 1850 the head of the Catholic Church in England, Cardinal Wiseman, after consulting both Lord John Russell and the Pope, proposed to create a new Catholic hierarchy for Britain. It was to be headed by an Archbishop of Westminster and bishops whose titles (such as the Bishop of Birmingham) did not at that time exist in the Anglican Church (the head of the Anglican Church is, of course, the Archbishop of Canterbury). Wiseman, who had only just been made a Cardinal of the Roman Church, the first such creation in over 400 years, also issued an undiplomatically enthusiastic pastoral letter claiming that 'Catholic England . . . begins now anew its course of regularly adjusted action round the centre of unity, the source of light and vigour'.

---

4 For the purposes of deciding the Gorham case, however, the Judicial Committee included the two Archbishops and the Bishop of London, all members of the House of Lords. Normally, of course, the doctrines of a religious body and their interpretation by individual clergymen could hardly have been the subject of lawsuits. As the Established Church, however, the Church of England was ultimately subject to civil law, a fact deeply resented by many clergymen from both the High and Low wings of the Church.

Rather surprisingly, an extraordinarily fierce storm then ensued. Anti-Catholicism had long been a surprisingly strong element in Protestant England's national character, and Wiseman's action and words, seen in the context of Newman's conversion and other events, unleashed a torrent of anti-Catholic abuse and even anti-Catholic rioting. In November 1850 the Prime Minister wrote an open letter, addressed to the Anglican Bishop of Durham, blaming the Pope for his 'aggression', attacking the Pope's attempts to 'fasten his fetters upon a nation which has so long and so nobly vindicated its right to freedom', and, for good measure, condemning the Oxford Movement for reintroducing 'the mummeries of superstition' to Anglicanism. Given Russell's long and honourable championing of religious freedom, this letter seemed as uncharacteristic as it was absurdly provocative, but it unquestionably caught a widespread mood of militant English Protestantism then at its flood. Several members of Russell's Cabinet actually wished to prosecute Cardinal Wiseman under a forgotten Elizabethan Act. The following year Russell produced a bill, which Parliament enacted, prohibiting the Catholic hierarchy from using the same names for its bishoprics as those already employed by the Anglican Church. Since the Catholics had pointedly avoided doing this, the Act served no purpose and was perfectly useless; it was repealed by Gladstone's government in 1871. Historians have long been puzzled by Russell's incongruous bout of anti-Catholic xenophobia. To be sure, Whig liberalism of the type Russell espoused, while it supported toleration for Catholics as a facet of religious freedom, was also generally hostile to the Catholic religion, seeing in it a superstitious medieval survival and deploring the support for political reaction almost always given at the time by the Roman church. On the other hand, some recent historians like T. A. Jenkins have viewed Russell's motivations as political. It was well-known that many Peelite Tories were champions of High Church Anglicanism which viewed Catholicism in a friendly or at least benign light, and Russell was trying to reinforce the Whig leadership of the liberal forces in Britain by contrasting his militant Protestantism with the equivocal position of the Whigs' potential rivals. Whatever the cause, the 'Papal Aggression' affair showed Russell at his least attractive.

The 1846–52 Whig government experienced some of its greatest difficulty, however, in the realm of foreign policy. Since the Napoleonic Wars, foreign affairs played remarkably little role in determining the fate of governments, and all of the great issues of the 35 years since Waterloo had concerned the British Isles alone. Most of the Russell government's difficulties in foreign policy stemmed directly from Russell's appointment of Lord Palmerston as Foreign Secretary. Palmerston had served as Foreign Secretary before, for no less than 11 years between 1830 and 1841. More will be said of this remarkable and controversial man in the section discussing his years as Prime Minister in 1855–58 and 1859–65. Palmerston was a British patriot, and increasingly conservative, at home; abroad he was a liberal, an opponent of absolutism, and (consistent with his domestic views) a militant champion of British interests, which he regarded as synonymous with progress. In the conduct of foreign affairs he was often truculent rather than diplomatic. Above all, he conducted Britain's foreign policy alone, taking heed of few.

Three incidents in Palmerston's Foreign Secretaryship under Russell stand out. In 1850 came the celebrated 'Don Pacifico' affair. 'Don Pacifico' (David Pacifico) was a Jewish Portuguese money-lender who claimed British citizenship on the grounds of being born in Gibraltar and who owned a house in Athens. When his house in Athens was pillaged by anti-Semitic mobs, Palmerston supported his case for compensation from the Greek government: Palmerston deplored this latest in a long record of Greek failure to honour its commitments to Britain. He ordered a blockade of the Greek coast by British ships. This he did without consulting France or Russia, leading to France temporarily withdrawing its ambassador from London. In June 1850 Palmerston defended his actions with a lengthy speech in Parliament which soon became one of the most famous of the nineteenth century, ending with the celebrated peroration: 'As the Roman, in days of old . . . could say "Civis Romanus sum" [I am a citizen of Rome], so also a British subject, in whatever land he may be, shall feel confident that the watchful eye and strong arm of England will protect him against injustice and wrong.' (Palmerston's words are often misquoted as 'Civis Britannicus sum'.)[5] Palmerston's speech produced an electrifying effect throughout Britain, as well as in Parliament, where a motion supporting his actions passed with a majority of 46. It was widely noted that middle-class Britain, normally pacifistic, strongly supported the Foreign Minister.

Palmerston also nearly came to grief in September 1850 when General Haynau of Austria visited Britain. Haynau was widely detested by British radicals for flogging women and committing many atrocities during the 1848 revolution. While visiting Barclay's Brewery in Southwark (one of the great sights of the capital), he was set upon by a mob of workers and thrashed. Palmerston was compelled to apologise officially to Austria, but in a lukewarm manner which showed that he had more sympathy with the workers than with the general. This outraged Queen Victoria, who long disliked Palmerston, and who now sought his resignation without success. Yet Palmerston was skating on very thin ice, despite his popularity. In December 1851 Louis-Napoleon Bonaparte carried out his famous *coup d'état*, abolishing the French republic of which he was President and declaring himself to be Emperor Napoleon III.[6] Without asking the permis-

5 It is notable that Palmerston acted to assist a foreign Jew with the most dubious grounds for considering himself a British citizen; this is unlikely to have happened even 20 years earlier.
6 According to Bonapartists, the son of Napoleon I who survived the Emperor but never reigned was actually Napoleon II.

sion of either the Cabinet or Queen, Palmerston acknowledged the government's 'entire approbation' of Napoleon's *coup*. At first glance this seems rather curious: Palmerston's belligerency would seemingly make him hostile to any Napoleonic restoration which entailed a reassertion of Napoleon's old military ambitions. Yet Palmerston apparently viewed Napoleon III, who lived for many years in Britain, as likely to be more friendly to Britain than any other possible regime would be. In any case, Russell as Prime Minister dismissed Palmerston over his actions. Palmerston had his revenge early in 1852, when he moved an amendment to a Militia Bill, opposed by Russell's government, which was carried by a vote of 136 to 125. Russell then resigned, and two days later the Earl of Derby formed the first of the three minority Protectionist governments which held office over the next 16 years.

While the Russell government of 1846–52 ended on a series of rather discordant notes, it must also be said that the closing years of his administration coincided with the very zenith of the mid-Victorian period, the 'age of equipoise' which followed the 'hungry forties' and in which Britain's stability contrasted so markedly with the unrest sweeping Europe. In 1851 the celebrated Great Exhibition, the first 'world's fair', was held in a unique 'Crystal Palace' – strongly presaging twentieth-century architecture – in Hyde Park (and later removed to and rebuilt in south London). An enormous display of industry and invention from around the world, especially Britain, it attracted hundreds of thousands of visitors; many were poor persons from remote parts of Britain who had never visited London before. The Great Exhibition did not receive universal endorsement when it was first proposed. It was opposed by many conservatives, who pessimistically feared that it could produce only unrest. One extreme Tory, Colonel Waldo Sibthorp MP, expected the Exhibition to bring only 'foreign assassins and venereal disease' to London! The previous year, in 1850, Alfred Tennyson succeeded the aged William Wordsworth as Poet Laureate. In contrast to Wordsworth, a radical during the early phases of the French Revolution who then became an extreme conservative and champion of rural England, Tennyson appeared to welcome mid-Victorian 'progress' and experienced the religious doubts then becoming so common among intellectuals. In 1851 it was very difficult to believe that Providence had not vouchsafed stability, progress and prosperity to Great Britain for some higher purpose. It was also very difficult not to believe that the old was constantly giving way to the new. In 1852 the aged Duke of Wellington died, and he was accorded the greatest, and most sincerely felt, state funeral (apart from the Sovereigns') seen between the burial services of Lord Nelson in 1805 and Sir Winston Churchill in 1965. 'The last great Englishman was dead', eulogised Alfred Tennyson, and so very many believed. The age of the giants had now passed; the age of relative pygmies, whether in government, cultural life or commerce, was in full flood. To many, Britain now mass-produced notable men and women as Birmingham mass-produced cheap tin trays, but they were less grand, and certainly less great, than before the machine age. It was hard to reconcile Britain's unquestioned prosperity and progress with this sense of decline, and, in a sense, for many intellectuals the rest of the Victorian age consisted of an extended attempt to make sense of these contradictory tendencies.

|7|

The minority Conservative governments, 1852–1868, and the rise of Disraeli

The split over the Corn Laws, although obviously disastrous to the Conservatives in the short term, did much less harm, in the long term, than one might have imagined. The Peelite faction of the Conservative party failed to exploit its strong position as one might assume it would; while superficially in a weak position the Protectionist Tories were actually much sounder than one might have supposed. Peel was forced to give up the Prime Ministership in June 1846, and never held office again. In the four years before his death, he declined to reunify the Conservative party or to organise the 'Peelite' faction of the Conservative party, with its men of talent and experience, as a separate party. Had Peel not died suddenly in June 1850 it is possible – though far from certain – that he would have become reconciled with his former colleagues, and there is some tentative evidence that he had begun to view Disraeli in a warmer light. In the event, most of the Peelites gradually but clearly began to drift away from the Protectionists and effect an ever-closer association with the Whigs and Liberals. At the general election of 1847, the first after Repeal, most Peelite candidates lost the support of the Conservative registration societies which existed to support Conservative candidates. Nevertheless, the 1847 general election had left the Conservative party, considered as a single unit, in a surprisingly strong position: together, the Peelites and Protectionists are generally believed to have won 327 seats in the Commons, compared with 329 for the coalition of Whigs, Liberals, Radicals and Irish members. Of course, the two wings of the party would not cooperate, and the Whig government under Lord John Russell continued in office until February 1852. Despite the unprecedented turmoil created by Repeal, in 1847 the two wings of the Conservative party did not achieve dramatically worse results than they had six years before in 1841, when they won the election.

Apart from the fact that the two wings of the party failed to reunite, the period between Repeal and the formation of the minority Conservative government was chiefly notable, on the Tory side of politics, for two things: the rise of Benjamin Disraeli and attempts by the Protectionist wing of the party to keep tariffs alive as a viable issue. In the six years between Repeal and the first minority Tory government, Disraeli evolved from an exotic, mysterious, but arguably brilliant backbencher to one of the first men of the party. He was still widely mistrusted by most Conservative backbench landowners, but he was in an immensely stronger position in 1852 than at the time of Repeal, and his claims to a senior position on the formation of the minority Tory government (he became Chancellor of the Exchequer) were unanswerable.

Benjamin Disraeli (1804–81; created first Earl of Beaconsfield in 1876) was probably the most unlikely man to rise to the highest ranks of European politics during the nineteenth century. A Jew by birth, Disraeli was converted to Anglicanism at the age of 13 with his family by his father, the famous and successful writer of anecdotage about famous authors, Isaac D'Israeli, but remained centrally conscious of his Jewish origins throughout his life. The younger Disraeli did not attend a public school or a university; he had no profession or business apart from writing novels (he was one of the most considerable Victorian novelists) and some singularly unsuccessful financial speculations. He owned no land and no country house until he was well over 40; he did not marry into the aristocracy or have any aristocratic connections. He was possibly the only major political figure of the nineteenth century to prefer the company of women to men, and not as potential sexual conquests, but as intellectual companions. (This singular quality might well have more fully marked Disraeli out as extremely peculiar, and untrustworthy, than his Jewishness, his novels, or his apparent lack of fixed principles.) Essentially, Disraeli was a pure intellectual and an adventurer, although one remarkably adept at sophisticated political intrigue and also, paradoxically, a man of deep if eccentric fundamental beliefs which animated his whole career. His career was the greatest *tour de force* in nineteenth-century political history. He was probably the most brilliant man to rise high in nineteenth-century British politics, although his legacy is confused and ambiguous.

The essence of the ambiguity surrounding Disraeli's legacy is that he is often seen as a 'Tory democrat', or even a 'Tory socialist', one who wished to lead a combination of the old Tory aristocracy and the urban working classes against the factory owners and their Whig-Liberal associates. There is more than enough truth in this familiar depiction to make it plausible. Both the 1867 Reform Act, which enfranchised the urban working classes, and the significant social legislation of Disraeli's great government of 1874–80, aimed at benefiting the trade unions and manual workers, bear this out. Yet there was also another Disraeli, often overlooked by romantic-minded historians, whose orientation is quite different. At all times, Disraeli supported all of the conservative forces and institutions of society, including the conservative middle classes, and he won office decisively in

1874 because much of the urban middle class, especially in London and the south-east (but also in Lancashire, especially Liverpool), had become Conservatives. His finances and budgets were always orthodox, and his hand-picked second-in-command and Chancellor of the Exchequer, Sir Stafford Northcote, was both a hereditary baronet and a City businessman, who had once been Gladstone's private secretary. One may romantically (indeed, perhaps accurately) view Disraeli's chief legacy as a union of the old aristocracy and the new working classes, a view favoured by many 'One Nation' Tories in the twentieth century, especially under Baldwin and Macmillan, and still often heard today. Yet it is probably more accurate to view Disraeli as one of the architects of the union of old money and new money – the old aristocracy and the new middle classes, especially in the south of England – which emerged triumphantly under Lord Salisbury, Disraeli's successor, and has been among the primary bases of the Conservative party's remarkable electoral success in the twentieth century. In view of the romantic notion of 'Dizzy' as the prince of Tory Democrats, it is important to be reminded how often he was no such thing. Given that the merger of the old aristocracy and the south of England middle classes would be perhaps the most salient feature of Conservative politics after the 1880s, Disraeli's other legacy may be seen as probably the more important.

Disraeli was also animated, throughout his life, by a genuine love of institutions and families of demonstrably long lineage. This love of the long-existing was derived from his Jewishness, which was at the core of his peculiar outlook. Disraeli saw an affinity between the unbroken history of the Jewish people, who had existed for 4000 years, and Britain's old aristocratic families. He indeed went further, and saw himself as a Jewish prophet, destined by Providence to lead the landed families of Britain. He was an anti-radical for the same reason: radicalism pointlessly broke historical continuities, replacing them with artificially constructed institutions, which lacked both the proven success and the legitimacy of those they replaced. Disraeli was a genuine conservative, the legitimate successor to Burke. Yet, as always, there was another very different side to his worldview here. He was always conscious that the nineteenth century had been a time when old dynasties fell and new ones rose, when new men, from novel backgrounds, replaced time-honoured elites. As a new man *par excellence*, Disraeli also welcomed this, and was particularly taken by a figure like Napoleon III, who had lived on an innkeeper's charity in England a few years before becoming French Emperor. It is pointless to try and resolve this, and the other contradictory elements in Disraeli's outlook, which were as unique and unclassifiable as the man himself.

In Parliament, Disraeli rose because he was the best debater by far on the Protectionist side. He became renowned, above all, for making the clever-clever, telling jibes at the Peelite and Whig front benches which the average backbench Protectionist squire was simply incapable of making; jibes indeed too clever for the solid, competent men of business and government experience around Peel. While Disraeli was initially mistrusted by his backbenchers, especially over his support for Jewish 'emancipation' (the right of practising Jews elected to Parliament to swear 'so help me God' rather than 'upon the true faith of a Christian' upon taking their seat), he also had powerful friends, particularly Lord George Bentinck and his relative the Duke of Portland, who in 1848 helped Disraeli to purchase a small estate, Hughenden, near High Wycombe in Buckinghamshire, enabling him to become a legitimate, if very peculiar, country gentleman and gain election as MP for Buckinghamshire.

Technically and officially, Disraeli only became undisputed leader of the Conservative party in the House of Commons in February 1852, with the formation of the minority Protectionist government under the Earl of Derby. From the split of July 1846 until December 1848, the official leader of the Protectionist Conservatives in the House of Commons was Lord George Bentinck, Disraeli's friend and protégé, who resigned from the Conservative leadership in December 1847 after he had supported Disraeli against his party over Jewish 'emancipation'. Rather than choose Disraeli as their leader in the Commons at this stage, the Protectionist MPs selected another Tory nobleman in the House of Commons, Lord Granby (who later became the sixth Duke of Rutland and was the brother of another of Disraeli's protégés, Lord John Manners). A nonentity who never held office in any government, he resigned the sole Protectionist leadership in the Commons only a month later, in March 1848. There then ensued a 'triumvirate' leadership (the only time there has been a joint leadership in either Houses of Parliament) consisting of Disraeli, Lord Granby, and J. C. Herries, who had held office in the Tory Cabinets of the late 1820s and early 1830s. Finally, in February 1852 Disraeli became the undisputed leader of the Protectionists in the Commons, a position he held until he went to the House of Lords in August 1876. Disraeli had been *de facto* leader of the Protectionists during most of this period, speaking on most of the important issues. Lord Aberdeen likened the curious 'triumvirate' which nominally led the Protectionists in the Commons for three years to that which had existed in France of the 1790s, consisting of two forgotten men, Sièyes and Ducos, and Napoleon Bonaparte.

While Disraeli was gradually but surely becoming undisputed leader of the Protectionist Tories in the House of Commons, he was not the leader of the party as a whole. From March 1846 until his death 22 years later in February 1868, the recognised leader of the Protectionist party as a whole was Edward Stanley (1799–1868), who went to the House of Lords in 1844 as Baron Stanley of Bickerstaffe and succeeded his father as fourteenth Earl of Derby in 1851. Although one of the least-known Prime Ministers of the nineteenth century, he was far more than a figurehead and deserves to be more famous than he is. Derby was originally a Whig aristocrat serving as Chief Secretary for Ireland and then Secretary for War and the Colonies from 1830 till 1834 under Lord Grey. There was nothing in his background or behaviour up to that point to suggest that Derby would begin a rightwards drift, and much to imply that he would remain a rather typical Whig aristocrat. Derby was the richest landowner in Lancashire – the Earls of Derby are often known as the 'kings of Lancashire' – and, as such, he was in close touch with local businessmen. Many, including Derby himself, saw him as a future leader of the party. Nevertheless, in 1834 Derby resigned from the Grey Cabinet over the issue of the reduction of revenues from the established Church of Ireland. He moved steadily to the right, serving in Peel's government as Secretary for War and the Colonies. Slowly but surely he broke with Peel over Protection, leaving the government when Peel declared in favour of a total repeal of the Corn Laws.

Derby was the natural leader of the Protectionist party, and so long as he was alive, there was no question of anyone but him leading the party; it was inconceivable that Disraeli could have succeeded as Prime Minister while Derby was alive and active. Handsome and accomplished – he produced an original translation of the *Iliad* which was reprinted six times – Derby was almost as great an orator and debater as Disraeli himself, who dubbed him the '[Prince] Rupert of Debate'. Enormously wealthy and powerful, a patron of the turf who won £100 000 in stakes on the racecourse, he provided even more to the legitimacy and viability of the Protectionist party than did Disraeli.

From 1846 until they first took office in 1852, the chief problem facing the Protectionist party was how to deal with the issue of protection itself when they returned to power. Between 1846 and 1852 the Whig government pushed free trade even further. In 1848 it passed the Sugar Bill, which removed the preference previously given to British West Indies sugar planters. In 1849 it repealed the last of the old-established Navigation Laws, which had required goods to be shipped into and out of Britain in British ships. Both laws barely passed through Parliament, especially the House of Lords, and some Protectionist activists like Lord George Bentinck looked forward to forming a rural-urban alliance of the agricultural, shipping and colonial interests to oppose free trade. In the agricultural sphere, the terrible Irish famine, and generally very depressed rural conditions in England, led to a revival of the Protectionist movement in Britain, with the formation, in May 1849, of the National Association for the Protection of British Industry and Capital. Although chiefly comprising Tory peers and landowners, it also included a number of urban businessmen. In 1848–49 Protectionist candidates won a series of important by-election victories, including a remarkable one at Cork, in Ireland. Many of the Peelite MPs in the House of Commons were now returning to the majority of Protectionist Tories, especially after Peel's death in 1850.

Despite all this, the Protectionists still lacked a coherent or straightforward approach to the tariff question. So powerful had the free trade lobby, and the free trade ideal, become, that a full-blooded return to protection appeared increasingly quixotic. As early as 1849 Disraeli made his famous remark that 'Protection is not only dead but damned'. Increasingly, however, the Protectionist majority of the Conservatives were compelled to find an alternative series of party desiderata and proposals which could take the place of protection as a central party programme. It has been said that at heart Derby was a 'protectionist in the country, neutral in a small town, and a Free Trader in the cities', and certainly most recognised that free trade was there to stay. Disraeli privately voiced a number of alternative policies to Derby and his other close friends. The most important of these was a sinking fund, that is the use of either the surplus from or a dedicated portion of the annual budget to gradually pay off the national debt, and thereby reduce interest rates. This idea would surface again and again in Conservative thought, and was actually enacted by Sir Stafford Northcote, Disraeli's Chancellor of the Exchequer, a quarter-century later. Another idea was the 'equalization of taxation', that is the financing of rates (local taxes) at the national level, again designed to reduce the burden on landowners. Both would, incidentally, have benefited businessmen and other persons of wealth as well, although both plans required that general taxes be raised initially to pay for either scheme. In any case, the Protectionist party was now actively looking well beyond agricultural tariffs, and had begun the process of making a much wider appeal than merely to the landed interest.

After a number of abortive attempts, a minority Protectionist government was formed early in 1852. This government was, upon its formation, one of the least prepossessing of any post-1832 administration. Only a handful of Cabinet ministers had held office under Peel (or anyone else), and no fewer than 17 of its members were sworn of the Privy Council on the same day (membership of which is a *sine qua non* for holding Cabinet level office). Very few of its ministers would have held governmental office at any rank had the Conservatives not split in 1846. The old and deaf Duke of Wellington, hearing the list of its ministers read out in the House of Lords, called out 'Who? Who?' upon hearing each name, and Derby's 1852 Cabinet has been known as the 'Who? Who?' government ever since. Choosing its most obscure single member might be difficult, but as good a candidate as any was Sir John Pakington, a hitherto unknown country squire who became Colonial Secretary. At a dinner party, Lord Derby the Prime Minister was asked by the hostess 'Are you sure that he is a *real* man?' Quick as a flash Derby responded 'Well, I think so – he has been married three times.' (Pakington proved to be an able minister and served with some distinction in the other two minority Conservative governments.) The new Home Secretary, Spencer Walpole, had only sat in Parliament since 1847; the Foreign Secretary, Lord Malmesbury, claimed that his only qualifications for the post were that he had edited the diplomatic correspondence of his grandfather. Disraeli himself described the first Derby government as a Cabinet with 'six Dukes of Buckingham'. It was High Tory, strongly Protestant, and Protectionist at heart.

The Cabinet was almost universally derided in the press and by intelligent commentators upon its formation, and, crucially, the remaining Peelite Conservatives remained aloof, a major sign that the breach between the two components of Conservatism was permanent. Its leading figures were, plainly, Derby as Prime Minister, and Disraeli, who became Chancellor of the Exchequer, a post for which he had no training or experience. When Derby offered him the post, and Disraeli demurred, Derby pointed out that 'You know as much as Mr. Canning. They give you the figures.' The key question facing the government was, of course, what to do about protection. Derby strongly favoured the introduction of a fixed duty on corn; Disraeli prevaricated in his views, and actually praised the benefits of free trade quite gratuitously in his speeches. In reality, the government, being in a minority, could pass nothing without the support of the free trade majority in the Commons and took office on the understanding that they would delay any new proposals until they held an election, which they agreed to do at the end of 1852. In the absence of any far-reaching initiatives, the minority Conservative government did pass a number of minor but useful measures, such as the granting of a constitution to New Zealand and a reform of the chancery courts. Disraeli was also obliged to frame a budget in 1852. This showed him at his most ingenious, although too clever by half. To placate the agricultural interest, he halved the malt tax. In an early bid to secure the support of the Radicals, he drew a distinction, in the levying of income tax, between 'earned' and 'unearned' incomes, the first time this had been done. He reduced the tax on tea. To pay for this he decreased the lower limit on liability to income tax from £150 to £100 and raised the House Duty. The budget, however, contained a number of other highly controversial features, and the envisioned surplus was almost wiped out by a last-minute need to raise defence spending.

Disraeli's budget was defeated by the anti-Protectionist majority in the House by 305 votes to 286 and the Derby government was forced to resign. The debate over his budget was also memorable in that, for the first time, Gladstone responded to Disraeli's proposals at length, the beginning of the most famous of all parliamentary rivalries. The general verdict on the minority Protectionist government was that it had been a good one, even a very good one, and this period of office did much to ensure the long-term success of the post-1846 split Conservative party. Lord Blake, in his famous biography of Disraeli (London, 1966), compared the 1852 Protectionist government with the 1924 Labour government, the first British Labour government in history, whose 10 months in office also proved its competence and fitness to rule. This is a good analogy, but perhaps a better one might be with Bonar Law's 1922 Conservative government, the 'government of the second eleven', formed when Lloyd George was overthrown by the Tories' backbenchers and formed without the inclusion of most of the

Conservatives' most brilliant men, such as F. E. Smith. It, too, proved itself capable of ruling successfully without their assistance, and it found its equivalent to Disraeli in the almost unknown Stanley Baldwin, made Chancellor of the Exchequer and soon to put his distinctive stamp on the party for a generation. Had the 1846 split not occurred, the leadership of the Conservative party for the rest of the nineteenth century would probably have been very different, but not necessarily more successful.

With the return of protection, especially in a full-blown form, now recognised by most members of the Derby government as improbable, Conservatives began to enunciate an alternative programme which might perhaps be seen as marking the origins of a modern, familiar Conservative platform. At the 1852 general election Disraeli produced a manifesto which stated the 'Principles of Conservative Progress' based around the assertion that 'the Crown of England shall still be a Protestant Crown', an obvious reference to the controversy over 'Papal Aggression'. Significantly, Disraeli called for the maintenance of the colonial empire, a generation before this became a keynote of Tory policy, and also announced that the Tories might agree to further parliamentary reform 'in the spirit of our popular, though not democratic institutions'. For the landowners, Disraeli called only for the equalisation of 'the burdens of the community' by fairer taxation.

Given the relative success of the Protectionist government and the biases of the electoral system, the Protectionists did fairly well in the election, gaining a few seats, but not quite enough to give them a majority. Precise figures cannot be given as they could today, but it would appear that Protectionist and Peelite Conservatives together won 331 seats in the new House of Commons, four more than in the previous Parliament, elected in 1847. The combined forces of the Whigs, Liberals, Radicals and Irish totalled about 323, seven fewer than in 1847.[1] As before, the Conservatives won a clear majority in England (251:216), and Wales (18:11), but fared poorly in Scotland and Ireland. Had the two Conservative factions been united, they could unquestionably have formed a stable government, but by this time the gap between them had become permanent, and the 40 or so remaining Peelite Conservatives now sided more and more openly with the Whigs and Liberals. In December 1852 a coalition government was formed, headed by the fourth Earl of Aberdeen, consisting of six Peelite MPs and peers (including Lord Aberdeen), six Whigs, and one Radical. This Cabinet was especially significant in that Disraeli was succeeded as Chancellor of the Exchequer by William E. Gladstone, still nominally a Peelite Conservative but, increasingly, not merely drawn to liberalism but to championing the Liberal cause.

Because of the Aberdeen coalition, the Crimean War, and the ascendancy of the virtually non-party figure Lord Palmerston (who became Prime

---

1 There were slightly fewer MPs in the new Parliament as one seat, St Albans, had been disenfranchised for bribery.

Minister in 1855), the Protectionist Conservatives did not form another government until February 1858, when Lord Derby again formed a short-lived minority ministry which held office for just over 16 months, until June 1859. The electoral circumstances in which the Conservatives[2] found themselves on this occasion were less fortunate than those of five years before: the 1857 general election proved to be a decisive victory for the Whigs and Liberals (and their former Peelite allies, now for the most part clearly associated with the Whig-Liberal camp), who won 373 seats compared with only 281 for the Conservatives. Palmerston fell over the most trivial and unexpected debate after losing a vote on whether to make the manufacture of terrorist bombs a felony rather than a misdemeanour. Palmerston wanted this change after an attempt on the life of Napoleon III by French terrorists using a bomb made in Birmingham, but found himself in the improbable position of being accused of 'trucking to France' by an unlikely parliamentary coalition of Radicals and Conservatives. Palmerston immediately resigned, and Derby formed a Cabinet fairly similar to that of 1852, although it did include General John Peel, Sir Robert's brother, at the War Office. Disraeli again became Chancellor of the Exchequer. Derby and Disraeli attempted, unsuccessfully of course, to woo Gladstone and the other Peelites back to the Conservatives. Since they failed in this, they remained in a clear minority during their term of office.

Nevertheless, the Conservative government did pass one important piece of legislation, the great India Bill which abolished the East India Company and placed the subcontinent directly under British government control. The bloody Indian Mutiny of 1857 had drawn attention to the inadequacies of previous British rule in the clearest possible way, but it was highly appropriate that a Tory government in which Disraeli was a prominent member should enact the India Bill. As well, the Tory government pro-ceeded in an unexpected way in an entirely different sphere, for it also attempted to pass a Reform Bill to change the basis of parliamentary representation. Although, as noted, Disraeli had foreshadowed such a move in 1852, it was still surprising to see a Conservative government proceeding with what inevitably would be perceived as a radical measure. To some extent this was a tribute to Disraeli's flexible, calculating mind, always attempting to find a way to out-manoeuvre the Whig-Liberals, in a manner presaging, perhaps, the way in which Churchill with his Gallipoli strategy attempted to win the First World War with flexible tactics. Another bout of parliamentary reform had been widely discussed since 1852. Even though the 1832 Act was seen, when passed, as a 'final' resolution of the electoral question, by the mid-1850s it was generally recognised that further reform, embodying an extension of the franchise up to universal manhood suffrage, was inevitable. Conservatives often felt disadvantaged

2 From this point on, the term 'Conservative' will be used to denote those formerly described as Protectionist Conservatives.

by the 1832 Act, which overrepresented boroughs at the expense of rural county seats.

In 1858–59 Disraeli and the Conservative Cabinet decided on a bill which made important, but not earth-shaking changes to the 1832 Act. The leasehold franchise in the counties was lowered to £10; a new £20 lodger franchise was created in both boroughs and counties; and 40 shilling freeholders in boroughs were obliged to vote in their own borough rather than in an adjacent county. Seventy seats were taken away from smaller boroughs, 18 of which were given to larger boroughs and 52 to the counties. The vote was automatically given to a number of new categories of men, including anyone with an income of £10 a year from government funds or owning £60 in a savings bank, as well as to all doctors, lawyers, university graduates, ministers of religion, and many schoolmasters. These 'fancy franchises' (in John Bright's phrase) were designed to ensure that all men of learning and property had the vote, and thus to overbalance the additional number of new voters. Disraeli's bill pointedly did not enfranchise very large numbers of workers. His proposals were defeated by 330 to 291 votes. The second minority Conservative government fell in June 1859 after losing a vote of confidence by 323 to 310. The coalition of Whigs, Liberals, Radicals and Irish, formed by the famous meeting at Willis's Rooms which is often seen as marking the beginning of the modern Liberal party, was small but adequate. Derby dissolved Parliament, and a general election was held in the summer of 1859.

The Conservatives again made some advances, increasing their estimated total number of MPs to 307, up from 281 two years before, while the Liberals and their allies now totalled 347, enjoying substantial leads in the English borough and Scottish seats. Lord Palmerston now resumed the premiership with a popular, centrist government of a type which many Tories had no trouble living with; on his sudden death at the age of 80, he was succeeded for eight months by the 73-year-old Lord John Russell (first Earl Russell since 1861). Gladstone, who had been the Chancellor of the Exchequer since 1859, was the Leader of the House of Commons and the driving force of the Whig-Liberal government. With the death of Palmerston, Gladstone's newly discovered reformist zeal came to the fore, and in early 1866 the Russell government attempted to put through its own reform bill.

This bill appeared fairly moderate. Its aims were to reduce the lower limit for voting in borough seats from £10 to £7, to enfranchise lodgers who paid £10 a year in rent, and to reduce the limit of the county franchise from £50 to £14. Had it passed, it would have increased the percentage of adult males who could vote from about one in five to one in four.

The Tories decided to oppose the proposal, moderate as it was. Given the Liberals' position in the Commons, they could easily have carried the measure. However, significant opposition to the proposal also emerged from conservative Whigs and Liberals, spearheaded by Robert Lowe

(1811–92; created first Viscount Sherbrooke in 1880), a brilliant but doctrinaire barrister who had lived in Australia and developed a detestation of democracy as a result. Lowe had held a variety of junior ministries but had never yet sat in a Cabinet. Nevertheless, he became the acknowledged leader of about 30 other conservative Liberals, a group dubbed by John Bright 'the Cave of Adullam', a Biblical reference to a place which included 'everyone that was in distress and everyone that was discontented'. The Adullamites argued eloquently that excessive democracy would bring corruption and ruination to British politics. Historically they were a highly significant group, for they represented the first time an important group of Whigs or Liberals allied themselves with the Conservatives because they regarded impending Liberal legislation as too radical. Nevertheless, no formal alliance was possible as yet between the Conservatives and the Adullamites (chiefly because Disraeli and Lowe detested one another), and Lowe served as Chancellor of the Exchequer and Home Secretary in Gladstone's 1868–74 government. The combination of Tories and Adullamites did make it impossible for the Liberals to pass a reform act, and led to the fall of the Russell government in June 1866. Since a general election had been held only the previous year, no election ensued, the Conservatives forming the third and most significant of their minority governments in this period, which held office from June 1866 until February 1868.

There is general agreement that the third minority Tory government was the ablest of the three, including for the first time Disraeli's protégé Sir Stafford Northcote and also Viscount Cranborne (the third Marquess of Salisbury), later Disraeli's successor as Prime Minister. Basically, however, it was fairly similar in composition to the two previous minority Tory governments, Lord Derby again becoming Prime Minister until he retired through poor health in February 1868; he was succeeded, at last, by Disraeli from February until December 1868. (It was on the occasion of kissing Queen Victoria's hand when he assumed office as Prime Minister that Disraeli made his famous remark that 'I have climbed to the top of the greasy pole'.) Prior to becoming Prime Minister Disraeli was, yet again, Chancellor of the Exchequer. Lord Stanley, Derby's eldest son and later the fifteenth Earl of Derby (1826–93), became Foreign Minister.[3]

The third minority Tory government of this period will always remain renowned for its passage of the 1867 Reform Bill, a very radical piece of legislation which chiefly enfranchised the urban working classes. Many historians have been perplexed at the willingness of a Tory government to initiate a measure far more radical than any which a Whig-Liberal government might have enacted, and there is no easy answer as to why the 1867 Reform Act was carried by a Conservative government. 'No one knows

3 The fifteenth Earl of Derby had an unusually chequered career. In 1862 he had been offered the throne of Greece by the Greek Parliament, which he declined. In 1880 he joined the Liberal party, leaving them again in 1886 during the Liberal Unionist split.

why Dizzy did it', Donald Southgate summarised the verdict over a century later. In February 1867 Disraeli gave a rather remarkable promise to Lord Robert Montagu, a right-wing MP, to bring in a reform bill as quickly as possible, before the Cabinet had even considered the terms of a bill, and Disraeli's aides, Dudley Baxter and Montagu Corry, had to produce statistical figures on the effects of any electoral reform almost on the spur of the moment. Throughout the country, with the death of Palmerston and the end of the long parliamentary 'truce', monster rallies on behalf of further reform, led by radicals like John Bright, were taking place, and the government feared a bout of mass unrest. Disraeli was personally keen to form a *de facto* alliance with the Radicals in order to frustrate Gladstone, and time and again accepted far-reaching amendments from Radical back-benchers in the course of the debate over the Act while blocking Glad-stone's more moderate proposals.

There is no doubt, too, that the Conservative party had little to lose and potentially much to gain from the type of electoral reform enacted in 1867; this was probably their overriding consideration. Under Britain's existing electoral provisions, enacted in 1832, the Conservatives had not won a parliamentary majority since the Peelite split over 20 years before and lost five general elections in a row. Disraeli and other Conservatives believed that there was an untapped constituency for their party among poorer urban workers who did not accept the Liberal-Radical ideology of the 'aristocracy of labour' and who were then largely without a vote. Thus, Disraeli's grand plans to 'dish the Whigs' had more than a superficial plausibility. Most of all, as things stood the Liberals and their allies already had a near stranglehold on Britain's borough seats. In 1859 the Liberals had won 202 borough seats in England, compared with 121 for the Conservatives; in 1865 the Liberal lead was 198 to 126. In Scotland and Wales the position was even more extreme, with the Liberals in a majority of 12 to 2 in Welsh borough seats at the 1865 general election, while in Scotland the situation could literally not have been darker for the Tories, with the Liberals electing all 23 borough seats in 1865. Whatever electoral changes the Tories enacted could hardly make the situation much worse and could potentially make things much better. Furthermore, the residual very small boroughs, sometimes virtually 'pocket boroughs' in the pre-Reform sense, more often belonged to Whig aristocratic families than to Tory landowners.

The 1867 Reform Act was thus genuinely radical, but of a rather machiavellian kind which chiefly affected borough seats in a way which might well help the Tories. As in 1832, it consisted of two separate parts, one liberalising the franchise and the other redistributing seats in Parlia-ment. It also contained separate Acts for England and Wales, Scotland, and Ireland with different provisions. In terms of persons entitled to vote, the Representation of the People Act 1867 (as it was officially known) most affected the borough franchise, which (in England and Wales) it extended to all male householders who were resident at that address for at least one year and who had paid their rates, and also to male lodgers who had occupied lodgings worth £10 a year and who had been resident there for at least one year. In the county seats, it broadened the franchise to include all male persons occupying lands worth at least £12 a year or owning land worth £5 or more. (In Scotland the lower limit was fixed at £14 a year.)

In terms of parliamentary seats, the 1867 Act (and the 1868 Act, affecting Scotland) disenfranchised six small boroughs returning two members (Honiton, Lancaster, Thetford, Totnes, Wells and Yarmouth), and five boroughs returning one member (Arundel, Ashburton, Dartmouth, Lyme Regis and Reigate), while it removed one member from 35 smaller boroughs previously returning two (the list included Andover, Bridport, Buckingham, Dorchester, Hertford, Leominster, Marlborough, Ripon, Tavistock and Windsor). Thus, 52 smaller boroughs ceased to exist. In their place, 19 new borough seats were created: Salford was to return two members instead of one; Leeds, Liverpool, Birmingham and Manchester were to return three members instead of two; Chelsea and Hackney, previously unrepresented, were to return two members each, and nine new borough seats were created (Burnley, Darlington, Dewsbury, Gravesend, the Hartlepools, Middlesbrough, Stalybridge, Stockton and Wednesbury). Tower Hamlets was divided into two constituencies (Hackney and Tower Hamlets), each returning two members. Finally, graduates of London Univeresity were to return one MP.

There was less alteration to the counties. The West Riding would henceforth return six members, Lancashire eight, and 10 populous counties (Cheshire, Derbyshire, Devonshire, Essex, Kent, Lincolnshire, Norfolk, Somerset, Staffordshire and Surrey) were to return six MPs each. In Scotland and Wales there was even less change. Two additional Scottish university seats were created, one additional MP given to Glasgow and Dundee, one additional member for Merthyr Tydfil; with other minor changes, eight new MPs were added. In all, 52 new seats were created, exactly balancing the number of seats disenfranchised. (In 1832, it will be recalled, no fewer than 143 seats were disenfranchised.)

Scholars have debated just how many new voters were added to the electorate by the 1867 Reform Act. It would seem that the total electorate in England and Wales grew from 1 056 659 in 1866 to 1 995 086 in 1869, an increase of 88 per cent. The county electorate in England and Wales grew by 45 per cent, while the borough electorate grew by no less than 134 per cent, although it was uneven in its distribution. In Scotland, the electorate grew by about 119 per cent (54 per cent in the counties and a remarkable 178 per cent in the boroughs) but in Ireland by only 8 per cent (3 per cent in the counties and 31 per cent in the boroughs). One adult male in three now had the vote in England, Wales and Scotland, one adult male in six in Ireland, a total of about 2 445 847 adult men.

As usual, there are two very different ways of viewing the 1867 Act. It can certainly be interpreted as thoroughly radical, creating, for the first time, a mass working-class electorate in Britain's cities and towns. Moreover, Disraeli was compelled to drop nearly all of his schemes for 'fancy franchises' and plural voting, intended to counterbalance the effects of mass democracy by giving extra votes to men of property and substance. University graduates could vote separately (as they could before) in an extended range of university seats, while a man owning property (especially business premises) in several constituencies could also vote more than once, but these provisions were far less comprehensive than most Conservatives and Whigs had hoped.

On the other hand, a more perspicacious view of the 1867 Act would show that it contained many features designed to advantage the Conservatives and injure the Liberals, especially the abolition of so many residual small 'pocket boroughs', often Whig and Liberal. It must be emphasised, too, that the Act did not establish manhood suffrage (or anything like it), and was not intended to. While the electorate in Manchester and Birmingham increased greatly in size, these and other large boroughs continued to be significantly underrepresented, returning just three MPs each. London in particular was less fairly represented than almost anywhere else, returning just over 20 MPs, including four returned by the business elite of the City of London. The whole of the East End of London returned exactly four MPs. Since these places almost always returned Liberal or Radical MPs in any case, it was difficult to see what gains the Liberal party could make as a result of the 1867 Act, or how the Tories could lose very much. Indeed, the effects of an enlarged Radical urban constituency would very likely be to move the Liberal party to the left, almost certainly driving out many of its Whigs and moderates as a result. A closer reading of the 1867 Act might well conclude that it was a diabolically clever piece of Tory gerrymandering.

It was at this time, during the debates over the 1867 Reform Bill, that the possibility of women securing the parliamentary vote was raised, and seriously debated, for the first time. During the latter stages of the debate over the Reform Act, John Stuart Mill, the great philosopher who had been converted to feminism by Harriet Martineau, introduced a bill to grant the vote to women. It was defeated by 196 votes to 73, by no means a bad result for so radical a measure. Britain had no female suffrage organisation and hardly any serious consciousness of women's political disabilities. Farsighted Tories, even in 1867, might well have seen that women's suffrage would almost certainly augment the Conservative vote, especially if only women ratepayers and property-owners had been enfranchised. The Conservative party's continuing hegemony in post-1918 British politics was based in part upon the 'gender gap' in electoral politics and the remarkable ability of the Conservative party to appeal successfully to the women's vote. With his vision and imagination, Disraeli might well have perceived this, especially given his lifelong preference for the company of women and his special relationship with Queen Victoria. But this was, of course, not to be, and women would have to wait for just over half a century to achieve their electoral rights.

Disraeli's first brief period as Prime Minister of a minority Conservative government was dominated by the Irish question. Gladstone, now about to lead the Liberal party as Prime Minister, was converted to the view that the Church of Ireland – the Anglican Church in Ireland – should be disestablished. Disraeli had also been coming to the view, after the first of the 'Fenian outrages' involving murders and terrorism by Irish nationalists, that some change in the position of the Irish Church was necessary, probably entailing a kind of joint recognition of the Church of Ireland and the Catholic Church in Ireland. Extreme Protestant and anti-Catholic sentiment within the Conservative party made this impossible, and when the 1868 election was held in November, Disraeli fought largely on a pro-Protestant, 'Church in danger' platform. The Conservatives were in a clear minority in the Parliament elected in 1865, and the 1867 Reform Bill had made electoral predictions especially hazardous. In the event, the Liberals won a significant victory, with their numbers increasing from about 360 in the 1865 Parliament to 382 at the 1868 election, Conservative numbers declining from 298 to 276. Conservative MPs increased significantly in the English counties (rising from 99 to 127) but declined sharply in the boroughs (from 126 to 93, compared with the Liberals' total of 198 in both elections), except in Lancashire. There the 'Tory working man' appeared to be reality and not merely fiction in places like Bolton, Salford, and even Manchester, where the Tory candidate Hugh Birley, the first Conservative elected since Manchester was enfranchised in 1832, topped the poll. The Celtic areas, however, proved to be a minefield for the Conservatives, with Scotland returning 52 Liberals compared with only eight Tories, Wales electing 22 Liberals and eight Conservatives, and Ireland 65 and 40. It should also be noted that the number of uncontested seats, where only one candidate was nominated, declined from 240 in 1859 to 194 in 1865 and to only 140 in 1868, the lowest number since 1832. With a considerable professionalisation of the party machinery now beginning, and the press focusing strongly on Disraeli and Gladstone as the great leaders of great parties, a recognisably modern British national political scene was coming into existence. Disraeli and the Conservatives resigned in early December 1868, and William E. Gladstone took office for the first time as Prime Minister of a Liberal government.

8

Lord Aberdeen and the Crimean War

After the fall of the first minority Conservative government in December 1852, Queen Victoria asked the Earl of Aberdeen to form a coalition government consisting of Peelite Conservatives, Whigs and Liberals. Aberdeen had served constructively as Foreign Minister in Peel's 1841–46 government. A committed free trade Conservative, he was widely acknowledged to be the leader of the free trade Conservatives after Peel's death in 1850. It is safe to say that George Hamilton Gordon, fourth Earl of Aberdeen (1784–1860), is the least-known Prime Minister of post-1832 Britain. Among nineteenth-century premiers, Peel, Disraeli and Gladstone remain legendary figures, known to all, and while most educated persons know at least something about Melbourne, Russell and Salisbury, even well-informed persons are unlikely ever to have heard Lord Aberdeen's name. Ask a thousand British people chosen at random to name Britain's Prime Minister during the Crimean War, and it would surely be surprising if more than four or five could possibly give the correct answer. In this, Lord Aberdeen resembles Lord Liverpool, Britain's other unknown wartime Prime Minister at the time of Waterloo.

Aberdeen was the first Scottish Prime Minister since Lord Bute in 1763. He came of an old aristocratic Aberdeenshire family (Lord Byron was his cousin) but lived and was educated in England, at Harrow, where he was a classmate of Palmerston's, and at Cambridge. William Pitt was a mentor after Aberdeen's father died and the latter entered Parliament as a Scottish representative peer in 1806 at the age of only 22. (Aberdeen never sat in the House of Commons.) A shrewd, intelligent and strikingly handsome man, he was a fairly typical Tory aristocrat whose ability led him to serve as Foreign Minister in 1828–30 and 1841–46. As Foreign Minister he was known, if for anything, as a constructive conciliator whose approach was the virtual opposite of Palmerston's provocative sabre-rattling. After 1846, Russell and the Whigs made overtures to Aberdeen to join the Liberal government, but these always came to nothing. In September 1852, however, while Derby and the Protectionists were in office, Russell and Aberdeen, representing many Peelite Tories, struck a deal enabling a coalition government of Whigs, Liberals and Peelites to be formed.

The price demanded by the Peelites for joining a coalition, and paid by the Whigs, was a high one. The incoming Cabinet contained six Whigs (including Palmerston) and six Peelites, with one Radical (Sir William Molesworth), although the Whig-Liberal contingent in the House of Commons outnumbered the Peelites by up to ten to one. It was, moreover, a government somewhat peculiarly put together. Most notably, Aberdeen made Palmerston Home Secretary rather than Foreign Secretary, a curious appointment occasioned by Queen Victoria's intense dislike of Palmerston's approach to foreign policy. As well, Aberdeen gave the Foreign Ministry to Lord John Russell on a strictly temporary basis: it was necessary for the success of the coalition to give Russell, as leader of the Whigs, a very senior post, but Russell's indifferent health led to a promise of a less strenuous position as soon as possible. Russell, indeed, had wanted to become a kind of joint Prime Minister with Aberdeen. In February 1853 Russell became Minister Without Portfolio and Leader of the House of Commons, the Foreign Ministry going to the fourth Earl of Clarendon, who proved less able and decisive than Palmerston was likely to have been. Nevertheless, Aberdeen's coalition government was universally seen as a particularly able one. In particular, Gladstone became Chancellor of the Exchequer for the first time, fresh from his successful parliamentary assault on Disraeli's handling of that office. Gladstone proved to be the archetypal and defining Chancellor of the Exchequer. He brought to that office a high competence and an approach to expenditure of legendary parsimoniousness, often termed 'cheese-paring', designed to produce continuing 'retrenchment' and reduction in expenditure, which put its stamp on the Treasury for the next 90 years. Giving the Exchequer to Gladstone in a coalition government also facilitated his transition from Tory to radical Liberal, from coming man to probable leader, and to legendary foil for Disraeli. The formation of a Whig/Liberal-Peelite coalition also marked a natural progression of the Peelites, as men of business and principle, into a constructive left-of-centre government.

Being only in a small minority in the House of Commons after the 1852 election, the Protectionist Tories were unable to make much of a dent in the Aberdeen government's strong position. Disraeli, always energetic, founded a progressive-Protectionist Tory newspaper in 1850, *The Press*, and attempted to reform the management of the party. Derby was in semi-retirement during the early years of the coalition and the inherent quality of the senior leaders in Aberdeen's government ensured its continuation without difficulty. Nevertheless, it had its fair share of internal difficulties. In particular, when Lord John Russell proposed another round of moderate parliamentary reform, Palmerston resigned in protest (although he subsequently withdrew his resignation), creating a major sensation for the government at the very moment when the events leading to the outbreak of the Crimean War were unfolding.

Prior to the outbreak of the Crimean War in May 1854, the Aberdeen government's focus of attention proved to be Gladstone and his budgets. Gladstone's 1853 budget is sometimes seen as the first ever delivered by a Chancellor of the Exchequer in the modern sense. For the first time, an attempt was made to calculate national income for seven years ahead (thus presaging modern analyses of the economy by many decades). Most remaining tariffs were lowered or abolished; a succession duty was enacted, for the first time taxing inherited land (as opposed to inherited personal property, which had been taxed since 1694).[1] Gladstone also announced his intention to retain the income tax for a further seven years, and included all incomes of £100 or more (previously, £150 or more) as liable to income tax, but lowered their rate from 7d (about 2.9 per cent) in the pound to 5d (about 2.1 per cent) over the seven-year period. Income tax was also extended to Ireland, previously exempted. By no means all of Gladstone's Cabinet colleagues approved the introduction of succession duty on land, but Gladstone persuaded them, and then convinced the House of Commons in a speech lasting nearly five hours which made his reputation as one of the greatest politicians of his day and the greatest financial manager.

In other spheres the Aberdeen government enjoyed less success and made less of an impact. The one exception to this, curiously, was Palmerston's administration of the Home Office. As Home Secretary Palmerston made vaccination compulsory, attempted to stem air pollution through the first Smoke Abatement Act, forbade the burying of corpses in a church (as opposed to a churchyard or a cemetery), abolished the transportation abroad of prisoners, and instituted the first juvenile reform schools and separate prisons for young offenders. He introduced the Truck Act, thus prohibiting employers from paying their workers in goods instead of money or compelling them to buy goods only in company shops. He removed many of the loopholes in the earlier Factory Acts. This was a notable record indeed: Palmerston was probably among the three or four greatest Home Secretaries of the nineteenth century. Yet he was also severe against would-be revolutionaries and violent foreign agitators, losing considerable support from radicals but gaining it from the conservative middle classes.

The years of the Aberdeen government also saw the issuance of a government report with momentous consequences for the future administration of Britain. This was the 'Report on the Organization of the Permanent Civil Service', signed in November 1853 and issued the following year and usually known as the Northcote–Trevelyan Report, from the names of its two authors, Sir Stafford Northcote and Sir Charles Tre-

---

1 It is a popular myth that death duties were first levied in 1894 by Sir William Harcourt. Some forms of death duties had then already existed for precisely 200 years. Harcourt's duties merely increased the level of taxes payable by large estates.

velyan.[2] This report laid the foundations for a highly competent Civil Service in which appointment and promotion would be based on merit. Hitherto, many appointments to the Civil Service were based on patronage – jobs given to relatives or friends of a well-connected aristocrat or MP, or to those to whom such persons owed favours. The Report recommended that appointment in future be on the basis of competitive examination, with higher positions open only to those aged between 19 and 25 who passed an examination of a literary type. Promotion inside the Civil Service was to be based upon merit rather than seniority. These proposals naturally caused a great outcry, and, on closer inspection, it is not necessarily obvious that examination results produce the best civil servants. It took 15 years, until 1870, for the Northcote–Trevelyan recommendations to become legally obligatory. As a result, the higher Civil Service in Britain quickly became the domain of clever university graduates, at least as measured by examination results. The new higher Civil Service as it emerged in late Victorian times was renowned for its complete impartiality and total freedom from corruption, and in these qualities could stand comparison with any similar group in the world. These values in themselves added immeasurably to Britain's reputation internationally, and to its stability at home. On the other hand, with some notable exceptions it was not renowned for its originality or lateral thinking: such terms as 'the Treasury view', for example, became synonymous with rigorous financial orthodoxy. Some have argued, in fact, that Britain's serious economic and political mistakes in the twentieth century were caused in part by the narrow viewpoint of its top civil servants. But the Northcote–Trevelyan reforms did eventually give over virtually the whole of the higher Civil Service in Britain to men almost always of middle-class rather than aristocratic background who in their youth were hard-working and intelligent, but normally lacking in private means of their own or wealthy connections. (Most of the senior appointments in the Foreign Office and diplomatic service, however, remained in the hands of traditional aristocrats or their close relatives until the Second World War.)

If the Aberdeen government is remembered for anything at all it was, however, for fighting the Crimean War. This was the only significant war which Britain fought between 1815 and 1899. Its origins were singularly unlikely, its results tragic and inconclusive, yet also strangely far-reaching.

The formal origins of the Crimean War were to be found in an implausible dispute over the custody of the Christian holy places in Bethlehem and Jerusalem, then a part of the Ottoman Empire. Custody had previously been shared by Greek Orthodox monks and Roman Catholic priests, but had, in the years prior to 1854, come to be exercised by the Greek Orthodox religion alone. This outcome pleased the Russian Czar but

2 Trevelyan was Assistant Secretary at the Treasury, and in effect head of its permanent staff. Northcote, later Disraeli's Chancellor of the Exchequer, had been legal assistant at the Board of Trade and private secretary to Gladstone.

displeased Napoleon III, anxious to drum up Catholic support for his sometimes unpopular regime.

Self-evidently, no British government would ever be likely to become involved in a war fought exclusively over these issues, but the questions involved ran far deeper, namely the future of the Ottoman Empire (Turkey and the considerable territories it owned) and the eastern Mediterranean, as well as Russia's increasing ambitions in the Near East and possibly India. Side-by-side with this question were British attitudes towards Czarist Russia. Russia was probably the most unpopular major power in Victorian Britain. The absolutist and autocratic rule of the Czar, Russia's increasingly oppressive role as 'the prison of nations', and its treatment of liberal campaigners for reform in Russia, made it repellent to almost all British liberals, while its apparent imperialist designs on the Near East and possibly in India also made it distrusted by many conservatives. Matters came to a head in 1853 when Russia sent troops into Romania, then a Turkish province, ostensibly as champion of Orthodox Christians in the Balkans. Turkey declared war on Russia in October 1853 and a month later Russia destroyed the Turkish fleet at Sinop on the Black Sea. British public opinion now became intensely aroused by what was depicted in the press as a 'massacre'. In December 1853 Britain and France agreed to cooperate to save Turkey from Russian invasion and, as a consequence, to attempt to keep the Russian navy from leaving their Black Sea port of Sebastopol. Russia withdrew its ambassadors from Britain and France; ultimatums followed, and, despite intense international negotiations, war was declared in March 1854. Many historians believe that Britain acted ineptly in bringing matters to such a pass: in particular, the absence of Palmerston from the Foreign Office (and, indeed, temporarily from the Cabinet, for he had just resigned over the government's parliamentary reform proposals) meant that less than able hands were at the helm. Britain acted irresolutely during the period prior to the war; on the other hand, Russia's long-term ambitions were likely sooner or later to lead to a major dispute with Britain over its role in the Near East and India.

The Crimean War has been criticised from that time to this as one of the most incompetent conflicts Britain ever fought. Indeed, it is the only modern war waged by Britain which did not produce a single well-known military leader. Britain's senior commanders in that war, such as Lord Fitzroy Somerset (first Baron Raglan, Commander-in-Chief of Britain's Crimean Expeditionary Forces) and James Brudenell (seventh Earl of Cardigan, who led the 'Charge of the Light Brigade') are remembered only by military historians, and then chiefly for their inadequacies and short-comings. Even the senior British commanders in the First World War, like Haig, Robertson and French, who are also chiefly remembered, rightly or wrongly, as 'butchers', nevertheless in August–November 1918 produced one of the most striking periods of military success in British history, while the leaders of the British forces in the Boer War, like Roberts and Kitchener, with reason or not became national heroes.

Wisely, the aims of the Anglo-French forces were extremely limited, being restricted to capturing Russia's prime Black Sea naval port at Sebastopol in the Crimea in order to deter the Russian fleet from attempting to capture Turkey's capital, Constantinople (now Istanbul). There were no grandiose calls of 'on to Moscow!', and Russia, under Austrian pressure, had withdrawn from Romania. Unfortunately, Britain was unprepared for a war of this kind. Britain had, of course, not fought a significant land war since Waterloo nearly 40 years before, and all of its military engagements were with colonial forces in the Empire. The military officers' ranks were still widely regarded as 'outdoor relief for the aristocracy' and highly inefficient. A combined naval and military campaign in the Crimea, hundreds of miles from the nearest British base, was obviously very difficult in the best of circumstances.

A direct Anglo-French assault on Sebastopol was impossible because of heavy Russian fortifications to the sea. The Allies decided to land on the Crimean peninsula to the south of the Russian port, which they successfully carried out in September 1855. The Allied forces numbered about 56 000 (26 000 British and 30 000 French soldiers), an extremely impressive piece of military transport by the standards of the time. The Russians numbered about 80 000. The Allies scored a resounding victory at Alma on 20 September but (due to French reluctance) did not pursue their advantage; in the meantime the Russians sank seven Allied ships, making an immediate continuation of the campaign very difficult. In October the Allies continued their gains and appeared to be in a position to seize their goal at Sebastopol.

The Russians countered this threat by launching two attacks, in October and November 1855. It was in the first of these, at Balaclava, that both the British Heavy and Light Brigades of Cavalry charged against the Russian line of horsemen in order to gain time for the main British counterattack.[3] The first of these cavalry charges is virtually unknown; the second, the subject of Tennyson's celebrated poem, is world-famous. Based upon ambiguous orders, the responsibility for which has been debated time and again, it was extremely successful but terribly costly in terms of British lives.[4] The courage shown by the Light Brigade, made immortal in Tennyson's surprisingly frank poem ('someone had blundered'), marked it out as one of the most famous battles of the nineteenth century.

The Russians tried again a few weeks later. Their numbers, potentially almost limitless, were reinforced by 120 000 soldiers. The Anglo-French forces had also grown and now numbered 65 000, with an additional 11 000 Turkish soldiers. Fierce fighting at Inkerman resulted in losses of

3 'Heavy' and 'light' refer to the size of the weaponry they carried.
4 Of 673 cavalry horsemen at the Charge of the Light Brigade, 113 were killed and 134 wounded. The last veteran of the Charge, however, died in 1936 at the age of 101.

2573 killed among the British troops compared with only 143 French dead. The Russian casualties were far greater. While the Allies could not be driven from the Crimea, they had now to face 'General Winter', as always the Russians' best soldier. Preparations for a winter encampment in the Crimea were meagre and the Allied position was unprotected. It was during this period that the Allies suffered their greatest losses, through lack of food, fuel, medicines, and other supplies. Parliament had previously cut expenditure for necessary provisions. Cholera, dysentery and other virulent diseases reached epidemic proportions and actually threatened literally to wipe out the Allies' forces altogether.

Into this grim picture there now emerged perhaps the most famous single figure whose fame stems from the Crimean War; she came from the most unexpected of quarters. Florence Nightingale (1820–1910), a well-connected friend of Sidney Herbert (1810–61; created first Baron Herbert of Lea, 1860), Secretary at War in Aberdeen's government, had trained as a nurse in Germany and France and had taken an interest in military nursing since her teenage years. William Howard Russell, *The Times'* Crimea correspondent (see below), advised her of the appalling conditions faced by the sick and wounded in the Crimea, and of the total lack of adequate medical care. In October 1854 Nightingale persuaded Herbert to send her and other British nurses to the hospitals at Scutari (now Uskudar) adjacent to Constantinople (and, of course, hundreds of miles from the Crimea; sick and wounded British soldiers had thus to be transported long distances from the battlefields). Her nightly inspections of the wards made her immediately legendary as 'the lady with the lamp': nothing like this had ever been known before in the British military. Nightingale arrived just in time to treat the victims of the battle at Inkerman, and she and her nurses did much (it is perhaps possible to claim too much) to improve conditions and restore British morale. At the end of the war, she received a subscription in her honour, which she used to found Britain's first school of nursing, at St Thomas's Hospital on the south bank of the Thames opposite Parliament. This, more than anything, represented her lasting and significant contribution to British society: formal education for what, in effect, became the first predominantly female profession. Nightingale, who was only 34 when she went to Scutari, lived as an invalid for over 50 years after the end of the war, becoming, in 1907, the first woman to receive the Order of Merit.

The horrors of the Crimean War, and the incompetence of the British authorities in preparing for them, became a matter of widespread public concern and debate in another innovation of the war, investigative journalism of a kind very familiar to us today but unknown prior to that time. The London *Times*, long known as 'the Thunderer' and already something of the 'newspaper of record', sent as its correspondent to the Crimea William Howard Russell (later Sir William, 1820–1907). Because the Crimea was now linked by telegraph to England, this was the first war ever fought by

Britain which was reported upon in the English press within days (indeed, hours) of any significant occurrence: in the Napoleonic Wars, despatches from Spain or Russia took weeks to reach London. To the speed of reportage Russell added a frankness also hitherto unknown, describing the horrors and sufferings of the battlefield and the army hospital with a grim clarity of a new kind, accounts which emphasised the appalling conditions faced by Britain's soldiers rather than depicting the war, as was almost always done in previous conflicts, as the noble clash of knightly warriors. Russell's reportage had an enormous, perhaps electrifying, effect upon British public opinion, galvanising hostility to an arguably unnecessary, certainly incompetently fought, conflict in a manner strangely presaging the undermining of America's Vietnam War through frank and brutal television portrayals over a century later. Indeed, the two conflicts had another important commonality, for the Crimean War also produced what might be described as the first anti-war movement of a modern kind, in which anti-war activists opposed the horrors of war and the unnecessary nature of the conflict, while feeling no ideological sympathy for the enemy power (in contrast, for instance, to British radicals who opposed the wars with France after 1789 because they supported the French Revolution). The best-known leaders of the anti-war movement which emerged during the Crimean campaign were Bright and Cobden, the two great champions of free trade a decade earlier. Bright, in particular, a devout Quaker, opposed the war for its own sake, pointing to the unnecessary and unjustified level of casualties, the fact that the Russian government, regardless of how awful it obviously was, was willing to negotiate, while the government of Turkey was the most corrupt and backward in Europe. Indeed, Bright went further, arguing (like Gladstone, in different circumstances, nearly 25 years later) that Britain ought to have supported Russia's efforts to champion the Christians of European Turkey instead of (as he put it) 'going to fight for Mahomet'. The leaders of the anti-war movement were assailed with abuse in the press, and their meetings often produced wild pandemonium. In February 1855 Bright delivered his best-known anti-war speech to the House of Commons, arguably the most eloquent parliamentary speech ever made during the nineteenth century, containing the famous passage:

> The Angel of Death has been abroad throughout the land; you may almost hear the beating of his wings. There is no one, as when the first-born were slain of old, to sprinkle with blood the lintel and the two sideposts of our doors, that he may spare and pass on; he takes his victims from the castle of the noble, the mansion of the wealthy, and the cottage of the poor and lowly . . .[5]

5 This passage was so moving that it was set to music (in *Dona Nobis Pacem*) by Ralph Vaughan Williams 80 years later. Bright, like Disraeli, was a great phrase-maker. At an unknown date during the American Civil War Bright, asked which side he thought would win, stated that he expected that the North 'would muddle through', the first time the phrase was ever used (and which, in effect, was what happened).

Anti-war sentiments during the Crimean conflict largely came from the northern middle classes, especially from some Dissenters.

On the other hand, it is probably fair to say that the majority of informed British public opinion remained pro-war until the end. Most newspapers supported the war, often in xenophobic terms. Most opinion-makers were fiercely anti-Russian, with demands for retribution the chief result of increased British casualties. Rather surprisingly, such people did not have long to wait. Throughout 1855, the Allied forces gradually took the upper hand against the Russians, and conquered Sebastopol, the goal of the war, in September 1855. Protracted diplomacy delayed a formal peace treaty until March 1856, when the Treaty of Paris guaranteed Turkish independence and neutralised the Black Sea. The autonomy of Turkey's Danubian provinces, eventually leading to the independence of Romania, was secured. Although this should have pleased Russia, it removed it as a direct guarantor (or, possibly, conqueror) of the Christian Balkans. Russian power was diminished and Napoleon III began to think of himself as truly having inherited his uncle's military genius, an illusion shattered in 1870 when he lost the Franco-Prussian War.

One of the more negative consequences of the Crimean War was its effects on British finance. Government expenditure on the military rose from £15.3 million in 1853 to £19.4 million in 1854, and then skyrocketed to £27.5 million in 1855, dropping to £23.5 million in 1856. It then declined to £20.7 million in 1859, but always remained above £20 million for the rest of the century. To his great credit, Gladstone as Chancellor of the Exchequer met the cost of the war from raising taxes rather than borrowing, more than tripling the amount raised by income tax. As a result, the debt charges payable by the government rose only fractionally, and the Crimean War did not add to its other regrettable features the saddling of future generations with the necessity to pay for it.

While in some important ways the Crimean campaign brought innovations to warfare, in other ways it was the last old-fashioned war, the final one fought with cavalry charges and with hand-to-hand fighting between individual troops, ironically preserving some notion of knightly conflict. In 1858 the Armstrong gun, the predecessor which in the long term led to the machine gun and heavy shelling, was introduced. In 1861 the Royal Navy completed building HMS *Warrior*, the first British armoured ship. HMS *Devastation*, often termed the prototype of the modern battleship, was completed in 1873. Many of these modernising trends in armaments came about directly as a result of the Crimean War. In all, about 24 000 British soldiers died in that conflict. A few years later the American Civil War of 1861–65 witnessed the deaths of 600 000 troops and the first battle between ironclad ships; the South was devastated for 80 years. Awful as the Crimean War was, it could not compare with future wars.

The greatest political casualty of the War proved to be the Prime Minister, Lord Aberdeen. In January 1855 J. A. Roebuck, a Radical MP, gave notice that he would move for a committee of inquiry to investigate the conduct of the war. On the same day, Lord John Russell resigned, angry at his diminishing role in the coalition. Other leading figures in the Cabinet were in disarray. On 29 January 1855 the Protectionists – nearly a majority in the whole House after the 1852 election – combined with the Radicals of the Liberal coalition to pass Roebuck's motion by a very large majority, 305 to 148. Aberdeen and his government promptly resigned, an inglorious end to what might have been, in other circumstances, a very promising government.

9

The zenith of Lord Palmerston, 1855–1866

Upon the defeat of Lord Aberdeen's government, Queen Victoria did everything possible to prevent Lord Palmerston from becoming Prime Minister. Given the fluid state of the political parties and the lack of an obvious alternative Prime Minister in the modern sense, the Sovereign had very considerable discretionary powers in choosing a head of government. The Queen was now 36 years old; she had reigned for 18 years, with increasing confidence, and knew her own mind. Her prejudices were shared (many say formed) by her husband, Prince Albert. Both detested Palmerston as wild and unreliable; his unsavoury private life, especially his reputation for casual seductions, did nothing to increase his royal esteem. Nevertheless, the Prime Minister also had to enjoy the confidence of the House of Commons, and the Queen's efforts to find an alternative premier were unsuccessful. Quite naturally, she made the first offer to Lord Derby as the Leader of the Opposition. Derby actually made considerable headway in forming a broadly based Conservative government which would have included, most remarkably, Disraeli, Gladstone and Palmerston in the same Cabinet. A reconciliation of sorts between Disraeli and Gladstone actually occurred. Nevertheless, Palmerston refused to join and nothing came of what might have proved one of the most extraordinary of British governments. Virtually every other prominent possible government leader was also considered – Russell, Clarendon, Lord Lansdowne. Finally, on 4 February 1855, the Queen sent for Lord Palmerston, who officially became Prime Minister two days later. The government he formed was fairly similar to that of Lord Aberdeen, with 8 of 13 Cabinet ministers continuing as before. The new government was basically Whig-Liberal, with initially a small Peelite contingent represented in the Cabinet by Gladstone, Sidney Herbert, Sir James Graham and the Duke of Argyll. Palmerston had wished to appoint Lord Shaftesbury, the great Tory Evangelical social reformer, to the Cabinet, but the Whig majority objected to his appointment as a Conservative. The small Peelite grouping in the new government did not last long: Palmerston was forced, much against his will, to accede to Roebuck's proposed committee of inquiry on the conduct of the Crimean War. The Peelites regarded this as a breach of normal practice and (with the exception of Argyll) they resigned. Gladstone was thus out of office until the formation of the second Palmerston government in 1859. In their place, Palmerston now headed a purely Whig-Liberal government, bringing in (among others) Lord John Russell, who had been sent to Vienna to negotiate a peace treaty, as Colonial Secretary with Palmerston acting for him while he was abroad. (Russell resigned in July 1855, angry at the direction the peace negotiations were taking.)

There is an element of paradox and irony in the careers of most notable nineteenth-century Prime Ministers. Gladstone, the High Church Tory, ended his days as the champion of British radicalism. Palmerston is far from being the least paradoxical such figure. He is best-known for the truculent British patriotism which he enunciated in the 1850s. At the time of the Don Pacifico speech Palmerston was 66 years old and had sat in the House of Commons for 43 years. He had held the post of Secretary of War for 19 years, being appointed as long ago as 1809, aged 25. He had held the position of Foreign Secretary for fifteen years (1830–34, 1835–41, 1846–51). He thus knew the strengths and limitations of British power as well as anyone else, and how unconstructive truculence generally was. Palmerston had been a Tory in the early part of his career, but then became a moderate Whig. He had supported the 1832 Reform Act but had strongly opposed further reform and mistrusted democracy. He was, in fact, the leading Whig most admired by Tories and was approached to join several Conservative governments of this time. He was a friend and mentor of Disraeli, and their outlooks were not miles apart. Yet Palmerston emerged as Prime Minister because he was the most popular leader in the country, popular especially with a part of the new industrial middle classes of the north of England. This opponent of further democracy was almost swept into office on a popular tide. In some respects he was the first notable British politician to court popularity with the masses.

Palmerston's name was Henry John Temple. His ancestors were English landowners in Ireland and his title was an Irish one (he was the third Viscount Palmerston), meaning that he was not a member of the House of Lords and could be elected to the House of Commons.[1] Nevertheless, like the Scotsman Lord Aberdeen, Palmerston was almost wholly English in his upbringing, being born in London and educated at Harrow and Cambridge

---

1 Under the Act of Union between Great Britain and Ireland of 1801, 28 Irish Representative Peers were elected to the House of Lords. They were elected by the whole Irish peerage and served for life. Many Irish peers also held English or United Kingdom peerages; these were automatically entitled to sit in the House of Lords. Irish peers not chosen as Representative Peers were eligible to stand for election to the House of Commons. Palmerston came into this class. No new elections to choose Irish Representative Peers have been held since 1922, and in the late 1990s there were about 50 Irish peers who could not sit in the House of

. . . continued

(as well as Edinburgh University) and owning large estates in Hampshire. (Indeed, of course, Palmerston became the personification of English nationalism.) Palmerston was lucky in his patrons, entering Parliament at the age of 22 for a pocket borough on the Isle of Wight belonging to a man named Sir Leonard Holmes who made it a condition of his gift of the seat that Palmerston should never visit the place! Almost immediately he was made a Lord of the Admiralty. Within two years he was offered (and declined) the Chancellorship of the Exchequer, while then accepting the position of Secretary at War (responsible for the administrative side of the War Office) in 1809, a position he held through changes of government and fortune until 1828. Palmerston became a moderate Whig because of his views on reform and Catholic emancipation, serving as Grey's Foreign Minister, and then continuing under Melbourne and Russell. During his remarkable career he held government office for no less than 48 years, serving in the very senior posts of Prime Minister, Foreign Minister and Home Secretary for 27 years in all. Palmerston was also a renowned, some would say notorious, ladies' man, a rake of rakes, widely known in the fashionable world of Regency London as 'Lord Cupid'. (There were no tabloid newspapers in those days.) In Regency England Society women like Lady Jersey and Princess Lieven were extremely influential as political hostesses who could help to make or unmake careers, and Palmerston's record of success in this department did him no harm. In 1839, a bachelor of 55, he married his newly widowed former mistress (by whom he was reputed to have fathered a child) Emily, Countess Cowper, sister of Lord Melbourne the Prime Minister and mother-in-law of Lord Shaftesbury the reformer. It proved a happy match, although Palmerston continued his philandering until he was past 80. Palmerston was also a familiar figure on the racecourse, and his general air of permanent Regency rakishness, carried on into old age and into the mid-Victorian period, caused many wrongly to underestimate him.

Palmerston, like Disraeli, lacked *gravitas*, that air of high seriousness of purpose notably possessed by Peel, Gladstone, Russell and Shaftesbury and so central to the fundamental values of Victorian Britain. Palmerston's combination of rakishness, a kind of populist nationalist demagoguery, and old age meant that many, even those who knew his strengths, saw him as a clown and a buffoon. 'The aged charlatan has at last attained the great object of his long and unscrupulous ambition', was Bright's comment. Disraeli was no less scathing, describing Palmerston as an 'old painted pantaloon [a theatre clown], very deaf, very blind, and with false teeth'.

Lords. The status of Scottish peers was somewhat similar. After the union between England and Scotland in 1707, the Scottish peers elected 16 Representative Peers from among their number. These served for the term of one Parliament only, not for life. Unlike the Irish peers, however, Scottish peers not holding a further United Kingdom peerage and not elected as Scottish Representative Peers could not be elected to the House of Commons. In 1963, all Scottish peers became entitled to sit in the House of Lords.

Most observers expected any government formed by Palmerston to fall within a year. Instead, he remained Prime Minister for nearly 11 years, with a gap of 16 months in 1858–59 when Lord Derby formed a minority Tory government. Palmerston relied upon his popularity in the country, the balance in size between the political parties and factions, and the disinclination of most Tories and many Whigs to enact far-reaching reform, to remain in office for so long. Palmerston was Prime Minister for much of what is sometimes known as 'the age of equipoise', the mid-Victorian zenith of Britain's stability and prosperity. He was far from its most obvious or likely symbol, yet there he was.

Most of the major problems and difficulties of the Palmerston government occurred abroad rather than at home. There was, first of all, the unfinished business of Crimea which had brought Palmerston to power. To a surprising extent, although Palmerston was regarded as something of a joke by the 'Establishment', his popularity among the middle and working classes was enormous and his coming to power was greeted as a relief by voters throughout the country, especially because of the enhanced prospects for peace and victory in Crimea. During the first few months of his government, events in Crimea continued to deteriorate further, and many of Palmerston's initial appointments were unfortunate. The aristocratic leadership of the British army came under severe criticism. As the Allies slowly but surely advanced, a peace treaty became inevitable. Both Russia and France were anxious to leave the war. Russia's Czar Nicholas I died in March 1855; his successor, Alexander II, was more amenable to peace (and proved himself to be one of the very few liberal Czars in the years before his assassination in 1881). Russia had suffered enormous casualties in the war, and the fall of Sebastopol was a reminder of its backwardness. Napoleon III, Emperor of France, saw his country as contributing far more resources and men to Crimea than had Britain; he viewed a lengthy, indecisive war as likely to produce unrest at home. Palmerston was less enthusiastic for an early peace, but pressure forced him to a compromise which made it appear that Britain had definitely won the war. A peace congress opened at Paris on 25 February 1855 and the Treaty of Paris, formally ending the war, was signed on 30 March 1855. The Crimean War began the process of removing both the Turks and Russians from the Balkans and helped to preserve the life of the Ottoman Empire for another 65 years. Yet within a few years there was considerable fear in Britain of France's military build-up and potentially aggressive intent. The Crimean experience reminded Britain that her international comparative advantage was as a naval and imperial great power, and did not rest in mounting large-scale continental military campaigns, where her generalship was mediocre if not incompetent. Britain fought no European wars, of course, until 1914–18; whether the quality of her generalship had improved in the ensuing 60 years has been endlessly debated.

The Palmerston government's areas of most intense concern during the late 1850s proved to be in Asia. The great Indian Mutiny broke out in 1857, and there was war with China in 1857–58. Britain had first gained a foothold in India several centuries before. By the mid-1850s it was on its way to establishing hegemony over the whole subcontinent. Until 1857, Britain's interests in India were administered by the Honourable East India Company, a remarkable chartered company (and private government) founded in the seventeenth century.[2] Originally the East India Company had enjoyed a legal monopoly over all British trade with both India and China. Its commercial monopoly with India ended in 1813 and with China in 1833. Most anomalously, however, the East India Company also held a second, vastly more important role, as the administrative unit governing Britain's growing territories in India. Technically, British territory in India was divided into three so-called presidencies, Bengal, Bombay and Madras, each of which had its own Governor and a separate army, while the supreme head of its territories in India was known as the Governor-General. The latter was normally a British aristocrat close to Britain's governing circles and appointed by the Cabinet. From 1848 to 1856 the Governor-General had been the Marquess of Dalhousie, who had served as President of the Board of Trade under Peel. From 1856 to 1858 it was Viscount (later Earl) Canning, Postmaster-General and a Cabinet minister under Aberdeen and Palmerston. The East India Company was also subject to the administration from Whitehall of the Board of Control, whose President was normally a Cabinet minister. Yet the Company enjoyed enormous governmental powers on the ground in India, so remote from Britain.

By 1857 Britain directly controlled about 60 per cent of the land area of what is today India, Bangladesh, Sri Lanka and eastern Pakistan. (It had not yet gained control over western Pakistan, Burma, Nepal or Bhutan.) The remaining 40 per cent of the subcontinent was technically in the hands of native or princely states, ruled by local maharajahs and nawabs. The princely states included Hyderabad and Mysore in the south, the Rajputana-Baroda areas in the north-west, and Kashmir in the far north. These native states were tied to Britain by treaties, and it was increasingly clear that Britain regarded them as subservient. Lord Dalhousie took over four native states in the years between 1848 and 1854 when their princes produced no heirs, as well as another state, Oudh, whose Nawab did indeed have heirs. Successive British administrators had, since the 1820s, also taken over more and more of the Indian subcontinent by direct conquest, especially at the edges in what is now Pakistan. In 1843 Sir Charles Napier, who was commander of Britain's army in the Bombay Presidency, conquered Sind, the territory where the Indus River meets the sea. By repute, Napier sent back a one-word message to London, the Latin

---

2 The word 'Honourable' was officially a part of the East India Company's title.

word *Peccavi* ('I have sinned' [Sind]).[3] Even then, Britain's commanding officers in India had a reputation for both eccentricity and vigour; many were religiously minded and nearly all believed that British rule in India would vastly improve the life of the native, especially in the amelioration of superstition and autocratic native rule of the most barbaric kind.

Britain found in India a society totally bewildering, alien and divided. The subcontinent had at least five major religions, often at war with each other: Hinduism (itself divided into innumerable sects and castes) was predominant, but what are today Pakistan and Bangladesh were strongly Muslim, while Ceylon (Sri Lanka) and Burma were largely Buddhist. There were, in addition, the two reformist breakaways from Hinduism: Sikhism and Jainism. Sikhism, which was predominantly found in the Punjab region of north-west India, was heavily influenced by Islamic concepts. It was remarkably progressive in its doctrines, and its soldiers, the Gurkhas, were renowned for their capability and, generally, for their loyalty to Britain. There were, in addition, small minorities of native Catholics and Protestants, and several communities of 'black Jews', especially in Cochin in the far south. Apart from this cultural diversity, nineteenth-century British administrators, increasingly influenced by Evangelical Christianity, found many traditional Indian customs, especially those associated with Hinduism, to be loathsome and barbaric. In particular, *suttee* (widow burning), abolished in the 1830s, and *thugee* (the murdering of people at random by religious devotees of the Hindu goddess Kali), suppressed in the 1840s, were regarded as simply intolerable (the term 'thug' is derived from *thugee*). As the population of India grew and grew, its wretchedly poor, illiterate population, underpinned by the incredibly barbaric Hindu caste system, seemed to many nineteenth-century Englishmen to be the last word in backwardness and bizarre superstition, only slightly removed from the stone age barbarians of central Africa, despite the unquestioned fact that India had produced a high, literate culture for millennia.

The British, especially those who were reform-minded, were in a genuine quandary about what to do with India's backward society. In the 1830s, British writers, especially Thomas Babington Macaulay, hoped to reform India's legal and educational system, making English the language of governance. On the other hand, the British authorities pointedly refrained from encouraging more than minimal Protestant conversionist activity in India, although most Christians presumably believed that India's heathen millions faced eternal damnation unless they were converted. While Britain suppressed the horrors of *thugee* and *suttee*, it deliberately did not interfere with any other aspects of native culture, leaving local structures of authority, education and religions strictly alone.

Despite this unwillingness to interfere, India under the East India Company was a powder-keg. The spark which ignited it was an unlikely one. In

3 It seems this famous story is untrue.

January 1857 a rumour spread that grease used for a new type of rifle cartridge introduced by the Indian army was made of the fat of cows (holy to Hindus) and pigs (unclean to Muslims). Cartridges had to be bitten into by troops prior to inserting into a rifle, and thus most native troops considered themselves polluted.[4] Trouble spread via native mutinies during the early months of 1857, fanned by proto-nationalist and fundamentalist religious grievances at Britain's modernising legal code, and its interference, however limited, with traditional customs, as well as with the extension of its area of rule. Britain's military rule was (and continued to be) accomplished with a surprisingly small force, consisting of only 40 000 British and 230 000 native soldiers. In May 1857 native troops mutinied at Meerut, near Simlap in northern India, and then marched on Delhi, technically the capital of India (the East India Company's headquarters were at Calcutta, adjacent to what today is Bangladesh), where they murdered every British person they could find.[5] Britain's response was surprisingly weak, a weakness occasioned chiefly by the lack of troops. Massacres of Europeans occurred frequently during the Mutiny, among them a particularly horrifying slaughter at Cawnpore in northern India where hundreds of British women and children were killed by a local ruler, the Nana Sahib. When British troops recaptured Cawnpore, they were so appalled by what they found that every rebel, or suspected rebel, was immediately killed. By early 1858, with the arrival of reinforcements under the leadership of Sir Colin Campbell (later Baron Clyde, 1792–1863) and Sir Hugh Rose (later Baron Strathnairn, 1801–85), the Mutiny was suppressed, although Rose's campaign in the Ondh continued until 1859.

The Mutiny led to drastic changes in the government of India. In 1858 Palmerston announced that the East India Company was to be abolished.[6] He fell from office before the change could be enacted, and Derby's government carried it through. Under the 1858 Act, the territories and property of the East India Company were transferred to the British government, with a newly created Cabinet position, the Secretary of State for India, responsible for India's government, assisted by a council of 15. (The first Secretary of State for India was Lord Stanley – son of the Prime Minister Lord Derby – later the fifteenth Earl of Derby.) The title of the Governor-General of India was changed to the altogether grander one of Viceroy (i.e. direct representative of the King or Queen) of India, with Lord

4 Lard (but not, apparently, cow-fat) was in fact used for grease, but was withdrawn once complaints began.
5 The mutineers installed Bahadur Shah, the King of Delhi (who lived in his ancestral palace on a pension provided by the East India Company), as the restored Moghul Emperor of all India.
6 The British government played little direct role in the Mutiny, being far too remote to influence events except long afterwards. There was no telegraph line to India until 1870, and any message of any kind to or from India had to be sent by ship which, of course, took many weeks. As a result, the Governor-General and military commanders enjoyed great freedom of action.

Canning, the old Governor-General, continuing as Viceroy until 1862.[7] More British troops were brought to India and greater centralisation of the Indian army under the Crown took place. The government encouraged an ever-expanding British commercial presence in India and stepped up the building of public works and railways. It is often said that the Mutiny induced in the British a nagging sense of mistrust of the Indians which never vanished, which heightened racism and diminished any notion that the Indians could be Westernised by education. On the Indian side, orthodox Hinduism was strengthened while fewer wholeheartedly accepted Western ideas. On the other hand, in 1853 the East India Company had opened the Indian Civil Service to competitive examination, and Indian candidates could henceforth be admitted, although there were very few until the end of the century. On balance, the Mutiny forced a kind of modernisation and professionalisation of Britain's rule in India and thus probably strengthened it, although the vogue of imperialism after 1870 appears to be only indirectly linked to the Mutiny.

The Palmerston government's other Asian trouble spot was China. Britain's attitude towards China had long been inglorious. British merchants, often acting in semi-legal ways, had progressively opened China to foreign trade, including the enormously lucrative trade in opium. At the beginning of Palmerston's premiership, so-called 'treaty ports' existed at Shanghai, Canton, and several other port cities where foreign trade was allowed, while Hong Kong was already in British hands. Traditional Chinese administrators and intellectuals bitterly resented this intrusion into the affairs of the 'Middle Kingdom' which, in theory, itself still ruled the world and regarded outsiders as barbarians. China itself was in the grip of an appalling civil war, the Taiping Rebellion, in which literally millions were killed. China's traditional Confucian Mandarin system of administration, under the Emperor, had hardly been modernised. It seemed to many only a matter of time before China became a colony of a Western power or powers (and somewhat miraculous that this never occurred). As in India, an unpleasant incident of some kind was obviously waiting to happen. In October 1856 a small Chinese-owned *lorcha* (a fast coastal shipping vessel) called the *Arrow*, officially registered as British (its owner lived in Hong Kong), was boarded by Chinese authorities and 12 of its crew (accused by the Chinese of piracy) were imprisoned. Asked to apologise by the British consul at Canton, the Chinese refused, although the crew was freed. Sir John Bowring, formerly a prominent Radical MP and close associate of Bentham, who was now Governor of Hong Kong, ordered Chinese forts near Canton to be bombarded, as a pretext to open China to unlimited free trade. The Chinese responded with murderous attacks on Englishmen and

---

7 This change should not be confused with the alteration, in 1876, of Queen Victoria's official title to include the designation 'Empress of India'. The two changes are not directly related.

the widespread destruction of British property in Canton (but not else-where). This was exactly the sort of international crisis testing British power which Palmerston relished, and both the *Arrow* incident and his response bear a close resemblance to the Don Pacifico affair. Palmerston ignored expert advice that Bowring had acted illegally, and announced that his government would support the Governor. In March 1857 Cobden brought a motion of censure in the House of Commons which was remarkable for enjoying the support, during debate, of Disraeli, Gladstone, Russell and Lord Robert Cecil (later Lord Salisbury the Prime Minister): in other words of Conservatives, Peelites, and many Liberals and Radicals. Palmerston responded with a spirited and truculent defence of his policy and a firm assertion of British power. Cobden's motion of censure was carried by 16 votes (263 votes to 247), a surprisingly narrow margin given the depth and quality of its support. Palmerston, too, had his supporters, especially among the 'silent majority' of backbenchers who loved this display of British patriotism.[8]

Most remarkably, Palmerston now decided to call a general election over these events in far-off China. Palmerston's electoral address contained one sentence which his supporters quoted in every constituency: 'An insolent barbarian wielding power at Canton has violated the British flag.' Palmerston's 1857 campaign is also important because, for the first time since the Reform Bill, a general election was being fought, in effect, over a single issue, with the Prime Minister of the time making it a national vote of confidence in his own personality and policies in a way which presaged the British political process of a century later.

Palmerston banked, in 1857, on receiving the enthusiastic support of the business middle classes who, despite the pacifism of a minority like Cobden and Bright, were essential patriots and certainly defenders of an aggres-sively expansionist British commercial policy. Palmerston was received enthusiastically in all commercial cities and especially in the City of London. His speeches bordered closely on demagoguery and he virtually claimed that his opponents supported the murder of Englishmen in China. In the end, Palmerston's coalition of Whigs and Liberals won an excellent victory, and certainly Palmerston scored a remarkable personal triumph. At the previous election in 1852, the Protectionist and Peelite Conservatives had won about 331 seats, the Whig-Liberal coalition about 323. (The two wings of the Conservative party could not agree to cooperate, of course.) In 1857 the Whigs and Liberals together won about 373 seats, the Con-servatives only 281. The Whig-Liberal coalition was triumphant in all parts of the country except Wales, winning a majority of 266 seats to the Tories' 201 in England and 38 seats to the Tories' 15 in Scotland. The nature of the Palmerstonian coalition shifted, however, reflecting the personal nature of Palmerston's triumph. Cobden and Bright were both defeated, and moder-

---

8 So, too, did Queen Victoria, previously a bitter opponent, who now firmly supported Palmerston.

ate, patriotic Liberals were returned for many of the big industrial seats. The Liberals also did well in traditional Tory county seats in the south of England. Palmerston appeared set to rule for many years to come. Nevertheless, general elections fought chiefly on foreign issues remained rare in British politics. For the most part, the patriotic chord benefited the leader who played it, as in 1900 and 1918, but was too unpredictable to use consistently.

Asia was not the only area of the world which rather surprisingly came to figure largely in Palmerstonian politics. Europe was also important. As noted in the section discussing the minority Conservative governments of this period, Palmerston temporarily fell from power in 1858–59 over a European issue. In January 1858 an Italian refugee who had lived in England, Felice Orsini, tried to assassinate Napoleon III in Paris, killing several bystanders. The French police discovered that the explosives he used had been made in England, and Napoleon demanded that the British government crack down on anti-French conspirators in London. Palmerston (rather surprisingly) obliged by introducing a Conspiracy to Murder Bill, which made it a felony to conspire in Britain to murder someone abroad. An amendment offered by Radical MPs, and supported by the whole of the Conservative party, was carried by 19 votes and Palmerston resigned on 25 February 1858, only 10 months after his singular general election win. The fluidity of British party politics at this time meant that no general election win was as solid as it seemed.

Palmerston returned to power in June 1859 when the minority Conservative government fell. Originally the Queen sent for the Earl Granville (1815–91), Whig of Whigs, grandson of the phenomenally wealthy Duke of Sutherland and closely related to all the other great Whig families, who had served as Foreign Minister in 1851–52 and more recently as Lord President of the Council under Palmerston. Granville was unable to secure the cooperation of Lord John Russell (although Palmerston was willing to serve under him), and the Queen was compelled to ask Palmerston to form a government for the second time. Thanks to negotiations which had taken place at Willis's Rooms shortly before, this government was deliberately designed to be more all-inclusive than any previous Whig-Liberal one apart from the Aberdeen coalition. Lord John Russell (created an Earl in 1861) was given the Foreign Office, Granville resumed the Lord Presidency of the Council, and Gladstone, now more or less a permanent Whig-Liberal rather than a would-be Tory, became Chancellor of the Exchequer once more. The chief novelty of Palmerston's second government was the inclusion of Radicals. Thomas Milner-Gibson, a Radical MP who had actually moved the amendment which brought down the first Palmerston government, was made President of the Poor Law Board. A fortnight later, he was made President of the Board of Trade, and another Cobdenite Radical, C. P. Villiers, was given the Poor Law Board. (Villiers had been one of the earliest and most dedicated champions of free trade and repeal

of the Corn Laws in Parliament, although, in background, he was a
wealthy aristocrat and brother of Lord Clarendon, a Whig Cabinet fixture.
Villiers died at the age of 96 in 1898.) More significantly, Palmerston
originally intended to offer the Presidency of the Board of Trade to Richard
Cobden, who declined unless John Bright was also included as a Cabinet
minister. But Bright's repeated attacks on the House of Lords, and his own
reluctance to serve, ruled him out. Thus, neither Cobden nor Bright served
in a Palmerston government, but Cobden was sent to France in 1860 to
negotiate the Cobden–Chevalier commercial treaty that greatly reduced
tariffs between the two countries. Both Cobden and Bright agreed to
support the second Palmerston government, which was given much less
trouble from the Radicals than his earlier one. Nevertheless, the second
Palmerston government, like every other government of this period, was
markedly aristocratic, comprising six peers (including two dukes) among
the 15 original members of the government. Apart from the six peers were
Palmerston himself, an Irish peer, Lord John Russell, two baronets and a
knight.

Palmerston's government quickly became involved in the struggle
between France and Austria over Italian independence and unity, and in the
struggle of the Italian states to throw off their despotic rulers and unite as
a nation. Napoleon III worked for the independence of the Italian regions
under Austrian rule, fighting and winning (although not decisively) a war
with Austria in 1859. Palmerston mistrusted Napoleon's intentions but also
gave general support to the Italian states (as did British public opinion, long
enamoured of Italy), then struggling under Cavour and Garibaldi, in their
efforts at unification. Many conservatives, as well as the Queen, continued
to support Austria. The force of Italian nationalism took on a life of its
own, and in 1860 Victor Emmanuel was made constitutional King of Italy,
although the area of central Italy around Rome, where the Pope ruled as an
autocrat, did not join the new kingdom of Italy for another 10 years.
Britain played no direct role in the unification of Italy, but did have a fairly
strong indirect influence. One of the important effects of the Italian crisis,
however, was renewed and serious fears of French intentions which were so
strong that, in 1859, Palmerston's government formed a new volunteer
defence movement of 150 000 men which became a major part of the social
organisation of late Victorian and Edwardian Britain. Palmerston originally
opposed forming rifle associations in industrial towns, fearing infiltration
by Chartists and revolutionaries, but encouraged them in the countryside.

In the very last years of Palmerston's government, the centre of European
crisis shifted to Germany, and to the efforts, spectacularly successful, by
Prince Otto von Bismarck to unify Germany, but in such a way as would
give German hegemony to the Protestant Prussian Hohenzollern dynasty
(and eliminate the Catholic Austrian Hapsburgs from a dominant role in
Germany) without bringing into the new German Empire millions of
hostile Slavs or producing a general European war which might have

overturned almost all ruling dynasties and established socialism. Very few men in history were sufficiently clever, cunning and resourceful to have accomplished these aims in a brief period of time: in Bismarck, however, Germany found a statesman of *realpolitik* whose like has seldom been seen before or since. Unlike his successors under Wilhelm II and the Nazi regime, Bismarck knew where and when to stop, and harboured no dreams of continental hegemony, still less of genocide and the enslavement of 'inferior' peoples. He was essentially a conservative who wished to preserve the monarchical and aristocratic order. Yet central to his aim was, necessarily, the unification of Germany outside of Austria under Prussian hegemony. But Prussia's traditions of militarism and its glorification of military victories in an era of imperialism and social Darwinism, combined with the incredible growth of Germany after 1870 as an industrial power of the first rank, saw Bismarck's legacy lead, in the twentieth century, to two world wars and the most diabolical crimes committed in modern history.

Of course, none of this was in any way clear in the early 1860s and the Palmerston government cannot be criticised for failing to see into the distant future. Yet by any standards Palmerston and his Foreign Minister, Lord John Russell, made serious mistakes in dealing with Bismarck's Prussia, which they simply failed to understand. Bismarck unified Germany by stages. In 1863–64 came the Schleswig-Holstein crisis, involving the future disposition of two duchies immediately to the south of Denmark. The question was a complex one: it was over this issue that Palmerston was reputed to have said, referring to the recently deceased Prince Consort and to a German professor who was then in a madhouse, that 'Only three men understand the Schleswig-Holstein question, one of whom is dead, the second insane, and I, the third, have forgotten all about it.' Nevertheless, Bismarck's intentions were not especially complex: he intended to drum up a war with Denmark in order to obtain Kiel and other parts of north Germany for Prussia, before turning on Austria (his ally against Denmark) in order to unify Germany under Prussian hegemony. We now know that German unification in the manner it was carried out represented the gravest possible threat to Europe and to the world. Had Britain and France taken a firm line with Bismarck over Schleswig-Holstein, innumerable future tragedies might have been prevented. Unfortunately the Palmerston government, and especially Earl Russell, the Foreign Minister, completely misread the situation, pointedly refusing to join Napoleon III in either convening a European peace conference or in going to war. British public opinion strongly supported Denmark, and the general view, in this time before the Franco-Prussian War of 1870, was that France would rout the Prussian army. In the event, Britain and France refused to intervene, and, in two weeks in mid-1864, Prussia defeated Denmark and took Schleswig-Holstein. Two years later it defeated its former ally Austria, Bismarck forming the North German Confederation under Prussian domination shortly after. In 1870 he routed France, Napoleon III being driven into exile, and the following year Wilhelm I of Prussia was proclaimed Emperor of Germany. Within a quarter-century Germany had overtaken Britain as the industrial giant of Europe, especially in the newer, technologically oriented areas of steel, chemicals and electricity. By 1914 all of Europe was at war. Palmerston, of course, cannot be blamed for failing to foresee any of this, but it is ironical that his uncharacteristic instance of non-intervention proved so disastrous in the long term.

In foreign policy, however, the years between 1861 and 1865 were dominated by Britain's response to a conflict in yet another part of the world, the American Civil War. This mighty struggle, which in many respects was the first modern war, fought with mass armies and modern means of mass destruction, saw British opinion deeply divided. Even in the 1860s many Englishmen already knew that they enjoyed a special relationship with their American kinsmen, and were well aware that, within a generation or two, the United States was likely to become the strongest power in the world in economic and perhaps political terms. Yet many British conservatives (and others) essentially supported the South, which had broken away from the Union after the election of Abraham Lincoln in November 1860 to form the Confederate States of America, hostilities beginning in April 1861 when Southern forces fired at a remaining Northern fort, Fort Sumter, in the harbour of Charleston, South Carolina. The slave-owning South represented a quasi-aristocratic society which many British conservatives admired, apologists for the South repeatedly making the point that their slaves were better treated than Britain's factory proletariat. Additionally, Britain derived most of its cotton from the South. Had the South succeeded in establishing its independence, it is likely that it would have turned even more significantly to commercial relations of all kinds with Britain, in preference to the Yankee capitalists and factory-owners of the North. As well, the South was traditionally in favour of low tariffs, while the North imposed very high tariffs on exports to America, and it could only be in Britain's interests for the South to win, especially as the Northern areas of the United States were already emerging as a full-blooded rival to Britain's manufacturing supremacy. Many Englishmen disliked 'Yankees' (Americans from the North) as pushy, gauche, ingenuous prigs with too much money; British 'Establishment' figures often looked upon Yankee businessmen as similar to captains of industry from Manchester or Liverpool, only 10 times richer and one-tenth as respectful. Had the South won, indeed, some sort of quasi-political association with Britain might conceivably have developed in the long run.

Nevertheless, British sympathy for the North was also strong. Above all, the South and its way of life was based in Negro slavery, whose undeniable horrors were hateful to most Britons, even those who admired the Southern planter aristocracy and regarded blacks as inherently inferior to whites (as the majority of British people certainly did). *Uncle Tom's Cabin* sold more copies in Britain than in America. An independent South might be a good thing for Britain, but it might equally well be good for Britain's European rivals, especially France. As the Civil War progressed, it became clear that in Abraham Lincoln the United States had found a leader without parallel in modern history, proof that a democracy could produce a head of state, from the most meagre of backgrounds, superior to any aristocrat. Lincoln, moreover, proved to be perhaps the most eloquent orator the English language has ever produced, one who combined stark simplicity with soaring eloquence in a way wholly different from the pompous and flowery rhetoric of the day. The Emancipation Proclamation, freeing the slaves in the Confederate states, promulgated by Lincoln in September 1862, gave the Civil War a noble purpose. Grant, Sherman and Sheridan became legendary military leaders to set beside the South's Lee, Beauregard and 'Stonewall' Jackson. The complete triumph of the North in April 1865, followed closely by the assassination of Lincoln, deeply affected many Englishmen. Although John Bright had never met Lincoln, he wrote that news of his assassination had affected him as greatly as the death that same month of Richard Cobden, his close associate for a quarter-century.

Britain's attitude towards the American Civil War was one of strict neutrality, proclaimed by Lord John Russell in May 1861. The proclamation of neutrality issued by Russell seemed to many to lean towards the South (for instance it referred to the 'States styling themselves the Confederate States of America', rather than the 'states in rebellion', as was always done by the North). Shortly before, the North had blockaded the South, using the American Navy to ensure that no Southern vessels could export cotton to Europe. This policy was obviously vital to the North's strategy of destroying the South's economic means of carrying on the war, and was effected with great efficiency. Yet it was almost certain to have deleterious effects on British-American relations. British ships were certain to run the blockade, while the status of Confederate citizens travelling abroad was ambiguous. Both matters brought trouble with them. In November 1861 Jefferson Davis, the President of the Confederacy, sent two negotiators, James M. Mason and John Slidell, to London to explain the Southern case. After journeying from the South to Havana, Cuba, they crossed the Atlantic on a British ship, the *Trent*. An American warship stopped the *Trent* and took custody of the two men. A major diplomatic incident ensued, with Britain coming to the brink of recognising the South and even of declaring war. An additional 15 000 British soldiers were actually sent to Canada. Tempers cooled, however, and the two representatives were allowed to travel to London with no lasting effect. Considerable trouble also ensued over persistent blockade-running and over an incident, in May 1862, relating to a ship being built in Liverpool for the South, known as the *Alabama*. This ship was allowed (through government incompetence) to sail despite strong American objections, again leading to a serious strain in relations.

The most important effect of the American Civil War on Britain, however, was to produce the severe 'cotton famine' of 1861–62. Most of the raw cotton used by the mills of Lancashire, where hundreds of thousands were employed, came from the American South. The Northern blockade cut supplies to Britain to a trickle, although its main effects were not felt until the end of 1861 as a great amount of cotton had been stockpiled in anticipation of the conflict. By early 1862, however, a quarter of a million people in Lancashire found themselves out of work, and supported chiefly by local relief or private charity. Yet British radical opinion, especially that led by John Bright, remained firmly on the side of the North and supported its opposition to slavery. Most cotton operatives of Lancashire still sided with the North, and the resolute stance taken by Lancashire did much to restore American sympathy for Britain. By 1862 fresh sources of cotton, from India and Egypt, started to arrive in Lancashire, although cotton exports did not reach their 1861 level until 1866. Britain's stance of neutrality in turn was significant in the North's victory. According to Bright, the news of Lincoln's assassination created the greatest sensation seen in Britain in 50 years. 'The whole people positively mourn', he wrote to Massachusetts Senator Charles Sumner. Increasingly, though certainly not at once, there would be many people who would see the destinies of the two nations as intertwined.

Even this does not quite exhaust the list of international areas of conflict in which the Palmerston government was compelled to take a stand. In 1863 a serious rebellion broke out in Poland, then ruled, or rather misruled, by Russia. It was suppressed with great harshness. Most Englishmen, including Palmerston, were sympathetic to the Poles and greatly deplored Czarist Russian oppression. While Palmerston joined France and Austria in international protests, Britain could do nothing more and certainly could not fight a land war for the liberation of Poland. As well, Palmerston had doubts about whether the Poles could actually govern themselves. Thus, nothing was done, and Poland did not achieve its independence for another 55 years. A longstanding dispute over the Ionian Islands, a group in the western Adriatic near Greece, and under British protection since 1815, was settled in 1862 when Britain gave the islands to Greece. In October 1861 came one of the most bizarre instances of direct British intervention overseas, a joint British-French-Spanish expedition to (of all places) Mexico, whose government had defaulted on interest owed to foreign bond-holders. Normally, the Monroe Doctrine, promulgated by American President James Monroe in 1823, which told Europe's powers to stay out of Latin America, would probably have deterred such an expedition, but America's military preoccupation with its Civil War, and the fact that the South occupied the area adjacent to Mexico, meant that the United States did nothing. The three European powers seized Mexican customs revenues to pay their debt-holders. Napoleon III had more grandiose ideas, wishing to establish the Archduke Maximilian of Austria as Emperor of

Mexico under strong French influence, something he actually attempted to do, although quickly failing, four years later. Had the South won the Civil War thanks to European help, it is possible, even likely, that Mexico would today have a Hapsburg king as its head of state.

Compared with the unusually diverse and difficult nature of the foreign policy questions facing Lord Palmerston and his ministers in his two governments, little of a dramatic nature occurred in domestic politics. Indeed, Palmerston's administration was widely seen then, and since, as a period when, by Palmerston's choice, no far-reaching measures of reform would be enacted. Nevertheless, some rather significant legislation was passed during the nine years and three months of his premiership. Probably the most significant was an Act, introduced in 1855 and passed in 1856, to permit all companies, apart from banks, to become limited liability concerns. All limited liability firms had to add 'ltd.' after their company name; banks were allowed to incorporate in 1858. Limited liability gave British companies the right to expand, by issuing shares for sale, without any liability for the debts or losses of the company being incurred by shareholders apart from the value of their shares. (In contrast, previously most owners or joint-owners of a company were private partners who were personally liable for the debts of their company.) In the long term, the growth of a modern corporate economy would have been impossible without a general right of companies to limited liability. Yet limited liability was remarkably slow in coming to Britain, given the early development of British capitalism. Private corporations (as limited liability companies are) were widely mistrusted, even by many wealthy businessmen, as likely to encourage slovenly management practice and fraud. Even after 1856, large-scale corporations were notably slow to grow in Britain compared with Germany and the United States, and did not become the characteristic mode of capitalist organisation in Britain until the twentieth century. Private partnerships and family-oriented concerns continued to be major features of British business life, even among well-known businesses, until the inter-war period and even, among merchant and private banks in the City of London, until the 1970s. Even today, Lloyd's of London, the celebrated transport and risk insurance enterprise in the City, consists entirely of private partners with unlimited liability to pay for insurance pay-outs for accidents on transport they insured, including catastrophic aviation and marine disasters where hundreds of millions of pounds are owed. The unlimited liability of Lloyd's of London partners almost brought it to ruin in the 1990s.[9] The failure of Britain to develop truly large-scale business and industrial corporations on the scale of America or Germany is

9 Lloyd's of London the insurance brokers should *not* be confused with Lloyds Bank, one of the 'Big Four' high street clearing banks with hundreds of branches throughout Britain. They are totally unconnected, the two Lloyds in their titles being different men. (Lloyd's of London was an obscure coffee house in the City where marine insurance brokers met in the seventeenth century; the Lloyds of Lloyds Bank were Quaker bankers from Birmingham.) Lloyds Bank is most definitely not an unlimited liability partnership.

often highlighted as one of the characteristic features of post-1870 British capitalism and, it is often suggested, a reason for the relative decline of the British economy in the twentieth century.

An important piece of social legislation was the Divorce Bill of 1857, which established a special civil court to try cases of divorce and placed the granting of divorces on a legal footing. Previously, divorces in England and Wales could occur through two means: a special Act of Parliament passed to allow a particular divorce, or a law suit at Common Law for 'crim. con.' ('criminal conversation', i.e. adultery). Special Acts of Parliament were exceedingly expensive and exceedingly rare – about one or two a year in the earlier nineteenth century. Suits for 'crim. con.' could only be brought by a husband whose wife had committed adultery, since adultery was deemed to be a legal 'trespass' on a husband's 'property'. Against the fierce opposition of most Anglican bishops and many politicians like Gladstone, the Palmerston government, following the advice of a commission of 1853, established a civil divorce court. Obtaining a divorce was by no means easy (although the number of divorces rose). A husband could obtain divorce by proving that his wife had committed adultery. For a wife to obtain a divorce, however, she had to prove that her husband had committed adultery *and* either desertion for two years, sodomy, rape, incest or bigamy. This blatant piece of what would now be described as sexism emerged chiefly from the fact that middle- and upper-class husbands could be expected, as a matter of course, to have casual affairs and encounters with prostitutes. Only if such husbands were also thoroughly detestable men was there anything out of the ordinary. Wives, in contrast, were supposed to be faithful and chaste at all times. Some influential men, including Gladstone, protested at the unfairness of the law, but public opinion accepted the 'double standard' as a matter of course, and no one then wished to open the 'floodgates' to easy divorce. The grounds for divorce were made equal for both husbands and wives only in 1923. The 1857 Act also permitted divorced couples to remarry, something whose legality was unclear before. By the late nineteenth century, the narrow grounds for divorce produced an enormous cottage industry which provided often fraudulent evidence of adultery, while the Divorce Act virtually created the private detective business, and Sherlock Holmes, if he had actually lived, might well have spent his time looking through hotel registers. Since newspapers could freely print all courtroom testimony, contested divorce proceedings became one of the few spheres where luridly frank sexual details could be reported in the press, and into the 1960s (when divorce virtually 'on demand' became legal) British newspapers used to devote many columns to reporting divorce proceedings almost verbatim, with a heavy emphasis on the salacious details, especially if Society figures were involved. Nevertheless, until the 1960s divorced persons were virtually shunned by polite society, and certainly until after the First World War divorce amounted to social suicide, and meant the ruin of any politician's career.

In 1857 as well, the system of the probating of wills in England and Wales was reformed and secularised. Until then, the probating of all wills had, extraordinarily, been a legal monopoly of the Church of England (even the wills of non-Anglicans). Probating was carried on in a special system of Ecclesiastical Courts, extremely complex and notoriously slow, administered from Doctor's Commons, a building in the City of London, with its own separate system of Ecclesiastical Court lawyers and judges (barristers, not vicars). The Church of England enjoyed a continuing source of revenues from this monopoly. In 1857 the entire system was changed, and a purely secular system of probate established, whose headquarters moved from Doctor's Commons to Somerset House on the Strand in 1873. This change, sooner or later affecting everyone with property, was an obvious counterpart to the civil registration of births, marriages and deaths enacted 20 years before.

A number of noteworthy changes also took place in the field of education. In 1856 a Committee of the Privy Council on Education, linking all government bodies concerned with education, was established. Its chairman, the Vice-President of the Committee of the Council on Education, was a government minister, although only rarely a Cabinet member. (The first holder of this position, W. F. Cowper, later Baron Mount-Temple, was a Whig politician.) Significant government commissions which enquired into elementary education, chaired by the Duke of Newcastle, into the public schools, chaired by Lord Clarendon, and into endowed schools, chaired by Lord Taunton, were held at this time, although it was not until 1870 that far-reaching changes in English elementary education were undertaken. In religious matters Lord Palmerston was instinctively a Low Churchman and, as the source of senior promotion in the Church of England, significantly strengthened the position of Evangelical Low Churchmen. However, he knew little of the actual trends of the Church of his day; it is said that he had never heard of the Oxford Movement until he became Prime Minister. He left all senior church appointments to his wife's son-in-law Lord Shaftesbury, the great Evangelical. The Palmerston government's frank preference for Low Churchmen was obviously unpopular among High Churchmen, including those in his Cabinet like Charles Wood, later, as Lord Halifax, one of the champions of the High wing of the Church, and Gladstone. Palmerston's explanation was that Low Churchmen were close to Dissent, which comprised one-third of the English population, and had a wide measure of popularity, while High Churchmen represented a tiny minority and verged too closely on quasi-Catholicism. Palmerston was always favourable to Catholic emancipation, but deeply opposed the intrusion of Catholicism, or of pseudo-Catholic ideas, into Protestant England.

On 14 December 1861 Prince Albert the Prince Consort died of typhoid at the age of only 42. In earlier years, Palmerston and Prince Albert had never been friendly, Palmerston resenting Albert's preference for conciliation in international affairs and his intrusions into parliamentary government. During Palmerston's Prime Ministership, however, they drew more closely together, particularly as Palmerston's love of military interventions became more muted. No one, of course, knows what might have happened had Prince Albert lived, and Disraeli's well-known remark that he would have given England 'the blessings of absolute government' are surely overdrawn. In intellectual and cultural matters Prince Albert was high-minded in the earnest and serious way of Victorian Britain; in international affairs he was a moderate though perceptible liberal. He lived an exemplary family life and was perhaps the first royal to pay scholarly attention to the Royal Art Collection. As the scion of a small princely house in Germany, it is possible – just possible – that he might have brought Britain's influence to bear against German unification on Bismarck's terms. His premature loss was genuinely and deeply felt. For the Queen, the loss was, of course, traumatic, and Victoria withdrew from public life for over a decade, re-emerging as a symbol of imperial unity only in the 1870s. During her withdrawal, a short-lived republican movement, closely linked with middle-class radicalism, grew up, but disappeared once Victoria re-entered public life. The late Victorian period, the years from the time of Disraeli's Crystal Palace speech of 1872 until the Queen's death in 1901, saw Victoria, the ageing queen, as central to the very being of the United Kingdom and the Empire. It is almost impossible to imagine anything else, yet this period might just as easily have been the age of Victoria and Albert.

Palmerston was nearly 81 when he died at his country house, Brocket Hall in Hertfordshire, in October 1865. There was a universal feeling that an age had died with him and that long-delayed measures of reform and change, considered impossible while Palmerston was alive, were now at hand. The first question, however, was who was now to become Prime Minister.

Shortly before Palmerston died, a general election was held which brought the Whig-Liberals a slightly larger majority than in the Parliament elected in 1859. About 360 Liberals were returned compared with 298 Conservatives. Liberals held a majority in all parts of the United Kingdom, including England, where they outnumbered the Tories by 246 seats to 225. These bald results are perhaps misleading, as about 40 of the Liberals were personally loyal to Palmerston but might not side with his successor.

Palmerston died before meeting Parliament. The Queen sent for Earl Russell rather than a younger man like Gladstone.[10] There was a universal sense that the *de facto* truce between the parties over issues like parliamen-

---

10 Lord John Russell was ennobled as Earl Russell in 1861.

tary reform had come to an end. It was also assumed by perceptive observers like Disraeli that any radical measures would produce considerable opposition in moderate Liberals and Whigs.

Russell's last government was formed in October 1865 and lasted until June 1866, a period of only nine months. Superficially, it differed little from Palmerston's government, with most Cabinet ministers holding the same posts. Gladstone, still Chancellor of the Exchequer and Leader of the House of Commons, was more important than ever. Since the 1865 election he had sat for South Lancashire rather than Oxford University, where his increasingly radical and democratic views were given greater centrality, and the former High Church Peelite Tory was about to emerge as the greatest leader of Victorian Liberalism. Russell also brought a number of important new figures into his short-lived Cabinet, especially the Marquess of Hartington (later the eighth Duke of Devonshire, 1833–1908) and the City banker George Joachim Goschen, but essentially his Cabinet was almost identical to Palmerston's, with its Whig bias.[11]

Russell's government was dominated by issues of parliamentary reform, particularly the search for a bill which would extend the franchise to many more urban skilled workers without bringing about a wildly radical transformation of the British political scene. Most proposals considered by the Cabinet revolved around lowering the franchise qualification to include all adult males paying £7 or more in rental in the boroughs. After much discussion, Gladstone, as Leader of the House, introduced a reform bill in April 1866. The bill also included a measure of redistribution, eliminating most of the remaining very small boroughs, and then increasing the number of country and large borough seats. Gladstone's bill produced sharp opposition from two quarters. A number of conservative, pro-Palmerstonian Liberals, led by Robert Lowe (those known as 'the Cave of Adullam') opposed any wide extension of democracy *per se*, fearing the dire consequences of enfranchising large numbers of poorly educated working men. As well, many Whig aristocrats and their relatives and supporters in the House opposed the disenfranchisement of the remaining small boroughs, for which many sat. Combined with the steady opposition (at this time) of the Conservative party, Russell's government had an extremely rough time, and was defeated over a proposal by Lord Dunkellin, an Irish landowner, to substitute the rateable value of property, rather than its rental value, as the basis for a revised county franchise. Dunkellin's motion, carried in mid-June 1866, united the Conservatives, 'Adullamites' and right-wing Whigs. Russell resigned, and Lord Derby formed the third and last of his minority Tory governments which, paradoxically, led by Disraeli in the Commons carried a much more radical and extreme measure

11 The 'Marquess of Hartington' is the courtesy title always borne by the eldest son of the Duke of Devonshire. Hartington was thus not a member of the House of Lords but an elected member of the House of Commons, sitting for South Lancashire. His name was Spencer Compton Cavendish.

of parliamentary reform the following year. Russell never held office again; in the 1866 discussions over parliamentary reform he proved himself to be a consistent radical, as in 1830–32. Gladstone now came into his own as the somewhat unexpected torch-bearer of Liberalism. Russell's ill-fated 1865–66 government knew bad luck in other respects: in 1866 the Austro-Prussian War broke out, and in the same year the crash of the prominent City bank Overend, Gurney and Co. precipitated a serious financial crisis. With the resignation of Russell and Lord Derby 18 months later, the way was cleared for Gladstone and Disraeli to dominate British politics. Neither had been an MP during the period 1830–32 when the Great Reform Act was debated and passed, and the British political scene now came into the hands of men who had only known the reformed Parliament, and, increasingly, of men younger still.

In the same month that Palmerston died there suddenly emerged one of the great controversies of Victorian Britain, the uproar surrounding the actions of Edward Eyre, Governor of Jamaica, in suppressing an uprising by its black population. In that uprising, 18 white men were killed, and Eyre, imposing martial law to restore order, hanged 354 of the black rebels after court martials; others were flogged and several settlements burned down. In Britain, liberal opinion was outraged, and a 'Jamaica Committee' was organised to prosecute Eyre for grossly exceeding his authority.[12] Comprised of a remarkable list of Victorian worthies, it was chaired by John Stuart Mill and included John Bright, Charles Darwin, Thomas Huxley and Leslie Stephen, representatives of British liberalism and humanitarianism. In response, a hardly less distinguished Eyre 'Defence Committee' was established, which included Thomas Carlyle, Charles Kingsley, John Ruskin and Alfred Tennyson as Vice-Presidents. The 'Defence Committee' was not motivated by racism or blind imperialism – Kingsley and Ruskin could fairly be described as on the political left – but chiefly by a belief that Eyre, an exemplary colonial governor, had been faced with an impossible situation and his punishment would be unjust. The Eyre controversy was one of the few which split Victorian Britain's intelligentsia down the middle, showing as well that imperial policy was a matter of moral concern at home, especially the treatment of non-Europeans. Despite a protracted campaign, the Jamaica Committee's attempts to prosecute Eyre failed to succeed.

12 Eyre had previously been Governor of South Australia, where he was known for his humane treatment of the Aborigines.

10

Gladstone's great government, 1868–1874

It is impossible today to like William Ewart Gladstone: we can respect him, even admire him, but no one can like him. He seems to embody in one man every unacceptable feature of Victorianism except sexual hypocrisy, and even that (unfairly) has been widely alleged. That Gladstone is unlikeable must inevitably be contrasted with the way we commonly view Disraeli. Disraeli's insincerity and initial lack of fixed convictions were legendary, yet he is now remembered as the founder of a coherent political philosophy, Tory Democracy, which dominated the Conservative party for a century after his death. Disraeli's sardonic smirk, characteristic of most photographs and portraits of him, virtually proclaims that he does not believe a word either he, or anyone else, is saying, and his private letters delight in highlighting ubiquitous hypocrisy. Far from demeaning Disraeli to posterity, these qualities mark him out as both recognisably modern and endearing. It is difficult not to think of Disraeli without being amused. Add to this Disraeli's storybook ascent from marginal Jewish intellectual and writer to Prime Minister and close confidant of the Queen, and one may readily see why he remains such a favourite, the supremely unVictorian Victorian. Our image of Gladstone, his great rival, is almost the precise opposite. To us Gladstone's high-mindedness is wearisome, his Christian view of politics hypocritical, his continuous political shifts devious and incomprehensible (whereas Disraeli's complete lack of high-mindedness makes his political shifts seem cleverly amusing). All of this is probably unfair, and it was not a view held in Gladstone's own time except by his political enemies. To millions of British people in late Victorian Britain, from millionaire industrialists to humble crofters and factory workers, Gladstone was the greatest statesman and leader Britain had ever produced, a hero, the 'Grand Old Man', without peer. Gladstone retired from politics in 1894 and died in 1898. For a decade after his death the Liberal party tried faithfully to reflect the spirit of Gladstone, and, despite the collectivist 'New Liberalism', the Liberal party continued to be well aware of his shadow until the 1930s and perhaps until the present time.

Gladstone's early life story is surprisingly like that of Peel's, whom Gladstone greatly admired and in a real sense modelled himself upon. Like Peel, Gladstone's father was an enormously wealthy businessman who had entered politics and been given a baronetcy, one of the first awarded to a businessman.[1] Peel had attended Harrow and took a double first-class degree at Christ Church, Oxford; Gladstone, 21 years younger than Peel, attended Eton and also took a double first-class degree at Christ Church, Oxford, where he was also President of the Oxford Union. Thanks to his father's influence, Peel had entered Parliament at the age of 21 for an Irish pocket borough; Gladstone entered Parliament just before his 23rd birthday for the pocket borough of Newark, controlled by the Duke of Newcastle, a friend of Gladstone's father. Both were initially arch-Tories (Gladstone was regarded as a Tory of Tories) who moved steadily to the left, eventually breaking with their party, Gladstone of course following Peel. Both were practical men of affairs, Peel's speciality being a reformed and efficient administrative apparatus, Gladstone's being finance and government spending. So many parallels may be found in their careers that it is difficult to believe that Gladstone was not very conscious of them, perhaps haunted by them.

To be sure, there were also many differences. Gladstone's ancestors were Scottish, and he imbued much of the seriousness of purpose and constant soul-searching of Scottish Presbyterianism, although he (like Peel) was a life-long Anglican. Indeed High Church Anglicanism, and religion generally, was central to Gladstone's world-view. Gladstone's father was a Liverpool merchant with extensive slave and plantation interests in the West Indies and British Guiana (Demerara); Gladstone made his name in early life in part by defending the West Indian slave-owners and their interests. Peel's father, a cotton manufacturer, represented the new British industrial elite. Gladstone's wife, Catherine Glynne, the daughter of a baronet who was distantly related to much of the Whig aristocracy, was higher-born than Peel's. Above all, perhaps, Gladstone was much more of an intellectual than Peel, writing an important pamphlet on the role of the Church and State in British society and a three-volume work on Homer in which he claimed that the Greek writer had anticipated the Doctrine of the Trinity. (Try to imagine a contemporary British Prime Minister producing works on either subject!) Gladstone centrally viewed the world through religious eyes; a cynic might say that this allowed him to see his own constant changes of viewpoint not as inconsistencies but as a continuing revelation of the unfolding of the Mind of Providence. Certainly he

---

1 While Peel the Prime Minister was the eldest son and inherited his father's title, Gladstone was a second son whose little-known elder brother inherited the baronetcy and most of his father's land.

believed that Providence was on his side. At the 1865 general election Gladstone lost his seat of Oxford University. Had he kept a diary, in a similar situation Disraeli would surely have made a joke. Gladstone, who kept a diary throughout his whole adult life, quoted (16 July 1865) Jeremiah: 'And they shall fight against thee, but they shall not prevail against thee, for I am with thee, saith the Lord, to deliver thee.' Gladstone often changed his position, sometimes radically, but always gave the impression that when he changed, God changed with him.

Gladstone wished, certainly in the first half of his career, to find a role for the Church of England in the governance of the country, and viewed the fortunes of the Church as possibly more important than those of Parliament itself. He gradually abandoned this position, but always continued to see the welfare of Christians, both in Britain and internationally, as one of his principal concerns. He regarded the political role of the Catholic Church throughout southern Europe as reprehensible. He strongly supported the forces of liberalism against reaction and oppression throughout southern and eastern Europe, most notably in the case of the opponents of the reactionary Italian kingdoms before unification and the Christian minorities under Ottoman rule in the Balkans. In economics, he was a classical liberal, committed to free trade, continuing government retrenchment, and *laissez-faire*.

There were a number of key turning-points in Gladstone's evolution from a Peelite Tory to an advanced Liberal. Gladstone came to have ever-growing confidence in the sense of responsibility of the skilled working classes, contrasting their thrift, sobriety and good sense in the mid-Victorian period with their reputation for unrest and wildness a generation before. In 1861 as Chancellor of the Exchequer Gladstone established the Post Office Savings Bank, enabling small savers, often skilled workers, to make deposits and withdrawals at any Post Office in Britain. The scheme proved to be a huge success, giving impetus to Gladstone's new-found opinion that enfranchising many skilled workers posed no threat to British stability. In May 1864, allegedly speaking for the Palmerston government in reply to a radical MP's motion for parliamentary reform, Gladstone stated: 'I venture to say that every man who is not presumably incapacitated by some consideration of personal unfitness or of political danger, is morally entitled to come within the pale of the constitution.' These words became famous (or notorious) at once; the last phrase was widely construed to mean that Gladstone favoured something like universal male suffrage. Gladstone was quick to deny this, and the Reform Bill introduced by Russell and Gladstone in 1866 enfranchised only about 400 000 new voters, compared with the one million or so added by Disraeli's 1867 Reform Act. Gladstone certainly spoke without the knowledge or approval of Palmerston, the Prime Minister, who immediately wrote to Gladstone to criticise him. Deliberately or not, however, Gladstone was marking out a clear area of disagreement between himself and the more conservative Whig-Liberals in Palmerston's government. At the 1865 general election, Gladstone was, as noted, defeated for his parliamentary seat of Oxford University. The Oxford University constituency was notably conservative, especially the many Anglican vicars entitled to vote by postal ballot, and Gladstone found it increasingly difficult to secure re-election. In the nineteenth century, voting in general elections took place over several weeks rather than on a single day, and it was still possible for Gladstone to secure a seat at the 1865 general election. He was offered one in Lancashire South and was elected, with some difficulty, four days after being defeated at Oxford.[2] In the course of an election address at Manchester Free Trade Hall, he declared: 'At last, my friends, I am come among you, and I am come among you "unmuzzled" ', meaning that his newly minted but enthusiastic radicalism could now be given free flow in a north of England industrial seat, whereas no MP for Oxford University could have enunciated these views and be elected.

Gladstone was now the darling of Britain's radicals (radicals in the nineteenth-century sense), especially skilled workers, radical industrialists, and those from the Celtic areas. Many middle-class Evangelicals admired his moral earnestness and religious view of politics. He continued to enjoy, rather oddly, some support from High Church Anglicans, normally Conservatives, and from many traditional Whigs. Yet Gladstone also inspired mistrust and even fear in many quarters. His ideological journeyings were unusual, to say the least. One is very familiar, then and now, with the flaming radical youth who evolves into a middle-aged man of arch-conservative views. There is nothing unusual in this; it is the norm. Gladstone moved in precisely the opposite direction. In 1833 Macaulay wrote a celebrated book review of Gladstone's work on Church and State which described him as 'the rising hope of [the] stern and unbending Tories'. Gladstone was then 24. In 1865, when Gladstone was 51, he announced himself to have been 'unmuzzled' and a radical democrat. Throughout most of the rest of his life he led the radicalised party, and was still a fixture at its head in the mid-1890s, when the Liberals seemed to many Tories to have moved a long way to socialism. 'An old man in a hurry' was, increasingly, the Tory view of Gladstone. As the left wing of the Liberal party increasingly flirted with active measures of redistribution, and as universal suffrage seemed increasingly inevitable, Gladstone came to be more and more distrusted by many members of British Society. Undeniably, his views puzzled many more. Gladstone's private life, though almost certainly impeccable, also gave rise to many rumours. For most of his adult life he went on night-time expeditions to London slums to 'reclaim' prostitutes to a Christian life. He was, apparently, absolutely sincere in this, but

---

2 Lancashire South returned three MPs. Gladstone finished third (out of six candidates) and was defeated there at the next general election in 1868.

it is difficult to imagine anything more likely to give rise to innuendo and slander. In 1930, 32 years after his death, Gladstone's sons fought a celebrated defamation suit against an author, Peter Wright, who claimed that Gladstone's sexual life was anything but pure and that he had fathered an illegitimate son.[3] To this day, it is widely assumed (without evidence) that there was more to Gladstone's sexual life than meets the eye. Again, Gladstone should be contrasted here with Disraeli or Palmerston, who cheerfully had a string of mistresses without being censured. It was Gladstone's presumed hypocrisy which has made it so tempting to believe the worst of him.

Gladstone's ascendancy to Liberal leadership in 1868 was made easier by a number of significant trends or events. At a meeting at Willis's Rooms in June 1859, all sections of the parliamentary Whig-Liberal party agreed to work together, and by 1868 there was a recognisably unified Liberal party, now including many former Peelites, which was ranged against the Conservative party led by Derby and Disraeli.[4] By the 1860s, Britain's left-of-centre party had evolved, as Ivor Bulmer-Thomas put it, from 'a large Whig party with some Liberals in it' in 1832 to 'a Liberal party with Whigs in it'. By this he meant from a party basically consisting in Parliament of aristocratic great landowners, their relatives and minions, to a party of landowners, businessmen and professional men, sometimes of self-made social origins, sometimes Nonconformist and from the north of England and the Celtic areas, who had in common adherence to radical nostrums, above all free trade, and to a common, but not necessarily universally-held, programme of reforms. Increasingly, business and professional men became more prominent among the Liberal party's MPs, although this change was surprisingly gradual. Between 1859 and 1869 (at least on one analysis) the percentage of Liberal MPs who were businessmen rose from 16.2 per cent to 24.4 per cent, while those with peerage connections or baronetcies declined from 30.2 per cent to 24.7 per cent, a perceptible but not revolutionary change. Lawyers among Liberal MPs in this period rose from 11.5 to 13.2 per cent. Including other occupational categories, by 1868 the majority of Liberal MPs were probably middle-class men (many of whom were extremely wealthy, of course) rather than landowners. This trend would become more and more evident during the remainder of the nineteenth century, so that by the 1890s (and especially after the Liberal Unionist split of 1886) a great landowner was increasingly a rarity in the

---

3 In English law, one cannot defame a dead person, and Gladstone's sons themselves wrote a defamatory letter to Wright, forcing him to sue them for libel; Gladstone's sexual behaviour became the main focus of the ensuing trial.

4 Willis's Rooms were a meeting place on Pall Mall, in central London, which could be booked for specific occasions such as the gathering in 1859. Formerly it had been Almack's, a famous gambling club of the Regency period.

Liberal party. This shift was, however, less evident at the Cabinet level. Cabinets had by definition to include many members of the House of Lords, who comprised generally one-half or nearly one-half even of late Victorian Liberal Cabinets, while the scions of aristocratic and landed families still enjoyed all of the advantages which had long enhanced their ascendancy: education in the ways of assured governance at a public school and university, great wealth, territorial influence, a recognisable name, and, above all, a much earlier start, with sons of aristocrats entering political life decades ahead of middle-class men with their way to make. Conversely, businessmen, with rare exceptions, continued to be seen as gauche, parochial and poorly educated beyond the counting-house and factory, lacking polished accents, *savoir-faire* and worldly wisdom. William E. Gladstone benefited from these broader changes by having a foot in all camps: by origin middle-class, a genius of competent Liberal finance, and increasingly radical, yet by marriage a Whig, an outstanding product of Eton and Oxford, a former Tory and a High Churchman. Gladstone also benefited from the relative lack of rivals, especially those from the Whig aristocracy. That the Whig aristocracy failed to produce any successors to Grey, Russell and Palmerston has been widely noted by historians. Lord Hartington was very much the ablest of the younger Whigs, and could easily have become leader of the Liberal party from the 1870s onwards had he wished. Gladstone also outlived his able Peelite contemporaries, like Sidney Herbert, many of whom died young.

The 1868 general election was the first held following the Second Reform Act, which enfranchised approximately 1 150 000 new voters, chiefly working men in the boroughs. As the authors of the Act, the Conservatives expected to do well, but were sadly disappointed. Already in a minority before the election, they fell further behind as a result, while the Liberals won a significant victory, winning 382 seats to the Tories' 276. The Liberals had a small majority (243:220) in England, but were dramatically ahead in Wales (22:8) and Scotland (52:8), as well as gaining a substantial win in Ireland (65:40). To a limited extent, however, Disraeli's reform gamble had paid off: there were strong Conservatives in working-class Lancashire, with Gladstone suffering the indignity of losing his seat. (For the next 12 years Gladstone sat for Greenwich, in south-east London.) The Tories also gained in the middle-class areas of London. In most other respects, however, the gamble had failed. Other working-class seats were heavily Liberal, while the characteristic Liberal (later Labour) hold on Scotland and Wales has been seen as dating from the 1868 election.

Realising that his position was hopeless, Disraeli resigned without meeting Parliament. The Queen immediately sent for Gladstone. In future years she might well have hesitated, but at this stage had no special animus against him. 'My mission is to pacify Ireland', Gladstone announced, rather unexpectedly, to a friend standing next to him when he received the

Queen's telegram.[5] He had first to form a government. In many respects Gladstone's 1868 Cabinet did not differ markedly from those of previous Whig-Liberal governments, containing six peers and Lord Hartington, heir to the dukedom of Devonshire, among 15 members. The peers included a duke (Argyll) and four earls (Ripon, Kimberley, Clarendon, and Granville), with Lord Clarendon holding the Foreign Secretaryship for the third time. The remaining nine members of Gladstone's Cabinet were members of the House of Commons, among them a number of businessmen and lawyers. John Bright, after being central to radical politics in Britain for 25 years, at last gained a Cabinet position, the Presidency of the Board of Trade. Bright was a Quaker, and was thus one of the very first Nonconformists to sit in a Cabinet. Gladstone's Cabinet also included the banker George J. Goschen and, from July 1870, another Quaker manufacturer, William E. Forster, as well as several lawyers and, remarkably, two men with Australian experience, Robert Lowe and H. C. E. Childers. Lowe was an Oxford graduate and barrister who had lived in Sydney during the 1840s, serving in its Legislative Council. Here Lowe became hostile to extreme forms of democracy, and is best-known as the most visible opponent of the proposed 1866 Reform Act on the grounds that working men were unfit to govern. Childers, like Lowe the son of a vicar but a Cambridge man, lived in Melbourne during the Victorian Gold Rush. Another key member of Gladstone's first Cabinet was Edward Cardwell (1813–86; created Viscount Cardwell, 1874), like Gladstone the son of a Liverpool merchant, like him a double first at Oxford, and like him a former Peelite Tory. In all, Gladstone was well-served by his ministers and his first Cabinet proved easier to manage than his subsequent ones, lacking, in particular, any prima donnas like Joseph Chamberlain who, in future governments, would give endless trouble.

Gladstone foreshadowed in 1867 that Ireland would be high on the agenda of any incoming Liberal government. His new views on Ireland took shape in the mid-1860s, during the period of the Fenian outrages. Founded in 1858, the Fenian Brotherhood enjoyed strong backing and financial support from Irish emigrants in the United States. In 1867 a band of 1500 Fenians tried, extraordinarily, to seize Chester Castle and were put down by a battalion of Guards from London. The Fenians attempted to rescue two of their kind from a London prison in December 1867, causing an explosion in which 12 persons were killed. Ireland also felt a deep sense of grievance in the agrarian sector, especially over rents still unpaid from the famine years and over absentee landlords. Yet Catholic Ireland and its bishops deplored the violence of the Fenians, which declined after 1867. Gladstone became convinced that timely and far-reaching concessions might win Catholic Ireland back to full loyalty to the United Kingdom.

5 Gladstone was chopping down trees on his estate when he received the Queen's telegram. This was one of his hobbies.

Gladstone's programme to win back Catholic Irish opinion comprised two measures in the religious and economic spheres. In a remarkably radical move, he proposed to disestablish the Church of Ireland (i.e. the Anglican Church in Ireland) and, as well, enacted a measure to guarantee Irish tenant farmers compensation for any improvements they made to their land if they were evicted for non-payment of rents. The disestablishment of the Church of Ireland was one of the most radical measures ever passed by Parliament in the nineteenth century. The case for disestablishment was, obviously, very strong: in 1861, out of a total population in Ireland of 5 799 000, no less than 4 505 000 were Catholics, or 77.7 per cent of the population. A total of 523 000, mainly in Ulster, were Presbyterians, about 9.0 per cent of the population. The established Church of Ireland had about 693 000 adherents, only 12.0 per cent of the population. (Some 77 000 persons belonged to other religious denominations.) Adherents of the Church of Ireland were numerous in and around Dublin and in parts of Ulster, but were virtually unrepresented throughout most of the south of Ireland, especially among the poor peasantry and tenant farmers. The Church of Ireland was closely associated with the Anglo-Irish Establishment centring around Dublin Castle, and was one of the most potent symbols of England's supremacy over Catholic Ireland. To Gladstone and his supporters it was obviously unfair, and in the long run untenable and counter-productive, to maintain the privileged position of a Church which included only one inhabitant in eight. Disestablishment was an easy, relatively painless way to remove a central grievance of the majority of the Irish people, entailing no *political* change or concession, but proving the goodwill of the Westminster government. Disestablishment in no way affected, of course, the rights of adherents of the Church of Ireland, but merely placed the Church on the same legal footing as Ireland's other religious denominations.

Disestablishment of the Irish Church was also consistent with a growing movement for the disestablishment of all of Britain's Established Churches, especially the Church of England. This movement was led in England and Wales by the Liberation Society (originally known as the British Anti-State Church Association), founded in the 1840s, which reached the peak of its influence in the 1860s. It was strongly supported by militant Nonconformists, then also at the zenith of their influence, especially in industrial England, and was also strong in Wales and Scotland. Nonconformists still felt a powerful sense of being, legally and *de facto*, second-class citizens in many respects, and their willingness to see the Anglican Church disestablished in Ireland, hopefully as a prelude to disestablishment elsewhere in Britain, overrode their hostility to Roman Catholics. In Ireland, the National Association, founded in 1864 and actively supported by the leadership of the Catholic Church, included disestablishment as an important part of its agenda.

Naturally, the disestablishment of the Irish Church met with considerable opposition from many Anglicans and conservatives. George Anthony Denison, a prominent Puseyite, termed disestablishment a 'revolution' in public affairs. The United Kingdom was a Protestant country: if Protestantism was not morally superior to Catholicism, what was the point of the Reformation? The Church of Ireland represented education and learning in a benighted land of superstition and backwardness; whatever abuses of pluralism and venality had been present in the Church had been ameliorated since the 1830s. Disestablishment of the Irish Church would leave Ireland as the only part of the United Kingdom, and one of the only places in Europe at the time, without an established religion. Appeasement would fail in this case as in all others: Irish extremists would never accept disestablishment as a final settlement, but would want more and yet more; so, too, would radical Nonconformists. Disestablishment showed that violence and terrorism paid off. It represented a typically immoral stance by the left in rewarding one's enemies and punishing one's loyal friends. Such were the arguments made by the Anglican and conservative opponents of disestablishment. Yet it was notable that their resistance to Gladstone's proposals was less strident than the response by British conservatives to changes by Parliament to the Irish Church hierarchy in 1833, which led directly to the Oxford Movement. This moderation was probably due to a realisation that the 1868 general election gave Gladstone a mandate for his plans, and perhaps to greater sensitivity to the Irish plight and to a growing sense of religious pluralism and toleration.

From the vantage point of 130 years afterwards, both Gladstone and his opponents were partly right. Gladstone's religious and economic reforms in Ireland did pacify that country for another generation. In the long run, however, the fears of the opponents of disestablishment proved well-founded. Disestablishment was not the concluding chapter of a period of hostility between England and Ireland but the opening of a campaign which led to complete southern Irish independence in 1922 and to all the troubles since. Despite disestablishment, Gladstone himself introduced a Home Rule Bill for Ireland 18 years later. The Church of Ireland – Protestant, yet retaining many Catholic forms – in some senses represented a middle way between Catholic Irish nationalism in the south, and Protestant extremism in the north.[6] It was also a Church which was not associated with any geographical area, although it was strongest in Dublin and the north. By removing its official status, Gladstone paradoxically turned the Irish question purely into one of the claims of two hostile, regionally based ethnicities, making the Irish question harder to solve, a running sore to this day. Furthermore, by conceding Irish Church disestablishment without a fight, Gladstone virtually made it inevitable that the

6 The Protestants of Northern Ireland are chiefly Presbyterians, not Anglicans.

unappeased forces of Irish nationalism would then concentrate their energies on further stages of *political* reform, especially the constitutional arrangements binding Ireland to the rest of the United Kingdom. A contrast might be made here between Ireland and Wales. In Wales, nationalists concentrated their efforts on achieving the disestablishment of the Anglican Church in Wales, but did not achieve their aim until 1919. No movement for a separate Welsh parliament, or for Welsh independence, grew up until Plaid Cymru was founded in the 1920s, and these did not become a significant force until the 1960s. Of course, the two situations were vastly different, but Gladstone's actions necessarily made it easier, not harder, for political independence (or 'home rule') to move to the centre stage of Irish nationalist desiderata.

Gladstone had introduced a bill to disestablish the Church of Ireland in March 1868, before the general election of that year. It passed the House of Commons, but failed in the House of Lords. Elected with a large majority in 1868, Gladstone proceeded with the Irish Church Act as a matter of priority, and it became law in July 1869. The leadership of the Irish Church could do little to thwart Gladstone's plans, and therefore attempted to obtain the best possible financial terms from the Liberal government. Under the Act, the Irish Church was disendowed: that is, it ceased to be given any income from the British government. The Act allowed the Irish Church to keep £14 million in property, and it actually ran a surplus thereafter, which it used for charitable and educational purposes. Bishops of the Church were henceforth to be elected by a Church Synod, rather than chosen by the Prime Minister. Gladstone's Act also had the paradoxical effect of ending the grant paid to Maynooth College, the Catholic seminary, and also a similar grant paid to the Irish Presbyterian Church. Freed of its connection with the English 'Establishment', the Church of Ireland held its own during the nineteenth century, although it has declined in relative importance in this century with the division in Irish society between the south and Ulster. The number of Church of Ireland clergymen also declined significantly, from 2265 in 1861 to 1617 in 1901, while the number of Irish Catholic clergymen rose from 3014 to 3711 in the same period.

Gladstone's other early measure of reform in Ireland concerned land tenure. In 1870 Gladstone passed a bill which limited the powers of landlords in Ireland to evict tenants, and guaranteed compensation to tenant farmers for improvements they made on their property; previously, they had no right to such compensation. Gladstone's Irish Land Act of 1870 also allowed government loans to be made to tenants to purchase their land. The Act was not particularly successful, being consistently evaded by unscrupulous landlords. The Act did nothing to consolidate small landholdings in Ireland, introduce economies of scale on the English pattern, or bring scientific agriculture to Ireland. The central problem of Irish farming was that there were too many small tenant farmers, who were often impoverished, a one-crop peasantry similar to that found in southern

Europe or the Third World, and radically different from the efficient, large-scale farming of England. Gladstone's Act affected this situation only marginally, if at all. Gladstone had also attempted several other reforms in Ireland as part of a package of changes, opening up Dublin University much more widely to Catholics, and reforming Irish local government. He also wished to nationalise Ireland's railways, as unlikely as this might seem.[7] These were defeated in Parliament, many Liberals defecting to the opposition over these proposals. Despite Gladstone's two important measures, in 1870 a 'Home Government Association of Ireland' was established with the aim of setting up an Irish Parliament. At the next general election in 1874 it returned 58 MPs to the British Parliament.

The first Gladstone government is often seen as completing the great programme of liberal reform initiated by Peel in the 1820s, in which the Great Reform Act, the abolition of slavery, and repeal of the Corn Laws were landmarks. Animated by a wish to limit, rationalise, and (consistent with the existence of Established Churches in Great Britain) secularise British government, it brought the liberal agenda nearly to its logical conclusion. Indeed, it is from the time of the first Gladstone government that 'retrenchment and reform' as watchwords of Liberalism are, first gradually, then rapidly, overturned in favour of collectivism and a greater role for the state, especially in the interests of the poor and the working classes. Gladstone's first government, while strongly committed to an agenda of state minimalism and *laissez-faire*, also contained some presaging of the later aims of Liberalism.

The most important and far-reaching reforms carried out by the 1868–74 government were in the field of education and within the army. For years, there had been widespread demands for reform of Britain's woefully inadequate system of primary education. In particular, it was widely felt that the North beat the South in the American Civil War, and that Prussia defeated Austria in 1866, because their soldiers were better educated. In 1870, nearly one-half of the age group of 5–13 year olds in Britain were not at any school, often being barely literate.[8] The others were either in state-aided, non-denominational 'British' schools or 'voluntary' schools (usually founded by a religious group, especially Anglican schools known as 'National' schools). With the granting of the franchise to most of the (male) urban working classes in 1867, their education, to make possible a minimum level of understanding necessary to conduct the public affairs of a democracy, became an absolute requirement. 'We must educate our masters', was Robert Lowe's famous, tart observation. The issue of primary

7 Gladstone was always very dubious about the efficacy of *laissez-faire* in the functioning of railroads and was earlier instrumental in passing legislation which would have allowed English railways to be nationalised.
8 The Newcastle Committee of 1859–61 had, however, estimated that only 4–5 per cent of children younger than eleven were *not* in some school.

education in England and Wales was clouded by two other issues. Education had always been a local matter and state schools would in the future be founded or funded at the local level, based in local taxes. More important was the religious issue, which had become central to any changes in Britain's educational system. Nonconformists, growing in strength and plainly of great significance in the Liberal party's electoral success, insisted that any public funding for elementary education be 'unsectarian' in nature and, in particular, that the Church of England not be favoured in any legislation on this question which called for the spending of taxpayers' money. In 1869 Joseph Chamberlain, a radical Unitarian manufacturer in Birmingham who later became one of the seminal figures in British politics, entered public life by helping to found the National Education League, along with other Nonconformist leaders like R. W. Dale, a prominent Congregationalist minister. Gladstone placed W. E. Forster, his Nonconformist Cabinet minister who was Vice-President of the Committee of the Privy Council for Education, in charge of producing a sweeping bill. Forster's famous Education Act, passed in April 1870, concerned only children under 13. It did not affect students of secondary school age, and no British government attempted to reform secondary education until 1902. Forster's Act grew out of the Report of the Newcastle Commission of 1859–61, which found the state of primary education woefully inadequate. It had recommended the establishment of 'Boards of Education' in counties and larger boroughs with powers to levy rates and assess educational results among students, but which would not affect the running of the schools themselves. Forster's Act in fact did not affect the running of any existing elementary school. It did, however, permit the establishment of locally elected school boards which were given the power to levy rates, build new schools, and appoint teachers. (Forster's Act allowed local governments to spend money on education for the first time.) These school boards could also make school attendance compulsory. School boards could be established where it was found that existing school provision was inadequate or where a majority of ratepayers requested it. Elementary education had not been free and was not necessarily to be free. It cost parents about 30 shillings a year per child. This fee was, however, waived for the very poor.

Against his own inclination, Gladstone acceded to a famous amendment by William Cowper-Temple, a prominent Whig MP who had served in many Whig-Liberal governments but who was now on the backbenches, requiring that religious instruction in any school established by any Board of Education should exclude any doctrine 'distinctive of any particular religious denomination'. This in effect limited religious education in Board Schools to the Bible and hymn-singing, which satisfied a part of the demands of the Nonconformists. It also led to the growth of a secular-oriented class of schoolteachers, greatly facilitated secular education, and, indeed, in the long term certainly contributed significantly to the decline of the strength of organised religion in England, both Anglican and Noncon-formist. In response to the National Education League, however, Anglicans had formed a National Education Union, and in response to its pressures Forster's Act also allowed school boards to pay the fees of poor children in Anglican schools out of local taxes. This provision was strongly opposed by Nonconformists, who continued to hold a lasting grievance against Gladstone's government. Nevertheless, Forster's Act was certainly one of the most significant passed by Parliament during the late nineteenth century, particularly in opening the way for a greatly increased government role in education, a field which became ever more important. Nevertheless, Britain failed to develop a unified national educational system until the twentieth century, remaining with a haphazard, locally organised structure. Since neither Gladstone's government nor any subsequent one addressed the issue of secondary schooling until 1902, Britain came through the nineteenth century with a secondary school system heavily private in organisation, which made upward social mobility from the working to the middle classes extraordinarily unlikely even for the very bright poor boy (or, still more, the very bright poor girl).

While Gladstone's government left secondary education alone, it did reform entry to Oxford and Cambridge, which in the past had been restricted to practising Anglicans.[9] In that year religious tests were totally abolished at both of the old universities by the Universities Tests Act, an obvious component of Victorian liberalism's belief in religious toleration and in 'the career open to talent'. Many of these religious tests had been partially removed in the 1850s, although until 1871 no non-Anglican could be appointed to any teaching position or fellowship at Oxford or Cam-bridge. By the early 1870s, Nonconformist and Jewish undergraduates were increasingly prominent among the best students at those universities, and the inability of the latter to offer them teaching posts despite their merits had become embarrassing. By coincidence or not, within 15 or 20 years of the 1871 reform the atmosphere of both universities had changed dramatically, so that an undergraduate from the 1840s or 1850s, returning in 1895, would have been bewildered by the changes he found. In the 1840s, Oxford and Cambridge were *primarily*, in effect, seminaries for Anglican vicars, based purely on classical learning and dominated by unmarried dons, most of whom were clergymen. By the 1890s the old universities had seen the emergence of the 'clever clever' High Table style of epigrams and witticisms, of a largely secular, facetious undergraduate style, eventually sometimes aesthetic and camp, and of a division of students

9 Until then, and certainly until the 1850s, matriculating (i.e. entering) students at Oxford had to swear their belief in the Thirty-Nine Articles of Anglicanism. At Cambridge this was required upon graduation: thus Cambridge had already had its share of Nonconformists and others who were prepared to attend the university, and take its examinations, but not formally to graduate. Of course any Nonconformist, Jew or Catholic who was prepared to declare their belief in the Thirty-Nine Articles was admitted (or graduated).

between 'hearties', interested chiefly in sport, and serious 'swots', often bright scholarship boys. The beginnings – but only the beginnings – of the modern role of universities primarily as centres of original research was also taken at this time. Of course many dons had written original and valuable works of research, but these were primarily in the classics and theology, which formed the older universities' core curriculum. Most strikingly and significantly, it is virtually impossible to point to a single seminal English cultural or scientific figure prior to the late nineteenth century who was employed as a university don, the leaders of the Oxford Movement being the most notable exceptions. If one draws up a list of the most prominent British thinkers and writers of the nineteenth century, with names like Darwin, Faraday, Mill, Dickens, Tennyson, and so on being to the fore, none worked at a university or did his research there. In 1871 Cambridge appointed James Clerk Maxwell as professor of experimental physics, the first time that a world-ranking scientist had been employed by one of the older universities. The situation in Scotland, where education was more progressive, was different, with such figures as Sir William Thomson (later Lord Kelvin), the great theoretical physicist, holding chairs (Thomson at Glasgow University from 1846), but British universities probably had much less of a commitment to pure research at this time than did continental or American universities. Except by reflecting the liberal and progressive 'spirit of the age', it should be noted that Gladstone's government did nothing to advance university research, and Gladstone's own view of the role of universities had been fashioned in the 1820s.

Nor did Gladstone's government have anything to do with the most radical change of all, the admission of women to the older universities. Women had been admitted to examinations and degrees at London University on the same basis as men from 1848 and also at the provincial university colleges, with their strong Nonconformist and secular traditions. This period, however, saw women undergraduates at Cambridge, with the formation in 1869 of Girton College and in 1871 of Newnham College.[10] Oxford led the way, its first women's colleges, Lady Margaret Hall and Somerville, having been founded in 1868 and 1869. Women's colleges and their students met with fierce resistance until the First World War or even later, their students not being, technically, members of the university, although they were allowed to attend lectures and sit for examinations. Unchaperoned meetings of male and female students were so discouraged as to be virtually impossible, and normal friendly relations between men and women were in the highest degree unusual until the inter-war years, if not until the 1950s. The women's colleges were built on the outskirts of the two university towns, deliberately kept as far as possible from the older men's colleges. Until the First World War, if not much later, the

10 Girton was originally founded at Hitchin, Hertfordshire, and moved to Cambridge in 1872.

ambience and atmosphere of the older universities was overwhelmingly masculine, the very presence of women being resented as an intrusion to be suffered as little, and as ungenerously, as possible. Modern notions of sexual freedom were, needless to say, unknown, and male undergraduates who wished for sexual experience frequented prostitutes in Oxford, Cambridge or London. In this atmosphere, homosexuality became a well-known feature of groups like the Cambridge 'Apostles' by the early 1900s.

As well as to the universities, the concept of the 'career open to talent' was applied by the Gladstone government to other areas. By an Order in Council of June 1870, virtually all new appointments to the permanent Civil Service were to be filled by open competitive examination.[11] Successful candidates were still likely to be those educated at public and grammar schools and the older universities, but grossly unqualified candidates henceforth stood little chance of appointment, although of course brilliantly original minds may well have done poorly at these examinations. Sociologically, this change (and the Civil Service reforms which preceded them) broadened the base of successful entrants to the administrative Civil Service to include talented boys from the whole middle class and a part of the lower-middle class who had done well at grammar school or a minor public school. It was, however, still virtually impossible for boys from the working classes to remain at school long enough to pass the Civil Service's entrance examinations.

One of the most important reforms of Gladstone's first government was in the organisation of the army. The Franco-Prussian War of 1870–71 – in which, most surprisingly, Germany simply thrashed the forces of Napoleon III, the Emperor abdicating (and fleeing to England) and Paris enduring the horrors of siege, Commune, and inglorious surrender – disturbed and excited Britain, even if from German unification in 1871 England did not draw the seemingly obvious inference that a superpower had emerged on the Continent whose expansion had to be resisted. British government expenditure on its army and navy actually declined between 1868 and 1872, from £27.1 million to £21.1, before rising again to £23.6 million in 1874. Fears over the readiness of Britain to fight another war, together with the Gladstone government's commitment to reform, both contributed to the far-reaching changes associated with the Secretary for War, Edward Cardwell. Cardwell introduced a series of major reforms in the army which modernised its structure to a significant extent. The most important was the Army Regulation Act of 1871 which abolished the purchase of commissions. For nearly 200 years commissions (whereby officer's rank was obtained) in the regular army could be purchased by open sale. Proponents

---

11 Entrance to the Foreign Office was excluded from this requirement until 1919. As a result, the diplomatic corps and the upper permanent staff of the Foreign Office were dominated by aristocrats and very wealthy public school and Oxbridge graduates until the Second World War. Certain technical appointments to the Civil Service were also excluded.

of this system claimed that purchase filled Britain's officer corps with gentlemen, generally of aristocratic or gentry background, who understood and respected Britain's traditional hostility to a standing professional army. These officers might at first glance have seemed untrained, but as Britain had won every war it had ever fought (barring only the American Revolution of 1775–83), they could hardly be termed incompetent. Opponents of purchase, of course, claimed that the system was manifestly unfair as well as counter-productive, keeping out talented but poor officers to make way for wealthy incompetents. Cardwell's reform was fiercely resisted by the army, and the House of Lords and the Liberals had to employ the subterfuge of a royal warrant to abolish purchase without financial compensation, forcing the Lords to pass their original bill which provided financial compensation for officers affected. Except for the Franco-Prussian War, with its lessons of the superiority of Prussian military professionalism, it is unlikely that purchase would have been abolished. Like university reform, Cardwell's reform was plainly in keeping with the notion of promotion by merit rather than status which now dominated liberal thought. Cardwell also introduced other changes to the army, including a reform of its staff, a revision of the nature of the territorial basis of the infantry, and a reduction in the length of service of regular recruits. His reforms made the British army more efficient. Nevertheless they were by no means as far-reaching as they might have been. The Duke of Cambridge, the Queen's cousin, remained Commander-in-Chief of the army until his death in 1895. A man who was opposed to all basic reforms in the military, his presence prevented wider changes. Secondly, Cardwell was unable to institute a modern general staff such as Prussia had, and which was one of the keys to Prussian military success. No British general staff in the modern sense came into existence until the twentieth century. Two or three other points about Britain's military in the later nineteenth century should also be noted. The army and the navy remained entirely separate and quite uncoordinated, with the Royal Navy being regarded, probably with accuracy, as the more important of the two services as well as the 'senior service'. The maintenance of Britain's Empire, as well as the freedom of the sea routes upon which its trade relied, depended upon the navy, and Nelson was a more potent symbol than Wellington. Britain's Indian army continued to have a semi-independent existence from its army at home. Finally, one fact entirely distinguished the military sphere *per se* in Britain from that in any other major European nation: it had no conscription, and was entirely dependent upon volunteers. Glorying in the army and in service in the army therefore never became the fetish in Britain that it was in Germany or France.

Gladstone's reforms also came in other spheres. A far-reaching Judicature Act of 1873, produced by Lord Selbourne the Lord Chancellor, fused the unwieldy court systems of England and Wales into one Supreme Court of Judicature, which still forms much of the basis of the court system of

England.[12] Gladstone's government also made one most important reform to the electoral system, the Ballot Act of 1872. This made voting confidential, by requiring each voter to fill their ballot in secret so that it was impossible to tell who had cast it. Such a procedure may seem as obvious as water running downhill, but – as extraordinary as this may seem to those unfamiliar with nineteenth-century elections – prior to 1872 voting was done in public and, indeed, hundreds of 'poll-books' survive for many dozens of parliamentary constituencies listing the names of electors and how they voted. Proponents of the old system claimed that this made voting more responsible, since it was a matter of public record; besides, why should anyone be ashamed of declaring how he voted? Members of Parliament voted openly in the House of Commons; no one dreamed of making their votes secret, or those of any other elected office-holders. It also prevented the 'stuffing' of ballot boxes with fraudulent ballots, as was common in America's cities, dominated by corrupt political machines. Opponents of the old system pointed out that it opened the doors to widespread corruption and influence-mongering, with, especially, tenant farmers and factory hands potentially threatened by their employers if they voted the 'wrong' way. In practice, in most of Britain the introduction of the ballot probably had little effect, and the Conservatives resoundingly won the next (1874) general election without any help from threats to voters of this kind by landlords or factory owners. In one part of the United Kingdom, however, the effects of the Ballot Act were, apparently, profound. This was in southern Ireland, where Catholic Irish tenant farmers and small owner-occupiers broke free of the domination of landowners in large measure because of the Act, their tactics masterminded by the rising star of Irish nationalism, Charles Stewart Parnell.

The left of the Liberal party was also active in formulating demands in other areas. The 1860s was the period when the issue of restricting the sale of liquor became an issue in Britain and America. Restrictions on the sale of liquor were demanded by an increasing portion of Nonconformity, and 'temperance' – the name by which the movement went – became, over the next 40 years or so, almost synonymous with political Nonconformity. Drunkenness was a common feature of many working-class homes and communities, and was regarded by temperance advocates as a supreme

12 Previously there had been three types of common law courts (Queen's Bench, Common Pleas, and Exchequer), and a Court of Chancery (itself divided into two 'instances' or sub-courts) to administer equity law. As well, three types of courts which derived from Roman law rather than common law also existed. These administered cases relating to admiralty and shipping, wills and probate, and divorces. Finally, a number of local courts and the Bankruptcy Court of London stood outside any of these courts. This sounds bewilderingly complex, and it was. Dickens' nightmarish depiction of the English legal system 40 years before Selbourne's reforms was based in part in the Byzantine complexity of the law as well as its notorious delays.

social evil. Nonconformist women were particularly active in this move-ment.[13] Solutions proposed by the temperance movement were varied, ranging from government licensing of public houses with drastic restrictions on their freedom to sell liquor to the prohibition of all alcoholic beverages, a solution more popular in America than Britain. In America 'prohibition' triumphed at the end of the First World War, and from 1920 until 1933 it was illegal to manufacture or sell *any* alcoholic beverage in the United States. Most historians believe that this resulted in the birth of organised crime in the United States; the 'Prohibition Amendment' to the Constitution proved so unworkable and unpopular that it was repealed 13 years after it was enacted.

In 1871 Gladstone's Home Secretary, H. A. Bruce (later Baron Aberdare), attempted to appease the temperance lobby by enacting a Licensing Act, but one which did not go far enough for pro-temperance groups. They favoured a 'local veto' – the right of local governments to stop the sale of alcohol in their areas – which Bruce's Bill did not include. Eventually, a watered-down bill was passed in 1872. Most notably, however, the Liberals' alliance with the forces of the temperance movement resulted in the growth of a counter-movement, led and funded by brewers and public house keepers, which greatly benefited the Conservative party. Although today's historians no longer believe that liquor interests were crucial in funding the Conservative party at this time, it seems clear that the alcohol industry, one of the largest and best-organised in Britain, increasingly threw its influence behind the Conservative party. Many Anglicans and others who were not influenced by Nonconformists also resented the temperance movement's attempts at massive social control, especially of the lifestyle of the common people, regardless of how well-intentioned it was. This attitude of opposition to temperance was summarised during the 1872 licensing debate in the House of Lords by Bishop C. W. Magee that 'England free [was] better than England sober'. As the linkages between Nonconformity, temperance and Liberalism grew stronger in the late nineteenth century, they produced a reaction which was probably stronger still.

The period of the first Gladstone government was a time of importance in the history of Britain's trade union movements. In 1868 the Trades Union Congress (TUC) was founded, its first conference, in Manchester, being attended by 34 delegates representing 118 000 members, chiefly skilled craft workers strategically placed in London and other large towns. Much later, Sidney and Beatrice Webb termed the leaders of these unions

13 It must be understood that there were at the time no 'soft drinks'. Water was often polluted and undrinkable, and the only beverages available to drink, apart from tea and coffee, were beer and spirits. Alcoholic beverages were thus the only available beverages which could cool one on a hot day. As a result, even small children drank beer, ale and stout without restriction. At the end of an enormously long day of grinding labour for a pittance in pay, alcohol became, as the famous phrase puts it, 'the quickest way out of Manchester' and other industrial slums.

the 'Junta', especially men like George Howell (the first Secretary of the TUC), George Odger and Robert Applegarth. The TUC was founded at a time of widespread hostility to unions and their association in the public mind with violent outbreaks such as the so-called 'Sheffield outrages' in 1865–66.[14] The mainstream of the Liberal party, either Whig or *laissez-faire* capitalist, had no love for trades unions. Nevertheless, advanced Liberal intellectuals like Frederick Harrison were sympathetic to the new forces of labour, while Gladstone and other Liberal leaders viewed the thrifty, reputable men of skilled labour as responsible citizens. In 1867 there occurred a major legal decision, *Hornby* v. *Close*, in which it was decided that trades unions were ineligible for the legal protection of the courts, unlike friendly societies, and thus had no legal protection against embezzlement by their officials or similar forms of robbery. The court decided that trades unions were, by their nature, bodies in restraint of trade and were hence ineligible, as the law stood, to legal protection.

The TUC was founded in response to this atmosphere. It was clearly inevitable that both the size and importance of the trade unions would grow. By 1874 the sixth TUC annual conference, in Sheffield, was attended by 169 delegates representing 153 societies with no less than 1 192 000 members. The TUC was thus already one of the largest organisations of any kind in Britain, and its potential influence was already enormous. As well, trade unionism was spreading beyond the so-called 'aristocracy of labour' to the unskilled. In 1872 Joseph Arch founded the National Agricultural Labourers Union, which claimed to have 10 000 members a year later. Agricultural workers were among the lowest paid, least well-educated, and most deprived of all British workers (for instance, virtually none could vote until 1884).

Gladstone's government did not respond to the growth of organised labour in any clear-cut way. In response to the *Hornby* v. *Close* verdict, Gladstone's government in 1869 passed a special Act of Parliament over-turning its far-reaching decision, but also appointed a Royal Commission on Trade Unions which reported that same year. It included both oppo-nents and proponents of unionism and, also in 1869, produced both Majority and Minority Reports.[15] The Minority Report was explicitly favourable to trade unions while the Majority Report was willing to endorse many of the aims of the unions. Gladstone's government wrestled with these differences of opinion, and in 1871 produced both a Trade

14 These occurred in the Sheffield cutlery industry, long among the worst and most unpleasant industries in Britain; the term refers to revenge taken by unionists against non-union employees and strikebreakers, including the throwing of cans of gunpowder down their chimneys.

15 It was sometimes the case that members of Royal Commissions could not reach agreement on an outcome and produced two final reports representing different, even contradictory, viewpoints. The most famous example of this occurred in 1909 with the Royal Commis-sion on the Poor Law. Its famous Minority Report recommended the scrapping of the 1834 Poor Law, a remarkably radical conclusion for the time.

Union Act, and, coupled with it, a Criminal Law Amendment Act affecting unions. By these measures, the trade unions were given legal recognition and – permanently overturning *Hornby* v. *Close* – were able to protect their funds under the Friendly Societies Act. On the other hand, all trade unions were still liable to criminal prosecution under an 1825 Act, and picketing of any kind by strikers or union members remained illegal.

The ambiguity of the 1871 legislation pointed to a deep division in Liberal ranks which would grow and grow until – it is hardly an exaggeration to say – it led, half a century later, to Labour replacing the Liberals as Britain's left-of-centre party. The Gladstonian Liberal party was divided into, on one hand, Whigs and advocates of *laissez-faire* capitalism who were, for the most part, hostile to unions, and, on the other hand, more advanced radicals who viewed the plight of the working classes as increasingly central to the political agenda. It is difficult to see how, in the long term, both components could coexist in the same party. The Conservative party was also sharply divided over the trade union question, but, under Disraeli and his successors, managed to handle it in a surprisingly skilful way.

The formation of the TUC also coincided with heightened trade union militancy, chiefly involving skilled craftsmen in issues of pay and hours of work. In 1871 a five-months' strike by Tyneside engineers led to the concession of a nine-hour working day, a gain extended to most other engineering works. Workers in a variety of other industries went on strike in the same year. It is quite possible that labour unrest would have reached massive proportions had not the economic recession which began in 1873, leading to increased unemployment, put a stop to it.[16] Yet the most famous strike of this period originated in a quite different source. In 1871 Robert Lowe, the Chancellor of the Exchequer, faced with the need to raise expenditure on the military as a result of fears generated by the Franco-Prussian War, decided to place a special tax on (of all things) matches.[17] As a result, and encouraged by match manufacturers in London, an enormous crowd of 'match girls' – unskilled, generally uneducated women workers in match factories, fearful that the proposed tax would destroy their employment – marched on the House of Commons. This crowd was dispersed by the police but affected MPs so effectively that Lowe was forced to withdraw his tax and instead raise income tax. This was presumably the first occasion on which women workers were instrumental in gaining a concession of this kind, even if they had the full backing of their employers. During Gladstone's first premiership, however, the new forces of labour

---

16 As a rule, strikes by trade unionists decline when unemployment is increasing (or high), and rise during times of full employment. Obviously, unions have much more trouble extracting increased benefits from their employers when business is bad than when it is good.

17 Lowe, an accomplished Latin scholar, wanted to include the pun '*Ex luca lucellum*' (roughly, 'money from light') on his proposed revenue stamps.

never flexed their muscles; in particular, they most definitely did not attempt to form a new socialist or working-class party such as those in the process of formation in Germany, France, and elsewhere in Europe. In Britain, working-class loyalty to Liberalism (and, indeed, as will be seen, to Toryism) remained strong for more than another 40 years, the goals of the trade unions were more moderate, and both parties appeared to be at least reasonably sympathetic to minimal trade union demands. Britain's prosperity, though threatened by recession, was still great, and the barriers, in income and lifestyle, between the higher part of the working class and the lower part of the lower middle-class were more blurred than elsewhere. Britain notably lacked a leadership element of radical trades unionists and their sympathisers committed to socialism, while workers chiefly ignored those theorists of socialism, like Marx and Engels, resident in Britain.

Gladstone's first government was more fortunate in its foreign policy concerns than were most of its recent predecessors. Indeed, very little affected it here. The Franco-Prussian War, although leading in the long run to a European catastrophe, had few direct consequences for Britain, apart from increased military expenditure. One important result, however, was that in mid-1870 Gladstone's government forced both France and Germany to reaffirm the 1839 treaty guaranteeing Belgian neutrality. Germany's violation of the 1839 and 1870 accords over this issue was, of course, the chief direct reason for Britain entering the First World War in 1914. In 1871 Gladstone's government also secured two major international treaties recognising, first, the binding force of treaties and, second, and more specifically, freedom of navigation in the Black Sea and the Danube, the latter seen as a partial victory over Russia in circumstances in which the defeat and revolution of France by Prussia had removed a traditional ally of Britain. In 1872 Gladstone's government also resolved the long-standing dispute with the United States over the ship the *Alabama*, left over from the American Civil War. After arbitration, Britain agreed to pay over £3 million in compensation to the United States, a vast sum by the standards of the day but far less than many influential Americans demanded. The *Alabama* settlement is widely seen as a turning-point in Anglo-American affairs: both countries agreed to settle any future grievances by negotiation, and relations between the two countries became progressively closer, with profound implications for the course of twentieth-century history. Britain's record in foreign affairs during the 1868–74 period was, in fact, peaceful and amicable, and it fought only one war, a punitive expedition in early 1874 under Sir Garnet Wolseley against the King of the Ashantis, a warlike tribe in what is now Ghana. It had the full support of Gladstone's government.

Gladstone's first government was less successful in its closing year of office, 1873–74, than before. In March 1873, despite its large majority in Parliament, the government actually lost an important vote in the Commons, over the reform of the University of Dublin in the interests of Ireland's Catholics. Gladstone resigned, suggesting that Disraeli form a minority government. He refused, and Gladstone was back in office for another 11 months. The government lost an unusual number of by-elections, showed signs of increasing strain, and Gladstone called a general election in January 1874. Campaigning largely on a proposal to abolish income tax, he lost with a very considerable swing against him, and resigned as Prime Minister in mid-February 1874. (Moreover, he barely held on to his seat at Greenwich.)

Gladstone was 64 when he left office, and temporarily retired from political life (though not from Parliament) a year later. Few could have imagined that he would still be Prime Minister 20 years after his 1874 defeat. There is a general agreement that Gladstone's first government was the best of the four he headed, and one of the best of Victoria's reign. It certainly was relatively free from deep troubles, and very probably marked the apogee of mid-Victorian liberalism. Yet it is also possible to dissent from the normal view of the government's success (although not of its overall competence, which was considerable). With the possible exception of Irish Church disestablishment, it passed no epoch-making legislation, and the long-term legacy of that Act is highly equivocal. Gladstonian liberalism had, in fact, exhausted itself by 1874: there were no more major reforms, in the interest of retrenchment and *laissez-faire*, to be made, and increasingly the ideology, if not the leadership, of the Liberal party came to be dominated by proto-collectivists. Increasingly, too, Ireland jumped, and jumped again, like a jack out of the box into which Gladstone had tried to place it in 1869, each time in a more grotesque guise. Only in foreign policy was Gladstone's government as fully successful as some historians believe. Here, indeed, the conclusion of a lasting *rapprochement* with America, and the maintenance of international peace after 1871, were great achievements. It is difficult, however, to avoid the conclusion that Gladstone's first government was not the stunning success that many believe, but that it appears to be so because Gladstone's subsequent governments were notably less successful.

|11|

Disraeli's ascendancy, 1874–1880

In February 1874 when he became Prime Minister for the second time but for the first time with a working majority, Benjamin Disraeli had been an MP for 33 years, a first-ranking figure on the British political scene for 28 years, and leader of the Conservative party in the House of Commons in effect since 1849, 25 years earlier. There are really few parallels in modern British politics for a man becoming Prime Minister with authority so late in his career, Winston Churchill being the obvious exception, along with Sir Henry Campbell-Bannerman and Harold Macmillan. There are even fewer parallels with Disraeli's achievement of dominating the intellectual life and political dynamics of the Conservative party for so long: certainly none of these three later Prime Ministers, or anyone else, dominated a party's thinking and philosophy for a comparable length of time. To be sure, it was (and is) rather difficult to be precise about what that philosophy was. In opposition during the years of Gladstone's first government, Disraeli did clarify his position considerably, although he spoke, characteristically, in an oracular, even prophetic style. Disraeli's most famous expositions of his considered, mature philosophy were given in two public speeches he made in April and June 1872, at the Free Trade Hall in Manchester and at the Crystal Palace in south London. In these Disraeli foreshadowed the centrality of public health legislation and of 'social . . . improvement' and, for the first time, referred to the positive qualities of the British Empire. The British people 'are proud of belonging to an imperial country, and are resolved to maintain, if they can, their empire'. In this speech Disraeli also hinted at even more radical proposals involving the Empire, among them an imperial tariff, an Empire-wide 'representative council' in London, and a 'military code' binding the colonies to Britain in wartime. Each of these proposals was literally revolutionary, representing in large part the policies desired by Joseph Chamberlain and other conservative imperialists a generation later. The suggestion for an imperial tariff, made at the very height of the hegemony of free trade, must have seemed utterly fantastic to many of his listeners. With these speeches, Disraeli relaunched the Conservatives as the party of what recent historians have termed 'imperialism and social reform', a potent, heady, mesmerising package, implicitly if not explicitly strongly nationalistic, which paralleled in some respects the right-wing continental ideologies which arose at the same time, although of course without any of their unacceptable features such as authoritarianism, militarism, xenophobia or anti-Semitism. Disraeli also explicitly termed the Tories the 'national party', foreshadowing in his domestic social policies the 'One Nation' Toryism which dominated Conservative ideology until 1979, over a century later.[1]

As Gladstone's government seemed to run downhill after 1870, Disraeli also renewed his hold on the Conservative party leadership. His Manchester speech included a witty attack on the Liberal front bench as 'a range of exhausted volcanoes'. Despite poor health and personal sorrows – his brother and wife died at about the same time – Disraeli was now ready to seize the political initiative. Nevertheless, the decisive nature of the results in the 1874 general election came as a considerable surprise. Several reasons have been offered for the heavy swing to the Tories. In 1869 George J. Goschen, as an afterthought to the 1867 Reform Act, proposed and carried a bill which allowed urban ratepayers who 'compounded' for their rates (a 'compounder' was a householder whose rates were included in his rent, and paid by the landlord) automatically to register as voters. 'Compounders' tended to be poorer than other ratepayers, and many Conservative officials believed that they were heavily Tory, perhaps because they were more reliant on the goodwill of their landlords. Disraeli had also gone to great lengths to improve and modernise the Conservative party's machinery. In 1870 Disraeli appointed the highly competent Sir John Gorst MP as Chief Agent; Gorst in turn built up the Conservative Central Office and such organisations of the party faithful as the National Union of Conservative Associations. As a result, for the first time one of Britain's major parties acquired a party machinery fit for the new democratic age. Beginning in 1867 annual conferences of the Conservative party were held at rotating venues throughout England. They were normally presided over by a great aristocrat, and allowed middle-class Tory supporters to mix, however briefly, with the aristocracy and leading MPs. Conservative party officials found that there was an enormous untapped reservoir of 'popular Toryism'. In Lancashire and elsewhere this tended to be religiously based in Anglicanism and anti-Catholicism, and in the south it tended to be based in suburban 'villa Toryism'. Somewhat later, the Tories began to tap women as active political beings for the first time. The Primrose League (named for Disraeli's favourite flower), founded in 1883, although primarily intended for men, was arguably the first popular political organisation in Britain to

1 Disraeli also took the opportunity to publish, in 1870, one of his best novels, *Lothair*, which contains thinly disguised portraits of Cardinal Manning and other notable Victorians.

admit women on a large scale. While women could not, of course, vote in national elections until 1918, the Conservative party had already built up an enormous clientele of committed women activists who must have been enormously influential behind the scenes. In all of these activities the Conservatives were far ahead of the Liberals. For example, the Liberal party (strictly, the National Liberal Federation) did not begin to hold annual conferences until 1877, while it did not appoint a National Agent with responsibilities similar to Gorst's until 1886, when Francis Schnad-horst, a Nonconformist draper from Birmingham with close links to Joseph Chamberlain, was given the job.

All of these factors made for a considerable, even overwhelming, Conservative victory at the February 1874 general election, the first clear and decisive win for the Conservative party since 1841. The Conservatives won 352 seats, the Liberals only 242. An absolute novelty was introduced into this Parliament in the form of 58 (some sources state 59) members of a new party, the Home Rule party, which aimed at achieving a separate government in Ireland. At the time the party was led by Isaac Butt (1813–79) a Protestant who had been professor of political economy at Trinity College, Dublin; he then became a barrister. Originally a Conservative, he was converted to 'Home Rule' (he coined the term) in the 1870s. Butt was a moderate in terms of tactics and strategy, and in 1878 was displaced as leader of the Home Rulers by Charles Stewart Parnell (1846–91), the greatest figure of nineteenth-century Irish nationalism, whose role and importance will be discussed below. Disraeli's 1874 triumph was based on a near-total grip by the Conservative party on England's county seats, where the Tories won 145 compared with only 27 for the Liberals. The Tories made very considerable gains in English borough seats, nearly matching the Liberals' total of 144 by winning 143. The Liberals, however, held their customary lead in Wales (19:11) and Scotland (40:20). The Conservatives did especially well in Lancashire and Cheshire, winning 34 out of 46 seats. Another portent for the future lay in their success in middle-class London and its suburbs. This occurred most strikingly in the City of London itself, the commercial and financial centre of the Empire. The City, which elected four MPs, had seldom returned a Tory member. In 1865, for instance, all four City MPs were Liberals, receiving about 50 per cent more of the vote than their nearest Tory opponent. In 1868 the City did return one Conservative MP compared with three Liberals. In 1874, however, three of the four City members elected were Tories, and by the mid-1880s the City was overwhelmingly and permanently Conservative. Many other middle-class seats in London went the same route. For example, in 1865 Westminster had returned two Liberal MPs (one of whom was John Stuart Mill) by substantial majorities. In 1874 it returned two Tories by majorities of nearly three to one. The same thing happened in such seats as Middlesex and East Surrey.

This new source of strength for Conservatism highlighted a number of important underlying considerations about British politics as it emerged from the 1867 Reform Act. Increasingly, social class became the predictable basis of political loyalties, with the Tories emerging as the party of the middle classes and the Liberals as the party of the working classes. This simple pattern was, however, interwoven with a considerable regional dimension: the Tories almost always did well in the south of England, in many (but not all) rural areas, and in regions like Lancashire, the west of Scotland, and Northern Ireland where there was a popular, often implicitly or explicitly anti-Catholic Conservative tradition. The Liberals did well in most (but not all) industrial areas, in most urban slums and mining seats, in the 'Celtic fringe' generally, and in some remoter rural areas like Cornwall and northern Norfolk where the traditional class of Tory squires had been weak. It did well in almost all areas where Nonconformity was strong.

The underlying class and regional divisions which came permanently to dominate British politics in the late nineteenth century had important implications for the type of programme both parties could pursue, and the nature of the popular appeal both could make. We have seen that Disraeli wished to reorient his party, in its domestic policies, towards activist social reform in the interests of the Conservatives as the 'national party'. However imaginative Disraeli's aim was, however, it apparently conflicted with the party's increasingly central presence as the party of the middle classes and, eventually, of virtually the whole of the British 'Establishment'. The Liberals, however, were potentially torn for opposite reasons: overwhelmingly dominated at the leadership level by Whig aristocrats, *laissez-faire* businessmen and successful professionals, it had necessarily to offer an increasingly radical programme to appeal to its working-class clientele, a programme which came more and more to embody elements of collectivism and to threaten the redistribution of income and wealth. While both parties therefore were faced by very considerable potential difficulties in aligning ideology, leadership and voter support, by and large the Conservatives were able to do this more successfully than the Liberals, and have on the whole continued to do this in the twentieth century more successfully than Labour.

The 1874 general election was also the first for which real statistics exist of popular voting throughout Britain. These show that, despite the Tories' decisive win in parliamentary seats, the Liberals outpolled them in popular votes, gaining 690 135 votes to the Conservatives' 635 303 in England, Wales, and Scotland, or 52.1 per cent of all votes cast. These figures have to be used with great care, however. There were 122 uncontested seats, where only one candidate stood and therefore no actual vote was held. (This number was considerably less than in any previous general election: in 1859, for instance, there had been 240 uncontested seats.) Qualifications for voting were not uniform, either in different parts of the United Kingdom, or as between county and borough seats. In the counties, where the Tories were strongest, fewer men were entitled to vote. The population of seats in the House of Commons still varied enormously, with no attempt made, before 1885, to equalise them. Nevertheless, it will be seen that while the Conservatives managed the vagaries of the electoral system well in 1874, they still had some way to go before they could assume themselves to be the majority party.

Gladstone resigned as soon as the results were known, and the Queen sent for Disraeli on 17 February 1874. There is general agreement that his new government was abler than any of the previous Tory governments seen after Peel's day, and was probably now a match, in debating skills, for the Liberals. Disraeli appointed a Cabinet of 12, consisting of six peers and six members of the House of Commons. The most notable members of Disraeli's original Cabinet included both old and new men. His long-serving and reliable deputy, Sir Stafford Northcote, became Chancellor of the Exchequer; the fifteenth Earl of Derby (formerly known as Lord Stanley) was reappointed Foreign Minister, a position he held in the minority Tory Cabinet of 1866–68, and the third Marquess of Salisbury (Robert Gascoyne-Cecil, formerly known as Viscount Cranborne, 1830–1903) became Secretary of State for India; Salisbury (then Lord Cranborne) had briefly held this position in 1866–67. Perhaps as brilliant as Disraeli (or possibly more brilliant still), Salisbury was to become Prime Minister and hold the office for nearly 14 years, as well as the Foreign Ministry for nearly 13 years, often in tandem with the Prime Ministership. The most talented of the new appointees included Richard Assheton Cross (later Viscount Cross, 1823–1914), a banker and solicitor from Preston, Lancashire, as Home Secretary, and Gathorne Hardy (later Earl of Cranbrook, 1814–1906), of a wealthy family of ironmasters, as Secretary for War. In the course of his six years as Prime Minister Disraeli added other new faces to his Cabinet. Some, like Sir Michael Hicks-Beach, ninth Baronet (later Earl of St Aldwyn, 1837–1916), came from traditional Tory circles in the landed elite. (Hicks-Beach became Chief Secretary for Ireland in 1876.) Others, however, came from newer social groups previously associated with the Conservative party only rarely. In 1877 Disraeli appointed William Henry Smith (1825–91; his widow was created Viscountess Hambleden after his sudden death) to the Cabinet as Chief Lord of the Admiralty.[2] W. H. Smith was the proprietor of the renowned multiple newsagency which still bears his name, although at the time the firm chiefly consisted of newsagencies at railway stations (he held the monopoly of bookshops and newsagencies at England's stations) rather than of high street retail shops. A generation previously, Smith, by origin a Methodist who had entered his father's newsagency firm at 16, would

---

2 It was apparently Smith whom W. S. Gilbert had in mind when he wrote, in *HMS Pinafore* in 1878, of the First Lord of the Admiralty 'who polished up the handle so carefully/that now I am the ruler of the Queen's Navy'. These lines are often said to have prevented Gilbert from receiving a knighthood like his collaborator Sir Arthur Sullivan.

almost certainly have been a Liberal rather than a Tory, but now managed to enter the highest ranks of Conservative politics, serving as First Lord of the Admiralty with considerable distinction.

Most of the important social legislation associated with Disraeli's great government was passed in 1875, a year afer the government came to power, and is strongly associated with R. A. Cross, Disraeli's Home Secretary, who proved to be one of the very greatest holders of that office in history. Cross's legislation included two important Acts affecting trade unions, an Artisans' Dwellings Act, a Sale of Food and Drugs Act, and the Public Health Act 1875. Each of these was important in its own right, but collectively they marked Disraeli's 1874–80 government as one of the greatest of the century for social reforms, giving considerable substance to Disraeli's heralding in 1872 of a Tory-led new era which would go beyond the Liberal party's *laissez-faire*. There were also other notable, but less far-reaching, pieces of social legislation. The two Acts affecting trade unions, the Conspiracy and Protection of Property Act and the Employers and Workmen Act, legalised peaceful picketing and enshrined in law the principle (recommended by the Minority Report of the 1869 Royal Commission on Trade Unions) that, in a trade dispute, a combination of persons could do anything which was not illegal if committed by one person, and limited any penalty for breach of contract by unions to the payment of civil damages, rather than criminal penalties. This finally did away with the old Combination Acts which made strikes and collective bargaining illegal or virtually illegal in law, and in a sense began the modern age of labour–management relations.

Disraeli's Artisans' Dwellings Act made powers available in the areas of slum clearance and the rehousing of their inhabitants to all boroughs; these had previously been restricted to a few large cities. The Sale of Food and Drugs Act, though somewhat watered down, forbade the use in food or drugs of anything 'injurious to health', and was the first important piece of British legislation in this area; it was not substantially amended until 1928. The Public Health Act of 1875 brought together and consolidated all previous legislation in the public health field. Like the Sale of Food and Drugs Act, it remained the basis of British legislation in this area for many years, until 1937. One of the most important political effects of these Acts was the beginning of cooperation and liaison between the Tory government and local municipal reformers, especially Joseph Chamberlain (1836–1914). Chamberlain, at the time the great reforming Mayor of Birmingham, was an advanced radical whose policies of 'municipal socialism' (local government ownership or close regulation of utility companies, slum clearance, and the extensive provision of local amenities) was far in advance of anything seen in Britain before. Chamberlain, at the time a vocal anti-Tory and opponent of Disraeli, developed a close relationship with Cross and George Sclater-Booth (later Baron Basing, 1826–94), another reforming Tory in Disraeli's Cabinet as President of the Local

Government Board, which greatly facilitated Chamberlain's efforts. While no one could have foreseen it at the time, only a decade later Chamberlain would leave the Liberal party and eventually become one of the most powerful ministers in the Unionist cabinets of the period 1895–1903.[3]

There were, as well, a number of other important pieces of social legislation credited to Disraeli's government. These include a Rivers Pollution Act in 1876, one of the very earliest laws concerned with environmental pollution, an Education Act in 1876 (which compelled parents of children aged 5–10 to send their children to school, where this was not already done, and obliged local governments to pay the school fees of very poor pupils), and a Factory Act in 1878. Perhaps the most famous social legislation of this era related to merchant shipping, owing to the efforts by Samuel Plimsoll (1824–98), a Liberal MP, to address the scandalous conditions of overcrowded merchant ships. Plimsoll campaigned vigorously for reform, on one occasion, in July 1875, shaking his fists at Disraeli in the House of Commons. Despite the weight of the shipping lobby, the Conservative government acceded to Plimsoll's demands, enacting a Merchant Shipping Act in 1876 which required all merchant ships to be seaworthy and to have painted on their hulls the famous 'Plimsoll Line' to aid detection of unseaworthiness.

In all, this was a remarkable record, and marked a turning-point in British social history. Nevertheless, Disraeli's social reforms clearly did not herald the beginnings of 'Tory socialism' or of a Welfare State. Most of Disraeli's reforms were permissive in nature rather than mandatory, that is, they empowered a local government to carry out reforms or expenditures but did not require it.[4] For instance, by 1881 only 10 of the 87 English and Welsh towns which had been given increased powers by the Artisans' Dwellings Act of 1875 had actually used them. More broadly, Disraeli of course made no attempt to create a state social welfare system (such as Bismarck was in the process of instituting in Germany at this time, chiefly as a counterweight to the popularity of the German Socialist party), and it is virtually inconceivable that either a Tory or Liberal government could have enacted any such schemes for another generation. As noted, Disraeli had to balance his, for the time, advanced social legislation (as limited as it would be by the standards of a later generation) against the fact that, electorally, the Conservative party was drawing its support from the middle classes, often from former Liberals disturbed by the 'collectivist' programme of advanced radicals, with increasing and striking success. In other aspects, therefore, Disraeli's programme reflected the new sources of the

3 As will become clearer later, the Conservative party was officially known as the 'Unionist' (or 'Conservative and Unionist') Party (that is, favouring the union of Great Britain and Ireland and opposed to Irish Home Rule) from 1886 until the 1920s.

4 In the United Kingdom, all local units of government and their powers are 'creatures of Parliament', wholly created by Parliament and liable to be amended or changed by Parliament at any time.

Tories' electoral strength and was as financially orthodox as anything Gladstone might have introduced. In particular, Sir Stafford Northcote, Disraeli's Chancellor of the Exchequer (who had formerly been Gladstone's private secretary), produced extremely conservative and traditional budgets. His great innovation in the fiscal field was the creation of the so-called New Sinking Fund in 1875. This was a special fund, derived from taxation, to be held as a unit specifically to pay off the national debt, then £27 million. This was a constructive and innovative idea, much appreciated by Disraeli's supporters but derided by Gladstone. Its central difficulty was that the fund could be raided by the Chancellor of the Exchequer whenever he needed money and did not wish to raise taxes. The fund proved, in fact, to be irresistible even to Northcote, who plundered it in 1879 to pay for expenses arising from the Zulu war.

It is often noted that Disraeli's social reforms came during the first few years of his government, while the last few years were relatively barren. There are several reasons for this. Disraeli was, by the latter 1870s, old and ill, as were many of his key ministers. In August 1876 Disraeli went to the House of Lords when Queen Victoria created him Earl of Beaconsfield, chiefly so that his workload would be lessened. (Disraeli continued as Prime Minister in the House of Lords until he lost office in 1880. References by either contemporaries or later writers to 'Lord Beaconsfield' or 'Beaconsfieldism' mean Disraeli and his policies.[5]) From 1877, great difficulty was caused to the government's ability to conduct business in the House of Commons by the policy of deliberate obstruction of parliamentary business perfected by Charles Stewart Parnell MP, the young leader of the Irish Nationalists. Parnell and his allies attempted to prolong debate as long as possible, once keeping the House of Commons in session for 26 hours. Disraeli and his ministers were at a loss to know how to deal with these novel tactics, and were ineffective in suppressing them by novel parliamentary rules. Violence and turmoil in Ireland itself also escalated in the latter years of the Disraeli government.

If social reform comprised one half of Disraeli's programme, the other half was imperialism and an enhanced centrality for the Empire. He and his government were also busy in office on this front. In late 1875 Disraeli purchased the shares in the Suez Canal owned by the bankrupt Khedive (King) of Egypt for £4 million. The Suez Canal had been built in 1869, chiefly by French engineering, and the French owned many of its shares. For Britain, the Canal represented the shortest route to India, the 'jewel in the crown' of the British Empire, and obtaining a controlling interest in the Canal was widely seen to be in Britain's strategic interests. Disraeli himself masterminded the purchase in secret, with the direct assistance of Rothschild's Bank, and received the subsequent approval of the Cabinet and

---

5 Beaconsfield is a town in Buckinghamshire not far from Hughenden, Disraeli's country house. It has associations with Edmund Burke, the founder of modern Conservatism. Disraeli's wife had been created Viscountess Beaconsfield in her own right in 1868.

Parliament as a necessary measure to forestall the French government from controlling the main route to India. Ownership of the Canal was widely regarded as the prelude to British occupation of Egypt, and perhaps other areas in the Middle East, but Disraeli made no further moves in this region.

In 1876 Disraeli took another, symbolic step towards enhancing the centrality of the Empire for Britain when he enacted the Royal Titles Bill, officially making Queen Victoria the 'Empress of India'.[6] Several reasons were given for this step. It was argued that the illiterate peasant masses of India would respect and be loyal to a ruler who bore the title of 'Emperor', as the native ruler of India had in former centuries. Giving Queen Victoria the title of Empress would also make her equal in rank to the Emperors of Germany, Austria-Hungary, and Russia (as well as France, if the Napoleonic dynasty were ever restored), rather than a mere queen.[7] Clearly, too, changing the Queen's title would add much greater centrality to the Empire in British official and popular consciousness, and cement the position and status of India within the Empire.

Disraeli's proposal attracted a surprising amount of hostility. He had not informed either the Liberals or the Prince of Wales. Many liberals saw the new title as 'unBritish', continental or even 'Oriental' in its grandiosity, and with more than a hint of despotism. Disraeli's overt use of the Queen and her titles was also resented. Nevertheless, the Royal Titles Bill was enacted, and Britain and its overseas possessions officially became an Empire.

The Royal Titles Bill is also significant in the evolution which was occurring at this time both in the overseas Empire in the eyes of Britain and in the role of the Sovereign in the British Constitution. It is well-known that the predominant view in Britain of many of its colonies had been that they were 'millstones round the neck'. The tenor of much British policy towards the Empire prior to the 1870s was that, apart perhaps from India, colonies were embarrassing backwaters, largely acquired by Britain during the bad old days of the Navigation Acts, slavery, and the chartered companies. Colonies settled by Europeans, like the Canadian provinces, New Zealand and the Australian colonies, were gradually given local self-government. Under Disraeli, and especially subsequent to Disraeli, a fundamental shift occurred in perceptions of the Empire in British consciousness. The Empire came to be seen as the primary vehicle of British power and influence in the world, its boundaries to be extended as far as possible, Britain's 'civilizing mission' to go hand-in-hand with its economic hegemony in these lands. The boundaries of the Empire were also pushed back to prevent other great

6 By this Act the words 'Empress [or Emperor] of India' were inserted in the official title of the Sovereign. Britain's monarchs continued to hold this title until Indian independence in 1948. Thus, in official terms, the British Empire began in 1876 and ended in 1948.
7 The titles 'Kaiser' and 'Czar' both mean 'Caesar', i.e. Emperor. Wilhelm I became 'Kaiser' (that is, Emperor) of Germany when the German states were unified by Bismarck in 1871. Previously he had merely been King of Prussia.

European powers – Russia, France or Germany – from grabbing these territories and thus threatening Britain's existing interests. By the early part of the twentieth century one-quarter of the globe was coloured red on the world map, denoting British rule, and the overwhelming majority of thinking persons in Britain regarded this as profoundly good, a sign of Providence's regard for the British people. This change in thinking, though gradual, may be centrally linked to Disraeli and his policies of 'imperialism and social reform'. Disraeli's government actually annexed relatively few new areas to the Empire, but was largely responsible for a profound long-term alteration in the way the Empire was viewed, although in the short term several military disasters on the fringes of the Empire made these policies temporarily unpopular.

The Royal Titles Bill also affected the position of the Sovereign and the monarchy: again, this was a landmark along the way rather than a seminal change. Following the death of Prince Albert in 1861, Queen Victoria went into something like total retirement, declining to perform virtually any public function for many years. As a result, by the early 1870s the Queen was intensely unpopular in many quarters, and a small, but increasing, portion of the population was actually in favour of a republic. The serious illness of the Prince of Wales (later King Edward VII) in December 1872 is often seen as marking a turning-point in the popularity of the monarchy (the Prince had a severe case of enteric fever, and was near death for a week). From that point on – and rather mysteriously, as the Queen had hardly changed her reclusive ways – the Queen once again became enormously popular, a popularity which continued until her death in 1901 and has carried the British monarchy until the present time, buffeted by unpopularity only on rare occasions such as during the First World War and as a result of the royal scandals of the 1990s. The Royal Titles Bill gave Victoria, and her successors down to 1948, a new, official role as head of the Empire which in a sense has been continued since in the monarch's role as head of the Commonwealth. Throughout this period, the Queen still exercised very considerable influence behind the scenes with her Prime Ministers. She had very decided views on politics, beginning as a Whig-Liberal and ending as a clear Conservative. This was reflected in, and was closely influenced by, her relationship with Disraeli and Gladstone: as is well-known, she doted on Disraeli and came close to detesting Gladstone. Nevertheless, both parties and all political notables in late Victorian Britain cooperated in the apotheosis of the monarchy as an institution as it emerged from the 1870s onwards. Disraeli, however, was instrumental in facilitating and giving official form to this process.

During its latter phases, Disraeli's government was chiefly preoccupied with foreign affairs. The British fought several important colonial wars, in South Africa and in Afghanistan. Under Disraeli, it was British policy to facilitate the creation of a South African federation of the British colonies and Boer republics there. This was largely resisted by the Boers, but in 1877 the bankrupt Republic of Transvaal, threatened with physical destruction by the well-armed black kingdom of Zululand, acceded to Britain's request. Sir Bartle Frere (1815–84), well-regarded in a previous role of leadership in India, was sent by the British government as High Commissioner. Frere believed that the warlike Zulus were a standing menace to the white colonies and delivered an ultimatum to their King, making demands to which he knew they could not agree. A British army, led by Lord Chelmsford, invaded Zululand and was disastrously defeated in January 1879 at Isandhlwana, with over 800 British soldiers killed by the Zulus. (On the same day, the British defeated the Zulus at Rorke's Drift.) In June, in retaliation, the British under Chelmsford, now better armed and manned, destroyed the Zulu army at Ulundi. There was general agreement that the whole war was disastrously mishandled, chiefly because of bad advice and poor leadership in South Africa.[8] The Zulu war clearly produced a lasting legacy of bitterness among many blacks in South Africa. By removing the Zulu threat, it paradoxically also had the effect of emboldening the Boers, who regarded the British as invaders, into long-term hostility to English rule.

In Afghanistan, a protracted series of conflicts with the local leadership, aimed at preventing this area from falling into Russian hands, seemed to be working. In 1878–79 three British armies crossed through the Khyber Pass and expelled Shir Ali, the local ruler. The Afghans gave over control of their foreign and military powers to the British, by mid-1879 resident in Kabul. In the second half of the year, however, Afghan soldiers took their revenge by storming the British legation in Kabul, slaughtering everyone there. Although the British once more got the upper hand, their armies being led by Major-General Frederick Roberts (1832–1914, later Lord Roberts, the victorious general in the Boer War), the massacre at Kabul, coming only seven months after news of the slaughter at Isandhlwana reached Britain, caused a profound reaction, fully exploited by Gladstone, at Disraeli's 'forward' policy on the borders of the Empire.

Disraeli's most famous involvement in foreign affairs did not concern the Empire but the continuing dilemma of what to do about the declining Ottoman Empire, and the threats posed both to European stability and to Britain's interest by the rise of local nationalisms and by the involvement and rivalries of the great powers, especially Germany and Russia. The passions aroused in Britain by these events over a two-year period,

8 One casualty of this war was the Prince Imperial of France (the son of Napoleon III, who had abdicated in 1871 and died in 1873), a volunteer with the British forces, who was killed in the Zulu war. He was the Bonapartist pretender to the French throne; from the time of his death much less was heard in France about the possibilities of restoring the Bonaparte dynasty.

1877–79, were extraordinarily intense and had lasting political consequences. They are also very complex and can be summarised here only in a
superficial way.

By and large, it remained a settled component of Disraeli's foreign policy
to support the continuing survival of the Ottoman Empire and to resist any
attempts to weaken it, especially any which would advantage, in particular,
Russia, traditionally seen as the greatest threat in the region to Britain's
interests, or Germany or France. This had been the traditional policy of the
Conservative party and of conservative-minded Prime Ministers like Palmerston. The attitude of the Liberal party was more ambiguous, but in
general it was less sympathetic to Turkey and far more sensitive to the
rights of the Christian minorities still under Turkish rule (they would say
oppression) in Europe. In the mid-1870s there began a series of nationalist
uprisings against Turkish rule throughout the Balkans, especially in what is
now Romania, Bulgaria, Serbia and Bosnia, all of which at the time
remained under Turkish rule or had, at best, a semi-independent status.
Most European powers, especially Austria-Hungary and Russia, were
anxious to extend their own influence in the Balkans, the Austrians in order
to augment their territories and the Russians as part of a 'pan-Slavist'
instinct of support for the Orthodox communities of the region. Disraeli's
attitude was very lukewarm, seeing Russian expansionism as the primary
threat both to Britain and to the stability of the Balkans.

In May 1876 an uprising by nationalist guerrillas in Bulgaria was
suppressed by Turkish mercenary troops known as the Bashi-Bazoks with
savage brutality then virtually unknown in modern Europe. It was widely
estimated that 12 000 Bulgarians were murdered; there were, as well,
innumerable cases of torture, rape, arson and deliberate destruction.
Disraeli's information on these events was very poor and inaccurate, with
British officials in the area widely seen as biased towards Turkey in their
reports. As a result, Disraeli described the massacres as 'large[ly] inventions'.

The events in the Balkans, as unlikely as this might seem, sparked one of
the great political campaigns of late Victorian Britain. After his defeat in
1874, William E. Gladstone had temporarily withdrawn from political life,
writing pamphlets on religious questions. He was no longer leader of the
Liberal party, and there was no reason to suppose that he would ever re-
emerge as a political leader. From Gladstone's retirement in February 1875
until April 1880 the leader of the Liberals in the House of Commons was
Lord Hartington (later the eighth Duke of Devonshire), a talented and
enormously wealthy Whig aristocrat who was much more conservative
than Gladstone on most issues. Hartington might well have become Prime
Minister on several occasions; he is said to have refused the premiership
three times. In personal manner brusque and unpleasant, he compensated
for these qualities with an obvious competence. From 1868 until 1891 the
Liberal leader in the Lords (who might well himself have become Prime

Minister) was George Leveson-Gower, second Earl Granville (1815–91), Foreign Secretary in 1870–74 and 1880–85, who was a close relative of Hartington's, although in personality a much more pleasant and outgoing man.

Early in 1876 Gladstone turned his mind to the atrocities committed by the Turks in the Balkans, and in August 1876 produced a pamphlet, *The Bulgarian Horrors and the Question of the East*, which denounced the Turks in violent terms and Britain's policy hardly less violently. In a phrase which has entered the language, the pamphlet called upon the Turks to clear out of the Balkans 'bag and baggage'. It sold 40 000 copies within a few days, and marked the rather improbable beginnings of Gladstone's triumphant re-entry into political life. Gladstone began an energetic campaign of public agitation and speeches on behalf of the persecuted Christian minorities of the Balkans, a campaign that continued and escalated until the Liberals' return to office in 1880. Disraeli was more cynical. Fearing the anti-British intentions of Russian pan-Slavic expansionism, he described Gladstone's pamphlet as 'of all the Bulgarian horrors perhaps the greatest', and greeted Gladstone's agitation with sarcasm. Gladstone followed his pamphlet with a speaking tour of Liberal rallies which revivified him and his party. He succeeded in carrying with him most Liberal intellectuals, the Nonconformist working classes, and much of Scotland, all of whom were enthusiastic in their support of beleaguered Balkan Christianity and in their condemnation of the Turks. Much criticism now came to Disraeli, some of it with an unwontedly anti-Semitic flavour, the Prime Minister regularly depicted as a mysterious eastern Jew in league with the heathen Turks against the persecuted Christians.

The tide, however, now began to turn against Gladstone and in the government's favour. A conference in Constantinople was called in December 1876 to January 1877 to agree on an internationally backed programme of reforms. Lord Salisbury, then the Indian Secretary and subsequently Foreign Secretary (and, later, Prime Minister), represented Britain. Russia threatened war unless Turkey agreed to withdraw from much of the Balkans. The conference failed, and a war between Russia and Turkey began in April 1877, continuing until January 1878. At the war's outbreak, Britain declared itself to be neutral. Turkey proved to be no pushover, and, as it did 40 years later when Mustapha Kemal made his immortal name, produced surprisingly successful generals who managed to hold the Czarist forces at bay. In Britain, mainstream public opinion, led by Queen Victoria, now turned strongly and sharply against Russia, with every old fear of the central danger to British interests in the Middle East and India by Russian expansionism having strongly revived. In late 1877 and early 1878, Turkey suffered a series of defeats, and Constantinople itself appeared to be threatened. The government obtained an extra £6 million for military expenditure, and it appeared more than likely that Britain and Russia would go to war.

The anti-Russian war fever of this period produced a profound wave of national patriotism which nearly cancelled out Gladstone's Bulgarian agitation and the radical support for the Balkan Christians he had engendered. Virtually the whole of the British 'Establishment' was anti-Russian, and if war had indeed come at this stage it would have enjoyed 'Establishment' support. At the mass level, however, a new and powerful, but potentially sinister and dangerous, mood of mass xenophobia also emerged, known then and now as 'Jingoism' from the famous music-hall song which summarised the popular mood of the day ('We don't want to fight/But by Jingo if we do,/We've got the men, we've got the ships,/And we've got the money, too!'[9]).

Fortunately or not, no war occurred. A peace treaty, unacceptable to Britain, was signed between Russia and Turkey in March 1878. At the insistence of Austria, a European conference was also convened, to begin in Berlin in June 1878. In the meantime, Disraeli called up British reserves and brought Indian troops to the Mediterranean. Disraeli's preparations led to the resignation from his Cabinet of the Foreign Secretary, the sixteenth Earl of Derby (the son of Lord Derby the Prime Minister in three minority Protectionist governments), who now joined the Liberal party, thus severing a historical link between the Conservatives and the Stanleys, Earls of Derby. In his place Disraeli made Lord Salisbury Foreign Secretary, placing in the Foreign Office the scion of one of the oldest prominent aristocratic families and one of the most astute Foreign Secretaries Britain ever produced.

From mid-June to mid-July 1878 Disraeli (now Lord Beaconsfield, of course), Salisbury, and the British Ambassador in Berlin, Lord Odo Russell, represented Britain at the Congress of Berlin, the most famous and impressive gathering of European leaders since the Congress of Vienna 63 years earlier. Germany was represented by Bismarck; Russia by Prince Gotchakov. The Congress of Berlin proved to be one of the great British diplomatic triumphs of the century. Like many successful international conferences, most of its main decisions had been arranged beforehand. At the Congress of Berlin, the territory of the independent Slavic states in the Balkans, especially the 'Big Bulgaria' which had emerged by the Treaty of San Stefano earlier in 1878, was whittled back, with Turkey continuing to hold the territory in the south Balkans north of Greece. Turkey's independence, and Turkish control of Constantinople, were again guaranteed, and thus Russian penetration of the Balkans and the Middle East was checked. Britain gained control of Cyprus, an important strategic island close to the Levant and Egypt, control which was not relinquished until 1960. More dubiously Austria-Hungary was allowed to take Bosnia-Herzegovina in the north-western Balkans, a Slavic region with no traditional attachments to

9 Although the word 'Jingoism' was new, the term 'By jingo' is much older, dating from not later than the 1820s.

Austria. The acquisition of this region proved to be a most doubtful gain, adding large numbers of unwilling Slavs to Austria's polyglot empire. In 1914 Sarajevo, Bosnia's capital, was of course to be the place where the First World War began, caused by local nationalists. In 1878, however, all of this was far in the future; to contemporaries, it appeared that the spread of Germanic influence into the Balkans was fully justified as a counter-weight against Russia.

Disraeli and the other British delegates seemingly emerged from the Berlin conference with virtually everything they sought; it was one of the greatest triumphs in the history of British diplomacy. 'The old Jew – there is the man!' was Bismarck's famous tribute. Upon his return to cheering crowds in London, and ever the phrase-maker, Disraeli now coined one of his most memorable: he returned from Berlin bringing 'peace with honour'.[10] The Queen offered Disraeli a dukedom, which he declined, and the knighthood of the garter, which he accepted provided that (as she did) the Queen agreed to award the garter at the same time to Lord Salisbury. This was Disraeli's greatest hour, the capstone of probably the most remarkable career in nineteenth-century British politics.

There was, however, still Gladstone to contend with. Gladstone was even more hostile than before, describing the acquisition of Cyprus as an 'insane covenant'. (It was in direct response to this that Disraeli described Gladstone as 'a sophistical rhetorician inebriated with the exuberance of his own verbosity'.) Nevertheless, and undaunted, Gladstone now began perhaps the greatest of his popular political appeals, the famous Midlothian campaign, which greatly assisted him and the Liberal party to win the 1880 general election.

Shortly after Disraeli's triumph at Berlin, Gladstone began his campaign in earnest. In early 1879 he decided to stand at the next general election for Midlothian rather than Greenwich. (Midlothian is the county in Scotland where Edinburgh is situated.) Its electorate was based upon the narrower county franchise than were borough seats, containing only 3600 electors, who would, on average, be wealthier than those in the boroughs. The switch was thus a risky one, but was made easier by the fact that Gladstone's move there, and his Midlothian campaign, were masterminded by Archibald Primrose, fifth Earl of Rosebery (1847–1929), a young, talented Liberal magnate who retained considerable territorial influence in the Midlothian region; 15 years later, Rosebery briefly succeeded Gladstone as Prime Minister. In late 1879, after his adoption for Midlothian, Gladstone returned to the centre of political debate with a vengeance, delivering a dozen or more major speeches on the way to Edinburgh and in Scotland. He vociferously attacked 'Beaconsfieldism' (his term for Disraeli and his policies) as well as introducing an anti-plutocratic theme, stressing the

10 Almost exactly 60 years later, Neville Chamberlain, consciously echoing Disraeli, repeated the phrase upon his return from the Munich conference. His use of Disraeli's words were shortly to haunt him.

social responsibility of great wealth. Gladstone's speeches attracted crowds running into the tens of thousands. They reunified the Liberal party behind Gladstone as its inevitable leader. They also marked a political innovation, the first time a party leader offered national policies in a series of peripatetic local speeches. This innovation, in particular, was viewed with alarm by Queen Victoria and marked a further stage of deterioration in their relationship.

Gladstone's Midlothian campaign was an important factor, but not the only one, in securing victory for the Liberals at the 1880 general election. After Berlin, Disraeli and the other Conservative party leaders took far too much for granted, underestimating the force of Nonconformity which had been aroused by Gladstone. National expenditure rose, due to the war scare, and the national debt rose with it. The 1870s witnessed a chronic national recession, which was compounded in 1879 by the beginnings of an agricultural depression, and a decline in land values, that may have lasted until after the Second World War. The weather in 1879 was the worst of the century. Disraeli and his ministers were old and sick, and, after about 1876, lost much of their parliamentary touch. Nevertheless, the decisive results of the 1880 general election came as a great surprise to most observers. By-election losses during the time of the 1874–80 government had been limited. The Liberals won about 334 seats, the Conservatives only 238, 112 fewer than in 1874. But to the Liberals' total there normally had to be added another 50 seats won by Home Rulers in Ireland. The Liberals thus won one of their greatest-ever wins; indeed, except for that of 1906, their last real win in their own right and without the assistance of independent or semi-independent allies like the Irish Nationalists and Labour. Conversely, the Conservatives won fewer seats in the House of Commons than at any election between 1832 and 1906 (although alone, the Protectionist Tories won fewer seats at several elections after 1846). The Liberals were triumphant in every type of seat except the English counties, the bedrock of Tory support, where the Conservatives won 118 seats compared with the Liberals' 54. In Wales (28 Liberals to 2 Conservatives) and Scotland (53 Liberals to 7 Conservatives) the Liberal triumph was virtually complete, and in Wales the 1880 general election has come to be seen as 'the end of feudalism' and the beginnings of a Liberal, then Labour, Welsh political identity in which the traditional landed gentry and the Anglican Church played virtually no role. The number of uncontested seats continued to fall dramatically, to only 67, 55 fewer than in 1874. In terms of votes actually cast, the Liberal triumph was not so one-sided. The Liberals received 55.2 per cent of the vote, the Conservatives 44.8 per cent. The total number of votes cast (1 969 816) was 36 per cent higher than in 1874 (in part because so many fewer seats were uncontested). Ironically, the increase in the Conservative vote – from 690 732 to 881 566, or 27.6 per cent – was significant, although not as great as the increase in the Liberal vote (from 756 386 to 1 088 250, or 43.9 per cent). Disraeli resigned soon after (but not immediately after) the election returns were known, without meeting Parliament. He advised the Queen to send for Lord Hartington, who was officially the leader of the Liberal party in the House of Commons. This was not to be: there was no other possible choice to head the new government than Gladstone. He had decisively triumphed, at least in the short run.

12

Towards the Home Rule crisis, 1880–1886

While it now seems inevitable that Gladstone, Prime Minister in 1868–74, should have headed the government again in 1880, he was not the first choice of Queen Victoria, with whom the decision lay. The Queen asked Lord Hartington to form a government. Hartington was officially the leader of the Liberal party in the Commons. After an indifferent beginning as leader, he emerged in the latter 1870s as a vigorous and energetic opponent of the Tories. Gladstone, however, made it clear that he would not serve under either Hartington or Lord Granville, the Liberal leader in the House of Lords, and so, after much negotiation, he was given the commission to form the next government, kissing hands on 23 April 1880. Gladstone formed a very traditional Cabinet, consisting of six peers and seven Commoners. Radicals continued to be notable for their rarity. Joseph Chamberlain at the Board of Trade, made nationally prominent by his activities in Birmingham and his Presidency of the National Liberal Federation, and in Parliament only since 1876, John Bright at the Duchy of Lancaster, and perhaps W. E. Forster, given the key position of Chief Secretary for Ireland, were the sole representatives of the radical wing of the party. One oddity of the new Cabinet was that for over two years, from April 1880 until December 1882, Gladstone, now over 70, held both the posts of Prime Minister and Chancellor of the Exchequer.

The 1880 election continued, but did not alter, the sociological trends in the Liberal party which had begun in mid-century. The best-known study of the economic interests of nineteenth-century MPs concluded that 159 Liberals in the 1880 House of Commons (about 45 per cent of all members) were landowners, a percentage not wildly different from a generation before, and still the largest single economic interest among the Liberals. Nevertheless, the Liberal landowners were now outnumbered by businessmen and professionals, especially MPs with an interest in finance, and by lawyers. Rather peculiarly, the number of Liberal MPs engaged as cotton or other textile manufacturers numbered only 20. Only two were described in this study as 'working men's representatives'. On the Conservative side, no less than 158 (of 238 MPs), about 66 per cent, continued to be landowners or their close relatives, although the number of businessmen on the Tory side was also constantly rising. The House of Commons elected in 1880 was probably the last one in British history in which landowners and their relatives comprised a majority of members. The Liberal Unionist split of 1886 drove most landowners out of the Liberal party, while after about 1900 the Tory party became primarily a businessman's party with a strong, although decreasing, landed element.

The years between 1880 and 1886 were seminal in the evolution of modern British politics, and the six years between the formation of Gladstone's second government and the Liberal Unionist split were as eventful as any in nineteenth-century domestic political history, although strangely devoid of far-reaching legislation apart from the Third Reform Bill in 1884. To a remarkable extent, too, and with the obvious exception of Gladstone, the mid-Victorian stage of British politics was now cleared, and a younger generation came to take its place. Among those who entered centre-stage in this period were, besides Chamberlain, such men as Sir Henry Campbell-Bannerman, Sir Charles Dilke, Sir William V. Harcourt and Lord Rosebery on the Liberal side, and Arthur Balfour, Lord Randolph Churchill, Sir Michael Hicks-Beach and Lord Salisbury the Prime Minister on the Tory side. H. H. Asquith entered Parliament in 1886; David Lloyd George in 1890.

For all practical purposes one issue dominated British politics in this six-year period, leading to the most far-reaching changes in the political landscape. That issue was Ireland. During these years, Ireland was increasingly ungovernable, and the question of what to do about it became central to political debate. To curb Irish unrest the Conservatives, in their previous administration, had passed a Coercion Bill which the Liberals had pledged to repeal. Unfortunately, the central grievances of the mass of Irish peasant farmers remained, especially an inability to pay their rents. Tenant farmers who failed to pay their rents were often evicted (over 10 000 in 1880) and a great wave of hostility towards landlords and the English swept the Irish countryside. A secret group of rick-burners and intimidaters, known from their mythical leader as 'Captain Moonlight', held sway. In September 1880 a particularly severe Irish landlord, Lord Mountmorres, was murdered in County Galway. After the 1880 election, Charles Stewart Parnell became leader of the Irish Nationalist group in Parliament. Parnell was far more radical than his predecessor Isaac Butt, and quickly emerged as a legendary Irish folk-hero, despite his English Protestant origins, his education at Cambridge, and his youth (he was only 34 in 1880). Parnell's response to Irish tenant eviction was to organise a campaign against the evictor, isolating him 'as if he were a leper'. As it happened, the first tenant-evictor to be given this treatment was named Captain Boycott, and a new word, unknown before, entered the language. A prosecution against Parnell and other Irish Nationalist leaders failed. In early 1881 the Liberal government (despite Gladstone's personal opposition) attempted to pass, and eventually succeeded in passing, a Coercion Bill of its own which suspended *habeas corpus* in Ireland and gave greatly increased powers to the Chief Secretary for Ireland. It was during the parliamentary debate over this bill that the Irish Nationalist contingent perfected its deliberate tactics of delay, prevarication and obstruction which almost made it impossible to conduct the business of Parliament. These tactics had been used by Irish MPs before, but now, under Parnell's lead, they became a hallmark of the Nationalists. Owing to obstruction the House of Commons was forced to sit for 41 continuous hours from 31 January to 2 February 1881, until the Speaker ended the debate.

Gladstone further attempted to win the support of the Irish masses for his policies by introducing a wide-ranging Land Reform Act, giving Irish tenant farmers fixity of tenure and establishing a new type of land court. The government also attempted to strike a far-reaching deal with Parnell (then serving a six-month term of imprisonment), by which Parnell would end crime and lawlessness in exchange for legislation cancelling the arrears of rents owed by 100 000 Irish tenants to their landlords. A secret, highly irregular deal was struck between the government and Parnell and his main supporters, releasing them from prison in exchange for cooperation over Gladstone's Irish programme. (It was known as the Kilmainham Treaty, from the name of the gaol in which Parnell was being held.) In protest, Lord Cowper, Lord-Lieutenant of Ireland, resigned, and his place was taken by John, fifth Earl Spencer (1835–1910), a long-serving associate of Gladstone.[1] At the same time, W. E. Forster, the Chief Secretary for Ireland, and a Cabinet minister, resigned, his place taken (at ministerial rather than Cabinet level) by Lord Frederick Cavendish, Hartington's brother and a Gladstone protégé.

The dealings between Gladstone and Parnell, though understandable and even enlightened if they worked, nevertheless deeply disturbed Conservative and Whig opinion. Worse was to follow. On 6 May 1881, following the pageantry in Dublin associated with the arrival of Earl Spencer, a small group of Irish terrorists known as the 'Invincibles' assassinated T. H. Burke, the Irish permanent under-secretary, and Lord Frederick Cavendish in Phoenix Park, Dublin. Burke was the terrorists' target. Both were stabbed, however, Cavendish being killed solely because he attempted to protect Burke. The killings deeply shocked and affected the whole of British society, making further concessions impossible. Gladstone's irregular transactions with Parnell were widely condemned. Gladstone's position was not helped by the revelation that Parnell, in writing to Gladstone to agree to the so-called 'Kilmainham Treaty', had used a sentence, subsequently omitted

1 He was known as 'the Red Earl' from the colour of his beard, although many Tories described his politics in similar terms. He was a collateral ancestor of Diana, Princess of Wales.

from his accounts of his actions to the House of Commons, expressing his willingness 'to co-operate cordially for the future of the Liberal Party in forwarding Liberal measures and measures of general reform'. It seemed as if Gladstone and Parnell had come to a shabby and improper agreement in order to help the Liberal party's radical agenda and electoral prospects.

Parnell, however, was not a terrorist; he deplored the Phoenix Park murders, and believed himself to be a likely future target of extremist Nationalists. (He often carried a revolver in his coat when in London, to protect himself from an expected attack.) In 1882 massacres and murders continued in Ireland. The government took resolute action, and the situation gradually quieted down. Parnell remained a hero to the Irish people, perhaps the greatest of the nineteenth century. Gladstone's actions pleased few except in his own party, alienating most Whigs and many other conservative elements in the Liberal party, who became deeply suspicious of Gladstone's long-term aims, convinced that Gladstone, backed by radicals like Joseph Chamberlain, intended to drive the Whigs and their allies out of the party.

The government's task of dealing with the Irish question, and the obstructionism of Parnell and his party, meant that there were fewer pieces of social legislation than in previous governments, Liberal or Tory. This may also have reflected the increasing divisions within Liberal ranks between Whigs and moderates on one hand, and radicals, with an agenda of increasing state activism, on the other. The most important piece of social legislation passed by the 1880–85 government was the Married Women's Property Act of 1882, giving married women the same rights over their property as unmarried women, and ending the injustices which arose from the fact that, previously, their husbands became the legal owners of all property owned by women on their marriages. This was an important step on the road to women's emancipation, although it should be emphasised that votes for women were seldom yet seriously contemplated by anyone, while no effective national organisation campaigning for women's rights had yet been founded. In 1882, too, came the Settled Land Act, greatly facilitating the legal ability of landowners, or their trustees, to sell land held in settlement (that is, in a legal trust made between several generations of the same family, entered into specifically so that the estates of the families of the great landowners could not be broken up). This Act had the support of most Conservatives, and its actual effects were probably very limited in practice. Nevertheless, it helped to place landownership on the same legal basis as the ownership of other property. Increasingly at this time, land-ownership and the 'land monopoly' became the targets of many English radicals, who saw them, and the social privilege they engendered, as crying out for radical reform. Other important pieces of commercial legislation, in the spirit of that passed since the 1840s, were also carried by Gladstone's government, among them a Bankruptcy Act and a Patents Act. In 1881 flogging was abolished as a punishment in the army and navy.

The early 1880s were a time of great parliamentary and extra-parliamentary sensations, even apart from the Irish question, leading to a widespread sense that the *gravitas* and seriousness of mid-Victorian political debate was fast becoming a thing of the past, a victim of the mass politics introduced in 1867, with all its dangers of demagoguery. Probably the greatest sensation of all was caused by Charles Bradlaugh (1833–91), an avowed atheist (or 'freethinker') and a well-known advocate of birth control at a time when its support was illegal.[2] In 1880 Bradlaugh was elected as Radical Liberal MP for Northampton. As an atheist, he nevertheless insisted on affirming the parliamentary oath, which ended in 'so help me God'. The Speaker of the House, Sir Henry Brand, referred the matter to a select committee of the House, rather than (as it is agreed he should have done) allowing Bradlaugh to affirm the oath, with the understanding that, if challenged, a court might have found this practice illegal. The select committee decided, by a majority of one, that Bradlaugh could not affirm the oath. Whether or not to seat Bradlaugh now escalated into one of the greatest parliamentary *causes célèbres* of the late nineteenth century. Bradlaugh's supporters claimed that the voters of Northampton should be allowed to elect anyone they pleased, that the House of Commons had ceased to be exclusively Protestant in 1829 and exclusively Christian (with the seating of practising Jews) in 1858, that 'freethinkers' (for instance John Stuart Mill, to say nothing of eighteenth-century MPs of the 'Hell-Fire Club' type) had sat in the House before, and that Bradlaugh was actually being punished for his advanced views on birth control. Bradlaugh's opponents – the majority of the House – were unwilling to accept the seating of a man who was opposed to the very concept of religion, especially as he combined these views with a very visible rejection of conventional sexual morality. The opposition to Bradlaugh was chiefly led by the so-called 'Fourth Party', a ginger group of radical Tories who (it is often suggested) could not care less about religion, using this affair as a means of splitting the Liberal party and (in particular) as a stick with which to beat the Conservatives' leaden leadership in Parliament. The Bradlaugh affair did indeed split the Liberals in Parliament, with many Evangelical Anglicans, Nonconformists and Catholic Irish Nationalists being appalled by Bradlaugh's demonstrative atheism and amorality. Bradlaugh was subsequently re-elected, although narrowly, as an MP for Northampton at three subsequent by-elections, in April 1881, March 1882 and February 1884, each time being denied the right to affirm the oath. Finally, after the general election of November 1885, the again victorious Bradlaugh was allowed to

2 In 1876 Bradlaugh and Mrs Annie Besant (1847–1933), a freethinker and radical, later an early member of the Fabian Society, still later the founder of Theosophy, a late Victorian philosophical movement emphasising mysticism, and lastly an advocate of Indian nationalism, republished an out-of-print pamphlet advocating and giving instruction about birth control. Under the laws of the time, Bradlaugh was convicted and sentenced to six months' imprisonment and a £200 fine, but the sentence was overturned on appeal.

take his seat after affirming the oath, on the ruling of the new Speaker of the House, Arthur Wellesley Peel. In 1886 Bradlaugh was re-elected yet again; he died five years later. In Parliament (just as one might suppose) he made no mark and was virtually unknown.

Another great sensation of these years emerged from the Conservative party, and specifically from the 'Fourth Party' mentioned above. When Disraeli went to the House of Lords in 1876 he was replaced as Tory leader in the Commons by his long-serving associate Sir Stafford Northcote. Although an able man, Northcote was not a good choice as leader, especially after the serious defeat of the party at the 1880 general election. Almost as soon as Parliament met, a ginger group of young Conservative MPs, determined to bait and bash both the Liberal government and their own Tory leaders in the House, arose. This was the so-called 'Fourth Party', led by Lord Randolph Churchill (1849–94) and Sir Henry Drummond Wolff, and joined by Sir John Gorst and Arthur James Balfour.[3] Their chief target was Northcote, viewed by them as a remote, antediluvian leader unfitted for the new democratic age. Churchill dubbed Northcote 'the goat' and labelled him, together with W. H. Smith, whom they viewed in a similar light, as 'Marshall and Snellgrove', from the London department store: representatives of the philistine commercial classes rather than traditional Conservatives of the governing class.[4] Churchill, an extraordinary and colourful figure, now briefly emerged as one of the formative, but very wayward figures in the Conservative party as it was entering the democratic age. The son of the seventh Duke of Marlborough and married to Jenny Jerome, the daughter of an American Wall Street millionaire (and, of course, the father of Sir Winston Churchill), Churchill was widely regarded as quite brilliant but quite unstable – if not something even darker.[5] He became the advocate of what had become known as 'Tory democracy', urging the championing by the traditional landed aristocracy of the working classes in the interests of both. These ideas were earlier, and in an earlier form, strongly associated with Disraeli, and Churchill and the 'Fourth Party' continued to idolise Disraeli, in contrast to their treatment of Northcote. Churchill, however, wished to take Disraelian policy even further, in 1884 explicitly likening his policy proposals to those of Bismarck in Germany ('he is the biggest man in the world'), advocating 'State Socialism and Customs revenue' (i.e. tariff reform) and a larger navy.

3 The other three parties were the Liberals, Conservatives and Irish Nationalists. The term 'Fourth Party' was a misnomer, since this group always remained within the Conservative party. Balfour (1848–1930) served as Prime Minister in 1902–05.
4 Northcote was, in fact, an eighth baronet with large estates in Devonshire, whose family had been landowners longer than the Dukes of Marlborough. He had, however, once been head of the Hudson's Bay Company.
5 Churchill was widely believed to have contracted syphilis as a young man. There is still some doubt as to what caused his clearly irrational behaviour during the later stages of his career, killing him at the age of only 45. It is clear that his personal physician believed him to have been suffering from syphilis and treated him for the disease.

Churchill wished 'a large investment of public money and a large amount of state intervention for the benefit of the masses of the people', to be paid for by the reintroduction of tariffs, including a tariff on corn (wheat), i.e. the re-repeal of the Corn Laws.

Churchill and the 'Fourth Party' saw themselves as inheriting from Disraeli the 'Mantle of Elijah' (from the biblical reference, and appropriate in view of Disraeli's Hebraic origins): that is, of being his authentic successors and following in the path he had first beaten 35 years before. From his place in the House of Lords, Disraeli (now the Earl of Beaconsfield) watched Churchill and his associates semi-approvingly, but always urged caution in their attacks on Northcote, who represented (in Disraeli's words) 'the respectability of the party'. It is not clear how Disraeli would have reacted had he lived longer. In April 1881 he died at the age of 76, having lived long enough to become a prophet and a hero to a younger generation. Robert Gascoyne-Cecil, the third Marquess of Salisbury (1830–1903), now succeeded Disraeli as leader of the Conservatives in the Lords and as the probable Prime Minister when the Conservatives next formed a government.[6] Salisbury, educated at Eton and Oxford, in his youth a journalist, was a brilliant man, possibly more brilliant than Disraeli. Deeply pessimistic, he deplored all of the democratic and levelling trends of the late Victorian period. In contrast to the alliance of the traditional aristocracy and the working classes urged by Disraeli and Randolph Churchill, Salisbury viewed the Conservatives as the natural party of all moderate, property-owning and anti-radical forces, and did perhaps more than anyone else to bring the middle classes and the south of England 'Establishment' into the Conservative party as their natural home. A complete cynic, he used all the new means of mass democracy to assist the Conservative cause. Salisbury's long suit, however, was foreign policy. He had served as Foreign Secretary in 1878–80, and would combine the offices of Prime Minister and Foreign Minister for 12 of the 14 years he held the premiership. Salisbury proved as able a diplomat as Britain ever produced. He was a worthy descendant of his remote but direct ancestor Lord Burghley, Queen Elizabeth I's great minister.

It is not necessarily true that the various factions in the Conservative party at this time were at daggers drawn. As we have seen, the Tories were far more adept and enterprising than the Liberals in adapting to the new democratic politics of the post-1867 period. They remained so in the 1880s. In 1883 the Primrose League was founded, with Churchill and Wolff in the vanguard of its organisers. The League was named for Disraeli's favourite flower, and existed to promote 'the maintenance of religion, of the estates of the realm, and of the Imperial Ascendancy of Great Britain'. There was thus nothing especially radical (to say the least)

6 Northcote continued as leader of the Conservative Party in the House of Commons until the formation of the minority Conservative government in June 1885, when he was succeeded by Sir Michael Hicks-Beach.

about its principles. It was, furthermore, organised in an elaborate hierarchy of 'Habitations' and 'Lodges' somewhat similar to the Freemasons and other fraternal orders so important at the time. Unlike them, however, it admitted women and was probably the first national political body to use the energies and abilities of women on any scale, thus utilising a previously untapped source of human resources of almost unlimited potential. By 1891 it had one million members, an extraordinary number for a political organisation. Essentially, the Primrose League was the semi-official national political organisation of the Conservative party. It gave an official role to the upper middle classes, especially to upper-middle-class women. It also organised popular entertainments which typically mixed political propaganda with slide shows of scenes of the Empire, and stage acts. Members of the working classes, especially in rural areas, comprised much of its audience, although power always remained with the middle classes. Churchill and his associates also attempted to gain control of the National Union of the Conservative Party. Churchill became its chairman, but entered into a protracted conflict with Salisbury and the established leaders of the Conservative party, resolved in 1884 when an unwritten concord was reached between Salisbury and Churchill whereby Salisbury would become head of the next Conservative government, and Churchill (rather than Northcote or anyone else) his chief deputy in the House of Commons, a remarkable feat for a man of 36, even the son of a duke, who had previously held no ministerial office of any kind.[7] Salisbury's peace offer was far-sighted in the extreme: it brought harmony to the Conservative party (the 'Fourth Party' no longer functioned after 1884), gave Churchill the opportunity to show whether he was a genius or a charlatan, and allowed the party to concentrate successfully on improving still further their growing organisational base. In 1885 the Conservatives appointed Aretas Akers-Douglas (later first Viscount Chilston, 1851–1926) – a protégé of Northcote, not Churchill – as Chief Whip, and 'Captain' R. W. E. Middleton (the title was apparently spurious) as principal Conservative Party Agent. Both were spectacularly successful, indeed legendary, and did much to ensure the great Tory electoral triumphs in 1886, 1895 and 1900.[8] Middleton's contribution, the creation of a large number of professional and regional agents, was startlingly modern, linking the grassroots with the party's centre in a particularly efficient way. Despite the rifts created by the

7 Lord Randolph Churchill was also in bad odour with the Prince of Wales at this time, as a result of a famous Society scandal in 1876, known as the Aylesford affair, which also involved the Prince, Lord and Lady Aylesford, and Churchill's brother the Duke of Marlborough. At one stage, Churchill attempted to blackmail the Prince of Wales over indiscreet letters written by the Prince to Lady Aylesford. Churchill was socially ostracised, temporarily fleeing to America. The affair also saw the involvement of Disraeli (as Prime Minister), the Lord Chancellor, and Lord Hartington as would-be peacemakers.
8 Middleton's retirement in 1903 was followed by the crushing 1906 defeat of the Tories. (Of course there were other reasons.)

'Fourth Party', by 1886 the Conservatives were better placed than the Liberals to enter the new era of mass politics which was then emerging.

There were sensations on the right; there was also thunder on the left. Both within the Liberal party and on the extra-parliamentary left, the early 1880s were a seminal period in the emergence of the collectivist (indeed, sometimes frankly socialist) ideas, virtually unknown before, which came to dominate the mainstream British left a few decades later. Within the Liberal party these new ideas are strongly associated with Joseph Chamberlain and his radical associates in Parliament like Sir Charles Dilke. Much of the Radical Programme (as it was known) of this period represented a continuation of the traditional political agenda of nineteenth-century radicalism: an extension of the franchise to the rural poor, land reform in Ireland, 'retrenchment' in foreign and imperial policy, possible reform and democratisation of the House of Lords if it blocked radical legislation. ('Mend them or end them' was John Bright's famous cry about the Lords, voiced in 1884.[9]) As a minister (he was President of the Board of Trade in 1880–85) Chamberlain was constructive in a useful way, impatient of the delays and half-heartedness of his Whig colleagues. In 1883 he carried a Bankruptcy Bill, creating a special Bankruptcy Department and official receivers in the Department of Trade. At the same time he carried an important Patents Bill, bringing this area under the supervision of the Board of Trade, reducing fees for poorer inventors, and thus protecting intellectual property.[10] Chamberlain was less successful in piloting through a radical bill securing the rights of merchant seamen, despite backing from both Radicals and the 'Fourth Party' and his own emotional commitment to this legislation.

There was nothing in Chamberlain's actual parliamentary performance to frighten anyone: what put the fear of God into Whigs and Conservatives were his statements elsewhere. In March 1883 Chamberlain was attacked (in moderate terms) by Lord Salisbury. Chamberlain responded, within 24 hours, with one of the most famous radical speeches of late Victorian England: 'Lord Salisbury constitutes the spokesman of a class . . . who toil not neither do they spin . . .'.[11] The fortunes of Lord Salisbury and his class 'originated by grants . . . for services which courtiers rendered kings . . . and have since grown and increased while they slept by levying an increased share on that [which] all other men have done by toil and labour to add to the general wealth and prosperity of the country'. This paragraph froze landowners and the 'idle rich' in their tracks, signalling an onslaught by radical industrialists and the working classes against the landed interest,

---

9 He would doubtless have been surprised to learn that the House of Lords still existed, in essentially the same form, 110 years later.

10 Chamberlain, as a screw manufacturer in Birmingham, had personally suffered from the inadequacy of the patent laws.

11 This is, of course, a quote from Jesus, although in the New Testament it is made admiringly.

a re-establishment of the old anti-Corn Law alliance. Cleverly, Chamberlain did not attack business wealth or industrial enterprise; on the contrary, he specifically linked these with the toil of the workers. Coupled with his remarks in early 1885 about a 'ransom' which the rich would have to pay to 'enjoy' their wealth, Chamberlain caused a sensation and marked himself out as the leader of the Radicals. Two years later, in 1885, he (and his associates like John Morley and Jesse Collings, another Radical MP from Birmingham) enunciated the 'Radical Programme', designed without the approval of Gladstone. It contained (perhaps for the first time in the British mainstream) measures deliberately aimed at the redistribution of property, especially a higher rate of taxation on large landed estates, but also a rise in direct taxes on all incomes, the encouragement of local governments to undertake schemes of housing and local improvements, to be paid for by higher rates, and free elementary education. Further down the line Chamberlain envisioned the disestablishment of the Church of England, manhood (but not women's) suffrage, and the payment of MPs, enabling trade union representatives to sit in Parliament. 'Society owes a compensation to the poorer classes of this country, that it ought to recognise [and] pay', stated Chamberlain. The Radical Programme also hoped to win the large class of small tenant farmers and agricultural labourers, enfranchised for the first time in 1884, for the left, promising measures of land redistribution (described, in a well-known phrase, as 'three acres and a cow' by Jesse Collings).

Chamberlain's programme inspired genuine alarm among Britain's Conservative forces. Chamberlain himself, a Unitarian screw manufacturer who had served as a successful Mayor of Birmingham, seemed the very embodiment of British urban radicalism.[12] Nevertheless, he also inspired considerable hostility among many Radical Liberals, who were jealous of his meteoric rise and mistrusted his long-term intentions. For instance, he had been flirting with some form of 'tariff reform' (an imperial tariff throughout the Empire) as early as 1882, at a time when free trade was virtually an article of religious faith among all Radicals, and would remain so for another 50 years. Similarly, Chamberlain's attitude towards the Irish Nationalists and their ultimate aims had always been negative. As early as October 1881 he publicly opposed any break-up of the Union between Britain and Ireland, specifically comparing Ireland with the South in the American Civil War. Seemingly a straightforward radical, Chamberlain was

---

12 Contrary to popular belief, however, Chamberlain was not a 'self-made man'. His father, a successful wholesale boot and shoe manufacturer, left £250 000 when he died in 1874 (around £13 million in today's money and twice as much as Joseph Chamberlain left at his death in 1914). Joseph Chamberlain attended University College School, a well-known London public school (albeit a day school rather than a boarding school; Chamberlain's Unitarianism precluded him from attending Oxford or Cambridge). Moreover, Chamberlain was a Londoner who had nothing whatever to do with Birmingham until he was 18.

in fact an extremely complex man who did not fit easily into any mould, as will shortly be seen.

Beyond Chamberlain and the Radical arm of the Liberal party these years also saw the appearance of even more extreme forces on the left. In 1879 Henry George (1839–97), an American land reformer and lecturer, published *Progress and Poverty*. The book reached Britain about two years later, almost coincident with Chamberlain's assault on the landowners, popularised by George's year-long lecture tour there. For a generation this curious work was perhaps the most influential extreme left-wing text in the English-speaking world, certainly more influential than Marxism. George believed that landownership was the root of all evil and the enemy of all progress. Land alone was the source of 'unearned increment' (George's phrase), the only important commodity which increased in value through no effort of its owners, but either by the bounty of nature (farming land) or by the growth of population (urban land). Land was thus the ultimate monopoly. George's famous solution was a 'single tax' on land, sufficient to remove taxation from all other forms of industry and commerce. This eccentric theory swept the British left, unquestionably capturing the radical mood of the time. It may have had a greater appeal in Britain, where there were few industrial monopolies or plutocrats, than in America. On the other hand, the appearance of George's book coincided with the beginnings of a severe agricultural depression in Britain, one which saw the value of land decline, in contrast to George's predictions.

A few years later, in 1884, the Fabian Society was formed, the first association of intellectuals in Britain dedicated to bringing about the triumph of socialism.[13] Among its earliest members were Sidney Webb, George Bernard Shaw and Graham Wallas. During the next few years, other notable left-inclined writers including Annie Besant, Beatrice Potter (Sidney Webb's wife) and H. G. Wells joined. The Fabian Society eschewed revolution and steered clear of the mystical, proto-'New Age', quasi-religious doctrines often found among bohemians of advanced views. Instead, the Society put forth practical plans for the growth of British socialism from the existing structure of society, as in the famous *Fabian Essays* of 1889, based upon solid research into poverty and inequality. Many Fabians had a strong belief in efficiency, especially 'national efficiency', which made them seem close to right-wing nationalist Tories; they often had an elitist, almost dictatorial streak which in this century saw some Fabians, especially Beatrice and Sidney Webb, admire Stalinist Russia (Shaw admired Fascist Italy). Fabian socialism was thus also close in spirit – and has seemed to some historians to be a descendant of – Benthamite Utilitarianism, which also attempted to replace the irrationality of the British *ancien régime* with rationality, and also advocated a strong cen-

13 The Fabian Society was named for the Roman general Fabius who defeated Hannibal by gradual, patient tactics. The Fabians believed that socialism was inevitable and would triumph by 'permeation' of the intelligentsia.

tralised bureaucracy. But Fabianism was very different in many respects from the mainstream of British liberalism and radicalism with their opposition to state control and their mistrust of central direction. It did, however, provide a means for middle-class socialists to join and participate in the radical wing of the late Victorian Liberal party and later the Labour party, in which it proved to be enormously influential.

Other extreme left-wing groups came into existence around this time. In the early 1880s H. M. Hyndman, a wealthy Cambridge graduate and formerly a Tory, was converted to Marxism, founding, in 1881, the Democratic Federation, renamed in 1884 the Social Democratic Foundation. Like the Fabian Society it advocated socialism; unlike the Society it organised working-class rallies and demonstrations, especially two somewhat violent rallies of the unemployed in Trafalgar Square in February 1886 and a huge demonstration of 50 000 in Hyde Park in February 1887. William Morris, the artist and writer, was briefly a member of Hyndman's group; so, too, was John Burns, in 1905 to become the first working-class Cabinet minister. Hyndman himself was a British nationalist and even a racist, a surprisingly common position on the advanced left of the time, perhaps because the evolutionary component of social Darwinism was then so ubiquitous a feature of intellectual life.

Karl Marx himself, who lived in London between 1848 and his death in 1883, had little or no direct impact on the British left, although his influence on the continental left was already profound. His famous collaborator, Friedrich Engels, also lived in Manchester (where he was a successful industrialist) until his death in 1895. Most British people, including intellectuals, paid no attention to their existence. Charles Darwin, for instance, was sent a copy of *Das Kapital* by Marx (who believed himself to have discovered the laws of history of a very similar kind to Darwin's discoveries about the laws of the natural world). Darwin apparently never read more than three or four pages of Marx's book. The British left at this time, and indeed at all times, was hardly influenced by Marxism, in contrast to the European continent's very different traditions. Nor did Gladstone's 1880–85 government pay much attention at all to these developments, however frightened many were by the spectre of socialism. Gladstone's government passed only one piece of legislation relating to trade unions, the Employers' Liability Act of 1880, which gave workers a right to compensation for injuries caused by the negligence of their employers. The Act attracted little attention or opposition. In general, trade union membership stagnated in these years, under Henry Broadhurst's conservative leadership of the TUC.

The rise of a left-wing intelligentsia, however marginal, did spark something of a right-wing reaction. In 1884 Herbert Spencer (1820–1903), regarded by many at this time as the most influential social commentator and philosopher in Britain, published *The Man Versus the State*, a hymn of praise to *laissez-faire* capitalism, and alarmist in its conviction that individual liberty was being whittled away. At about the same time Lord Elcho (later the eleventh Earl of Wemyss, 1857–1937) founded the Liberty and Property Defence League, again convinced that confiscatory socialism was coming to Britain by leaps and bounds. While many on the right desired the maintenance of *laissez-faire*, others viewed *laissez-faire* as the problem, not the solution. In 1881 a National Fair Trade League was established, headed by the Tory MP for Preston, William Farrer Ecroyd, a Burnley worsted manufacturer. This body was apparently the first in over 30 years to advocate a British tariff; it advocated a reciprocal tariff in retaliation for tariffs placed by other countries on British exports. The previous 15 years had seen the United States and Germany forge ahead behind high tariff walls. Not surprisingly, some British intellectuals and politicians began to ask whether such policies might not be relevant to Britain's economic fortunes, already seen by some as in decline, and especially when linked with a tariff barrier around the British Empire. Such ideas were, however, still heresy; it took another 20 years for them to be openly advocated by a leading British politician.

The most important single piece of legislation passed by the Liberal government of 1880–85 was the Third Reform Act, the Reform Bill of 1884 (whose very important redistribution provisions were actually passed in 1885). A year before the 1884 bill became law, however, the government enacted an electoral measure of some importance, the Corrupt and Illegal Practices Act 1883, which was designed to crack down hard on illegal and semi-illegal practices and political corruption in electoral campaigns. Corrupt activities, including the overt bribing of electors, had been rife throughout British electoral history, although as the electorate expanded and ideologically based mass political parties emerged, naked corruption of the old kind became more difficult and more expensive. Throughout the nineteenth century, too, parliamentary constituencies had occasionally been disenfranchised entirely for gross electoral corruption. The chief aims of the 1853 Act were to lessen electoral expenses and increase penalties for corrupt practices. Stringent limits to the maximum electoral expenses which a candidate could incur, and to the number of electoral assistants who could be employed, became law, and very severe penalties were enacted for corrupt practices. For instance, candidates found guilty of such practices were excluded from holding any public offices for seven years, and were perpetually excluded from representing the constituency in which the offence occurred. As a result of the 1883 Act, electoral expenses reported by all parliamentary candidates declined drastically, from £1.8 million at the 1880 general election to only £773 000 by 1895. Successful petitions claiming bribery at parliamentary elections decreased even more drastically, from 22 in 1868 to zero by 1886. The 1883 Act was a powerful, if little-noticed, force in the growth of the modern party system. Since wealthy individual candidates could no longer use their money freely to win over the electorate, the party machine and ideological-based mass electoral appeals became more important, as did the activities of constituency agents. By and large, too, the act advantaged the poor at the expense of the rich, and the orthodox party man at the expense of the independent candidate.

The Third Reform Bill was enacted chiefly to remove the distinction between the borough and county franchises. In the boroughs, most working men had received the vote in 1867; in the counties, however, voting was on a much narrower franchise. There was, objectively, no reason why this distinction should exist, and the reforms made by the Gladstone government aroused less hostility than did either of the two Reform Acts. On the other hand, in 1867 the vote was conceded to urban working men and householders because they had allegedly proved themselves to be a stable force, increasingly property-owning, saving part of their earnings and joining friendly societies, while the agricultural labourers, who would be the chief group to benefit from the 1884 Act, were still too poor and too uneducated to be seen as a force for stability in the same way. For centuries the latter had (with periodical Captain Swing-like uprisings) done what the landlord and farmer had told them to do; but by the 1880s many advanced Liberals had great hopes of making them into a radical electoral force to displace the dominance of the aristocracy from the countryside.

That there would be some electoral reform was promised by all Liberal leaders during Disraeli's premiership. Gladstone, something of a conservative in these matters, was in no great hurry to enact a new reform bill, which was drawn up only after pressure by Radicals. Originally the 1884 bill had dealt only with the franchise, omitting any redistribution of parliamentary seats. This original bill passed through the House of Commons in April 1884 and indeed passed its third reading by a unanimous vote. The Act then went to the House of Lords, where the Tory majority, led by Lord Salisbury, insisted that the franchise reforms of the Act must be coupled with a wide-ranging redistribution of parliamentary seats. As in 1832, Radicals then began a campaign against the Lords, using such cries as 'the Peers Against the People'. Both Gladstone and the Conservative leadership were anxious to compromise, and a series of surprisingly friendly meetings in October and November 1885 between the leaders of the two parties produced a compromise Act which then passed through Parliament. The meetings between the leaders of the two parties was the first time in parliamentary history that government and opposition leaders had ever met to reach a private compromise about a controversial bill.

The Representation of the People Act 1884 had two distinct parts. It changed the basis of the franchise in Britain so that the householder and lodger franchise created for the English boroughs in 1867 was extended to the counties, and also created a new franchise for those occupying lands or tenements worth £10 or more a year. This component of the Act vastly increased the number of men entitled to vote. The best estimate is that the electorate in England and Wales grew from 2 618 000 in 1883 to 4 381 000 in 1886, an increase of 67 per cent. In the English and Welsh counties, the growth of the electorate was even sharper: from 967 000 to 2 538 000 in the same period, an increase of 163 per cent. In Scotland the electorate grew from 310 000 to 551 000 in the same period, an increase of 240 000 or 77 per cent. The effects of the Third Reform Act were most pronounced, however, in Ireland, where the electorate grew from 224 000 to 738 000, thus adding 514 000 men to the electoral roll and increasing the Irish electorate by 229 per cent. This vast new Irish electorate was (outside of Ulster) intensely loyal to Parnell and Irish Nationalism, while Ireland retained the same number of seats in the House of Commons (100) as before, far more than it was entitled to on the basis of its population. As a result of the 1884 Act, about two-thirds of the adult males in England and Wales were now entitled to vote, about three-fifths of Scotsmen and one-half of Irishmen. It must, however, be noted that this was still not universal suffrage: it is generally believed that as late as 1914–18 as many as 40 per cent of adult males could not vote (generally because they had moved in the recent past) while, of course, no women could vote in national elections, although some (as will be discussed) could vote in local elections.

As sweeping as the franchise clauses of the 1884 Reform Act were, it can be argued that they were less significant than its clauses which redistributed parliamentary seats. In effect, and with only limited exceptions, the United Kingdom was divided exclusively into single-member constituencies, with MPs no longer representing a town or community but a specific constituency (e.g. St Pancras North; Suffolk North-West) with its own local political geography. The great cities of Britain, especially London, now, for the first time, were given the number of MPs to which they were entitled on a population basis. The remaining very small borough seats were disenfranchised, and, again for the first time, all parliamentary seats became roughly equal in size (bearing in mind that Scotland and Ireland were deliberately overrepresented).

In England and Wales, no fewer than 79 boroughs disappeared and were merged into their counties, with 36 additional boroughs returning two members deprived of one seat. In return, the number of seats allotted to London was increased from 22 to no less than 62. Liverpool now returned nine MPs, Birmingham seven, Manchester six, Sheffield and Leeds four each. Each of their many seats was entirely separate from the others. Most crucially, as class boundaries solidified in Britain's cities and towns, distinctive class-based residency patterns emerged which became the recognisable basis of the electoral fortunes of each seat: South Kensington would return a Conservative to Parliament 99 per cent of the time, just as Whitechapel would always return a Liberal (later Labour) member. In a few seats, however, the old pattern, of the town as a whole voting for two (or three) MPs, still persisted. Twenty-five middle-sized cities, ranging in population from Bradford and Hull to Preston and Stockport, continued in this category.

This new arrangement was both proposed, and enthusiastically supported, by the Conservative party, which indeed would not have allowed the 1884 Reform Act to pass without its endorsement. The Tories saw the novel redistribution of seats as differentially assisting them in a variety of ways. In their view, it gave them a rock-solid base of support in the rural seats and, most significantly, in the middle-class seats of London and the provincial cities and their suburbs, now so much more numerous. By eliminating most small boroughs and two- and three-member towns, the Act weakened the Whigs, who were strongest either in the remaining smaller boroughs or in two-member constituencies where they were selected to 'balance' a Radical member. As Radicalism grew ever stronger in the Liberal ranks, and the electoral basis of Whiggery eroded, the reasoning of the Tories was that the Whigs would thus sooner or later join the Conservative party in great numbers: as events unfolded, it proved to be 'sooner' than 'later'. To be sure, most Conservatives would have preferred no change, and a Liberal party dominated solely by Radicals made it near-certain that a truly radical Liberal government would eventually be elected (as became the case in 1906). Furthermore, the newly enfranchised agricultural labourers might indeed show themselves to be extreme radicals rather than pliant creatures of the local landed elite. Nevertheless, on balance the Conservatives probably achieved as much from the 1884 Reform Act as did the Liberals, and the next 21 years were a time of Conservative electoral hegemony. For this to be achieved, however, a realignment of political forces was necessary and was achieved only two years later. It is also noteworthy that many Radicals, like Joseph Chamberlain, also opposed the system of single-member constituencies instituted in 1884, which eroded their dominance in the big cities by creating middle-class Tory enclaves.

As controversial as Gladstone's policies in the domestic sphere often were, the most contentious acts of the 1880–84 Liberal government were in foreign policy. Together with most Liberals, Gladstone was reluctant to embrace the concept of an expanding Empire. Unlike many Nonconformist radicals, Gladstone was not a pacifist or semi-pacifist, but he preferred to keep Britain out of foreign entanglements and did not properly understand the new spirit of large empires and power politics that had entered the European scene in the wake of Bismarck. Nevertheless, Gladstone's government became entangled in a series of colonial activities of the most controversial kind, in Egypt and in what is now the Sudan, south of Egypt. Britain and France had entered closely into Egyptian affairs, Britain following Disraeli's purchase of a major interest in the Suez Canal in 1875. In the early 1880s Egypt was still technically a part of the Ottoman Empire, although its ruler in the 1870s, the Khedive (Ismail Pasha), was in effect an independent ruler. Apart from its crucial geopolitical position and its unrivalled historical associations, Egypt was of interest to the British and other Europeans because of the size of its national debt (owed chiefly to wealthy British and European bond-holders, including Gladstone). In 1879 Britain and France, acting together, deposed Ismail Pasha, and put his son Tewfik Pasha on the throne. This act, plus the corruption and backwardness endemically surrounding the Egyptian government, produced a nationalist backlash, probably the first of importance in the Middle East, in the form of a revolt in 1881 led by Colonel Arabi Pasha. Arabi was a native Egyptian, unlike the Khedive (of Albanian Muslim ancestry), or the Turks, Circassians and Greeks who dominated Egyptian society at this time. In September 1881 the Khedive's palace was surrounded, and he was forced to concede a constitution. For the next eight months a very confused situation arose, in which France, due to internal political pressures, largely withdrew from the joint role it had been playing diplomatically in Egypt with Britain, leaving Britain as the dominant European force. In May 1882, however, Britain and France both sent fleets to Alexandria, the main Egyptian seaport, as a precaution against further nationalist violence. The following month, nationalist rioting, instigated by Arabi, broke out in Alexandria, and 50 Europeans were killed. The British naval commander, Admiral Frederick Beauchamp Seymour (later first Baron Alcester), received government permission to use force to keep order, while the French fleet was suddenly called back to France, giving Britain a free hand. An ultimatum to Arabi to desist from strengthening Egyptian fortifications went unanswered, and on 11 July Seymour bombarded Alexandria for ten hours. Gladstone, a bitter opponent of Disraeli's purchase of the Suez Canal shares six years before, now turned the super-imperialist, and decided on a full-scale military expedition to conquer Egypt. He enjoyed the support of most of the Cabinet, especially the younger Radicals Joseph Chamberlain and Sir Charles Dilke, already strong imperialists. John Bright, however, a Quaker and a pacifist, resigned the day after the bombardment. Bright never held office again, and four years later was a prominent member of the Liberal Unionist contingent which split with Gladstone over Irish Home Rule.

The expedition to conquer Egypt was headed by Sir Garnet Wolseley (1833–1913; later first Viscount Wolseley), an able and experienced commander who put in a sparkling performance, perhaps the most successful colonial military mission that Britain mounted during the nineteenth century. Assisted by the military reforms of the previous 12 years, Wolseley landed over 16 000 British troops in Egypt and destroyed Arabi and his forces at the Battle of Tel-el-Kebir on 13 September 1882, losing only 450 men. Cairo was taken and Egypt became a semi-official British Protectorate, effectively a part of the British Empire, remaining in the British sphere perhaps until Nasser's revolution of 1952. The other European powers were frozen out. A year later, in September 1883, Major Evelyn Baring (1841–1917; later first Baron and first Earl of Cromer), of the famous merchant banking family which had married into the Whig aristocracy, a financial member of the Council of the Viceroy of India, was made British Consul-General in Egypt, serving as its ruler in all but name until 1907. (Egypt still also retained a Khedive (King) until King Farouk and his son were deposed by Nagub and Nasser in the early 1950s; apart from a Consul-General, Britain also appointed a High Commissioner in Egypt, the first, from 1884–85, being Lord Northbrook, Evelyn Baring's uncle.) Gladstone was exultant at Britain's signal victory.[14]

The triumph in Egypt was, however, to be followed quickly by a long-remembered fiasco. South of Egypt was a vast area, the Sudan, nominally under Egyptian control but gripped by anarchy. In 1881 a former Egyptian government official in the Sudan proclaimed himself to be the Mahdi (Messiah), leading a revolt against Egyptian misrule in the area. (On hearing of the revolt, Gladstone proclaimed the Sudanese 'a people rightly struggling to be free'.) The Egyptian government responded to the revolt, in 1883, by sending an Indian army officer on the staff of the Khedive and stationed in Khartoum, General William Hicks ('Hicks Pasha', as he was known in Egypt), to destroy the Mahdi's territory in the remoter parts of the country. Unwisely Gladstone's Cabinet declined to oppose the move, despite strong advice from British officials on the spot that it was certain to fail. On 5 November 1883 Hicks Pasha and his forces were destroyed and killed. No one really knew what to do. Early in 1884 it was decided to send General Charles George Gordon (1833–85) to secure the British base at Suakim on the Red Sea. General Gordon was a remarkable man, the epitome of the Victorian soldier-Evangelical. He had won 33 battles during the Taiping Rebellion of the 1860s, and also had already a wide experience of fighting in the Sudan. A convinced, Bible-inspired Evangelical, he did much good work in England for the education of the poor and was renowned for his fearless incorruptibility. Upon reaching Egypt, Gordon was sent to Khartoum, where he miscalculated his campaign badly, attempting to commission a former slave-trader, Zobeir Pasha, to hold Khartoum while he chased the Mahdi. This plan was vetoed by the British government; the Mahdi made further strong gains; and Gordon was isolated in Khartoum. Plans were advanced in London to send an expedition to relieve Gordon, but the Cabinet, deeply immersed in passing the 1884 Reform Act, prevaricated unreasonably. Gladstone must bear the primary responsibility for what occurred.

In August, Wolseley was finally ordered to relieve Gordon. Wolseley was in England and mounting the expedition took time. His forces reached Cairo in September but took three months to make their way to Khartoum. They reached Khartoum on 28 January 1885, only to find that Gordon had been killed by the Mahdi two days earlier. Two things now ensued. In

---

14 Gladstone himself owned £41 000 worth of Egyptian bonds in 1881, a very large share of his private portfolio. With the success of his Egyptian campaign, Gladstone's stocks appreciated greatly. Recent historians have estimated that he earned £7500 alone (£375 000 in today's money) on one-third of these bonds in a few months.

Britain, a wave of popular hostility against Gladstone swept the country; a motion of censure against the government failed by only 14 votes. Secondly, very shortly after, before the British government could decide what to do, Britain suddenly came to the edge of war with Russia over an aggressive incident in Afghanistan. This sudden crisis (unlike the Sudan well-handled by the government so that a compromise became possible within a few months) made it impossible to pacify or retake the Sudan, an event delayed until 1898, when Sir Herbert Kitchener (1850–96; later first Baron and first Earl Kitchener of Khartoum), a major in Wolseley's Khartoum expedition, finally took the Sudan for Britain.

Meanwhile yet another domestic issue, the longest running sore of all, now surfaced again with a vengeance. This was, of course, Ireland, where a climax was about to be reached which would influence the shape of British politics for generations to come. In the early months of 1885, the Liberal government was losing its hold on power, weakened by the disaster at Khartoum, but still more by events in Ireland. Joseph Chamberlain, as President of the Local Government Board, entered into the Irish question by attempting to put forward a scheme of enhanced local government powers in Ireland. The Cabinet was bitterly divided on the scheme, in the end rejecting it. Chamberlain and Dilke offered their resignations when the government was defeated on 8 June 1885, on a vote amending the budget offered by Sir Michael Hicks-Beach, the Tory politician. Most Irish members and six Liberals voted with the Tories, while many Liberals abstained, defeating the government by a vote of 264 to 252.

The Irish Nationalists had sought an alliance with the Tories, and Parnell held extended discussions with Conservative leaders over measures of Irish reform. The Tories ultimately rejected any far-reaching plans but enjoyed considerable Irish goodwill and were certainly not, at this point, viewed as unalterably hostile to the Irish.

Although not strictly necessary, Gladstone took his defeat on 8 June 1885 as a vote of no confidence and resigned the next day. After protracted negotiations, on 23 June 1885 Lord Salisbury formed a minority Conservative government which lasted until 28 January 1886. Salisbury thus now became Prime Minister for the first time; in addition he also became Foreign Minister, his primary field of interest but an enormous burden.[15] The chief novelty of the new government was the spectacular emergence of Lord Randolph Churchill, who entered the Cabinet at the age of 36 as Secretary of State for India. Sir Michael Hicks-Beach became Chancellor of the Exchequer and leader of the Conservative party in the House of Commons, while Sir Stafford Northcote, the butt of so many 'Fourth Party' attacks, was ennobled as the Earl of Iddesleigh and given the extremely

15 As noted, Gladstone had combined first the premiership with the position of Chancellor of the Exchequer from the formation of his 1880 government until December 1882, when the burden simply proved too great and Hugh Childers was appointed to the Exchequer for the remainder of the Liberal government.

curious position of First Lord of the Treasury.[16] Most of the other Cabinet ministers were stalwarts of previous Conservative governments, although Sir Hardinge Giffard (1823–1921), a new appointment, was made Lord Chancellor as Lord Halsbury, and remained a fixture in extreme Tory legal circles for the rest of his long life. Lord Carnarvon was given the key post of Lord-Lieutenant of Ireland. The new Cabinet contained eight peers and eight members of the House of Commons, roughly the same number as in the past and suggesting little democratisation at the highest Tory levels.[17] The 'Fourth Party' was represented in the new government, but was anything but central. Arthur Balfour (Salisbury's nephew) became President of the Local Government Board but was not a Cabinet minister, while Sir John Gorst was made Solicitor-General.

The new Tory government was, of course, a minority one which still reflected the significant Conservative defeat in 1880: there had been no general election since then. It thus existed wholly on the sufferance of the Liberal and Irish members, and its very existence, given the substantial Liberal majority in the Commons, was somewhat mysterious. While a general election could have been postponed until 1887 (seven years after the previous one), it was more likely to be held if the minority Tory government was defeated, as it almost inevitably would be. The future of Salisbury's government depended in large part on its Irish policies, and here the Tories struggled to produce a viable policy. Traditionally, the Tories favoured taking a firm line over Ireland, deplored Irish nationalism, and had close links with the Anglo-Irish elite. Nevertheless, one of the most curious features of the short-lived Tory government of 1885 was that it flirted with the Irish Nationalists, abandoning its hardline policies and sponsoring a far-reaching land purchase scheme (Lord Ashbourne's Act), designed to create a genuine peasant proprietorship. Secret talks were held between Lord Carnarvon, the Irish Secretary, and Irish leaders, including Parnell. Nothing, however, came of these, although a surprising amount of good-will existed at this stage between Parnell and the Tories. It is well-known that Parnell would have preferred Home Rule to have come from the Tories, who could carry the House of Lords and the Anglo-Irish 'Establishment' with them rather than the Liberals.

The Irish question dominated Salisbury's minority government to such an extent that little else was accomplished. Late in 1886 Lord Randolph

16 British Prime Ministers are officially known by the title of 'Prime Minister and First Lord of the Treasury'. The two positions have occasionally been divided from each other (they were to be in the period 1895–1902, when Salisbury was Prime Minister and Arthur Balfour First Lord of the Treasury), but this was normally done only when the Prime Minister sat in the Lords and the First Lord of the Treasury in the Commons (constitutionally, the Commons initiates all money bills). In this case, however, Northcote was peculiarly given the position of First Lord of the Treasury but also sent to the House of Lords at the same time.

17 Moreover, of the eight MPs in the new Cabinet, seven were close relatives of peers or were baronets or knights. The only member of the Cabinet not from these categories was W. H. Smith, Secretary for War.

Churchill, the Indian Secretary, annexed Upper Burma (the northern two-thirds of today's Burma) for the Indian Empire. Upper Burma was an incompetently ruled independent kingdom which France had been eyeing from its possessions in Indo-China. The local King, Theebaw, had shown disturbing friendliness to France, entailing the confiscation of British property in order to transfer it to the French. The usual pattern of a British ultimatum (October 1885), followed by an expedition of 10 000 Indian army troops (November), and annexation (January 1886) followed. Upper Burma was largely Buddhist or animist in religion, and thus sat uneasily with the Hindus and Muslims of the subcontinent, developing separately and eventually achieving independence separately. Upper Burma was Britain's last substantial imperial acquisition on the Indian subcontinent.

In November 1885 Parliament was dissolved and a general election, the first after the Third Reform Act, held during the period 23 November to 19 December.[18] A number of important factors influenced the outcome of the election. Within the Liberal party, there was considerable bitterness and divisions from both wings of the party. On the left, Chamberlain stormed the country with his 'Radical' (or 'Unauthorised') Programme, appealing to the working classes and agricultural labourers. On the right of the party, Whigs and moderates like Hartington and Goschen were increasingly uneasy with the direction the party inevitably seemed to be taking. By and large Gladstone did his best to appease the Whigs, forcing Chamberlain to accede to only a minimal programme of reforms in the event the Liberals won the election (which was widely expected). Gladstone is also often accused of deliberately placing Ireland on the back-burner, and certainly of concealing the momentous change in his thinking on Ireland which became known soon after the election. While no one among the Liberal leadership either expected or hoped that the party would split, the ideological differences within their ranks were now becoming very difficult to conceal or paper over. The greatest surprise in the 1885 general election was, however, provided by Parnell and the Irish Nationalists, who pointedly endorsed the Conservatives. Two days before polling began Parnell told Irish electors in Great Britain to vote for the Conservatives.

The results of the 1885 general election were both surprising and indecisive. The creation of new urban middle-class seats, and the bitterness of many to Gladstone's handling of the General Gordon affair, together with Parnell's endorsement, led to gains for the Conservatives in Britain's urban areas, while Chamberlain's 'Unauthorised Programme', especially the campaign among agricultural labourers launched by his ally Jesse Collings for 'three acres and a cow', led to Liberal gains in the rural areas. In Great Britain there was, overall, a considerable Liberal victory, with the party winning 321 seats to 250 for the Conservatives, while Independent

18 The election was called when the formalities of the Reform Act, especially the compilation of new electoral rolls, was completed.

Liberals (4), Scottish Crofters (4), and Liberal-Labourites (5), won 13 more. Comparisons with the last election, in 1880, are difficult because of the Third Reform Act, but the Conservatives appeared to have won nine more seats in England than in 1880, two more in Wales, and one more in Scotland, while losing ten seats in Ireland. This seemingly clear-cut victory for the Liberals, however, was completely negated by the fact that Parnell and the Irish Nationalists won 86 MPs, exactly balancing the gap between the Tories and the Liberals. (Parnell's advice to Irishmen in Britain to vote Conservative is believed to have given 25–40 extra seats to the Tories.) Thus, while the Liberals still formed the largest single party in the new House of Commons, even with its smaller allies it did not constitute a majority of elected MPs, and was potentially very vulnerable. In terms of the popular vote, the results between the two parties were actually much closer, with the Liberals gaining 47.4 per cent of all 4.6 million votes cast (2 199 998), the Conservatives 43.5 per cent (2 020 927), and the Irish Nationalists 6.9 per cent (310 608).[19] In England itself, the Conservatives gained 47.5 per cent of the vote compared with 51.4 per cent for the Liberals.

As was often the case in those days, the Conservative minority government did not resign at once but met Parliament. On 28 January 1886 Salisbury's government was defeated on Collings's amendment proposing to give agricultural labourers 'three acres and a cow'.[20] The next day Salisbury resigned; on 1 February 1886 Gladstone formed his third government, which lasted until he resigned on 20 July 1886. In general, it closely resembled his previous government. Sir William V. Harcourt became Chancellor of the Exchequer, Gladstone not repeating his previous experiment of combining the two offices (although he was, curiously, also Lord Privy Seal). Lord Rosebery (Archibald Primrose, fifth Earl of Rosebery and first Earl of Midlothian, 1847–1929), the rising hope of the moderates within the party, although a loyal Gladstonian and only 38, became Foreign Secretary.[21] Another future Liberal Prime Minister, Sir Henry Campbell-Bannerman, entered the Cabinet for the first time as Secretary for War. Chamberlain was insultingly given the Local Government Board, one of the most junior Cabinet posts, albeit one where his constructive talents could be shown. Gladstone's relatively small Cabinet of 14 contained six peers and eight Commoners, about the same as in previous Liberal administrations. It was, however, notable for some very prominent omissions. John Bright, increasingly disaffected with Gladstone, was offered no post. Hartington and Goschen, even more disturbed by the tenor of Liberal

19 As always in nineteenth-century elections, popular vote totals are somewhat misleading because of plural voting and uncontested elections, although the number of uncontested seats in 1885, 39, was the lowest total of the century.

20 On the vote to bring down the minority Tory government, however, 18 Whig Liberals voted with the Conservatives, while no fewer than 76 Liberals abstained or were absent.

21 Rosebery had previously held Cabinet rank very briefly, in February–June 1885, as First Commissioner of Works.

policy and by the so-called 'Hawarden Kite', described below, also refused to serve. The lack of enthusiasm displayed by Hartington, regarded by many moderates as the Liberals' natural leader, rather than the aged Gladstone, was highly significant. Sir Henry James, the Liberals' most prominent barrister, pointedly declined the Lord Chancellorship. In February 1886 came another crushing blow for the success of the new Cabinet: Sir Charles Dilke, a Radical regarded as much more likely than Chamberlain to lead the Liberal party after Gladstone, was named as co-respondent in a particularly lurid and salacious divorce proceeding (*Crawford* v. *Crawford*), which effectively ended his promising career.[22] Nevertheless, Gladstone's government did begin with many advantages. In January 1886 Gladstone, aged 76, had already become a living legend, self-evidently the greatest active British politician. Involved in politics since just after the 1832 Reform Act, he was dubbed the 'Grand Old Man' (usually abbreviated as 'GOM') by Henry Labouchère in 1881, and remained, to millions of ordinary Britons, 'The People's William', the champion of democracy, progress and liberalism. And while Parnell made active overtures to the Tories, a Liberal-Irish alliance – one which would have enjoyed a huge parliamentary majority – was still more likely.

The next six months were, however, to be of decisive importance for the future of British politics. At some stage in the latter half of 1885 Gladstone became convinced that Home Rule for Ireland, along the lines demanded by Parnell and the extreme Irish party, was necessary to secure the future of relations between Britain and Ireland. No one really knows when, or why, Gladstone made this decision, which he most certainly did not announce in the 1885 election campaign. As noted, Gladstone was an old man in 1885, a national figure almost above politics, and little given to explaining in detail the numerous changes of policy which marked his career. In his defence, historians have suggested that Gladstone hoped that the Tories would be bold enough to grant Home Rule themselves, and that also he expected to win a large majority in the 1885 election which would itself naturally turn to Home Rule. On 17 December 1885 came the so-called 'Hawarden Kite' ('Hawarden' was Gladstone's country estate), a newspaper interview given by Gladstone's 32-year-old son Herbert to journalists from the *Leeds Mercury* in which it was stated that Gladstone had now decided on a policy of Home Rule. Historians have argued whether the 'Kite' was a deliberate ploy on Gladstone's part or an inadvertent leak by the press (the latter is more likely). As a result, however, the fat was in the fire. The 'Kite' made it possible for Parnell and the Irish party to withdraw

---

22 The divorce case included allegations that Dilke had had 'two girls' in bed with him simultaneously, and that Dilke had taught Mrs Crawford 'every French vice'. (In those days, 'France' and 'vice' were virtual synonyms.) The precise nature of this 'French vice' was left to the imagination. Rumours arose at the time, and have persisted ever since, that Dilke was the victim of a deliberate conspiracy, instituted either by Rosebery or Chamberlain, his arch-rivals for future advancement.

its support from the Tories and deliver it to Gladstone, thus making his third premiership possible. Politics reached an unusually confused state of flux, with, especially, schemes being mooted for Lord Hartington to form a right-wing Liberal government.

Gladstone, however, managed to form his government after all. It was dominated by the Home Rule question, which now took the centre stage of political life. From the previous November, Gladstone had composed elaborate schemes for a new constitutional framework for Ireland. He was centrally motivated by the fact that it was impossible to hold Ireland against its will, especially in the new democratic politics which emerged as a result of the 1884 Reform Act, and that a timely, far-reaching concession could still secure Irish loyalty for the Union and bring about a cessation to the violence which had plagued Irish life. Self-government had been progressively given to the white colonies without destroying their loyalty to the Crown – if anything, their loyalty to Britain grew – and there was no reason why Ireland should be different. Having conceded Irish Church disestablishment in 1869, as well as significant measures of land reform, there were no concessions which Britain could make apart from Home Rule; the alternative was continuing repression and coercion, which would obviously fail in the long run.

The Home Rule Bill drawn up by Gladstone was more moderate than one might imagine; it also had some curious features. An Irish Parliament was to be established, with the Westminster Parliament reserving all matters affecting the Crown, foreign policy and defence, customs and excise, and religious establishments. In exchange, Ireland was to lose all of its members in the Westminster Parliament unless a revision of the Home Rule Act was discussed. Peculiarly, the Irish Parliament, to meet at Dublin, was to consist of two 'orders' sitting and voting together, an elected lower order, and an appointed upper order, to include 28 Irish peers. This strange constitutional structure was designed to appease the conservative, pro-Union elements in Irish society. From taxes raised in Ireland, a portion was to be spent on defraying one-fifteenth of United Kingdom expenses on 'imperial' purposes, with the remainder to be used as the Dublin Parliament saw fit. Apart from the Home Rule Bill, Gladstone also drew up at the same time a major scheme to buy out all Irish landlords, entailing the expenditure of £120 million. It is not clear why Gladstone turned to such a far-reaching scheme of Home Rule at this time. Radicals like Chamberlain suspected that he did so to avoid introducing any of the measures in the Radical Programme. Gladstone's whole career, however, contained a series of sudden, dramatic lurches of this kind and he clearly believed that his scheme would permanently resolve the Irish question.

Gladstone's first Home Rule Bill produced one of the greatest sensations in the history of British politics, perhaps the greatest sensation between the 1832 Reform Act and the declaration of war in 1914. On 26 March 1886, when Gladstone made his proposals known to his Cabinet, Joseph Chamberlain and another leading radical, Sir George Otto Trevelyan, the Secretary for Scotland, resigned from the Cabinet, chiefly over the proposal to remove Irish MPs from Westminster. Chamberlain also specifically cited 'the security of the Empire' as a major reason for his resignation, claiming that Home Rule 'will lead in the long run to the absolute national independence of Ireland', causing Britain to 'sink to the rank of a third rate power'.

The Imperial and Great Power themes – that Home Rule would inevitably lead to the break-up of the United Kingdom and the decline of the British Empire – were indeed important ones in the litany of the anti-Home Rule forces, but not the most powerful. In late 1885 and early 1886 the most powerful component of the anti-Home Rule campaign emerged from the fertile brain of Lord Randolph Churchill; it was a factor so significant that it continues to this day to delineate the Irish question. Until this time, the province of Ulster, and of its largely Protestant population, played little or no role in debate on Ireland. It was Churchill who made Ulster central to the Home Rule question. For obscure reasons, Churchill decided that 'if the GOM [Gladstone] went for Home Rule, the Orange card would be the one to play'. He visited Ulster in February 1886, where he coined the famous phrase 'Ulster will fight, and Ulster will be right'. In March he coined the phrase 'the Unionist party' to describe all of the anti-Home Rule forces, including Liberals disaffected from Gladstone's policies. Churchill also did his best to woo the disaffected Liberals into an anti-Home Rule coalition.

Gladstone introduced the first Home Rule Bill on 8 April 1886 in a speech lasting over three hours, to scenes unprecedented in Commons history, with every seat in the Commons taken before noon, although Gladstone did not begin speaking until 4.30 p.m. A lengthy debate on the terms of the bill ensued for the next few weeks. Debate hardened, with Lord Salisbury declaring in the Lords that the Irish 'like the Hottentots' were 'incapable of self-government'. The General Assembly of the Presbyterian Church passed a strong resolution against the bill, and a Solemn League and Covenant for Ulster was drawn up to resist an Irish national government.[23] Proponents of the bill claimed that by removing all unreasonable grievances it would make Ireland loyal to the Union; opponents, that it would inevitably lead to an independent Irish republic. Gladstone made the point that Ulster was loyal because its Protestant inhabitants had nothing to complain about; remove the grievances of the Catholics, and they would be loyal, too. While the mainstream of Liberal opinion remained loyal to Gladstone, both Whigs and Radicals in the Liberal party made increasingly loud noises of discontent. In May, Lord Hartington

23 The original Solemn League and Covenant was an alliance made in 1643 between Scottish Presbyterians and the English Parliament. Another Ulster Covenant, signed by most of the Protestant inhabitants of Ulster, was composed in 1913 to resist the Home Rule Bill due to come into force in 1914.

appeared at a great London gathering to oppose the bill with Lord
Salisbury, the first time the leader of the Whigs joined forces with the
Tories. In the same month John Bright came out against the bill, claiming
that it would 'consign' Protestant Ireland 'to . . . the Irish party now sitting
in Parliament'. Actually to defeat the Home Rule Bill would, however, not
be easy. It would require 50 or more Liberal MPs to vote against the
measure. Mass parliamentary dissent over so important a bill had not
occurred since the Corn Law vote of 1846, and was far less likely to take
place as the machinery of mass democratic politics hardened.

In the end, at 1 a.m. on 8 June 1886, 93 Liberals voted with the
Conservatives to defeat the second reading of the bill, 343 to 313.
Gladstone decided the same morning to call a general election, fought with
unusual vehemence.[24] Historians have long debated who were the anti-
Home Rule Liberals – who quickly, and permanently, became known as
Liberal Unionists. One can point to four types of men likely to desert
Gladstone. First and foremost were the Whigs – that is, the old landed
aristocrats who had led the party from before the time of the 1832 Reform
Act. With few exceptions, most now left the Liberal party; most soon
became Conservatives. This represented a continuation of a long-term
trend. In 1884 John Bateman's *Great Landowners of Great Britain and
Ireland* listed all of the largest landowners (2000 + acres) in Britain,
together with their clubs. At the time, and even before the Home Rule Bill,
856 belonged to London clubs affiliated with the Conservative party, 348
to Liberal clubs, a 71:29 per cent majority for the Tories. In 1880 there
were 159 landowners among the Liberal MPs; in 1885, 92; in 1886, 59; in
1900 only 30. A year after the Home Rule vote, in 1887, Liberals in the
House of Lords numbered only 63 out of 501 peers who declared their
political allegiances. While all Liberal governments until the First World
War continued to contain a significant number of great landowners and
aristocrats and their close relatives (up to nine out of 20 members of
Asquith's Cabinet, formed in April 1908, could be so described), the great
majority of the traditional landed aristocracy were henceforth firmly Tory.
In particular, the Whig aristocracy – very rich and powerful, but consistent
reformers, even radicals – now disappeared in a full-hearted way.

Secondly, an important component of the Liberal Unionist rebels consisted of financial and commercial magnates, often millionaires, associated
with the City of London. George Joachim Goschen (1831–1907; later first
Viscount Goschen), a wealthy, articulate City banker of German descent,
and a major figure in Gladstone's first government (but disaffected and out
of office after 1874), was typical of this type of Liberal Unionist. To a
significant extent, the Liberal Unionist split marked the movement of

24 It was during the election campaign that Randolph Churchill memorably described
   Gladstone as 'an old man in a hurry'.

commercial and financial wealth, especially in the City of London, from the Liberal to the Conservative party, its natural home ever since.

A third element among the Liberal Unionists consisted of Liberal MPs from Scotland, and other areas of high Presbyterian, pro-Ulster sentiment. For a generation, Liberal Unionism brought a vanguard of Scottish MPs in seats which might otherwise be Liberal into an alliance with the Conservatives. For example, at the 1895 general election Scotland returned 39 Liberal MPs, 17 Tories, and 14 Liberal Unionists, who by then were full supporters of the Conservatives.

The fourth major element in Liberal Unionism was the most unexpected, namely Joseph Chamberlain and his group of anti-Home Rule Radical MPs. A small group of eight or ten consisted of Chamberlain's close personal followers (including John Bright and Jesse Collings) in Birmingham, personally loyal to Chamberlain himself. A larger group, another 35 or so MPs who had voted against Home Rule, were seen as Radicals without necessarily being part of Chamberlain's band of followers. Some looked to a large British Empire and deplored Gladstone's measure as likely to lead to Irish independence; others were Nonconformists who were uneasy with a Catholic-dominated Ireland. Many of these wished quickly to reunify the Liberal party and never envisioned themselves as permanently leaving the Liberal ranks. For the Whigs, City magnates, and Chamberlain and his followers, however, the break was to prove permanent.

The Liberal Unionist split was one of the great turning-points in modern British politics. Its most important consequence was to begin the process by which all elements of the British 'Establishment' were to be found in the ranks of the Conservative party, especially the London-based south of England upper middle classes and, of course, the landed aristocracy. This process of reunification reversed the 'unnatural' situation which had existed since 1832, of a left-of-centre Liberal party led by aristocrats and consisting in significant part of wealthy, well-established businessmen. As we shall see, the split gave the Conservative party and its allies electoral dominance for 20 years, and provided many of the foundations of the Conservative party's electoral hegemony throughout most of the twentieth century. It also speeded up the process by which the Liberals moved to the left, embracing the collectivist 'New Liberalism' and pioneering the Welfare State after 1906, although the Liberal party arguably never moved as far to the left as Radicals hoped and Conservatives feared. Finally, it delayed a solution to the Irish question, and helped to create a self-conscious separate national identity in Ulster whose consequences, to this day, remain both important and unresolved.

|13|

The era of Lord Salisbury, 1886–1895

After his defeat over the Home Rule Bill Gladstone dissolved Parliament and called a general election. This was held in July 1886, that is, only seven months after the 1885 general election.[1] The election was, in effect, a referendum on Gladstone's Irish policies, a referendum he lost, although perhaps not decisively. (It was during the election campaign that John Bright, a talented phrase-maker to the end and now a Liberal Unionist follower of Chamberlain, coined the phrase 'Home Rule is Rome rule', and latent anti-Catholicism, never far from the surface in Victorian Britain, played a major role in the campaign.) In a House of Commons of 670 members, the Conservatives elected 316 MPs, just under a majority in their own right. However, the number of Liberal MPs elected decined precipitously, from 334 in 1885 to only 190 in 1886. In their place, a substantial bloc of 79 Liberal Unionist MPs was elected, as well as the usual contingent of 85 Irish Nationalists. The Conservatives were predominant in England, winning 277 seats to only 123 for the Liberals, 55 Liberal Unionists, and one Irish Nationalist.[2] In Scotland, the Liberals won 43 seats (down 15 from the previous election), the Tories 10 and the Liberal Unionists 17. Only in Wales did Liberalism remain triumphant, with 24 Liberal MPs, six Tories and four Liberal Unionists. In Ireland, apart from the Nationalist contingent, 15 Tories and one Liberal Unionist were elected, chiefly from Northern Irish seats. The eight university seats (as usual) represented a virtual clean sweep for the Tories, returning eight Conservatives and one Liberal Unionist. In terms of popular votes, there was a clear, perhaps dramatic swing to the Conservatives and Liberal Unionists, who together

---

1 This period of seven months between two general elections was the shortest in modern history. Other brief intervals between general elections include April 1831–December 1832; January–December 1910; December 1923–October 1924; and February–October 1974.
2 The Irish Nationalist MP strangely elected for an English seat was T. P. O'Connor, elected for a heavily Irish district of Liverpool (bizarrely named Liverpool-Scotland) at every election between 1885 and 1924, and not retiring until 1929, after Irish independence.

polled 51.4 per cent of the vote (1 521 000 votes cast out of 2 974 000), compared with 1 354 000 (45.0 per cent) for the Liberals, and 3.5 per cent for the Irish Nationalists. These figures, if anything, understate the Tory share of the vote, for no fewer than 118 Conservatives and Liberal Unionists (105 in England alone) were elected unopposed, compared with only 40 Liberals (and 66 Irish Nationalists). Since candidates were likely to be unopposed only in very safe seats, it is likely that, had they been opposed, they would have been elected by substantial majorities, increasing the Tory share of the vote. Because of the large number of unopposed returns, as well as the fact that the party machines were forced to fight an election less than a year after the previous one, and with no advance warning, turnout declined significantly, from 81 per cent of eligible voters in 1885 to 74 per cent in 1886, the lowest percentage of the electorate at any election between 1885 and the First World War. Some of these, too, may well have been normal Liberal voters who abstained on what was in effect a referendum on Irish Home Rule.

The course of the next Parliament would thus depend greatly on what the Liberal Unionists would do and how they defined themselves. If they were simply a group of normally loyal Liberals who objected to Glad-stone's misguided Irish proposals, then reunion was possible, indeed likely, and the combined total of Liberal and Liberal Unionist MPs would make any Tory government insecure, especially as the Irish Nationalist bloc would almost certainly favour the Liberals. If, however, the drift of the Liberal Unionists away from Gladstonian Liberalism represented some-thing more fundamental and permanent, then the Tories would have no trouble conducting a government for the life of that Parliament. Indeed, if the Liberal Unionist split actually represented a kind of Peelite rupture in reverse, permanently moving substantial numbers of former Liberals to the more right-wing party, then a profound political earthquake had just occurred, giving the Conservatives something like normal majority status which they had not enjoyed since 1832. This question was also com-pounded by the fact that the Liberal Unionists were themselves divided into factions ostensibly having little in common, with the Chamberlainite radicals being on the far left of politics and very unlikely candidates for permanent alliance with the Tories. At the 1886 general election the Whig and radical wings of the Liberal Unionist group established separate election organisations, the Liberal Unionist Association under Lord Har-tington, and the Radical Unionist Committee (later renamed the National Radical Union) under Chamberlain. The two groups agreed not to oppose each other at the poll and, more significantly, reached an electoral pact with the Conservatives under which the 79 Liberal Unionists elected in 1886 had been unopposed by Conservative candidates.

The one certain outcome of the 1886 election was that the number of MPs who opposed Home Rule totalled 395, the supporters of Home Rule only 275. Gladstone was thus forced to resign, which he did on 20 July

1886, and Lord Salisbury became Prime Minister for the second time. Salisbury first offered the premiership to Lord Hartington, the leader of the Whigs, who declined chiefly on the grounds that Chamberlain was not invited to join the Cabinet at the same time. (Salisbury does not appear to have been especially anxious, at that stage, to see either man as his Cabinet colleague.) Most of his ministers were familiar ones. Sir Stafford Northcote, now the Earl of Iddesleigh, initially became Foreign Minister, Lord Cross (formerly Sir Richard Cross) took the Indian Office, while the key post of Chief Secretary for Ireland went to Sir Michael Hicks-Beach. The most sensational appointment was that of Chancellor of the Exchequer, given unexpectedly to Lord Randolph Churchill, who now reached the zenith of his influence. Churchill also became Leader of the House of Commons, and was widely assumed to be on the high road to the premiership. The Home Office was given, also unexpectedly, to the Roman Catholic QC Henry Matthews (1826–1913; later first Viscount Llandaff), an ally (though not a Liberal Unionist) of Chamberlain from Birmingham. Matthews was the first Roman Catholic ever to hold one of the very senior Cabinet positions in modern times, which helped to deter criticism that the new government was anti-Catholic. Newcomers to Cabinet rank were few, the most notable being the long-serving Tory stalwart Henry Chaplin (1840–1923; later first Viscount Chaplin) as President of the Board of Agriculture. Very notably, the new Cabinet initially contained no Whigs or Liberal Unionists, and looked very much like any other Tory Cabinet, containing seven peers and seven Commoners (five of whom were either baronets or the sons of peers).[3]

Rather unexpectedly, most public attention during the first year of the new government focused not on Ireland but on Lord Randolph Churchill's performance as Chancellor of the Exchequer. By 1886, Churchill, still only 36, was showing signs of unpredictable behaviour and was heavily in debt. Unquestionably brilliant, he was also unstable and demonstrated a continuing nervous, restless energy. At first Churchill proved a successful Chancellor of the Exchequer, though he was also a very unorthodox one, and appeared to be entrenched in his office. In his first budget, Churchill initially produced a radical set of proposals, reducing the standard rate of the income tax from 8d in the pound to 5d, cutting military expenses, raising death and succession duties and luxury taxes, and increasing local government expenses. These changes, of the kind that a fairly radical Liberal Chancellor might produce, aroused considerable Cabinet hostility. Churchill also picked a series of incessant quarrels with other members of the Cabinet, especially Lord Iddesleigh, the Foreign Minister, concerning

3 One curious Cabinet survival from the formative years of the modern Conservative party was Lord John Manners (1818–1906; he became the seventh Duke of Rutland in 1888), Disraeli's old protégé from the days of the 'Young England' movement in the 1840s, who served as Chancellor of the Duchy of Lancaster throughout the entire 1886–92 government.

British policy in the Balkans, and W. H. Smith, the Secretary for War, both of whom he had long detested. Matters came to a sudden and surprising head at the end of 1886. Churchill's proposals for the budget included a clear reduction of £1.3 million in military expenditure. The navy minister reluctantly acceded to them, but W. H. Smith, on behalf of the army, adamantly refused to do so. On 20 December 1886 Churchill wrote a letter to Lord Salisbury making it clear that he would resign unless Smith gave way. Salisbury had grown weary of Churchill, and was glad to get rid of him, while Churchill had told only a few confidants of his letter, and had not rallied support among his potential allies like Hicks-Beach. As a result, Salisbury accepted Churchill's resignation on 22 December 1886. It seems clear, however, that Churchill issued only a threat to resign in his letter. On receiving Salisbury's letter, Churchill informed the editor of *The Times* newspaper, who published it as a sensational scoop before the Queen knew of it. Naturally, this was the political sensation of the day, but Tory opinion was sharply divided as to what to do. It was widely feared that the government could not survive, although Churchill certainly did not have the widespread public support he imagined.

Only a political master-stroke could restore the stability of the government. Here Salisbury, a politician of extraordinary skill, rose to the occasion by appointing (after a good deal of backstairs negotiations) George Goschen as Churchill's successor. Goschen, one of the leading Liberal Unionists, was a respected authority on finance and a wealthy City banker, as able a replacement for Churchill as anyone could wish. Goschen would, moreover, carry a good deal of moderate Liberal Unionist opinion with him into the Tory camp, without compelling Salisbury to pay the heavy price that the accession of Hartington or Chamberlain at this stage would have done. The possibility of Goschen as his successor was mentioned to Churchill at a luncheon engagement a few days after his resignation. 'I had forgotten Goschen', Churchill said, strongly suggesting that he believed that Salisbury, unable to find a competent replacement, would be forced to surrender to Churchill's demands. Churchill never held office again; his health and, indeed, his sanity ran downhill steadily thereafter until his death at the age of only 45. For the Salisbury government, and possibly for the Conservative party, Churchill's resignation was a major turning-point, arguably the end of radical 'Tory democracy' and the real beginnings of the Conservative party as containing all of Britain's moderate forces.

Goschen's appointment led to further changes in Salisbury's Cabinet. The most dramatic circumstances surrounded the end of Sir Stafford Northcote, Earl of Iddlesleigh, formerly Disraeli's faithful lieutenant. Goschen had insisted upon Iddesleigh's removal from the Foreign Office as the price to be paid for his own agreement to join the government; Goschen felt that Iddesleigh was incompetent. Salisbury acceded, appointing himself to the Foreign Office (as in 1885–86) on the day that Goschen's appointment was announced in January 1887. At the same time, Salisbury again separated the offices of Prime Minister and First Lord of the Treasury, installing W. H. Smith as First Lord. Iddesleigh was given no new position, and, during his final interview with Salisbury at 10 Downing Street, he suffered a fatal heart attack and died. Salisbury received much criticism, and the stocks of the government did not rise for some time. Probably the most successful new minister appointed to the Cabinet at this stage was Salisbury's nephew Arthur James Balfour, who entered the Cabinet for the first time as Secretary for Scotland in November 1886 and then made his mark as Chief Secretary for Ireland from March 1887 until November 1891, following Hicks-Beach's retirement through ill-health. There were a few more notable changes to Salisbury's second Cabinet, especially Balfour's appointment as First Lord of the Treasury following W. H. Smith's death in October 1891, but in the main the Cabinet remained fairly stable until it left office in August 1892. Apart from Goschen, it failed to include any important Liberal Unionists, who remained apart and unclear of their future.

The history of the Liberal party during the years 1886–92 revolved around attempts to achieve reunification and to find a new sense of direction after losing significant support from both wings, especially from its Whig and moderate supporters. Initially, very few of the Liberal Unionists believed that the split in the party was permanent. Indeed, except for the unpredictable conversion of the 77-year-old Gladstone to Home Rule, there would, presumably, have been no split. The position of Chamberlain and his supporters was particularly anomalous, given that they might have been expected to have supported Home Rule and welcomed the decision of the Whigs and right-wing Liberals to leave the Liberal party, clearing the way for a Radical takeover of the party. Early in 1887 Chamberlain and Sir G. O. Trevelyan held a series of meetings with Liberal leaders, known as the Round Table Conference, aimed at Liberal reunion. Convinced that he would certainly become Prime Minister one day, Chamberlain proved stubborn (as did Gladstone). Salisbury threw a lifeline to Chamberlain of a curious kind, inviting him, in August 1887, to negotiate a fishing agreement between Canada and the United States (as implausible an assignment for Chamberlain as one could imagine). Chamberlain succeeded well, returning from America not only with a treaty but with his third wife, Mary Endicott (after a two-year unsuccessful courtship with the future Beatrice Webb).[4] By 1892 Chamberlain remained the absolute master of the Birmingham political machine, and had now moved some considerable distance towards a working alliance with the Tories, whose local government reforms in this period he admired. Apart from continuing personal hostility to Gladstone, Chamberlain and his followers

---

4 Chamberlain married the well-connected Mary Endicott in an Episcopalian church in Washington DC, showing that he had moved far from his original Unitarianism.

also supported many of the claims made by Ulster on Protestant religious grounds. Chamberlain's growing sympathy for imperialism, to be given full reign in the years 1895–1903, also plainly had much in common with the late Victorian Conservative party. On the other wing of the Liberal party, the prospect of reunification with the Whigs was *a priori* much less likely. During the years 1886–92 Liberalism thus contracted significantly into a smaller core. Nevertheless, most of the central support of the Liberal party in these years remained, especially among Nonconformists and in the 'Celtic fringe'. While the Liberals lost many of their very wealthy and landed supporters, they gained a large portion of the educated professional classes, many shopkeepers and small businessmen, and most trade unionists. In October 1891 the Liberal party adopted a series of measures it intended to enact when it next came to power, known as the 'Newcastle Programme'. It included a reiteration of the party's commitment to Home Rule, and the disestablishment of the Churches of Wales and Scotland, further suffrage reform on the basis of 'one man, one vote', local vetoes on the sale of drink in areas where a majority were teetotal, the creation of district and parish councils, and minor reforms of this kind, including an Employers' Liability Act covering accidents at work. This was not a very inspiring or a very coherent programme, nor was it especially radical. (In fact, virtually none of it was enacted by the Liberal government which held office in 1892–95.) The Liberal party would probably have declined as an electoral force earlier than it did without the commanding figure of Gladstone, still at its helm. The removal of Chamberlain, Hartington, Dilke and others from the trajectory of Liberal leadership during these years did leave the way open for others to move into senior positions who might well never have reached the heights: the next four Liberal leaders – Rosebery, Harcourt, Campbell-Bannerman and Asquith – were none of them pre-ordained to succeed without the earthquakes of these years.[5]

Rather surprisingly, given its centrality to British politics up to 1886, the affairs of Ireland did not figure as prominently during the 1886–92 government as one might have expected. There was, for instance, at first surprisingly little violence in Ireland, where one might well have expected the defeat of the Home Rule Bill to have led to an orgy of unrest and civil strife. (The previous year, in mid-1886, serious rioting had erupted in Belfast, which was widely attributed to the pro-Ulster campaigns of the Unionists.) Irish Nationalists instead organised a 'Plan of Campaign' aimed at a united front by tenant farmers against eviction. The new Conservative government responded with a draconian Crimes Act, the brainchild of Arthur Balfour, the new Irish Secretary, who as a result became known as 'bloody Balfour'. At the same time the carrot was offered as well as the stick, in the form of a new Tenants Act making some concessions to Irish farmers. In rural Ireland, conditions again descended into lawlessness as the

5 Lord Hartington succeeded his father as the eighth Duke of Devonshire in 1891.

Crimes Act took effect, with a new outburst of violence and rioting. By 1891, Balfour's policies of coercion had worked and violence decreased. The last year of Salisbury's second government saw more concessions to the Irish tenant farmers, especially a far-reaching Land Purchase Act.

After the defeat of Home Rule in 1886 it appeared that some degree of commanding authority had been lost by Parnell. The leaders of the 'Plan of Campaign', William O'Brien and John Dillon, were more radical than Parnell. In gaol a few years later, O'Brien refused to wear prison clothes and demanded recognition of Irishmen convicted under the Crimes Act as 'political prisoners', presaging the later demands of the IRA. Parnell's reputation, however, appeared to have sunk to its lowest point in April 1887, when *The Times* newspaper published a photograph of a hand-written letter, allegedly by him, in which he apologised to his supporters for having to denounce, against his actual convictions, the Phoenix Park murders of 1882. The letters, if true, would have irreparably destroyed Parnell's reputation among almost all Englishmen. (*The Times* also published damaging allegations against other leading Irish Nationalists.) In fact they were clever forgeries. Parnell declined to sue *The Times* for libel, fearing that no London jury would be impartial. Another Irish MP, also libelled by *The Times*, did sue for defamation, and at his trial in July 1888 he further alleged that letters of a similar kind by Parnell had been forged by *The Times*'s barristers. Parnell demanded an inquiry by a select committee of the House of Commons, but was forced to settle for a special inquiry by three judges (all opponents of Irish Nationalism) to investigate the claims made by *The Times*. In February 1889 the actual forger, one Richard Piggott, a disreputable Irish journalist motivated by money, broke down in the witness box and admitted that all the letters published by *The Times* had been forged by him.[6] The commission of three judges reported in February 1890, entirely vindicating Parnell and the other Irish leaders attacked by *The Times*. Thus, in the course of the first four years of the 1886–92 government, Parnell's reputation among the English public had shifted from that of a troublesome Nationalist leader to a mendacious apologist for terrorism and then, thanks to the fall of Piggott, to that of the victim of a terrible injustice, a kind of Irish Dreyfus. In mid-1890 there is no doubt that English public opinion had shifted in Parnell's direction, such that a general election at the time might well have seen Home Rule enacted.

Yet just at this moment the wheel of fortune was about to turn full circle again for Parnell, this time bringing about the effective collapse of his career. In November 1890 he was named as co-respondent in a divorce case

---

6 Piggott fled to Spain and committed suicide before he could be arrested for perjury. *The Times* paid out nearly £300 000 (around £15 million today) in legal costs, damages to Parnell and others, and payments for Piggott's forgeries.

brought by Captain W. H. O'Shea against his wife Katherine.[7] Mrs O'Shea had in fact been Parnell's mistress since 1881, and had borne him three children (none of whom survived). As with the case of Sir Charles Dilke, the public revelation of this scandalous situation (although many politicians had long known of it) threatened Parnell's prospects in the most harmful way imaginable, especially among English Nonconformist supporters of Gladstone and Home Rule. Among the multitude of Parnell's Irish followers, opinion was sharply divided: many were willing to follow his lead whatever happened, but for others, especially among conservative Catholics, the scandal of Parnell's private life outweighed his charismatic leadership. The Irish Nationalist parliamentary party debated the matter and divided between a majority of 44 MPs who no longer wished to be led by Parnell, and who were now headed by Justin McCarthy MP, and a minority of 26 who remained loyal to Parnell. A by-election at Kilkenny in December 1890 between a supporter and an opponent of Parnell saw the anti-Parnellite candidate elected by a two to one majority, with the Catholic clergy turning strongly against Parnell. The matter remained unresolved when, in October 1891, Parnell (who had a heart condition) died suddenly at the age of only 45. The Irish Nationalist movement was deprived of its greatest leader, and his successors were unable to bring about the goal of Home Rule until after the First World War. The final scandal of Parnell's life probably also weakened support for Home Rule among many English moderate Liberals.

In its domestic policies, the second Salisbury government was often cautiously reforming and sometimes rather radical. The Chancellor of the Exchequer who succeeded Churchill, George Goschen, cut income tax and raised death duties. He did not pursue the sharp cuts in military spending which Churchill had proposed, raising revenue from a variety of new sources to cover expenditure. Goschen is best remembered, however, for his so-called conversion of the national debt in 1888. Under this procedure, £558 million of the British National Debt was redeemed and reissued to creditors at 2.75 per cent rather than 3 per cent. This saved the government about £1.4 million in annual interest, about 5 per cent of the charge on government debt. Goschen and most of his colleagues were strict Gladstonians in finance, viewing any reduction in government expenditure as a good thing unless it could be proved otherwise. Goschen's resolute fiscal orthodoxy also helped to reassure the middle classes of the Tory government's *bona fides* as guardians of their interests.

---

7 Although known as 'Kitty O'Shea', Mrs O'Shea was (like Parnell) in fact an upper-class Anglican whose father was an English baronet and whose brother was Field-Marshal Sir Evelyn Wood; she was also the niece of a Lord Chancellor, Lord Hatherley, and in 1889 had inherited nearly £150 000 (£8 million today) from a wealthy aunt. Her only Irish connection was that her husband came from the Anglo-Irish 'Establishment'. Parnell's own background was similar.

Rather surprisingly for a government determined to prove itself conservative in nature as well as name, Salisbury's 1886–92 ministry was responsible for a far-reaching record of reform in local government. Given the Gladstonian and *laissez-faire* bias against any unnecessary expenditure or radical measures by the central government, local governments were, in the main, the chief *locus* of experimental and radical measures, especially those pioneered by Chamberlain in Birmingham. Yet the structure of many local government areas remained undemocratic and unreformed. In the rural areas, power still resided with the Lord-Lieutenants and local JPs, almost invariably chosen from the aristocracy and gentry. Although it was the largest city in Europe, London had no real government of its own, the Metropolitan Board of Works, dating from 1855, dealing primarily with public works contracts. The President of the Local Government Board, Charles T. Ritchie (1838–1905; later first Viscount Ritchie of Dundee), a jute merchant from Scotland, piloted the Local Government Act 1888 through Parliament. This wide-ranging measure, extraordinarily comprehensive and radical for a Tory government, had three main provisions. It established elected county councils in every county, while boroughs with more than 50 000 inhabitants (over 60 in all) were excluded from these county councils and re-established as country boroughs in their own right, with their own elected governments (most had, of course, existed long before 1888). These measures were extended to Scotland in 1889. Finally, the government of London was completely reorganised, with the urbanised areas of Middlesex, Surrey, Essex and Kent comprising a new unit of local government, the London County Council, elected at municipal elections throughout all of London. The London County Council (or LCC as it was invariably known) lasted from 1889 until 1965 (when the Greater London Council, or GLC, was established), gaining a world-wide reputation for clean, enlightened, and progressive government.[8] The newly established local units of government could raise their own revenues by local rates, and had control of their own police forces, as well as responsibility for state schools, local welfare and the usual prerogatives of local government. Overall expenditure on local government was very considerable, amounting to £101 million in 1900 (of which £41 million was raised by local rates), compared with £140 million for the United Kingdom government (of which £121 million was spent on the military). Women who were

8 While all large cities had Mayors or Lord Mayors, however, it should be noted that the LCC had no Mayor, the head of London's government being the leader of the party with the majority of seats on the LCC. Each of the London boroughs (such as Westminster, Islington, Lambeth, etc.) continued to exist, with their own borough council and local mayors. In addition, it should be clearly noted that the City of London, the historical 'square mile' containing Britain's financial headquarters, remained largely outside of the LCC (and the GLC) and was (and is) governed by its own pre-democratic body of officials, chosen by the City livery companies. The Lord Mayor of London was (and is) actually the Mayor of the City of London alone, not of the whole of the London metropolis.

ratepayers in their own right could vote in elections for the new county councils (as they had done in borough municipal elections since 1868), but could not sit on these newly established local government bodies until 1907 (although they could serve on borough and parish councils and local school boards from 1894). The newly established bodies shifted power away from the local gentry and opened the way for the widespread participation of working-class and Labour councillors even before the First World War. The Act also created a new, and potent, political arena at the local level, and made democracy a reality in local government. British local government, and particularly in big cities, was largely if not entirely spared the endemic corruption of American city machine politics, but instead often became a kind of laboratory for experimental innovations in government, especially in London.

The Salisbury government also produced reforms in other areas. Most importantly, in 1891, under the Assisted Education Act, it abolished all school fees in state elementary schools. In part its motives were progressive, but in part it stemmed from a fear that any future Liberal government would abolish fees in the secular board schools, leaving church-affiliated schools at a disadvantage, since they would be forced to continue to charge. The government also made some minor but progressive changes to hours of work in the Factory Act of 1891, which, for instance, raised the minimum age for children employed in factories from 10 to 11. In 1889 Treasury grants became available for the first time to universities in England other than Oxford University, and a number of other extensions of education funding were made. The Tories also established a Board of Agriculture in 1889, and greatly reformed the system of tithe payments, long a contentious issue among Nonconformists. Together, these measures established some claims, perhaps considerable claims, for the Conservatives as a party of 'Tory democracy', but in a manner which did not alienate the middle classes. One effect of this group of reforms was to make it possible for Chamberlain and his group of radical Liberal Unionists to join fully with the Conservatives, although Chamberlain held office in a Tory Cabinet only after the 1895 general election. Nevertheless, the Conservatives – or Unionists, as they were more commonly known – seemed more and more like a centre party and perhaps like the natural governing party than the Tories had before 1832.

The end of the 1880s and early 1890s coincided with a rather severe economic downturn, known at the time (and sometimes since) as the 'great depression', although of course today that term is almost invariably applied to the vastly greater economic catastrophe which overtook the whole world in the decade after October 1929. The Index of Industrial Production for Britain (as determined by economic historians several generations later on a scale in which production for the year 1831 equals 100) rose from 423 in 1880 to 515 in 1888, but then declined to 491 in 1892 and 479 in 1893 before rising again. Net national income also declined, from £1405 million in 1890 to £1336 million in 1894, before beginning to rise. This downturn was exacerbated by the agricultural depression of the 1880s, by the effects of foreign tariff barriers raised against British exports in Germany, America and elsewhere, and by the rapid industrialisation of Germany and the United States, which eliminated former markets for British manufactured goods and created new rivals in traditional areas of British commerce like Latin America. In November 1890 Baring Brothers, one of the very greatest merchant banking houses in the City of London, crashed and was rescued with difficulty only after the Bank of England and rivals like Rothschilds organised a rescue operation. Just before the beginnings of the recession of the later 1880s there occurred one of the formative experiences in British trade union history, the London Dockers' Strike of 1889.[9] The workers of the London docks knew a regimen of chronic poverty: they were casual workers, ununionised, and resident in the largest slum in Europe, where there were always more labourers available than work for them, depressing wages even further. The aim of the Dockers' Strike was to secure a standard wage of 6d an hour, about 25 shillings for a 50-hour week, less than £70 a year for a worker employed full-time. By the later 1880s, too, many among the well-educated classes of London had discovered the existence of the chronically poor. The Fabian Society, various Christian Socialist and settlement house movements, and the Radical 'Unauthorised Programme' had brought the question of poverty before the middle classes, and a seemingly well-justified case like that of the dockers actually enjoyed very widespread support among the London middle classes, especially as the outcome of the strike would not directly affect them. Cardinal Manning, the Roman Catholic Archbishop of Westminister, also played a notable part in the strike settlement. Led by Ben Tillett (1860–1943), Tom Mann (1856–1941) and John Burns (1858–1943; an MP 1892–1918 and the first working-class Cabinet minister, from 1905–14), three of the greatest trade union leaders of their day, it resulted in a victory for the dock workers after a month of striking: the concession of the 'docker's tanner'.

The earlier part of this period was an era of considerable growth in trade union membership generally, although growth was largely halted by the recession of the early 1890s. Membership in the TUC increased from 633 000 in 1886 to 1 470 000 in 1890, while the number of unions affiliated to the TUC in these years grew from 122 to 311. There then ensued a period of decline of several years, so that by 1894 there were 1 100 000 members of the TUC and 179 bodies affiliated to it. The late 1880s are best-remembered, however, as the beginnings of the 'New Unionism', hallmarked by the unionisation of unskilled and semi-skilled

9 It is often pointed out that this occurred before the recession began, and was the result of very poorly paid workers becoming intolerant of their low pay in prosperous times. It should also be noted that in February 1886 mobs of the unemployed had smashed shop windows and caused mayhem in London's West End. The Dock Strike, in contrast, was confined to the East End.

workers beyond the skilled artisans traditionally forming the majority of unionists, and organised by industry rather than craft. Apart from the Dockers' Strike, the efforts by Will Thorne in 1889 to organise workers at the Beckton Gas Works in East Ham, resulting in the reduction of the working day from 12 to 8 hours, and the foundation of the Miners' Federation of Great Britain in the same year, were pointers to the new ambitions of the unions. On the other hand, Keir Hardie's attempts to found an Independent Labour Party in 1892–93 came to little, most workers remaining absolutely loyal in their political affiliations to the older parties, especially the Liberals. Large-scale employers were not slow, however, to realise the dangers to them of heightened union militancy, and reacted by creating such bodies as the Shipping Federation, formed by leading shipowners in 1890, and the Employers Federation of Engineering Associations in 1896. The process of the amalgamation and cartelisation within some British industries, chiefly in order to meet the foreign challenge but also to deal more effectively with trade union militancy, began then as well.

Lord Salisbury's *forte* was foreign policy; in this area he was the acknowledged master. During the years 1886–92 there was surprisingly little animosity among the major European powers. Nevertheless, in 1890 the young Kaiser Wilhelm II pointedly dismissed Bismarck, the skilful helmsman of Germany's policies for 30 years, and installed men in his place who were manifestly his inferiors, especially in their shrewdness regarding where to place limits on Germany's foreign policy ambitions. Wilhelm's gaucherie and hot-headed and provocative braggadocio about Germany's intentions to dominate Europe eventually led to a fundamental reorientation of Britain's central foreign policy goals in Europe from hostility to France and Russia to alliances with both, with the aim of stopping Germany from dominating Europe. This led, a quarter of a century later, to the First World War, in which perhaps 12 million men were killed and the political foundations of Europe altered forever. For Salisbury, however, all this was in the future and unknowable, and international compromise was the order of the day. Between 1886 and 1892 Britain acquired much of Nigeria (1886), joint control with France of the New Hebrides (1888), Tonga (1889), parts of South-West Africa and Zanzibar (1890), and Nyasaland and Northern Rhodesia (1892). Responsible government came to Western Australia (1892) and the Federation movement began in Australia, aimed at unifying the six colonies of that continent into a single nation. While Germany and France also annexed substantial areas of Africa and the Pacific in these years (for example, Germany gained control of Tanganyika in 1886), by and large what has become known as the 'scramble for Africa', was decided peacefully. The Anglo-French Colonial Conference of 1887, the Anglo-German Treaty on East Africa negotiated by Salisbury in 1890, and various treaties along the same lines between Britain and France and Portugal signed in 1890–91, decided the boundaries of colonial Africa without conflict. It has long been debated what centrally motivated Britain: at base, it was probably a desire to forestall other European powers from interfering with British India and the hegemony of the Royal Navy; as well, Britain was determined not to lose out on colonial gains compared with other powers. In Europe, this was the period when France and Russia were reconciled (despite the fundamental differences in their forms of government and political ideologies), largely in order to stop German expansionism in the Balkans and elsewhere. Salisbury initially disapproved of Franco-Russian friendship, reflecting Britain's traditional hostility to Russian ambitions in the Balkans. Indeed, Britain came very close, in 1889, to joining openly in alliance with Germany against France. At this stage, Salisbury was as committed to international peace, and as opposed to secret alliances, as any Radical pacifist. For the time, it seemed as if Salisbury's skilful diplomacy could secure international peace for an indefinite period ahead.

The year 1887 saw the 60th anniversary of the Coronation of Queen Victoria in 1837. This event, the Queen's Golden Jubilee, was celebrated by a grand public ceremony on 21 June 1887, the likes of which had never been seen before and formed one of the best-remembered events of that time. More than 30 foreign kings and princes, together with most heads of government of the self-governing colonies, were escorted with the Queen and her entourage through the streets of London in an endless procession, watched by hundreds of thousands of spectators. The number of Indian soldiers, and their obvious loyalty to the Empress of India, was widely noted. A month later came the Queen's great review of the Royal Navy at Spithead, an event which caught the public imagination as much as the Jubilee procession. Nothing like this had ever been seen before: few British monarchs had reigned for half a century and the last one who did, George III, had celebrated his Jubilee in 1809 (a year early) by holding a private church service at Windsor and attending a fireworks display at Frogmore. Queen Victoria's Golden Jubilee, together with her even grander Diamond Jubilee ten years later, linked the official constitutional role of the Queen as Head of State with her new position as head of the Empire.

Despite the apparent achievements and successes of Salisbury's second government, it was gradually but perceptibly losing popularity by 1890–92. A string of by-election defeats, some in normally safe Tory seats, marked these years. As noted, the economy was not performing well and labour militancy increased. Salisbury's government had hardly settled the Irish question and it had not succeeded in bringing most Liberal Unionists into the government. In June 1892 Salisbury asked for a dissolution of Parliament, and a general election was held between 4 and 26 July 1892. Most Liberals supported the 'Newcastle Programme' of Irish Home Rule and church disestablishment in Scotland and Wales, possibly the first time that a major party, at a general election, was committed to a single

programme. The election saw substantial gains for the Liberals and significant losses for the Unionists, although the latter remained the largest
single party. After the election, the Unionists held 314 seats (compared with
394 in 1886), the Liberals 272 (compared with 191).[10] The 1892 election
saw the usual Unionist majority in England (262 Unionists compared with
189 Liberals), and the normal heavy Liberal majorities in Wales (31:3) and
Scotland (50:20). Only 60 seats were uncontested. Slightly more votes were
cast for the Unionists (2 159 000, or 47.0 per cent of the total vote of
4 598 000) than for the Liberals (who won 45.1 per cent of the vote, a total
of 2 088 000). Since most of the uncontested seats were in safe Tory
constituencies, it is possible that they would have won a majority of the
popular vote had every seat been contested. Nevertheless, Salisbury found
himself in a parliamentary minority since there were also 81 Irish Nationalists, who would naturally support the Liberals against the Unionists. On 11
August 1892 the government lost a vote of confidence soon after the new
Parliament met, and Salisbury resigned the same day.

Gladstone became Prime Minister for the fourth time on 15 August
1892. The Queen, as usual, wrote of the prospect 'with much regret', but
placed no obstacles in his path. Gladstone was nearly 82 when he became
Prime Minister in 1892, the oldest man to head a government in modern
British history. Gladstone had been imminently expected to retire for nearly
the previous 20 years, and agreed to become Prime Minister yet again only
because of his deep commitment to Irish Home Rule. There was serious
disagreement as to Gladstone's fitness to head a government. He was
unquestionably in remarkable health for a man of his age, was in full
possession of his faculties, and obviously had a unique experience of
government. Yet his eyesight was rapidly failing, and it was clear that he
was now an old man.[11] For the Liberal party, it would clearly have been
preferable if there had been an heir-apparent to Gladstone, but there was
no single figure capable of uniting the party, and the defection of both
Hartington and Chamberlain in 1886 removed the party's strongest potential leaders.

Despite everything, Gladstone formed a reasonably strong Cabinet of 17
which looked very similar to previous Gladstone Cabinets. Although most
aristocrats had left the party, the Cabinet (like all of Gladstone's previous
ones) had its share of hereditary landed peers in Lords Kimberley, Rosebery, Ripon and Spencer. With the Lord Chancellor, Lord Herschell, there
were thus five peers in the Cabinet. This was, however, by far the lowest
total of aristocrats in any Cabinet in history. Even if the members of the
Commons from landed and gentry backgrounds were considered, among

10 The Unionist contingent consisted of 268 Conservatives and 46 Liberal Unionists,
   compared with, respectively, 317 and 77 in 1886.
11 During the 1892 general election campaign Gladstone had been struck in the eye, and
   nearly blinded, by a woman in Chester who threw a hard piece of baked gingerbread at
   him while he was driving in an open carriage. The woman was never identified.

them Sir William V. Harcourt at the Exchequer, Sir George O. Trevelyan at the Scottish Office, and A. H. D. Acland as Vice-President of the Board of Education, nearly one-half of the Cabinet now consisted of middle-class men, professionals or men of business. Several were quite distinguished in their own right, for instance James Bryce (1838–1922, later first Viscount Bryce), the Regius Professor of Civil Law at Oxford from 1880 until 1893, who became Chancellor of the Duchy of Lancaster. Two newcomers to the Cabinet were, however, of especial note. Henry Fowler (1830–1911; later first Viscount Wolverhampton), President of the Local Government Board, was a solicitor and the son of a Methodist minister. He had been the dominant figure in Wolverhampton, a grim industrial town about 10 miles from Birmingham, but had declined to join Chamberlain and his circle in 1886. The most talented new member of the Cabinet, however, was Herbert Henry Asquith (1852–1928; later first Earl of Oxford and Asquith), who had entered Parliament only six years earlier and had never held any office before Gladstone chose him to become Home Secretary, one of the most senior Cabinet posts. Asquith, the son of a Congregationalist woollen merchant in the West Riding, had attended a minor public school in London but then made a brilliant name for himself at Balliol College, Oxford, and as a leading barrister. Still under 40 when he joined the Cabinet, his progress was certainly augmented by his second wife (his first wife had died young), the celebrated Margot Tennant, the brilliant if eccentric doyenne of Society who was fortunate enough to be the daughter of the richest businessman in Scotland;[12] she was a great favourite of Gladstone's, who flirted with her in his old age. Asquith proved to be perhaps the most successful member of the Cabinet and, of course, a future Prime Minister.

Gladstone's most controversial appointment, however, was his Foreign Secretary, Lord Rosebery. Often compared (like Lord Randolph Churchill) to a spoiled child, Rosebery made enormous trouble over his place in the Cabinet, changing his mind several times about accepting office before finally accepting the senior position of Foreign Minister at the age of 45. A great favourite with the Queen, two years later he became Gladstone's unlikely successor.

Gladstone assumed office as obsessed with Home Rule as in 1886. The Second Home Rule Bill came to occupy most of the attention of Gladstone's final government for its 18 months. The measure proposed by the government differed somewhat from the bill defeated six years earlier. In the new bill, 80 Irish MPs were to continue to sit in the Westminster

12 Margot Asquith's father was the chemical manufacturer Sir Charles Tennant, whose factory chimney was the tallest structure in Glasgow and who left over £3 million (around £175 million today) when he died in 1906. Tennant also had another rather unusual distinction: he was the father (by different wives) of children born 53 years apart, apparently a record interval for monogamous countries. One of Margot Asquith's half-sisters (and Asquith's sister-in-law), Baroness Elliott of Harewood, did not die until 1995!

Parliament, but without the power to vote on legislation not affecting Ireland. The nature of the proposed Irish Parliament was also different, with no role envisioned for the Irish peerage. The bill took an enormously long time to pass through the Commons Committee, and was obstructed every inch of the way by Unionists. It passed its second reading in April 1893 by 43 votes, 347 to 304. The Second Home Rule Bill was as notable as was the previous one for failing to take into account the fears of Protestant Ulster, which had if anything hardened since 1886, and a most legitimate criticism of Gladstone's proposals was that they attempted to do justice to one minority at the expense of another. It was also the case that the bill would have failed without the contingent of Irish MPs, being in a minority of about 48 among English and Welsh MPs.

The bill next went to the House of Lords, where the result, on 8 September 1893, was a foregone conclusion. The bill was defeated by an overwhelming margin, 419 to 41. The great majority of hereditary peers voted against the bill, as did all of the Church of England bishops present for the vote. It was far from clear what Gladstone could do next. Constitutionally, of course, the House of Lords was within its rights, while, until the 1911 Parliament Act, it could not be overridden by the House of Commons. Gladstone could dissolve Parliament (which he wished to do) and hold a general election on a 'Peers vs. the People' battle cry, but the peers in this case probably represented the people of Great Britain more accurately than did the Commons. Gladstone's Cabinet strongly advised against a dissolution, with few viewing Irish Home Rule as obsessively as their leader or wishing to risk office for its sake.[13] In fact, Irish Home Rule was not passed by Parliament until 1912, the Liberals ignoring it in the years 1906–10 when they held office with an absolute majority. Only after the two 1910 general elections, when the Liberals were dependent upon the Irish contingent to remain in office, did they get around to enacting Home Rule again.[14]

Early in March 1894 Gladstone decided to retire. Apart from old age and ill-health, there was no clear-cut reason for his retirement at this stage, which took his colleagues by surprise. (The ostensible reason was a minor disagreement with his Cabinet colleagues over raising taxes to spend on increased armaments.) There is a well-known story of Sir William V. Harcourt taking from his pocket a paper 'yellow with age' which he had written years before for this occasion. The entire Cabinet was in tears. Upon receiving word of his retirement, Queen Victoria pointedly declined

---

13 Gladstone apparently wished for the Commons to enact an Employers' Liability Bill, knowing it would be rejected by the Lords, and then hold a general election on the question of the powers of the House of Lords.

14 The 1912 Home Rule Bill was to take effect in 1914 but was postponed when the First World War broke out. As amended in 1914, the bill also excluded Ulster from its provisions for six years, but then automatically included the province in the workings of the bill. Britain teetered at the brink of a civil war in 1914 over the Home Rule question, with Ulster troops at the point of mutiny.

to offer Gladstone a peerage, perhaps the only time in history when a retiring Prime Minister was not offered ennoblement, normally automatic.

Nor did the Queen ask Gladstone for his views on a successor, again something which she would surely have done with any other premier. Gladstone, it seems, favoured Earl Spencer as his successor; the most plausible successor was probably Sir William V. Harcourt (1827–1904), the Chancellor of the Exchequer, who later served briefly as leader of the Liberal party in 1896–98. Harcourt, who was blustering and unpleasant in manner, was unpopular with his colleagues. In any case, and without consulting anyone, the Queen sent for Lord Rosebery, who formally became Prime Minister on 5 March 1894, the 10th man to hold the office under Queen Victoria, and the first born after she had reached the throne in 1837. Archibald Philip Primrose, fifth Earl of Rosebery and first Earl of Midlothian (1847–1929), was one of the strangest men ever to become Prime Minister in modern times and one of the least known. Rosebery was favoured in his origins, wealth and intelligence, and was perhaps more fortunate still in being favoured by his contemporaries, especially in the press and general public. Most politicians receive unfair abuse from many quarters while they are active, and are only assessed objectively and sympathetically after they are dead. Rosebery's reputation was the reverse: in his lifetime he was for decades regarded as the coming man, a perpetual 'golden boy', and was almost without criticism from the press, especially the right-wing press to whom he was one of the few acceptable Liberals. He was also a genuine hero in Scotland, especially in Midlothian (the area around Edinburgh) where he ruled supreme almost in the manner of Chamberlain in Birmingham. For a generation after he resigned as Prime Minister in 1895 he was still regarded as the most likely figure to head any non-party government, and was offered (and, typically, declined) the position of Minister Without Portfolio in Lloyd George's 1916 wartime government. Since his death, his negative features, especially his spoiled, sulking demeanour and his obvious lack of commitment to most of the values of the late Victorian Liberal party, have dominated most discussions of Rosebery's career.

Although the scion of one of the oldest and grandest Scottish landowning families, Rosebery was educated at Eton and Oxford and, rather implausibly, married Hannah Rothschild, the principal Rothschild heiress, in 1877.[15] This brought him close to the London plutocracy. Rosebery's lifestyle was deplored by many Nonconformists, especially his very visible patronage of the turf (he was one of the greatest racehorse owners of his

15 The match was opposed by both families on religious grounds. Disraeli gave the bride away and the Prince of Wales, among others, was a guest. As a result of the marriage, Rosebery was given the great Rothschild mansion at Mentmore, Buckinghamshire, as a wedding present. Rosebery's annual income from all sources after his marriage was around £140 000 (that is, over £7 million in today's money each year).

day). He was unquestionably a very talented man, who wrote interesting works of history and *belles-lettres*, but both his political judgement and his basic beliefs were questioned by many Liberals. He had been personally loyal to Gladstone (organising the 'Midlothian Campaign') but was very cool to Home Rule, deplored many of the advanced radical nostrums of his day, and was a dedicated imperialist (as were many of the leaders of the Liberals at the time). As a peer, he did not have to contest elections, while the main office he held before becoming Prime Minister, the Foreign Secretaryship, was also irrelevant to domestic concerns. Had Rosebery been more skilful, he might have been a success (as Lord Salisbury, another peer, obviously was), but he was notoriously petulant and, moreover, found himself the head of a minority government whose days were probably numbered.

Rosebery's Cabinet was virtually identical to Gladstone's, although Lord Kimberley, the Lord President and Secretary for India, became Foreign Secretary and H. H. Fowler moved to the India Office. Rosebery's administration, which lasted for 14 months, is remembered chiefly for one thing, the famous taxes imposed by Sir William V. Harcourt in his budget of 1894. Harcourt needed revenue for military and domestic purposes and was warm to the growing chorus on the left that the rich would have to pay a 'ransom' for the privileges they enjoyed. He raised income tax by a penny (while also increasing the lower limit below which incomes were exempt) but most famously raised and extended death duties, making land liable to tax at the same rate as other forms of property (previously it had been taxed at a lower rate) and relating the level of death duties to the global value of a deceased estate rather than to the size of a legacy or the relationship of the legatee to the deceased. While levels of taxation were very low by later standards – only 8 per cent on millionaire estates – Harcourt's death duties caused an enormous storm, especially as they were seen to be only the prelude to ever-higher levels of taxation by future left-wing governments.

In other spheres, Rosebery proved reluctant to proceed with Home Rule and actually stated that 'before Home Rule is conceded . . . England as the predominant member of the three kingdoms will have to be convinced of its justice', a statement which Irish Nationalists took to be a condemnation of its passage but which Rosebery insisted was simply a descriptive statement of what the Nationalists would have to do to succeed. In 1894 (just before Rosebery took office), Henry Fowler passed another Local Government Act which established democratically elected parish councils, nearly 7000 throughout England and Wales. An important novelty of Fowler's Act was that some married women, as well as all unmarried women who were ratepayers, could vote for all government bodies and also *be elected* to them, the first time women were legally entitled to be elected to any government bodies in Britain. By the First World War, a very considerable female electorate actually existed in Britain at the local level: suffragettism, of course, concerned the rights of women to vote at parliamentary elections.

Foreign affairs were fairly quiet during this period. In 1894 Uganda was formally annexed by Britain after the chartered company formed to exploit it went into financial difficulties. Rosebery led the Cabinet imperialists, and he had many allies. He avoided trouble with France, which wished to annex Siam, an independent state between British India and French Indo-China. Rosebery proved vigorous on this occasion, and Siam (Thailand) remained the only state in south-east Asia which never became a colonial possession. Britain also sensibly sided with Japan in its long-running conflict with China. For humanitarian reasons, Rosebery strongly protested to Turkey at the massacres of Armenians in its territories in 1894, risking the traditional alliance with the Ottomans.

All of this was a rather meagre set of achievements, and there was a strong feeling that the government could not last long. The end came on 21 June 1895, when Sir Henry Campbell-Bannerman, a highly competent War Minister, lost a vote in the Commons over his alleged failure to procure more cordite (smokeless explosive) for the army.[16] Rosebery resigned and, on 25 June 1895, Salisbury became Prime Minister for the third time. Neither Rosebery nor Harcourt ever held office again. Gladstone, aged 88, died in 1898. The Liberals did not return to power for 10 years.

16 On the same day Campbell-Bannerman had secured the retirement of the aged Duke of Cambridge, Queen Victoria's cousin, as Commander-in-Chief of the Army, in the teeth of resistance by the Queen. Cambridge, Commander-in-Chief since 1856, is generally seen as a reactionary who resisted all modern reforms. He was replaced (from 1895 to 1900) by Lord Wolseley, a highly successful professional soldier.

14

The era of Lord Salisbury, 1895–1902

Lord Salisbury formed his third government at the end of June 1895. On 8 July he dissolved Parliament, and called a general election which was completed by the end of July. In forming his government, Salisbury had one great advantage largely denied to his previous administration: the presence in his Cabinet of crucial Liberal Unionists, especially the eighth Duke of Devonshire (as Lord Hartington had become) as Lord President of the Council and, more remarkably, Joseph Chamberlain as Colonial Minister, the position for which he is now chiefly remembered. To contemporaries who had followed Chamberlain's career since his radical Birmingham days, it seemed as implausible that he could ever sit in a Tory Cabinet as it did 34 years later when Ramsay MacDonald also headed what was, in effect, a Tory government. As well, George Goschen became First Lord of the Treasury, and Lord Lansdowne (Henry Petty-Fitzmaurice, fifth Marquess of Lansdowne, 1845–1927), a prominent Liberal Unionist peer, became Secretary for War.[1] All the other ministers were Conservatives. As he did before, Salisbury combined the offices of Prime Minister and Foreign Secretary. He did this for over five years until Lord Lansdowne became Foreign Minister in November 1900. Arthur Balfour became First Lord of the Treasury, the government's leader in the House of Commons, and Salisbury's most obvious successor. The Exchequer went to Sir Michael Hicks-Beach, regarded as the government's best debater in the Commons apart from Balfour. Lord Cross, Disraeli's great Home Secretary, became Lord Privy Seal and a link with the past, while Aretas Akers-Douglas, the organiser of Conservative victories and Chief Whip, entered the Cabinet as First Commissioner for Works. Numbering 19, the Cabinet was exceptionally large. At the end of the nineteenth century, and 140 years after the British

1 The most prominent Liberal Unionist barrister, Henry James, first Baron James of Hereford, was to have become Lord Chancellor, but was prevented by Lord Halsbury, the arch-Tory former Lord Chancellor, who insisted on being reappointed. Lord James joined the Cabinet as Chancellor of the Duchy of Lancaster 10 days after its formation.

industrial revolution began, it is notable that nine Cabinet ministers (including a duke and two marquesses) still sat in the Lords, while of the 10 Commoners, three were close relatives of peers, two were hereditary baronets, and two (Henry Chaplin and Walter Long) were very large landowners, although untitled. The Cabinet did include three former businessmen, Chamberlain, Goschen and C. T. Ritchie, which was actually more than in any previous Conservative-dominated ministry. It is also notable that no changes were made in any Cabinet position for over five years.

The 1895 general election proved to be the Conservatives' greatest electoral triumph since before the 1832 Reform Act. The Conservatives secured 341 MPs in their own right, more than half of the House of 670 members. They were, however, joined by their 70 Liberal Unionist allies, giving the Unionists 411 MPs in all. The Irish Nationalist contingent of 82 MPs was still there, while the Liberals were reduced to only 177 MPs. In England the Unionists outnumbered the Liberals by 342 to only 112. The Liberals continued to be dominant in Wales, outnumbering the Unionists by 25:9, and by a lesser margin in Scotland (39:31). In England, the Liberals remained strongest in their traditional areas of greatest strength – the West Riding, the north-east, Cornwall and Norfolk.[2] Elsewhere, the Liberals were virtually eliminated, winning, for example, only 12 seats in Greater London out of 62. (In London, the Liberals lost 21 of the 34 seats they had gained in the 1892 election.) As usual, the popular majority was not as great. The Unionists received 1 781 000 votes, or 49.2 per cent of the 3 622 000 cast, while the Liberals received 1 658 000 votes, or 45.8 per cent. (The remainder went to Irish Nationalists and Independent Labourites.) Nevertheless, this certainly understates the Unionist percentage of the vote since no fewer than 185 seats were uncontested, of which 130 were won by Unionists and only 11 by Liberals. Since uncontested seats were normally each party's safest seats, it seems likely that, if every seat in the United Kingdom had been contested, the Unionists would have won 55–60 per cent of the vote.

The 1895 election (and the 1900 general election, whose outcome was very similar) marked the climax of the progressive reorientation of the middle classes into the Conservative party, thus – very roughly – bringing the 'Establishment' back to the situation which had existed before 1832.[3] In middle-class seats, the Unionists were now virtually hegemonic. Among 18 predominantly middle-class seats in Greater London, the Conservatives won every seat, apparently by an average majority of about 65 per cent,

2 Although these were remote rural areas, down to the twentieth century they were regions of strength for the Liberals rather than for the Tories. They had few 'squires', were heavily Nonconformist, and were poorer than most other rural areas.
3 There were still components of the middle classes loyal to the Liberals, especially in the Celtic areas, among Nonconformists, and among a growing section of the intelligentsia. Most of them remained outside the Conservative party until the inter-war period.

although this is difficult to ascertain since eight of the seats were uncontested. This represented a swing of 9.6 per cent since the 1885 general election, 10 years earlier. The Conservatives also won all 16 seats in the London area which contained a mixture of middle-class and working-class voters, by an average majority of about 55 per cent. Similar results were recorded in almost all other seats where the middle classes were significant. But the Tory sweep also extended to largely working-class seats as well. For instance, they won 12 of 13 cotton-spinning constituencies in Lancashire and its environs (Bury, Oldham, Stockport, etc.), 10 of 11 seats in Greater Manchester, and 11 of 12 seats on Merseyside (where the Orange Protestant vote was significant). Even in the 24 working-class seats in London, chiefly in the East End and South London, the Unionists won 16, although they had never been especially strong in these areas. Moreover, the party machinery, under Akers-Douglas and Captain R. W. E. Middleton, the party's Principal Agent, was in tip-top shape.

The man who achieved this remarkable success, Lord Salisbury, was an implausible and unlikely source of victory. Of all the modern leaders of the Conservative party, Salisbury was the most negative, pessimistic, and cynical about the possibilities of the established classes in society remaining in control, or, indeed, with their wealth intact in a democratic age which would, in his view, inevitably turn to socialism and confiscatory politics. Unlike Disraeli, with his policies of 'Tory democracy', or later 'One Nation' Conservatives like Stanley Baldwin, the theme of Salisbury's political ideology was the necessity of the propertied and established classes to fight a continuing rearguard action to deter or delay the inevitable triumph of radicalism. Salisbury once titled a magazine article he wrote 'Disintegration', and claimed that party politics were 'civil war with the gloves on'. The British political system, moreover, lacked the checks and balances to radical democracy built into the American system by its Constitution. Institutions which served this purpose in Britain, like the House of Lords, lacked ultimate legitimacy. It was the proper role of the Conservative party, therefore, to provide the drag on so-called 'progress' (that is, towards socialism) which America's basic governmental framework guaranteed.

There are two questions which might be asked of a politician with these views: how did he prove so electorally successful and how did he master British politics so well? The central irony of Salisbury's career is, of course, that despite his loathing of democracy, with Baldwin and Mrs Thatcher, he proved to be one of the three most electorally successful political leaders in post-1832 Britain. One may conclude that Salisbury was far too pessimistic about the effects of democracy on popular Conservatism, overlooking all the sources of mass Conservative loyalty, from imperialism to popular Protestantism, which the Conservative party employed so skilfully. In his dealings with other politicians, from Chamberlain and Gladstone to Randolph Churchill, Salisbury's cynicism complemented his grasp of both strategy and tactics. He was, in particular, a master of giving a man he did not like the right amount of rope to hang himself, and of using those he did like to best advantage. Few British politicians have ever been as accomplished at this as Salisbury.

The electoral success of the Conservatives was greatly assisted by the failures, during the decade between 1895 and 1905, of the Liberals. Bitterly divided and without a single recognised national leader, they appeared as well to have run out of ideas. The Newcastle Programme's extension of what were essentially mid-Victorian radical nostrums was attacked by Rosebery (the party's own leader) as consisting of (in his vivid phrase) 'fly-blown phylacteries'. Home Rule was electorally unpopular outside of Southern Ireland, while the party had not really adopted much in the way of the collectivist 'New Liberalism' which might appeal to the working classes. Gladstone's (presumably final) retirement in 1894 rid the party of its greatest legend, whose presence as leader of the Liberals in a general election was probably worth a couple of percentage points in the popular vote, as unpopular as he was with the 'Establishment'. In contrast to the Tories, the machinery of the Liberal party was relatively poor, with Robert Hudson, the replacement for Francis Schnadhorst, the party's Agent who retired in 1892, no match for him. In particular, relations between the overwhelmingly middle-class candidates and full-time workers for the party, and its supporters in the trade unions and working class, remained unresolved. Nevertheless, the Conservatives under Salisbury were able to exploit this situation with great skill.

The years of Salisbury's third government, and indeed most of the 10 years of Tory rule between 1895 and 1905, are best remembered, however, chiefly for one man and one event: Joseph Chamberlain and the Boer War. In a sense, as much as the Age of Salisbury (and he was no figurehead, but a brilliant leader and strategist), this period was also the Age of Joseph Chamberlain. Modern British political history offers no parallel to the situation which existed between 1895 and 1903, in which arguably the dominant figure of the government held a relatively minor Cabinet portfolio, and yet was literally able to sway the future of nations and the success of armies. Moreover, Chamberlain was already 69 years old in 1895; his eldest son, Austen Chamberlain, also entered the Ministry, as Financial Secretary to the Treasury, in 1900, and entered the Cabinet in 1903. Joseph Chamberlain was offered the Exchequer by Salisbury in 1895 (an appointment which would surely have displeased many Tories), but turned it down in favour of the Colonial Office, a post normally held by little-known ministers for whom the Prime Minister of the day was obliged to find a place. In previous times, before the cult of the Empire became central, its duties were among the least central of the Cabinet. Chamberlain, given enormous leeway by Salisbury, made it into the focus of the government's activities.

The dispute which led to war had been brewing for some time. The situation in southern Africa was complex, but may be summarised briefly in the following way. In the 1890s the southern tip of Africa consisted of four states: the Cape of Good Hope (or Cape Colony), Natal, the Orange Free State, and the Transvaal.[4] The Cape Colony had been in British possession since 1814, Natal since 1843.[5] The two Boer-dominated states, Transvaal and the Orange Free State, were founded between 1835 and 1856 in the wake of the so-called 'Great Trek' by 10 000 Boer cattlemen and farmers to the north of the Cape Colony in 1835–37, the Orange Free State gaining recognised independence in 1854 and the Transvaal (known initially as the South African Republic) in 1856.[6] These two states fought constant wars with the local natives, especially the Basutos. Most Boers would have preferred to remain as independent farmers, but were faced with sudden transformation following the discovery of diamonds after 1867. In 1871 the British annexed the diamond region (Griqualand) of the Orange Free State, and in 1877 annexed the South African Republic, although the Boers, under the leadership of Paul Kruger (1825–1904), retained much local control and achieved independence again in 1881 after a revolt. Germany showed much interest in South Africa at this time, and annexed German South-west Africa in 1884. From 1880 the diamond trade had been progressively organised from the Cape by two rival British corporations, the Barnato Diamond Mining Company (founded by Barney Barnato, 1852–97, a London Jew) and the celebrated DeBeers Mining Corporation, the instrument of the renowned Cecil Rhodes (1853–1902) and Alfred Beit (1853–1906). (These two groups merged in 1888.) Rhodes, British-born and a member of the Cape Colony's Assembly, and its Prime Minister in 1890–96, had grandiose visions of vast British possessions in Africa, of the formation of a federal South Africa under British rule, and of a world-wide condominium of Britain, the United States and Germany to govern the world in the twentieth century. This volatile situation was compounded by the discovery, in 1886, of gold seams of unparalleled richness at Witwatersrand in the southern Transvaal, leading to the foundation of Johannesburg, and a vast immigration of gold seekers from around the world. Rhodes's influence was enhanced still further by the charter he secured from the British government in 1889 for the British South Africa Company, giving it virtually unlimited powers, both economic and political, in the areas to the north and east of the Transvaal.

The attitude of Kruger and the Boers of the Transvaal to all this was, at base, obviously hostile, but not untinged with support for the economic consequences of the discovery of gold, which brought tens of thousands of persons (including many Englishmen) to the Rand (as the Witwatersrand

---

4 In addition, there was the independent native kingdom of Swaziland, and the two native states of Bechuanaland (annexed 1885) and Basutoland (a protectorate from 1871 and a colony since 1884).

5 The specific aim of annexing Natal was to protect the natives against harm at the hands of the Boers.

6 A number of smaller Boer republics, later absorbed by the Transvaal, were also formed at this time.

became known). A few became enormously wealthy. The migrants, known to the Boers as 'Uitlanders' (foreigners), probably outnumbered the relatively small Boer population (some contemporaries have put their numerical majority at up to ten to one, but this figure has been disputed by recent historians). That they had no political rights was a central source of their grievances and a cause of much subsequent trouble. The government of Transvaal was transformed from one of the poorest states in the world to one of the wealthiest. Kruger was able to import competent Dutch civil servants, to buy armaments, and, more ominously, to flirt diplomatically with Germany. He was also engaged in an immediate dispute with Britain over the coastal strip between Transvaal and the sea, known as Tongaland, which was annexed by Britain, denying the Boers an ocean seaport.

Cecil Rhodes now actively stirred up trouble with the Boers, in particular arming Dr Leander Starr Jameson (1853–1917), the administrator of Rhodes's Chartered Company, to launch a raid against the Transvaal Republic with the aim of overthrowing it and bringing the state under British rule. The raid, launched with 470 police from the Chartered Company and Bechuanaland, began in late December 1895, and was quickly put down. It was obviously illegal and led to Kaiser Wilhelm II cabling Kruger to congratulate him on destroying the 'armed hordes' of the raids. (This telegram is known as the 'Kruger Telegram', and was not a thoughtless whim of the Kaiser's, but a deliberate attempt by Germany to meddle in southern African affairs.) British public opinion was now aroused in two directions at once. A wave of anti-German, anti-Kruger 'Jingoism' swept the country, especially in London, but there was widespread condemnation from Liberal sources of Rhodes, the British government, and, especially, of Chamberlain's role in the Jameson Raid. A parliamentary committee of inquiry (of which Chamberlain was a member) was established (but not until early 1897) to look into the Raid. Chamberlain strenuously denied knowing anything of it in advance. The Liberal members of the committee did not go to extreme lengths to ascertain the truth, probably because the Rosebery government had itself been conniving with Rhodes, possibly for similar ends. There was (and is) a mystery concerning the contents of seven 'missing telegrams'. The committee voted to censure Rhodes but exonerated Chamberlain. Most recent historians believe that he knew much more than he admitted. Anti-British opinion naturally hardened in the two Boer republics, while, especially in London and in the wake of the 1897 Jubilee (see below), pro-imperialist sentiment grew in Britain, particularly in ruling circles.

After a year's hiatus in southern Africa, Kruger was triumphantly re-elected as President of the Transvaal. He increased his own powers, and of course reiterated his opposition to political rights for the 'Uitlanders'. In the meantime the British sent out a new and vigorous High Commissioner for South Africa, Sir Alfred Milner (1854–1925; later first Viscount Milner), a German-born, though British-educated barrister and civil servant (his previous position was Chairman of the Board of the Inland Revenue), who had also previously run the finances of Egypt. Remarkably competent, and an arch-imperialist, he closely sympathised with the 'Uitlanders' and their grievances. In November 1898 an English workman in South Africa was killed by a Boer policeman, deeply alienating 'Uitlander' opinion, and a mass petition, signed by over 21 000 British subjects on the Rand, demanding equal rights, was sent to Britain in March 1899. After a good deal of delay it was officially taken up (that is, accepted with a measure of approval) by the British Cabinet in May 1899, after vigorous urging by Milner. The British government then held a series of protracted negotiations with Kruger and his officials in an attempt to compel the widening of the Boer franchise to include Britons on the Rand. These came close to succeeding, but finally broke down at the end of September 1899 when Kruger blocked any chance at compromise.[7]

It now seemed clear that war between Britain and the Boer republics was near. From June 1899 Chamberlain – the minister in charge of South Africa – began planning for troop reinforcements to add to the 15 000 British troops in the Cape Colony and Natal. The British case was that the two republics were already under British control, according to the Convention of London of 1884 which defined relations between these states. If they were, indeed, under British control, then the deprivation of the right to vote or other basic rights among British citizens was plainly illegal. The Boer case was that they had not agreed to British 'suzerainty' in the 1884 treaty, although they had done so in an earlier Convention of 1881. If there was no British 'suzerainty', the Boers could define the franchise in any way they wished and could treat with any foreign powers they wished. Plainly, behind this legal argument was the fact that the British coveted the two Boer republics for the Empire, while the Boers wanted to remain outside.

On 9 October 1899 Kruger sent an ultimatum to the British demanding that they withdraw their troops from Transvaal's frontiers and return their reinforcements on the way to South Africa. The Orange Free State joined the Transvaal on 11 October and war broke out the following day.

It might well have seemed as if any war between the British Empire and the two Boer republics would end in the rapid annihilation of the latter, and there were indeed good reasons for believing that this was the most likely outcome. Leaving aside the size, strength and majesty of the British Empire, and Britain's control of the oceans, it was also the case that Britain enjoyed a universal reputation for military competence. Despite its lack of conscription or of a standing home army, Britain might well indeed have possessed

---

7 The chief advocate of compromise (that is, of making five years' residency the basis for the franchise) within the Boer community was the 29-year-old Attorney-General of the Transvaal, Jan Christian Smuts (1870–1950). Smuts later became the pro-British Prime Minister of the Union of South Africa, a member of the British War Cabinet during the First World War, and, in 1945, wrote the Charter of the United Nations! He was also a Boer general during the Boer War and a philosopher of note.

the best smaller army in the world in 1899, and no one thought at the time (as the image took shape 25 years later) that Britain's generals were narrow-minded, incompetent, antediluvian Colonel Blimps. Nevertheless, there were factors on the other side. When the war broke out, the Boers actually outnumbered the British forces by over two to one. The first group of British reinforcements, numbering 47 000, would take several months to arrive and prepare themselves for battle. The Boer army was equipped with modern German and French weapons, and was fighting on its own territory in terrain in which the British were not at home. The Boers were mobile horseback marksmen, ideally suited for the type of war they were fighting. As well, Britain's reputation for recent military excellence derived from colonial wars with Asian and African armies hardly removed from savagery; the most recent British war with Europeans was in Crimea over 40 years earlier, when Britain hardly distinguished itself. The military aim of the Boers was to push through Natal and capture Durban on the coast.

The war lasted 32 months, until 31 May 1902, and was anything but a walk-over for Britain. Its earlier phase, before the British could bring large-scale reinforcements from overseas to bear, consisted chiefly of Boer victories. In particular, the British were besieged by the Boers in three fortified towns or areas, at Mafeking on the Bechuanaland border, Ladysmith in the Orange Free State, near Basutoland, and Kimberley, also in the Orange Free State, on the border with the Cape Colony.[8] To make matters worse, the Boers won a series of stunning victories, especially at Magersfontein near Kimberley, during what quickly became known as 'Black Week', 10–15 December 1899; nearly 3000 British soldiers were killed in this week alone, a number without precedent since the Crimean conflict.

The British commander in South Africa, Sir Redvers Buller, was then replaced by Field-Marshal Lord Roberts (Sir Frederick Roberts, 1832–1914; later first Earl Roberts), a veteran of the Indian mutiny with distinguished service throughout the Empire.[9] The highly competent General Lord Kitchener (Horatio Herbert Kitchener, 1850–1916, later first Earl Kitchener of Khartoum), fresh from his victories at Omdurman (see below), served as his Chief of Staff. Roberts arrived in South Africa on 10 January 1900. While Buller continued to lose battles and men disastrously, especially at Spion Kop (25 January 1900), where 1700 British soldiers were killed, the tide had now turned in Britain's direction. The Boer general, Cronje, surrendered with 4000 men on 27 February, the day before Ladysmith was relieved. In May Roberts occupied the principal Boer cities of the Transvaal, Johannesburg and Pretoria, and in the same month, on 17

8 The defence of Kimberley was headed by Colonel (later General) Robert Baden-Powell (1857–1941; later first Baron Baden-Powell), subsequently celebrated as the founder of the Boy Scouts, which he began in 1908.
9 Roberts's only son was killed during 'Black Week'. It was just after this that Queen Victoria made her celebrated remark to Arthur Balfour that 'we are not interested in the possibilities of defeat; they do not exist'.

May, Mafeking was relieved after a 217-day siege. When news of the relief of Mafeking reached Britain, an unprecedented saturnalia of spontaneous street celebrations and jingoistic patriotism broke out in London, an event which became legendary to all who lived through it as 'Mafeking night'. (This gave rise to the word 'mafficking', to rejoice with boisterous street demonstrations, which is still occasionally heard.) Nothing like 'Mafeking Night' had been known in England in the memory of anyone then alive, and the wildness of the celebrations possibly exceeded those known at the end of the two World Wars. Also in May 1900, the British overran and formally annexed the Orange Free State, renaming it the Orange River Colony. Finally, in September 1900 the Transvaal itself was formally annexed to Britain as the Transvaal Colony.

Yet the war was to drag on for another 18 months. Although Kruger fled to Europe in September 1900, the remaining Boer commanders organised a campaign of guerrilla warfare against the British, one of the first times that this familiar tactic of modern conflict had been used. Small forces of Boers repeatedly raided the Cape Colony, destroying railway tracks, telegraph lines, and attacking military posts. Kitchener, Commander-in-Chief after November 1900, erected a line of fortified blockhouses and, much more controversially, herded 120 000 Boer women and children into what were named 'concentration camps', where over 20 000 died from disease.[10] By ruthless action, the Boer guerrillas were eventually forced to submit, although the end of the war did not finally come until the Treaty of Vereeniging on 31 May 1902. By the end of hostilities the British had no less than 300 000 troops in South Africa (double the total size of the British army in 1890), and had been forced to raise the number of men recruited into the army from 155 000 in 1895 to 421 000 in 1901. The cost of the Boer War was also astronomical: expenditure on the army increased from £18 million in 1895 to £61 million in 1900, while even expenditure on the navy rose from £19 million to £29 million in the same period. In all, the Boer War cost Britain about £222 million; nearly 5800 soldiers were killed and 23 000 wounded. Hicks-Beach, the Chancellor of the Exchequer, paid for the war by an increase in the income tax and other direct taxes, which rose rapidly so that, for the first time in British history, revenue from direct taxes was greater than revenue from indirect taxes. In the final analysis, Britain acquitted itself fairly well in the Boer War, especially considering the latter's remoteness and the terrain in which it was fought. Yet there were reasons for grave disquiet: the early and late successes of the Boers, the incompetence of some military leaders, and especially the lengthy period

10 These 'concentration camps' obviously had nothing in common with those used to commit mass murder by Nazi Germany and other totalitarian regimes. Nevertheless, the appalling conditions in the South African 'concentration camps' were deliberately hushed up by the British military (although not by the British government, which was sympathetic to the plight of their inmates when attention was drawn to their condition). Miss Emily Hobhouse, an English social investigator, was instrumental in ameliorating conditions for the Boers.

necessary to subdue as inconsequential a pair of states as one could imagine. Moreover, victory on the veldt gave promotion, during the next 14 years, to cavalry officers who would prove totally unsuitable to leading Britain in the kind of war fought in 1914–18. Some lessons were learned, but not enough.

During his tenure at the Colonial Office Chamberlain proved to be a dynamic and innovative administrator, with a grand vision of an increasingly unified Empire, developing economically and politically. While Chamberlain was instrumental in both fomenting and orchestrating the Boer War, he was something of a moderate in his policy towards the Boers, and until the last minute sought a compromise. He was highly critical of the muddle and inefficiency of the War Office (for which he had no direct responsibility) during the later, guerrilla-based phases of the conflict. Apart from the Boer War – widely known as 'Chamberlain's War' – the Colonial Secretary did much to further the 'imperial dream'. In 1897 Chamberlain convened a Colonial Conference, the first held for 10 years, to coincide with the Queen's Diamond Jubilee celebrations. It was attended by the premiers of 11 self-governing colonies, including those of Canada, the Australian colonies, New Zealand, and of the Cape and Natal in South Africa. Chamberlain wished to see the eventual creation of an imperial federal Parliament, an idea coolly received by the self-governing colonies. He set in motion the improvement of health in the tropical Empire, and was indirectly responsible for the discovery, by Ronald Ross (a student under the Medical Adviser to the Colonial Office; he was working in India), that malaria was spread by mosquitoes, eventually saving millions of lives, and for other public health improvements in the tropical Empire. In 1899 Chamberlain established the renowned London School of Tropical Medicine, as well as a privately funded school of tropical medicine in Liverpool. He was also responsible for beginning the modern economic development of the British West Indies, a neglected backwater for the previous 60 years, through his appointment of a Royal Commission on this subject in 1897. Chamberlain's startling vision of Imperial Preference – a tariff barrier around the whole Empire, thus contradicting Britain's pervasive free trade orthodoxy – was not, however, proclaimed until after the end of the Boer War and Salisbury's retirement.

During the years 1895–1900 Britain also found itself in a number of serious diplomatic imbroglios with other powers. The most implausible was that which erupted, for the most unlikely of reasons, between Britain and the United States. In December 1895 President Grover Cleveland, in a message to Congress, sent Britain what amounted to an ultimatum concerning a long-standing border dispute between British Guiana and Venezuela. Cleveland, drawing on the Monroe Doctrine, announced that an American commission would decide on the boundary and impose it regardless of Britain's wishes. Happily, Cleveland, a Democrat, did not stand for re-election in 1896, and his successor, William McKinley, a

Republican, proved more amenable to reason. Britain acted with considerable restraint, and the Treaty of Washington of 1897 and its subsequent adjudication in 1899 largely supported the British case. Chamberlain used considerable skills behind the scenes to bring about an amicable agreement.[11] The Venezuela border dispute marked a turning-point of extraordinary importance, not merely in relations between Britain and America, but in the history of the world. After its settlement, relations between the old and new English-speaking powers improved steadily and soon evolved into a *de facto* 'special relationship', based upon common ancestry, language and culture, which probably proved to be the most important determining factor in international diplomacy in the twentieth century.

Relations between Britain and France, meanwhile, also soured. Britain was slowly but surely advancing down the Nile Valley, conquering as she went. But France, the second greatest imperial power, was also advancing from French West Africa. In March 1895, just before Salisbury came to power, Sir Edward Grey, the Under-Secretary for Foreign Affairs in the previous Liberal government, had denounced French expansionism into British territory. The French took no notice, continuing to expand into the Nile Valley. In September 1898 Lord Kitchener, leading the expedition against Khartoum, encountered the French force under Captain Marchand at Fashoda, on the White Nile in southern Sudan. He handed the French a written protest regarding their presence, but took no further action. When word of the 'Fashoda incident' reached Britain, however, it nearly led to war. By February 1899, France, lacking either foreign allies or the stomach for a pointless war with Britain, gave way and evacuated the White Nile area. In March 1899 the Anglo-French Convention defined the limits of the spheres of influence between the two powers. As with the dispute with America, Britain's diplomacy paid untold dividends, with relations between the two traditional rivals steadily improving, so that a formal agreement, virtually a treaty, between Britain and France, the 'Entente Cordiale', was concluded in 1904 and the two countries were allies in 1914.

In this period, the British also finished their uncompleted business in the Sudan, where, in 1885, General Gordon had been massacred by the Mahdi. In June 1885 the Mahdi died, and was succeeded by the Khalifa Abdullah el Taashi, who conquered the whole of what later became the Anglo-Egyptian Sudan. Nothing was done until 1896, when Kitchener, the Sirdar (Commander) of the Egyptian army, organised an expedition to conquer the Sudan. Surprisingly, Salisbury and Chamberlain were lukewarm, although the extraordinary defeat of the Italian army by the Ethiopians at Adowa in the same year helped to concentrate minds. Kitchener advanced by short, relentless stages down the Nile, building a railway line (to bring supplies) as he went. In September 1898 he conquered Omdurman and

---

11 Normally, of course, the Foreign Secretary would deal with disputes with foreign powers; in this case, however, British Guiana was dealt with by the Colonial Office.

Khartoum, routing the Khalifa; an Anglo-Egyptian Condominum was proclaimed over the Sudan, which became known for nearly 50 years as the Anglo-Egyptian Sudan.[12] In 1896, Ashanti (later part of the Gold Coast and still later of Ghana), a troublesome inland African kingdom, was also conquered by the British. As well, the British East Africa Protectorate (later most of Kenya) came under direct British control at this time.

All of these colonial developments culminated in the second, or Diamond, Jubilee of Queen Victoria in June 1897. Far more in keeping with the 'spirit of the age' than even 10 years previously, the Diamond Jubilee was attended by 11 colonial premiers. The aged Queen drove through six miles of packed streets to St Paul's Cathedral, where an open-air service of thanksgiving had to be held since the Queen was too frail to climb the building's steps. This was one of the earliest historical occasions to be recorded on motion pictures.

Given the centrality of imperial and foreign events during Salisbury's 1895–1900 government, not surprisingly domestic legislation took a back seat, but here again what there was was achieved largely through Chamberlain's influence. In 1897 he passed a Workmen's Compensation Act, which introduced the general principle that accidents at a workplace had to be paid for by the firm concerned, this as a normal rule rather than as the product of an intricate lawsuit over the precise definition of negligence. The law was originally fairly restricted in scope but gradually widened. The Unionists, however, narrowly missed an opportunity to do something far more important. Chamberlain had long wanted a state old-age pension, similar to that which Bismarck had enacted in Germany. A Royal Commission appointed by the Liberal government in 1892, reporting three years later, had recommended only further study of the matter. In 1896 Chamberlain was instrumental in appointing a second Royal Commission on this subject which, in its 1898 report, recommended against adopting such a pension. Chamberlain persisted, and had a parliamentary select committee appointed which, in 1899, recommended a narrowly based scheme, but one which was not too different from that actually enacted by Lloyd George a decade later. The costs of this scheme, however, simply could not be met during the Boer War, and the plan died. Thus, the origins of the 'Welfare State' were finally to be found during the famous Liberal government of 1905–14 (and especially after Campbell-Bannerman's retirement in 1908), although the Unionists could easily have begun it themselves and nearly did. Some reforms were also made to agricultural rates, but in general the Salisbury government did not enact the reforms backed by Chamberlain.

The period of the Conservative ascendancy from 1895 to 1900 also saw what was probably the nadir of the Liberal party between Grey's accession to the premiership in 1830 and the Lloyd George–Asquith split in 1916.

12 Although the government of Egypt had a nominal independence (and residual links to Turkey), it was effectively under British control by this time, and Britain became the effective sovereign of the Sudan, which achieved independence in 1956.

The party was demoralised, without strong leadership, and lacking in effective policies. It was also, worse still, bitterly split over the Boer War. Lord Rosebery, the Liberal leader, constantly bickered with most of his colleagues and was literally not on speaking terms with his former Chancellor of the Exchequer (and effective successor), Sir William V. Harcourt. In August 1896 the Turks conducted an appalling massacre of Armenians in Constantinople, in which 6000 were murdered.[13] This brought Gladstone, now nearly 87, temporarily out of retirement, and the possibility was seriously entertained that the 'GOM' might yet again re-enter politics. Rosebery, a moderate on the 'Eastern question', resigned as leader of the Liberal party a few months later, in October 1896, nominally as a result of differences with his colleagues over Turkey. He never held office again, although for the next six or seven years he was regarded as the leader of the Liberal Imperialists, a close associate of H. H. Asquith, Richard Haldane, Sir Edward Grey and others. Then he drifted into a long twilight, and did not join the Liberal government in 1905, although he was still only 58. 'I must plough my furrow alone', he said mysteriously. The leadership of the Liberal party was now divided between Harcourt in the Commons (he had been leader of the party in that chamber since 1894) and Lord Kimberley (John Wodehouse, third Baron and first Earl of Kimberley, 1826–1902), Foreign Secretary in Rosebery's Cabinet in the Lords. (Kimberley remained as leader in the Lords until his death.) Harcourt was generally recognised as the actual leader of the party. Like Rosebery, Harcourt was also notoriously touchy and difficult with colleagues, and he, too, resigned as leader of the party in the Commons over a minor issue in December 1898. The leadership rivals were regarded as Sir Henry Campbell-Bannerman (1836–1908) and H. H. Asquith, with Asquith giving way to Campbell-Bannerman as the senior man, Asquith having to spend his time at the Bar as a highly successful QC. While Campbell-Bannerman was associated with the anti-Boer War camp and Asquith was a well-known 'Liberal Imperialist', there was actually very little difference in their general outlooks. As Prime Minister after 1905, however, 'C.B.', as he was known, proved to be a neo-Gladstonian advocate of retrenchment, while Asquith, who became premier three years later, introduced the 'New Liberalism' with a strong measure of collectivism and state expenditure.

Even worse was to follow for the Liberals, for the Boer War came close to tearing the party asunder. Throughout its history the Liberal party has had considerable difficulty in dealing with patriotism and patriotic emotions, with many radicals, especially Nonconformists and intellectuals, essentially opposing patriotism as an unworthy and atavistic emotion. Such men had still more trouble in coming to terms with military power or warfare, and more still in dealing with conflicts which (like the Boer War)

13 This was a prelude to the much more barbaric massacre of Armenians in the Ottoman Empire during the First World War, in which over one million Armenians are believed to have been murdered.

were not obviously necessary and waged in self-defence. Such wars were in their view generally conducted by bullies, the strong conquering the weak. On the other hand, the late Victorian Liberal party also contained an influential group of leaders who accepted British imperialism as a good thing, a progressive and uplifting extension of British government and democracy to Britons overseas in the white colonies, and of British civilisation to the non-European Empire. Far from being atavistic, large empires and states were at the forefront of progress, with the most advanced states, such as the United States and Germany, being continental in size or aspiring to world-empire status. These were fundamental differences in philosophy which threatened to split the Liberal party. In favour of the war were the 'Liberal Imperialists' such as Rosebery, Asquith, Richard Haldane and Sir Edward Grey, while opposing them were the so-called 'Little Englanders' or 'pro-Boers', especially John Morley and David Lloyd George (1863–1945, subsequently first Earl Lloyd-George of Dwyfor), 20 years later himself the Prime Minister of a successful wartime coalition, but in the latter 1890s, as a rising backbencher, a firm and courageous opponent of the Boer War. Lloyd George (and many other Welsh radicals) saw in the Boers a small Protestant nation like their own whose independence was threatened by an overweening England, just as Welsh autonomy had been extinguished by England.[14] As well, many, probably most, radicals and leftists opposed the Boer War, including the Independent Labour Party and radical intellectuals like J. L. Hobson, who linked the Boer War with 'finance capitalism' and the drive by 'plutocrats' in London to increase their profits.[15] On the other hand, many of the leaders of the Fabian Society, like the Webbs and George Bernard Shaw, actually supported the Boer War, viewing the growth of 'progressive' empires with favour.

Allied with the 'pro-Boers' was the new leader of the Liberal party in the Commons, Sir Henry Campbell-Bannerman. In June 1901 he made the simple most famous remark of the war when, commenting on the revelations of widespread suffering in the 'concentration camps', he asked in a speech at Bradford: 'When was a war not a war? When it was carried on by methods of barbarism in South Africa.' There was nothing unreasonable in these words, if applied to the unfortunate 'concentration camps'. But imperialists took them to refer to the war as a whole, implying that

---

14 During the post-1945 period, until multi-racial democracy came to South Africa in 1994, the Boers were chiefly known for their hardline racism, and it may be wondered that radicals would empathise with the Boer republics. At the time, however, the Boers were not especially known for their view of black inferiority, which was held ubiquitously by the white world.

15 A good deal of radical opposition to the Boer War had strong anti-Semitic overtones, with the Jewish financiers in South Africa, like Beit and Barnato, being singled out by the radical press for especial venom, and often linked with the 'degenerate' English aristocracy. This anti-Semitic edge was very alien to British politics, and quickly disappeared.

ordinary British soldiers were barbarians. This drove imperialists to fury, and the nation's atmosphere turned very nasty. Lloyd George was nearly lynched during an anti-war speech in Birmingham in December 1901, and a riot ensued in which two people were killed.

In September 1900, at the time when it appeared that Britain had decisively won the Boer War, Salisbury called a general election, several years before it was actually due. It was the first of three general elections known as the 'khaki' elections, from the colour of British military uniforms.[16] Chamberlain and the Tories were frankly anxious to capitalise on the patriotism surrounding the war, something which the Liberals naturally regarded as unfair, and not without reason. Nevertheless, five years had passed since the previous election, and the Tories had lost the usual number of by-elections. The election took place in the first half of October 1900. It resulted in a virtually identical result to the 1895 poll, a very significant win for the Unionists. The two wings of the Unionist party took 402 seats, nine fewer than in 1895; the Liberals won 184 seats, up seven from the previous poll. The Irish Nationalists won two seats and there were two wins for the Labour party, formed as an independent party that year (see below). The Unionists actually won a slightly higher percentage of the overall vote, 1 468 000 out of 3 523 000, or 50.3 per cent, while the Liberal vote, 1 572 000, declined slightly to 45.0 per cent. However, as in 1900 this actually understates the scale of the Unionists' victory, since there were even more unopposed returns than in the previous election: 163 on the Unionist side and 20 among the Liberals. Had all these seats been contested, it is again likely that the Unionists would have secured 55–60 per cent of the total vote, a higher percentage than any party ever achieved in any election in the twentieth century except 1931 (and possibly 1918). The Liberals did regain some lost ground, especially in Wales, but also lost some ground, especially in Scotland, where the Unionists won a majority of seats, 36 out of 70, and in previously Liberal seats influenced by the war, like Portsmouth and Plymouth. Among the middle classes, the Unionist vote was higher than ever; one historian has calculated that there was a further swing of 5.7 per cent in the 18 middle-class constituencies in London, and a swing of 5.8 per cent in London's mixed middle-class and working-class seats. The 1900 general election marked the high-water mark of the ascendancy of the late Victorian Conservative party: after this, it was downhill all the way, full recovery occurring only after the First World War when Labour and the Liberals split the non-Conservative vote.

16 The other two 'khaki' elections were held in December 1918, just after the end of the First World War, and in July 1945, just after V-E Day but before Japan had been defeated. The first resulted in a great triumph for the ruling Lloyd George government, but in the second, of course, Churchill was decisively but unexpectedly defeated by Labour.

15

The end of Conservative hegemony and the rise of the Liberals, 1902–1906

Following the 1900 election, Lord Salisbury (who was now 70) reorganised his government, relinquishing the Foreign Secretaryship in favour of Lord Lansdowne. C. T. Ritchie took the Home Office, and a number of others joined the Cabinet – St John Brodrick (1856–1942; later ninth Viscount and first Earl Middleton) at the War Office during the latter stages of the Boer War, the sixth Marquess of Londonderry as Postmaster-General, Gerald Balfour (Arthur's brother, and Salisbury's nephew) at the Board of Trade.[1] Despite these changes, Salisbury was now clearly on the decline as leader. In January 1901 Queen Victoria died after a reign of over 63 years. Only the elderly could remember a time when she had not been Queen. She seemed a permanent part of the British constitution and, indeed, of the British terrain. Unpopular after Albert's death and her withdrawal from public life, she lived to enjoy enormous popularity as a living monument. Her eldest son and heir, Edward VII (1841–1910), who reigned from January 1901 until May 1910, had waited 40 years to assume a position of responsibility, and was nearly 60 when he became King. An intelligent and far-seeing man, he was also renowned (in private) for his dissipations, over women – he was a celebrated philanderer – food and drink, gambling, and the racetrack. He had, for instance, been present at the most famous Victorian scandal at the card table, at Tranby Croft, in 1891, and twice gave evidence in court over Society scandals. Excluded from any real position of authority by his mother, he was popular and had a real authority in foreign policy, which he used for peaceful purposes, derived from his being a close relative of the ruling houses of Germany, Russia and many other countries. While Queen Victoria had evolved politically from a Whig to a barely disguised Tory partisan, Edward was something of a Liberal, a friend of Gladstone, who preferred the company of self-made

1 It will be seen that the social composition of the Cabinet did not change. So many of Salisbury's relatives were given positions in the Cabinet that it became known as the 'Hotel Cecil', after a leading West End hotel ('Cecil' was Salisbury's family name).

men and *nouveaux riches*. For decades after his death, millions recalled the nine years of his reign with genuine nostalgia as the 'good old days', and the Edwardian era (like his mother, Edward gave his name to a historical period) is still normally seen as a time of luxury and wealth, of genuine happiness for the upper classes against a background of political unrest and turmoil which ended (four years after his death) in European catastrophe.[2]

The date of Edward's coronation was set for June 1902, but had to be postponed until August when the King became seriously ill with appendicitis. In July 1902, however, Lord Salisbury resigned, and was succeeded by his nephew Arthur Balfour (Leader of the House of Commons since 1895), who was Prime Minister from 12 July 1902 until 4 December 1905.[3] Balfour's three and a half years as Prime Minister proved to be a political disaster almost without parallel in modern British history, such that at the 1906 general election the Unionists lost nearly 250 seats while the Liberals gained 216.

Arthur Balfour, whose mother was Lord Salisbury's sister, was the son of a wealthy Scottish landowner. Educated at Eton and Cambridge, he was renowned both for his languid aestheticism and his sharp mind. Unmarried, and regarded (wrongly) by many of his contemporaries as effeminate, Balfour was a strikingly clever intellectual who wrote serious, well-regarded works of philosophy and maintained an interest in science and (like many of his contemporaries) in psychic research. In Parliament, he was a brilliant and very skilful debater, among the very best of his time, and he belied his reputation for dilettantism by proving to be a strong, indeed ruthless, Secretary for Ireland. After giving up the leadership of the Conservative party in 1911, Balfour continued to serve in Cabinet posts for many years (he served in the Cabinet as late as June 1929, 55 years after he first entered Parliament), and was Foreign Secretary during the First World War and post-war years, 1916–19. A strong philosemite, in 1917 he was the author of the famous 'Balfour Declaration' promising the Jews a national home in Palestine (newly conquered by Britain from Turkey), and

2　In 1902 Edward initiated the Order of Merit, an order of chivalry for persons eminent in literature, science, the arts, and other spheres. Recipients, limited in number to twenty-four, place the initials 'OM' after their names but do not receive a title. This award is decided by the Sovereign, and was one of the earliest given to women: Florence Nightingale was given the OM in 1907 at the age of 87.

3　Balfour remained as leader of the Conservative party until he resigned, after three general election defeats, in November 1911. When Salisbury retired, the eighth Duke of Devonshire became leader of the Unionists in the House of Lords, although he, too, resigned from this post over the tariff reform controversy in October 1903, and was succeeded by Henry Petty-FitzMaurice, fifth Marquess of Lansdowne (1845–1927), who served until 1916. Salisbury was the last Prime Minister to serve from the House of Lords (although technically Sir Alec Douglas-Home sat in the Lords as the fourteenth Earl of Home for a few days at the start of his term of office in 1963 before disclaiming his title).

was thus one of the fathers of the State of Israel. He was an adept, skilful and subtle politician, whose term as Prime Minister was in many ways fruitful, and there was no reason why he should have proved to be a political failure in that office. He was, however, also a considerable trimmer – 'he nailed his colours firmly to the fence' was one famous description of Balfour – who lacked either the forceful personality or unassailable position to marginalise dissent within the party or to command events outside of Parliament.

Balfour's Cabinet naturally overlapped very considerably with his uncle's. Most of his changes were minor. There was one exception. Austen Chamberlain (later Sir Austen Chamberlain, 1863–1937) joined the Cabinet as Postmaster-General. The eldest son of Joseph Chamberlain, who had intended him to be his political heir, Austen was educated at Rugby and Cambridge, and was fully a part of the British 'Establishment'. Although he later held a wide variety of offices, including Chancellor of the Exchequer and Foreign Secretary, and was leader of the Conservative party briefly in 1921–22, he never attained the highest office, and, while competent and intelligent, lacked both his father's brilliance and audacity. 'He always played the game and always lost it' is the famous verdict on Austen Chamberlain's career.[4] The other new members of Balfour's Cabinet, appointed between 1902 and 1905, were, with the possible exception of Lord Onslow at the Board of Agriculture, surprisingly lacklustre, and few made much of a subsequent impact. Balfour himself had no obvious successor. Not the least of his failings, and the source of subsequent difficulties in the Conservative party, was his failure to identify and promote younger men of high talent. Andrew Bonar Law, a future Prime Minister, and Sir Edward Carson, possibly the party's best debater, held ministerial but not Cabinet positions; Lord Curzon was in India as Viceroy during Balfour's administration; Winston Churchill, then a Tory, remained on the backbenches and, as described below, left the party over tariffs in 1904, becoming a Liberal for the next 18 years. When the Conservative party eventually regained office over a decade after the 1906 débâcle, only a minority of its leading men had any previous Cabinet experience.

The Balfour government's main troubles came from three sources: from Joseph Chamberlain's scheme to enact Imperial Preference, which caused deep splits within the party, from hostility by Nonconformists generated by the Education Act of 1902 and other matters, and from the alienation of

---

4 Austen's younger half-brother was Neville Chamberlain (1869–1940), who is regarded as an outstanding Minister of Health and Chancellor of the Exchequer, but, of course, had the misfortune to have been Prime Minister at the time of the Munich Agreement and the outbreak of the Second World War. Unlike his elder brother, Neville attended Birmingham University rather than Cambridge and was then sent off by his father to head (unsuccessfully) a sisal plantation in the West Indies for several years. Unlike Neville, Austen was a militant anti-appeaser and an early, outspoken opponent of Hitler. He might well have changed the course of history if he rather than Neville had been Prime Minister in the 1930s.

many trade unions by the Taff Vale decision, described later in this chapter, and the rise of the Labour party.

To his credit, Chamberlain never conceived of the conquest of the Boer republics in South Africa merely in terms of greed and territorial expansion for their own sake, but always as part of a constructive vision of a united and progressive Empire. For years, he had been flirting with the overt abandonment of free trade in favour of a major, indeed grandiose, plan for an imperial tariff – a tariff around the whole British Empire – leading to a much greater degree of imperial unity and eventually imperial federation. In November 1902 Chamberlain visited South Africa, making a point of touring the Boer colonies. He had also already been actively proposing a system of reciprocal tariffs with the colonies, especially Canada, over corn (wheat), a kind of partial revival of the old Corn Laws. In May 1903 Chamberlain formally broke ranks with the entire free trade tradition of modern Britain, announcing in a major, widely heralded speech in Birmingham that he had been converted to a far-reaching plan of Imperial Preference, with tariff retaliation against foreign governments which kept out British goods.

Chamberlain's plan was indeed a bold and far-reaching one. His long-term aim was to mould the whole Empire into a single vast economic and military unit, able to meet the considerable threats posed by the United States, Germany and Russia, the obvious superpowers of the twentieth century. In a sense, Chamberlain's grand plan represented the strategy of what might be termed the battle for third place in twentieth-century geopolitics. He, like many others, realised that the United States was already destined to be one of the Great Powers of the new century, and would probably be joined by the vast continental Empire of Russia, if Russia, rather than collapsing, successfully modernised. The race for third place as a great power was between Germany, then furiously industrialising, and Britain. But Britain had never realised the potential of its world-wide Empire and was steadily declining economically, at least in its manufacturing industries. Its free trade policies left it unable to exclude foreign goods, especially those from Germany and the United States, despite the fact that these countries imposed tariffs against Britain. The long-term decline in Britain's manufacturing base was compounded by the huge increase in debt as a result of the costs of the Boer War.

Imperial Preference would also have another outcome which was regarded by Chamberlain as just as important as any other. It would produce fuller employment and higher wages for the British working classes, while the revenues generated by tariffs could be used for measures of social reform such as old-age pensions. Imperial Preference represented a non-socialist method of achieving social reforms benefiting the working classes: it did not entail higher taxes on the rich or a collectivist political agenda. Such reforms would be financed by 'making the foreigner pay', as tariff reformers put it. It was thus a constructive Conservative alternative to

Labour's socialism, and was seen as such by its supporters for many decades.

Chamberlain's aims were supported by a large number of younger Conservatives, who, for decades, kept alive a vision of imperial unity. Eventually, in 1932, during the Great Depression, a kind of Imperial Preference was indeed enacted. Many economic historians believe that Britain's tariff was important to ending the Depression in Britain so that the latter 1930s were relatively prosperous. When Chamberlain first proposed Imperial Preference, however, it had catastrophic effects on the fortunes of the Conservative party. Tariff reform (as his proposals were generally known at the time; the debate over tariffs at this time is also referred to as the 'fiscal question') was entirely rejected by the whole of the Liberal party, to whom free trade still remained almost an item of religious faith. Free traders used all of their traditional arguments in countering Chamberlain. They insisted that tariffs hurt those who enacted them, by raising prices and limiting consumer choice; that tariffs would lead to local cartels and monopolies, augmenting inefficiency and backwardness; that Britain had become the 'workshop of the world' under free trade, and if Britain's position was declining (which was arguable), the solution lay in more efficient industries, not in tariffs. Free traders were not slow to point out the self-contradictions in the 'social reform' component of Chamberlain's vision, noting that if tariffs worked effectively there would be no revenue for social welfare, while if tariffs raised significant revenue, they were not efficiently excluding foreign goods. The most politically telling point made by the free-traders, however, was that tariff reform aimed to reverse the legacy of Corn Law repeal by enacting a tariff on bread and other foodstuffs. 'No tax on bread' became one of the most successful catch-cries of the free traders, with a potent effect on the working classes. Free traders also pointed to the extreme (and rather surprising) reluctance of most of the self-governing colonies to warm to Chamberlain's scheme, and to the difficulties of persuading Canada, Australia, New Zealand and other self-governing Dominions to sacrifice their own economic interests for the Mother Country.[5]

Chamberlain's proposals thus had the unintended effect of uniting the previously disunified Liberal party. But they also had the arguably more serious effect of splitting the Unionists, and in particular of making the task of the Prime Minister almost impossible. To free traders in the Cabinet Chamberlain aimed at taking the party over and moving it in a quite

5 At the Colonial Conference of 1902, where Chamberlain first floated his plan in a preliminary way, the colonial ministers specifically declared 'free trade within the empire' to be 'impractical'. Many self-governing colonies were already in the process of formulating their own tariff arrangements with their neighbours, for instance Canada with the United States. The two largest Australian colonies, New South Wales and Victoria, traditionally had opposing attitudes to tariffs, with the former pro-free trade and the latter pro-tariff.

revolutionary direction. While the Tories had, in 1846, supported protection, no one had seriously advocated a reversal of the doctrine of free trade
for half a century. Free trade had many staunch supporters in the government, especially among Chamberlain's former Liberal Unionist colleagues.
It was unlikely that so radical a policy as the general adoption of tariffs
would be adopted without a general election victory, even assuming that
Cabinet agreement could be reached on such a programme, while tariffs
had plainly not been mentioned at the previous general election in 1900.
Chamberlain did have some supporters for his programme, most notably
Andrew Bonar Law (1858–1923), an influential junior minister who later
became Prime Minister, but surprisingly few front-line Tories supported
him, his main backers being intellectuals and party activists outside of
Parliament. On the other hand, it was probably the case that most Tories
were at least mildly sympathetic to Chamberlain's ideas, while only a
minority were as committed to free trade as were the Liberals.

Arthur Balfour found himself in a very difficult position. At first he
prevaricated, but in September 1903 announced a programme of his own,
in which retaliatory tariffs would be enacted against foreign countries
erecting tariffs against British goods, but he explicitly ruled out either an
imperial tariff or any tariff on foodstuffs. This programme pleased no one.
It was, in fact, a last-minute response to a wave of poorly handled Cabinet
dismissals and resignations earlier the same month. By the end of September 1903 Joseph Chamberlain, the Duke of Devonshire, C. T. Ritchie,
and two other Cabinet ministers had resigned, neither Chamberlain nor
Devonshire ever again holding office. Balfour continued his tightrope act by
appointing Austen Chamberlain as Chancellor of the Exchequer (although
he never enacted any tariffs in the two years he held this position) and
Devonshire's nephew and heir Victor Cavendish (1868–1938; later ninth
Duke of Devonshire) as his deputy. Joseph Chamberlain then launched a
great campaign on behalf of his policies, forming a Tariff Reform League
and a Tariff Reform Commission of sympathetic economists to provide
intellectual ammunition. Tariff reform enthusiasts launched a campaign
against pro-free trade Tories, driving up to a dozen pro-free trade Conservative MPs out of the party.[6] Balfour made statements increasingly
sympathetic to tariff reform, but was unable to rebuild a united party. By
the time of the 1906 general election, the Conservatives appeared hopelessly divided on this crucial question. In modern democracies, party
disunity, especially within a party with a weak leader, is virtually an
automatic prelude to electoral disaster, as, more recently, Labour discovered in the early 1980s and the Conservatives in the late 1990s. The

6 The most notable pro-free trade defection (as a result of personal commitment, not tariff
  reform pressure) was Winston Churchill, who quit the Conservative party in early 1904 to
  join the Liberals. Churchill served as a Liberal minister for most of the period between 1905
  and 1922 before rejoining the Conservatives in 1924.

Conservatives' disunity contributed enormously to their 1906 election débâcle.

The Tories also managed to alienate the large and influential Nonconformist section of the community. While Nonconformists had been heavily Liberal in the past, by the late nineteenth century, as sociological differences between Anglicans and Nonconformists narrowed, many Dissenters became increasingly sympathetic to the Tories. Religion *per se* (apart from Ireland) was certainly becoming less central and more marginal to political debate. Most evangelical and conversionist Protestant energy increasingly focused on winning the heathens of the tropical world to Christianity; high hopes were entertained, in the early twentieth century, of an increasingly Christianised world, often with good reason. In contrast, by the Edwardian period far less effort was devoted to winning denominational supporters in Britain. Many intellectuals were now agnostics; many more educated people now considered religion a purely private matter, with religious questions notably banished from dinner party conversation. Nevertheless, religion was still an enormously important matter to millions of people.

The immediate cause of Balfour's troubles in this realm was the Education Act of 1902, largely devised by Sir Robert Morant, a leading civil servant. It was designed to deal with some legal flaws in the provision of state secondary schooling as it stood, and did so in a sweeping way, by giving enlarged powers to local authorities to provide secondary education; moreover it abolished the school boards. However, it also brought the voluntary (i.e. religious-based) schools under the authority of local governments, using ratepayers' money, for the first time, to pay their teachers. This pleased Anglicans and Catholics, but incensed Nonconformists, who objected to public rates being used to pay denominational schools. Nonconformists particularly objected to the lease of life the Act gave to Anglican schools in country areas, where there was often no Nonconformist alternative. Joseph Chamberlain, still a champion of Nonconformity (although not a practising one), attempted to modify the Act but failed. The Nonconformists, led by Dr John Clifford, a Baptist minister, launched a campaign of passive resistance against the payment of rates to accomplish the purposes of the Act which lingered until the 1906 election.

Nonconformist hostility to the Education Act was only the tip of a great iceberg of dissenting and Evangelical Anglican hostility to the religious trends of the day, seemingly supported by the Conservative government, which has long been underestimated by historians. Within the Church of England, High Church quasi-Catholic ritual and usage was apparently winning the upper hand during the late nineteenth century. High Church Anglicanism was increasingly favoured by many Oxbridge graduates and by an important component of the upper classes. Many Low Church Anglicans and Nonconformists, however, found its success deeply alarming, raising the spectre of illegal, 'Romanist' rituals, unfair and secretive clerical power, and thinly veiled homosexual and other deviant sexual practices allegedly associated with the High Church wing. While similar charges had been voiced since the start of the Oxford Movement in the 1830s, they were frequently heard again at the end of the Victorian period, in works like Walter Walsh's *Secret History of the Oxford Movement*, which sold 12 000 copies in the first year of its publication in 1897.

Nonconformists also felt a deep sense of continuing grievance at the fact that they were still excluded from the Established institutions of England. During the 150 years since the rise of 'New Dissent', the industrial revolution had made many Nonconformists wealthy. Those several generations removed from the 'self-made' ancestor who founded the family fortune were, by the early twentieth century, thoroughly respectable. Yet Nonconformists still formed no part of the official religious component of the British 'Establishment'. There was, in other words, a considerable incongruity between the wealth and status of middle-class Edwardian Nonconformists, which was an important factor, when added to the others, in producing the great Liberal victory of 1906. As well, Chamberlain's resurrection of Protection, especially the protection of agricultural products, appeared to some Nonconformists to comprise a subtle way of favouring the Anglican squirearchy and the Anglican Church itself, which was still a considerable owner of land, often relying on rents for its income.

The third source of erosion of Tory support in this period was in the ranks of labour and the trade unions. The years 1900–05 witnessed a number of important developments in these areas. During the 1890s membership in the TUC remained fairly stable at just above one million. In the early years of the twentieth century it grew more rapidly, reaching over 1.5 million by 1905. This still represented a small portion of the British labour force of over 16 million (of whom 11.5 million were males) but organised labour was constantly growing in strength. Unlike most continental countries, Britain had never had a socialist party or one based in the trade unions. By 1898–99, however, key leaders of the old, unsuccessful Independent Labour Party were now successfully agitating for a broadly based Labour party. Such a body was formed, at least in embryonic form, at a famous meeting of trade unions and socialist societies at the Memorial Hall in Farringdon Street, London, in February 1900. Delegates established a 'Labour Representation Committee' (LRC) whose explicit aim – moved by Keir Hardie – was 'a distinct Labour Group in Parliament [with] their own Whips'. The Secretary of the LRC was a young socialist activist, James Ramsay MacDonald (1866–1937), who, 24 years later, became Labour's first Prime Minister. Fabian socialists – middle-class socialist intellectuals – were disproportionately influential in this group from the beginning.[7] Little notice was taken of the LRC at the time. Labour – as the new political

---

7 One foundation member of the LRC was George Bernard Shaw, the famous playwright. Many Fabians supported the Boer War and were actually not far removed from Chamberlain's overall programme.

grouping was known – elected only two MPs in 1900. However, in the constituencies where trade unions were powerful, especially in parts of Lancashire, South Wales and Tyneside, Labour soon found itself strong enough to enter into a working agreement with the Liberal party. The Liberal party looked upon Labour as an extension of itself and continued to hold the whip hand in its dealings with Labour until after the First World War. (Why Labour replaced the Liberals as Britain's left-of-centre party is probably the most heavily debated single question in twentieth-century British political history.)

Two specific issues further increased the influence of the new Labour party. In South Africa, a truly bizarre issue aroused fierce hostility among British workers, remote as they were from the scene. Because of a shortage of African labour to work in the mines of the Transvaal, the Balfour government, heavily influenced by Lord Milner, allowed the introduction of nearly 50 000 Chinese coolie labourers into South Africa. They were paid virtually nothing and forced to live in closed compounds where drug addiction, prostitution and homosexuality soon became rampant. Extraordinarily, the question of so-called 'Chinese slavery' on the Rand became a burning cause on the British left, possibly because the victorious conclusion of the Boer War had left them without an imperial issue of similar strength. Trade unionists believed that the Chinese 'slaves' were introduced merely to undercut the pay not only of African labourers but of white Europeans, and that this limitless international army of yellow 'slaves' might be sent around the world to undercut workers' pay. (Lloyd George later campaigned against the introduction of 'Chinese slaves on the hills of Wales'.) Nonconformists campaigned against the alleged low moral standards of the Chinese coolies, and the pervasive social Darwinistic atmosphere of the time did nothing to dampen populist fears of the sinister 'yellow peril'. Although Balfour and his advisers could not have foreseen the popular reaction to Chinese labour in South Africa, in 1906 it became another nail in the Tories' coffin.

The other issue which aroused Labour was the Taff Vale decision of 1901. Prior to this legal decision in the High Court, trade unions had been afforded absolute protection for their funds under the Trade Union Act of 1871. Under the famous judgment in the case of the *Taff Vale Railway Co. v. Amalgamated Society of Railway Servants*, it was held that a trade union could be sued by employers (or anyone else) and its funds confiscated as damages if the case went against it. The Amalgamated Society (a railway union) lost £32 000 in costs and damages. This aroused the trade union movement for Labour as nothing else had done, and greatly increased the success of Labour candidates at by-elections before 1906. Soon after the Liberals' 1906 election victory the Taff Vale decision was reversed by the Trade Disputes Act 1906.

The Balfour government did have some notably successful achievements and indeed proved to be more activist, after the Boer War ended, than its predecessor. These accomplishments included the Irish Land Purchase Act of 1903, which continued, with a substantial grant, the policy of creating farmers' ownership of the land. Ireland remained relatively quiet during this period and, indeed, proved to be largely somnolent until the Liberals were once again forced, after 1910, to rely on Irish Nationalist votes to remain in office. A Licensing Act of 1904 tried, with some success, to reconcile the demands of both publicans and the anti-drink lobby. An Unemployed Workmen Act of 1905 established 'Distress Committees' in most areas to investigate and relieve unemployment. With only very limited powers, it relied in part on voluntary contributions to assist the unemployed, and was thus considerably different from the quasi-Welfare State schemes of the future Liberal government. Balfour's most constructive reform was his reorganisation, in 1903–04, of the Committee of Imperial Defence, created in 1902, into a modern instrument for the conduct of war, headed by the Prime Minister and including the relevant Cabinet ministers, heads of the military, and other experts, with its own staff and secretariat. In 1904 important reforms were also made in the army, with the abolition of the post of Commander-in-Chief and the establishment of a modern General Staff and Army Board. The Balfour government's appointment of Sir John Fisher (1841–1920; later first Baron Fisher) as First Sea Lord set in motion the modernisation of the Royal Navy.

There were also great changes in foreign policy. Wisely or not, Britain increasingly joined in the treaty alliances which divided Europe into two hostile camps and produced an irreversible chain reaction of mobilisation when war came in 1914. With hindsight, it might have been far better if Britain had remained outside of the alliance system altogether, but no one in this period could possibly have foreseen the bloody stalemate of 1914–18, nor the horrors of trench warfare. In January 1902 Britain rather oddly entered into a formal alliance with Japan. This was done chiefly to signal Britain's displeasure at any Russian drive into Manchuria or Korea. In April 1904 came the extremely important Anglo-French Entente, settling all differences in the colonial sphere between the two powers, and paving the way for the wartime alliance. The famous visit of King Edward VII to Paris in May 1903 did much to alter previously hostile French attitudes to Britain. There were some in Britain, for instance Joseph Chamberlain and Lord Rosebery, who would have preferred an alliance with Germany rather than with France. All efforts at achieving such a pact, however, were defeated by Germany's obvious expansionism, particularly her greatly enlarged navy, and by the truculent statements of her leaders, especially the Kaiser. Until the Boer War, an alliance between Britain and Germany was at least a possibility, but thereafter it became progressively more unlikely.

The Balfour government also faced a difficult economic situation. The output of Britain's leading products such as cotton, coal and steel stagnated. So did exports, while imports rose. Unemployment probably increased, although there are no reliable figures. The government lost an unusually large number of by-elections between 1900 and 1905, 26 in all, to both the Liberals and Labour. Nevertheless, nothing prepared the party for the electoral catastrophe ahead. There were, of course, no public opinion surveys of voter intention at the time (the earliest were not undertaken until the late 1930s), and there was no accurate way of gauging the mood of the electorate.

While all of these events were, broadly, very helpful to the prospects of the Liberals, they had many troubles of their own. Their leader, Sir Henry Campbell-Bannerman, was widely regarded as weak, almost a stopgap. Many people expected Lord Rosebery to return, sooner or later, to the party's leadership. The party's leading imperialists distrusted Campbell-Bannerman, and in September 1905 Asquith, Grey and Haldane, the three most prominent advocates of the imperial position apart from Rosebery, met at Relugas, Sir Edward Grey's fishing lodge in Morayshire, and agreed that none would serve under Campbell-Bannerman in any future Liberal government unless he went to the House of Lords, leaving effective control of the government to Asquith and the imperialist wing of the party. As well, shortly afterwards Earl Spencer became seriously ill and retired from politics. He was widely respected and might have served, in Rosebery's stead, as a compromise Liberal Prime Minister. The issue of Home Rule continued to divide the Liberals, and the party remained without any real policies.

In this atmosphere, on 4 December 1905 Balfour took the unexpected step of resigning. Campbell-Bannerman and the Liberals were then called upon to form a minority government. The Tory expectation was that Liberal divisions ran so deeply that they would be unable to form one at all or, if they did, it would be bitterly divided and would quickly fall from office. In the event, Campbell-Bannerman managed to put together a very reasonable government when he became Prime Minister on 5 December 1905, with Gladstonian fixtures like Lords Ripon and Elgin and John Morley complementing newer men of talent like Asquith (Chancellor of the Exchequer), Grey (Foreign Secretary) and Haldane (Secretary for War). Radicals were in a small minority, David Lloyd George (President of the Local Government Board) being the most prominent. John Burns became President of the Local Government Board, the first working-man ever to sit in a British Cabinet.

The new government immediately called a general election, held from 12 January to 7 February 1906. The election produced one of the greatest routs in British political history: a comprehensive Conservative defeat, to use the term employed in remarkably similar circumstances 91 years later. Completely reversing the results of the two previous elections, the Liberals won 400 seats, the Conservatives only 157. The greatest novelty of the election, it was universally agreed, was the election of 29 Labour MPs supported by the LRC, plus another 24 Labour MPs unaffiliated to this body. The Liberals were triumphant almost everywhere, outnumbering the

Tories 38:19 in the County of London, 107:45 in the rest of southern England, 59:27 in the Midlands, 102:31 in the north of England, 33:0 in Wales, and 58:10 in Scotland. As usual, the result in popular votes was much less decisive. The Liberals won 2 758 000 votes out of 5 627 000 cast, or 49.0 per cent of the vote, while their Labour allies won 330 000 or 5.9 per cent. The Tories managed to win 2 451 000 votes, or 43.6 per cent of the vote, a respectable enough figure but one which, under the 'first-past-the-post' electoral system, produced many fewer victorious seats.[8]

Although the supporters of Joseph Chamberlain emerged as the dominant force within the Conservative party (Chamberlain being triumphantly re-elected in Birmingham), he himself suffered a paralysing stroke in July 1906, and remained on the political sidelines until his death in 1914. Meanwhile the Tories drifted through two more electoral defeats (thanks to Labour and the Irish) in the two 1910 general elections, and suffered continuing internal turmoil. So deep was the Conservative malaise over the next decade that some recent historians, most notably E. H. H. Green, have viewed the party as facing the real prospect of disintegration by 1914. Such a view may well, however, be much too pessimistic: Bonar Law, who became leader of the party in 1911, proved to be an able head who reformed the party's machinery; the Irish Home Rule Bill which was due to come into effect in 1914 would have removed most Irish MPs from Parliament; the Tories were winning many by-elections and, on balance, were also doing well in local elections. The London County Council, for instance, had possessed a Liberal majority until 1907, but then elected a Conservative majority which increased in 1913, the last election before the war.[9] On balance, it seems likely that the Conservatives would have won any general election held (as was due) in 1915.

Meanwhile, the Liberal government which took office in 1905 proved to be one of the greatest and most memorable in British history, laying the basis for the Welfare State, especially after Campbell-Bannerman died in 1908 and was succeeded by Asquith, and taking the country into the First World War. It is well-known, too, that it faced many domestic challenges, even crises, such that perhaps the most famous account of this period ever written (in 1936) was entitled *The Strange Death of Liberal England*. The never-ending Irish question (which was at the point of erupting into civil war in 1914), votes for women, continuing and often violent labour unrest, the role of the House of Lords, and the need for costly rearmament to meet the threat posed by Germany, became hallmarks of the next decade. Electorally, the Liberals, though sound enough, faced a possible long-term challenge by Labour which eventually caused their decline as a major party from 1922 onwards. Had the Liberals lost a general election in 1915, it is

---

8 The Irish Nationalists won their usual 83 seats on a grand total of 35 031 votes, with 74 of their MPs running in uncontested elections.
9 On the LCC the Liberals were known as 'Progressives' and the Conservatives as 'Municipal Reform Moderates'.

possible that the electoral challenge from Labour would have emerged even earlier.

In 1906 there were three competing visions of a British future in the political marketplace to replace the *laissez-faire* society of the nineteenth century. Chamberlain and others on the right offered a nationalistic, imperialistic, right-wing vision of a powerful world-empire unified economically by tariffs, and increasingly linked by closer political and military ties. The 'New Liberalism' offered the vision of something like the Welfare State, with responsibility for poverty and the other failures of capitalism increasingly borne by the state, although with free trade capitalism and a freely linked Empire still intact. Labour, though its vision remained confused and half-formed, increasingly offered more nationalisation and certainly more power for the trade unions. Over the next 75 years, all of these visions would be tried, at least in modified form. None produced the utopian outcomes for which its progenitors hoped, and all were eventually questioned. It is also arguable whether these implemented visions made much of a difference, in the long term, to Britain's fate in war and peace.

PART II

SOCIAL HISTORY

|16|

British population growth,
1750–1914

Population growth was probably the most important social reality affecting the nature of British life between 1750 and 1914. The facts are extraordinary. In 1750 the population of England and Wales was probably around 7.5 million; by 1861 it had increased to 20 million and by 1911 to 36 million. Between 1801 and 1911 Scotland's population rose from 1.6 million to 4.8 million. Ireland's population, estimated at 5.4 million in 1801, climbed to 8.2 million in 1841 before the Potato Famine and its consequences produced, perhaps uniquely in nineteenth-century Europe, extraordinary demographic decline, with Ireland's population reduced to 6.6 million in 1851 and then falling still further to only 4.3 million in 1911. (This was the total population of southern and northern Ireland: the number of Roman Catholics in Ireland, chiefly in the south, declined from 6.4 million in 1834 to only 3.3 million in 1901.) Population growth and change affected every aspect of British economic and even political life. It was one of the most important causal linkages to industrialisation; it made possible the growth of great cities like Manchester and Birmingham and increased the population of London, always larger than any city in Britain, so strongly that London still probably remained the most populous city in the world, and certainly in Europe, at the outbreak of the First World War.

Economic and social historians have long known of the key importance of population growth to Britain's development after 1750, but have endlessly debated many features of both its causes and consequences. One of the most keenly debated topics of controversy about population growth in Britain after 1750 was why it occurred at all. Logically, a country's population can only be increased by one or more of a very limited number of factors: a rise or decline in the birth and death rates, or a change in the rate of immigration or emigration. But which of these was most likely to have been primarily responsible for the great rise in Britain's population?

If an intelligent observer, without further evidence, were to be asked whether a rise in the birth rate or a decline in the death rate was the chief reason for the increase in England's population after about 1750, that person would probably point to a decline in the death rate as the likely cause: in pre-industrial societies, one might well reason, birth rates are as high as they can possibly be, while death rates may be reduced through the effects of modern medicine and better nutrition. As reasonable as this conclusion plainly is, rather remarkably it is mistaken. The weight of modern scholarship in historical demography has shown that it was, almost certainly, an increase in the birth rate which was the key mechanism in fuelling the exceptionally rapid increase in English population growth in the eighteenth and early nineteenth centuries. We owe this conclusion to the very important research of E. A. Wrigley and R. S. Schofield and their group of Cambridge University demographers, which appeared in their major work *The Population History of England, 1541–1871: A Reconstruction* (London, 1981; a revised edition, with an introduction answering the critics of the original work, appeared in 1989). For the period before the registration of births, marriages and deaths began in England and Wales in 1837, Wrigley and Schofield rely for many of their conclusions on the entries of baptisms, marriages and burials recorded in the registers of 404 Anglican parishes. These historians were well aware of the possible inaccuracies in their pre-1837 sources and devoted the first 154 pages of their book to discussing this question. Their conclusions have been widely – although not, perhaps, universally – accepted by historical demographers.

According to Wrigley and Schofield, birth rates (and, more significantly, fertility rates, that is, the number of children produced by each woman of child-bearing age) rose significantly in the eighteenth century because a significantly higher percentage of men and women married, and married at a younger age, than during the seventeenth century. Specifically, the percentage of persons aged 40–44 in England who had never married declined from about 27 per cent in the 1680s to only 5 per cent in the 1790s (and then began another upward trend). The mean age of first marriage of women apparently declined by about three years between the late seventeenth and early nineteenth centuries, from about 26.5 to about 23.5 (other researchers have suggested even sharper levels of decline, from about 28 to 22.6 in the same period). It was the combined effects of these two trends – more and younger marriages – which accounted for most of the increase in fertility in England; fertility rose, broadly, by about 50 per cent between the seventeenth and early nineteenth centuries.

Why the age of marriages fell while the likelihood of marriage rose is a much-vexed question, but it is believed by many historians to be related to contemporary changes in both agriculture and manufacturing in which children became an economic asset from an early age and in which the earning power of male artisans and manual workers reached its peak in their twenties and early thirties, rather than at a later age. It might also be related to a breakdown of the older type of apprenticeship system in which the master of the business-cum-household may have rigidly controlled the behaviour of his apprentices. While a decline in the death rate did occur in this period – and, especially, in the ratio between births and deaths – this was not sufficient, according to Wrigley and Schofield, to act as the 'trigger' for the enormous increase in population which occurred in England during the eighteenth century. Neither the diminution in plagues occurring at this time nor the effects of smallpox inoculation and other gains in medical knowledge (whose extent may be critically debated) could have had this effect. Between 1700 and 1820 the birth rate in England rose from about 32 to about 42 per 1000 people, while the death rate declined only from about 26 to 24 per 1000 people.

There is, however, one very important factor on the 'death rate' side of the equation which deserves some mention: the demographic position of London. Throughout modern history, from the sixteenth until the late eighteenth century, there were always many more deaths than births in London. Although London contained probably only about one-tenth of England's total population, the negative demographic balance of London was so important as to alter the entire population profile of England. In the quarter-century 1675–99, for instance, London (according to Wrigley and Schofield) witnessed 181 465 more deaths than births. In the rest of England in this period, however, there were 92 626 more births than deaths. Overall, throughout England (including London) there were there-fore 88 839 more deaths than births. London's terribly negative demo-graphic profile, in other words, altered the entire demographic position of England.

In the last quarter of the eighteenth century, however, the negative demographic status of London altered quite fundamentally, and the na-tional capital now saw more births than deaths (as did the rest of the country, at an increasing rate). It is difficult to explain this change, which may be related to a number of unrelated factors. These include the spread of smallpox inoculation; new, purer supplies of water in London; the growth of newer, relatively more salubrious suburbs on the fringes of the capital; and the emergence of the northern industrial areas as a magnet for the restless. For whatever reason, London then added significantly to England's population growth.

Steady growth of the English population as a whole began in the late 1730s and the growth rate itself – as well as the absolute number of people – accelerated almost without a break from the 1760s until the mid-1820s, when rates of population growth began to decline (see Table 16.1). Initially, the overall size of the English population grew steadily but not dramat-ically. The total population of England (excluding Wales, Scotland and Ireland) is believed to have totalled about 5 058 000 in 1701. It reached 5.5 million in the late 1730s, and 6.0 million around 1757. Climbing to 7.0

million in 1780, 8.0 million around 1794, and 9.0 million in 1804, growth continued at a rate without precedent, so that it had reached 13.3 million at the time of the 1832 Reform Bill, 16.7 million during the Great Exhibition of 1851, and about 20.3 million when the 1867 Reform Bill was passed. Gross reproduction rates – the number of children born to a couple – rose steadily and remarkably throughout this period, increasing by about 50 per cent.

From about the mid-1820s, however, the rate of population increase (although not, of course, the total population) now went into reverse and began to fall. During the quarter-century 1801–25, the crude birth rate in England and Wales was 40.2 per 1000 people. This declined to 35.8 in 1851–75, 32.3 in 1876–1900, and to only 24.0 in the quarter-century 1901–25. (In the twentieth century, rates declined still further, falling to under 15.0 in recent decades.) Demographers point to several reasons for this decline. The number of persons never marrying, which, as noted, declined dramatically during the eighteenth century, rose significantly. By the 1860s about 11 per cent of persons aged 40–44 had never married, more than double the percentage 50 or 60 years before. It seems likely that the structure of affectional and courtship patterns became both more difficult and more formal in nineteenth-century Britain, a trend which accompanied growing urbanisation. Couples had fewer opportunities to meet; hours of work became longer; workplaces became larger, more impersonal, and perhaps more closely supervised. Evangelical and Nonconformist religious practice discouraged extramarital affectional relationships which did not lead to marriage. In addition, it is likely that spinsters and bachelors became more visible as common types, and accepted as such. Unmarried 'aunties', teachers, governesses, household servants, and seamstresses were to be found in numbers. A male-only associational world, centring in the middle classes around the club, and in the working classes around the pub, grew up: by the late nineteenth century the clubland bachelor was a familiar figure (and one who has attracted remarkably little attention from historians). Most certainly, the majority of these bachelors were not homosexuals (although a homosexual underground existed in late nineteenth-century London), but simply middle-class men who were either uncomfortable in the presence of women or who found the company of males of a similar background more satisfactory, presumably accompanied by resort to prostitutes, who existed in very large numbers in London and other British cities.

As well, by the late nineteenth century England was experiencing what is termed the 'demographic transition', from a pattern of population growth in which there were very high birth rates, early marriages, and large families, accompanied by a continuing high death rate, to a pattern of population growth whose hallmarks were lower birth rates and smaller families, side-by-side with lower death rates, especially among children. England was probably the first society to undergo the 'demographic

Table 16.1 Population of the United Kingdom, 1801–1911 (× 1000)

Year	Population	Increase in Decennial Period	Percentage Increase
	England and Wales		
1801	8893	–	–
1811	10 164	1272	14.3
1821	12 000	1836	18.1
1831	13 897	1897	15.8
1841	15 914	2017	14.5
1851	17 928	2013	12.6
1861	20 066	2139	11.9
1871	22 712	2646	13.2
1881	25 974	3262	14.4
1891	29 003	3028	11.7
1901	32 527	3525	12.2
1911	36 070	3542	10.9
	United Kingdom		
1801	15 896	–	–
1811	17 907	2011	12.7
1821	20 894	2987	16.7
1831	24 029	3135	15.0
1841	26 731	2702	11.2
1851	27 397	666*	0.2*
1861	28 927	1530	5.6
1871	31 485	2558	8.8
1881	34 885	3400	10.8
1891	37 733	2848	8.2
1901	41 459	3726	9.9
1911	45 221	3762	9.1

* This very low increase was the result of the losses from the Irish Famine and subsequent emigration.

transition' in its full form, although France during the nineteenth century was famous (in some quarters notorious) for its unusually low level of population increase (the population of France rose from about 26 million in 1789 to only about 40 million in 1914, despite the fact that few Frenchmen emigrated overseas; in contrast, and despite the onset of the 'demographic transition', the population of England and Wales increased from about 9 million to about 36 million in the same period). During the nineteenth century France experienced some, but not all, characteristics of the 'demographic transition'; in particular, it failed to see a lowered death rate, especially among children.

The 'demographic transition' in England extended over a very long period – perhaps over the century between 1825 and 1925 – and was not fully evident until the latter part of the nineteenth century. Birth rates began a steady decline in England and Wales around 1870, declining from about 35 per 1000 at that date to about 25 per 1000 in 1900, and then to only 15 per 1000 by the mid-1920s. The decline in death rates began at almost precisely the same time and followed a broadly similar historical evolution, dropping from 22 per 1000 in 1870 to 16 per 1000 in 1900 to 12 per 1000 in the mid-1920s. It is clear that there was a connection between the two sets of figures, and that the key link was probably the decline in infant and child mortality. The infant mortality rate in England and Wales declined from 167 per 1000 in the quarter-century 1801–25 to about 150 per 1000 during the rest of the nineteenth century, and then spectacularly to 105 in the quarter-century 1901–25 (and to under 15 today). One result of this was that life expectancy at birth rose steadily throughout the nineteenth century, from about 37 years of age in the early nineteenth century to 41 in 1871 to 50 by 1910 (and to 75 today). The relationship between a couple having fewer children on the one hand and lower infant mortality on the other is that if it seems likely, or indeed near-certain, that a child will live to become an adult, fewer need to be born for at least one or two to survive to adulthood.

That couples could limit the number of children strongly implies that birth control was in widespread use. Little is known of a definitive nature about this topic, and the use of artificial birth control means was illegal throughout the nineteenth century and severely discouraged by Church and State. Nevertheless, condoms and other artificial means of birth control were sold before the 1870s in large cities. In 1877 Charles Bradlaugh, the self-proclaimed atheist MP, and Annie Besant, a radical thinker and activist, were tried for obscenity for republishing an old pamphlet on birth control, inadvertently generating enormous sales for the pamphlet. It seems likely that, by 1900, many, perhaps most, middle-class couples limited the number of children conceived by one or another means. There is considerable evidence that the British middle classes began to limit the size of their families from the third quarter of the nineteenth century chiefly in order to reduce the cost of educating their offspring, especially boys, at fee-paying schools or via apprenticeships.

The rate of population growth in England was affected as well by a number of other factors. As the British population shifted from rural areas to the cities, rates of population growth slowed as well, cities generally having lower birth rates and higher rates of infant and child mortality than country areas. Emigration from England, and other parts of the United Kingdom, was of course substantial throughout the whole of modern history from the seventeenth century onwards, chiefly to the United States but later to other parts of the temperate Empire such as Canada, Australia and New Zealand. Migration to Britain from overseas was small during the nineteenth century, but never non-existent. There were always political refugees ranging from the extreme right (like the future King Louis XVIII and other members of the French Royal Family) to the extreme left (like Karl Marx), while, after about 1880, significant numbers of continental Europeans, especially Russian Jews following the pogroms of 1881, arrived in many of Britain's cities, particularly in the East End of London, which, by the 1890s, had become predominantly Jewish (and Irish) in many neighbourhoods. It is very important to realise that, until the Aliens Act of 1905 was passed, Britain *had no immigration restrictions of any kind*, and literally any number of foreigners could settle in Britain, regardless of this country's economic or social circumstances.[1] (The United States also had virtually unrestricted immigration until 1921; in the early years of the twentieth century, more than one million immigrants settled in America annually.) The Aliens Act restricted, but did not forbid, immigration to Britain from outside the British Empire; it did not interfere with settlement in Britain by citizens of the Empire (including non-Caucasians). Migration to Britain by British Commonwealth nationals was only restricted in 1961, following considerable pressure to decrease the number of non-whites allowed to settle in Britain from the West Indies and the Indian subcontinent.

Throughout the nineteenth century, however, many more Britons emigrated overseas than foreigners who settled in the United Kingdom. The average net migration totals (emigrants minus immigrants) in England rose from an average of about 7000 a year in the early 1800s to nearly 25 000 per year by the mid-1860s. While this number was small compared with the overall English population, migrants were disproportionately drawn from the young and energetic, who would have been most likely to produce children. By the late nineteenth century, Britain had clearly seen the beginnings of its 'demographic transition', although this process was not completed until after the First World War.

Demographic change in Scotland was similar, but not identical, to that in England and Wales. There is considerable evidence that Scotland did not experience a 'population explosion' during the later eighteenth century on the same scale as in England. The best evidence available to us (and it is less reliable than the evidence for England) suggests that the population of Scotland grew by about 28 per cent between 1755 and 1801, compared with 45 per cent in England. No one knows why this was so, and a host of reasons, ranging from considerably higher rates of mortality and shorter lifespans, owing to Scotland's harsh climate, to later ages of marriage caused by a more primitive, less abundant economy, have been offered. It is also possible that rates of emigration from Scotland, especially among young men, were consistently higher than in England.[2] During the nineteenth century differences between the two countries continued, with Scotland's ratio of population compared with that in England and Wales

1 The term 'Aliens' in 'Aliens Act' is a legal term for persons who are not citizens of Britain or the British Empire. It has no pejorative connotations.
2 Throughout the nineteenth century, very small crofters were often forcibly removed from farms in the Highlands (and sent overseas especially to Canada) in order to make the lands yield higher rents through sheep-farming and deer-hunting. These 'Highland Clearances', which continued until the 1880s, became notorious.

continuing to decline consistently. In 1801 Scotland's population
(1 608 000) represented 18.1 per cent of the total population of England
and Wales (8 893 00). By 1861 its ratio had declined to 15.3 per cent, and
by 1901 to only 13.7 per cent (4 472 000 compared with 32 528 000 in
England and Wales). This was possibly due to a consistently higher death
rate in Scotland, although, curiously, rates of infant mortality in Scotland
were actually lower than in England. As noted above, Scotland may have
experienced much higher comparative rates of emigration than England
did. Another curiosity of demography in Scotland was that it saw consistently higher rates of illegitimacy than in England, normally almost twice
the English rate. The reasons for this are unknown, but may reflect the fact
that marriage, in the Church of Scotland, is regarded more as a legal
contract than a sacrament, and that a higher average age of marriage in
Scotland, productive of lower birth rates overall, was paradoxically also
responsible for more pre-marital sex and hence more pre-marital pregnan-
cies. It is ironic that nineteenth-century Scotland, with its fierce and
intrusive Calvinist morality, was so remiss in this aspect of moral behaviour.

By 1901, the population of Great Britain was nearly three and a half
times larger than it had been a century before, having grown from
10 501 000 to 36 999 000 despite continuing emigration. (These figures do
not include Ireland, whose population because of the Famine and its
attendant large-scale emigration had actually declined, from about
5 395 000 to only 4 459 000.) This increase was absolutely without parallel in previous recorded history and it must, naturally, have had the most
profound consequences for all aspects of British life, including its social and
political histories. The most immediate effect of continuing population
growth, however, came in the economic sphere, where historians have long
debated the connection between population growth and economic growth.
Since population growth accompanied an unprecedented period of continuing economic growth so spectacular as to be known as the 'industrial
revolution', it is only natural to assume that population growth was a
'good thing'. Historians have offered a number of linkages between
population increase and economic development in post-1750 Britain.
Plainly, a growing population increased demand for goods and services of
all kinds. It led to a younger, more flexible society, and provided many
more potential operatives for factories and mines.

While an increasing population would have led to important benefits for
the British economy, it is, however, important to realise that not all of the
outcomes of population growth were necessarily positive. During the first
half of the nineteenth century the population of Ireland increased as rapidly
as that in other parts of the United Kingdom, yet in the 1840s Ireland
suffered a demographic catastrophe without parallel in nineteenth-century
Europe, the 'Potato Famine', in which perhaps one million Irish people died
of starvation and disease, and another million or more emigrated. There

were numerous differences between Ireland and England at this time, but perhaps the most significant was that rural and peasant Ireland had witnessed no industrial revolution. This would suggest that British economic growth was itself the chief cause of British population increase, and would have been unsustainable without it. In today's Third World, population increase without equivalent economic development is often the norm, leading to even greater poverty. Population growth in itself was thus insufficient to have automatically produced economic growth, or even to have been a positive contributory factor to continuing economic growth. Indeed, the thrust of intellectual debate in Britain at the time was very much to emphasise the extremely negative effects of population growth, and the fact that population growth could simply not be sustained in the long term without some kind of catastrophe, a notion which, of course, we associate strongly with Rev. Thomas Malthus (1766–1834). Malthus made the famous point that while natural resources increase – if at all – at an arithmetic rate, human population, if unchecked, increases at a geometric rate, far faster. Malthus believed that any human population growth would therefore inevitably be checked by some kind of demographic catastrophe such as a great plague, unless later marriages led to a lower birth rate. (Malthus ruled out birth control as a 'vice' and contrary to Christian practice of his time.) He and his contemporaries were often aware of the potentially negative effects of unprecedented population increase.

Moreover, large-scale population increase would also have made human labour more readily available and hence cheaper, giving entrepreneurs less reason to invest in labour-saving machinery which replaced human labour because it was more efficient and cheaper in large-scale production. Yet the period of unprecedented population increase in Britain after 1750 also saw an industrial revolution occur side-by-side with a 'population explosion'. Linking the two phenomena is thus even less straightforward, and more puzzling, than at first glance.

The best explanation of this apparently strange paradox is that British entrepreneurs and inventors *still* found it cheaper to invest in labour-saving machinery despite the apparent cheapness and availability of human labour. Machine-made goods could be produced in such volume, and with such mechanical regularity, that they were almost automatically cheaper, and their production and distribution more regular, than old-fashioned domestic production such as was normal before the introduction of the new machinery. Inventors and capitalists knew that labour-saving machinery was almost invariably more productive, certainly in the long term, than human labour, although the degree of readiness to introduce new techniques varied from industry to industry. Even so, this process took a remarkably long time, with many phases of industrial production not mechanised for decades after industrialisation began. The handloom weavers, who continued to weave cotton goods by hand for 40 or 50 years following the mechanisation of the spinning half of the process of cotton goods production, provide perhaps the most famous example of long-delayed mechanisation.[3]

Secondly, economic expansion itself created new employment opportunities in great numbers; indeed, in numbers which far outstripped anything possible in a pre-industrial economy. These ranged from jobs in the factories themselves to employment in other novel forms of industry like the railways to positions in a greatly expanded service sector. Employment in most, if not all, occupational categories increased steadily in Britain during the nineteenth century. Inventions and innovations were responsible for increasing the number of males employed in railways from about 2000 in 1841 to about 212 000 in 1891, and of males employed in metal manufacturing, machinery and related trades from 396 000 in 1841 to 977 000 in 1891. In other fields, the increase was gender-specific, with greatly increased opportunities for women in the textile industry alongside only very limited increases for males. Females employed in the textile industry rose from 358 000 in 1841 to 795 000 in 1891, far outstripping the rise for males in the same period from 525 000 to only 593 000. Nevertheless, virtually every occupational field rose in numbers during the nineteenth century, the number of males employed even in agriculture rising from 1 243 000 in 1831 to 1 422 000 in 1891.[4] Overall, the occupied labour force in Britain rose steadily during the nineteenth century, with the number of occupied males increasing from 5 093 000 in 1841 to 10 010 000 in 1891, while the number of occupied females rose in the same period from 1 815 000 to 4 489 000, remarkable levels of increase.

Finally, the white Empire and the United States provided a potent 'safety valve' for excess members of the labour force throughout the nineteenth century. A potentially explosive situation, in which mouths to feed threatened to outstrip gainful employment, was unquestionably dampened by the fact that one could always take oneself and one's family away to far-off lands, but places which were English-speaking, drew their laws and culture

3 The manufacture of cotton goods took place in two phases, spinning and weaving. Spinning, in which raw cotton was processed into usable threads, was mechanised in the late eighteenth century. Weaving, the actual manufacture of the clothing or other cotton goods, was not mechanised until the 1840s. Tens of thousands of handloom weavers (i.e. those who wove cotton goods by the traditional process) became redundant almost overnight. The number of handloom weavers in the cotton industry declined from about 200 000 in 1834 to 110 000 in 1841 to only 43 000 in 1850; only about 3000 were left by 1862. The decline of handloom weaving has long been seen, especially by critics of British industrialisation, as one of the great tragedies of the industrial revolution.

4 The number of males employed in agriculture peaked at about 1 788 000 in 1851 before declining, although the decline even in this area was not as precipitous as one might assume. All figures for employment (derived from the decennial censuses) should be used by scholars with considerable caution. Figures for female employment, for instance, almost certainly undercount women in domestic industries. Administrative and managerial positions may or may not be tabulated separately from their particular industry. Part-time and semi-retired workers are not indicated as such, and nor are the unemployed. The large Victorian 'underclass' of criminals, beggars and prostitutes is never frankly reported in the censuses: the censuses have no category for prostitutes, for example. Usable figures for employment are not really available prior to 1841.

directly or indirectly from Britain, and were themselves rapidly expanding frontier societies. The United States, Canada, Australia, and other places of potential British emigration also had the merit of being relatively new societies, with more fluid social structures, and lacking in rigid class barriers or obstacles to upward social mobility such as increasingly existed in Britain.

Population growth on a scale without precedent in history thus posed no threat to the stability of British society; only in Ireland, lacking a modern industrial base, did demographic catastrophe ensue, however much such a cataclysm was predicted by Malthus and other pessimistic observers of recent population trends. Nevertheless, unprecedented population growth did have many profoundly disturbing effects upon Britain's social structure, which led directly to much of the social and political tensions of the nineteenth century. Perhaps three such changes stand out as being of especially far-reaching importance. Population growth radically disturbed the demographic balance within the existing county structure of Great Britain. As the counties were the primary unit of local government, and comprised the basic framework for parliamentary representation, this change was of considerable importance, in and of itself, in upsetting Britain's old regime. Britain's counties had evolved as units of local governance which were, approximately, as populous as one another and whose county towns were fairly similar in size and function. Britain's first census in 1801 – taken after half a century of unprecedented population growth – found that, among the 43 counties in England, 32 had populations of between 88 000 and 274 000. Only six counties contained fewer than 88 000 inhabitants, while, more importantly, only four (Devonshire, Lancashire, Middlesex, and the West Riding of Yorkshire) held more than 274 000. In 1801 the populations of largely rural Cornwall (192 000), Shropshire (170 000) and Wiltshire (184 000) were not markedly different from the populations of industrialising Northumberland (168 000) or Warwickshire (207 000). The county towns of all counties, often overgrown market towns to which were added county administrative functions, were mainly fairly similar. Recognisably similar rural gentries and old-fashioned urban elites comprised the governing circles of each county, London being the obvious exception.

By 1901, however, enormous differences in the size of counties had become normal. While almost all counties had grown in size during the nineteenth century, some had increased astronomically. In 1901 there were eight counties in Britain with a population of one million or more: Greater London (most of which was officially constituted as the London County Council in 1889) headed the list with 4 536 000 inhabitants, closely followed by Lancashire with 4 373 000. The West Riding of Yorkshire had a population of 2 843 000, while Durham (1 017 000), Essex (1 084 000), Staffordshire (1 184 000), Warwickshire (1 053 000) and Lanarkshire in Scotland (1 136 000) had all surpassed the million mark. Twelve other counties in England, as well as Glamorganshire in Wales, had populations of between 500 000 and one million. On the other hand, in 1901 the populations of 15 English counties remained at less than 200 000, with Rutland containing only 20 000 inhabitants, and two Scottish counties (Kinross-shire with 7000 and Nairnshire with 9000) having fewer than 10 000. Traditional county government, and the rule of the traditional elites, was virtually impossible in the larger counties, while, in fact, cities throughout Britain had assumed growing local governmental powers from the mid-1830s onwards. While counties, especially rural counties, continued to enjoy both legal and ceremonial authority, population growth in and of itself had swept aside their age-old functions.

Most of the growth (though certainly not all) had taken place in the large cities, and the central single facet of the geographical venue of demographic change in nineteenth-century Britain was the growth of cities and the urbanisation of much of the British nation. The growth of Britain's cities is, however, often misunderstood. Apart from London – very much an exception to everything – Britain had no truly large city, and most of the urban growth in the nineteenth century took place in medium-sized but still significant urban centres with populations at the opening of the twentieth century of between 50 000 and 300 000 or so. Even Britain's new larger cities were still surprisingly small.

Table 16.2 lists the 15 largest cities in Great Britain at three dates between 1801 and 1911 and contains many surprises, especially for the earliest set of figures. In 1801 London was a monster colossus which simply dwarfed any other British city; it is easy to see why Cobbett termed it 'the great wen [pimple]'. London was then nearly 13 times larger than Britain's second largest city, Manchester (with Salford), while, rather unexpectedly, the third largest was Edinburgh. Such key industrial centres as Manchester, Glasgow and Birmingham had much less than 100 000 inhabitants each, while other future centres of industry like Bradford, Nottingham and Leicester are not on the list at all. At that time, naval ports like Plymouth and Portsmouth, earlier centres of industry like Norwich, and an upper-class watering place, Bath, were among Britain's very largest cities. One might ask why such places as Manchester and Leeds remained so small 30 or 40 years after the industrial revolution began. A major reason was probably that steam power in factories was not yet the norm for manufacturing industry: most factories were situated near sources of running water, often in the countryside.

By 1861, however, most of the well-known industrial cities had grown considerably and now clearly comprised most of Britain's largest urban areas. Growth continued strongly throughout the rest of the nineteenth century, with three cities, London, Manchester and Glasgow, having populations of one million or more. Yet it will also be seen that what manifestly had no counterpart in nineteenth-century industrial Britain was anything resembling the demographic situation in the Third World today,

Table 16.2 Fifteen largest British cities in 1801 1861 and 1911 (× 1000 people)

1801

1.	Greater London*	1117	9.	Sheffield	46
2.	Manchester (inc. Salford)	89	10.	Plymouth	40
3.	Edinburgh (inc. Leith)	83	11.	Norwich	36
4.	Liverpool	82	12.	Newcastle upon Tyne	33
5.	Glasgow	77	13.	Bath	33
6.	Birmingham	71	14.	Portsmouth	33
7.	Bristol	61	15.	Hull	30
8.	Leeds	53			

1861

1.	Greater London	3227	9.	Bristol	154
2.	Manchester (inc. Salford)	501	10.	Belfast	122
3.	Liverpool	472	11.	Plymouth	113
4.	Glasgow	443	12.	Newcastle upon Tyne	109
5.	Birmingham	351	13.	Bradford	106
6.	Leeds	207	14.	Hull	98
7.	Edinburgh	203	15.	Portsmouth	95
8.	Sheffield	185			

1911

1.	Greater London	7256	9.	Belfast	384
2.	Manchester (inc. Salford)	1035	10.	Bristol	357
3.	Glasgow	1000	11.	Brighton	288
4.	Liverpool (inc. Birkenhead)	884	12.	Hull	278
5.	Birmingham	840	13.	Newcastle upon Tyne	267
6.	Sheffield	465	14.	Nottingham	267
7.	Edinburgh	424	15.	Stoke-on-Trent	235
8.	Leeds	453		(and pottery towns)	

* Figures for the approximate area of what became the London County Council in 1889; Greater London had no official borders in the early nineteenth century.

with millions and millions of former rural-dwellers crowding into gargantuan cities, so that by the 1990s the populations of Cairo and Mexico City had apparently reached 20 million.

Only in London was there a parallel to today's Third World situation, and London's amazing growth while *lacking* a factory infrastructure does indeed bear a resemblance to later trends. But no such growth truly occurred in other British cities, even those at the heart of the industrial revolution, nor in other commercial centres like Bristol and Liverpool. The reasons for this may be debated, but probably centre in the continuing relative prosperity and labour-intensive economy of Britain's rural areas, the fact that population growth was spread around many large but not gigantic, medium, and smaller cities owing to the spread of industry in many parts of the country, and the 'safety valve' provided by the white Empire and the United States for surplus labour.

Beneath the first rung of Britain's largest towns were a host of somewhat smaller cities where a good deal of nineteenth-century urban growth occurred. Cities like Cardiff, which increased in population from 6000 in 1831 to 182 000 in 1911, Blackburn (12 000 to 133 000 in the same period), Leicester (17 000 to 227 000) and Oldham (12 000 to 147 000), showed remarkable rates of growth often outstripping Britain's largest cities. Phenomenal rates of growth were indeed common among many cities of roughly this size, with Gateshead increasing from 9000 to 117 000 in the same period, Swansea from 10 000 to 144 000, while Middlesbrough, which literally did not exist until the 1830s, grew from 6000 in 1841 to 120 000 in 1911. Most cities which grew at this pace were chiefly industrial in nature, often in areas like the north-west of England, the mill towns around Manchester, and south Wales, which developed strongly in the mid to late nineteenth century. Others were middle-class cities in the south of England, like Brighton, transformed by the patronage of the Prince Regent and then by good railway connection from a minor resort with 7000 inhabitants in 1801 (and known by its old name of Brighthelmstone) to a premier commuter town, resort, and retirement centre, its population swollen to 131 000 in 1911. Bournemouth, an even posher high-toned resort and retirement centre far outside of London's commuter belt, evolved from a tiny fishing village as late as 1861 to a city of 79 000 in 1911.

Not every British town shared fully in demographic expansion at this level nor, indeed, experienced any but meagre growth. Older market towns without newer industries experienced unremarkable – indeed, surprisingly limited – population increases. Colchester grew in size from 16 000 in 1831 to 38 000 in 1901; Exeter from 28 000 to 47 000 in the same time-span; King's Lynn from 13 000 to only 20 000; Yarmouth from 25 000 to 51 000. Towns of this sort, often on old coastal trade routes, which had been local commercial centres for centuries, now stagnated. So, too, did Cambridge (21 000 to 38 000) and Oxford (21 000 to 49 000).

Unique and apart from everything else was London. The population of Greater London already totalled 1 117 000 in 1801.[5] This figure doubled in 40 years, reaching 2 239 000 in 1841. It has been noted, however, that the rate of increase of London's population between 1821 and 1841 was clearly slowing down. It grew rapidly again only after the railways and omnibus network extended the geographical limits of London's dimensions. Greater London's population then doubled again, to 4 770 000, 40 years later, in 1881. Growth was still extremely strong in the late Victorian and Edwardian period, although at a lower rate, with Greater London's population reaching 7 256 000 in 1911, just before the War. London's

5 The Greater London area, a region used by the Censuses and other official investigations for statistical purposes, was virtually identical with the boundaries of the London County Council as it was established in 1889. It extended from Hampstead and Stamford Hill in the north to Streatham and Sydenham in the south, and from Poplar and Lewisham (south of the Thames) in the east to west Kensington and Wandsworth (south of the Thames) in the west, but not beyond this area.

growth, indeed, continued until the Second World War, peaking at nearly 9 million in 1939. (It has declined since then, and, in the 1990s, totalled about 6.5 million.) The growth of Greater London from the 1830s onwards was augmented by the development of a transport system, based upon mainline and commuter railways, horse trams and then motorised trams and buses, and finally the underground network, probably without parallel anywhere for its density. One of the most important effects of the development of London's transport network was to make commuting possible for all classes of society; another – as will be discussed – was to accentuate the geographical bifurcation of London into areas for the rich and the poor.

Factors like the growth of London's transport system which facilitated the capital's remarkable population increase were, however, balanced by other factors which limited London's rate of increase after the late Victorian period. Heights of buildings in inner London were legally restricted to 80 feet in the 1890s, unless special planning permission was obtained; London never acquired the skyscrapers of New York or Chicago until the 1950s. Middle-class commuting began from areas in the Home Counties outside of Greater London. London's relative lack of factory industry compared with the industrial areas of the north limited working-class employment. From the 1930s, the notion of a Green Belt of undeveloped land at the fringes of London, to be left untouched for future generations, took shape, and was made legal, with considerable areas of outer London off-limits to developers. London's population growth rate was affected by the slow-down in Britain's total population growth which began in the mid-nineteenth century.

Two important demographic facts about the size of London do, however, stand out in even the most cursory comparative look. Throughout the nineteenth century and well into the twentieth, London was almost certainly the largest city in the world, and certainly the largest in Europe. In 1911, for instance, when the population of Greater London was 7 256 000, the next largest city in Europe was Paris, with only 2 888 000 inhabitants, followed by Berlin (2 071 000), Vienna (2 031 000), St Petersburg (1 908 000) and Moscow (1 481 000). As well, London united virtually all of the most significant political, economic and social functions of Britain's capital city in a way which only a few other great cities could boast. New York, Moscow (until 1918), Melbourne and Sydney in Australia, Toronto and Montreal in Canada, were the largest cities in their respective countries but were not their nation's capitals. Berlin and Vienna contested over several centuries for supremacy of Europe's German-speaking lands; Rome was Italy's national capital (from 1870) but never its economic or, perhaps, cultural centre. Only in Paris was there a parallel to London, and the effects of the 1789 French Revolution were to centre French political life in Paris even more decisively than before. But in both relative and absolute terms, Paris was far smaller than London, numbering perhaps 2.5 million in the late nineteenth century compared with London's 6 million or more. In contrast, London was Britain's governmental, legal and administrative capital, the centre of the Court and Society, the financial centre of the Empire, its retailing headquarters, the home of its newspapers, publishers and entertainments, and Britain's primary commercial entrepôt. It was, finally, the centre of governance for Britain's vast Empire. Only a handful of roles eluded the nation's capital: while London was a considerable manufacturing centre, most manufacturing industry was situated elsewhere, especially in the north of England, a division fundamental to the evolution of British society. England's two old universities were near London, but not in it. Scotland, Wales and Ireland were, in the final analysis, ruled from London, but contained unquestionably separate institutions. The great ports of the Royal Navy, and commercial ports like Liverpool and Bristol, had developed separately. Nevertheless, the list comprising London's attributes as Britain's capital in a very real and ubiquitous sense is a formidable one, perhaps without real parallel elsewhere.

The growth of Britain's cities and its other urban areas led to a number of very important changes in social structure and modes of authority, some of which are less obvious than others. As we noted above, the formal and informal structures of governance at the county level became outmoded with unprecedented population growth, and were simply unable to accommodate the tremendous growth which occurred in the formal structures of traditional governance. If this was the case at the county level *per se*, it was still more true of the structure of urban administration. Especially from the start of the nineteenth century, cities grew – and grew – without traditions, but with an economic and social structure of a new type, which could simply not be accommodated by the existing framework of parliamentary and local government. This was so, above all, in the new industrial towns of the north of England. Relying on steam technology and factories as the basis of their manufacturing industries, led by men who often had no connections with the traditional elites but who comprised a new type of urban elite group, often predominantly Dissenting in religion, these new industrial towns normally posed the most determined challenge to Britain's old regime. Moreover, the more radical and dramatic the nature of the demographic and social change which occurred in these cities and towns, the less well they could be accommodated by the old structure. It is unlikely that parliamentary and local government reform would have come in the 1830s if industry had not transformed towns like Manchester, Birmingham, Bradford and Leeds, especially during the 15 or 20 years after Waterloo, when steam factories became commonplace.

While the growth of a new urban manufacturing elite was crucial to political change, equally important was the emergence of a new type of working class often employed in factories and workshops in the new industrial cities, in mines and the growing transport system. It is easy to stereotype the group characteristics of the new working classes, or to exaggerate the extent to which they marked a break with the past, but the distinctive features of the working classes were often as different from what was common in the past as those of the new factory owners. These included a rigorous and methodical regulation of hours and conditions of work, pay rates which were normally distinctly below even those of the lower middle classes, a clear differentiation of skills among the higher working classes and a lack of training of any kind among unskilled workers, and the growth of trade unions. Another frequent characteristic of the new working classes was their basis in gender and age. In cotton factories – perhaps the most distinctive form of the new manufacturing industries – women *always* outnumbered men. In 1835, for instance, Britain's cotton factories employed 119 000 females of all ages (including 52 000 girls under 18) and 100 000 males of all ages (including 43 000 boys under 18). By 1890 the gender gap had become even more pronounced, with 334 000 females (of whom 99 000 were under 18) compared with only 208 000 males (of whom 67 000 were aged under 18). In industries such as cotton, adult males were typically more highly paid than were women or, of course, children, and monopolised the more skilled or responsible jobs.

British demographic change was thus of very great importance, in and of itself, in disturbing the country's traditional modes of governance in ways which could not well be accommodated without very great change to Britain's constitution. But the growth of population in itself also produced another important challenge to the settled order of things not directly related to the previous points. If the population of a country doubles, while national output of goods and services remains the same, the standard of living of the average person will be cut in half. (This assumes that there has been no change in the distribution of wealth or income between rich and poor.) If the population of a country doubles, but that nation's output increases by less than the rate of population growth, the average person will experience a decline in living standards. One of the key debates in modern British social and economic history, argued and rehearsed by many of the leading historians of this century, concerns the 'standard of living' question, especially the living standards of the working classes during the industrial revolution from about 1790 until 1850 (when virtually everyone agrees that living standards rose). The debate over this question is complex, and cannot be fully discussed here. There is, however, one point about any discussion of the 'standard of living' question which is very relevant here. Since Britain's population rose in this period continuously and at a pace without precedence, the output of goods and services in Britain had necessarily to have risen *even faster* than population in order simply to provide the same living standards to the average person as were normal before the continuous population explosion got underway. (This generalisation ignores the separate question of income distribution, as well as the role of technological innovation and novelties.) For the economy to have expanded *even faster* than the population – which doubled in the 50 years between 1811 and 1861 – is asking a lot, especially as population increase was continuous, while economic growth was fitful, and subject to the normal cycles of boom and bust of any capitalist economy, as well as to the vagaries of war, political change, and foreign trade shifts. It is at least highly possible that there were periods, perhaps long periods, during Britain's era of industrialisation when population increase exceeded economic growth. If this was the case, it was, in and of itself, a powerful source of unrest and disturbance within British society. Indeed, much of the instability within British society in the first half of the nineteenth century can be seen as having its origins in population growth alone. Conversely, it might well have been a *sine qua non* for a continuous rise in living standards that population increase should only occur at more manageable levels: perhaps we may conclude that the standard of living of the average person in Britain could have risen, especially over the medium to long term, only if population growth levelled off. This levelling off did not occur until very late in the nineteenth century, after the 'demographic transition' had taken hold. Perhaps only then could living standards rise for nearly all.

17

Social class in Britain, 1815–1905

That nineteenth-century Britain was radically unequal is self-evidently true. For many, the differences in power and wealth between, on one hand, the very rich and others holding dominant positions in the British Establishment, and, on the other, the great majority of people for whom the economic changes of the industrial revolution brought only want and misery, was the central salient feature of nineteenth-century life. Yet against the existence, and possible growth, of economic and social inequality in Britain must be set the growth of parliamentary democracy and the gradual, but almost continuous, growth of civic and political rights. It may well be that important trends in equality and inequality in nineteenth-century Britain produced contradictory long-term results. For the past 150 years social theorists and sociologists have attempted to explain and measure the nature of social inequality. To generalise, four prominent main approaches to these questions have emerged in the past century and a half, and it might be worth considering them briefly before examining the nineteenth-century British situation. The earliest and most famous theory of societal inequality is Marxism – the body of doctrines enunciated between the 1840s and 1890s by Karl Marx (1818–83) and Friedrich Engels (1820–95), and which, of course, became the most influential political ideology of the first half of the twentieth century, although, with remarkable suddenness, it now appears to have vanished without trace. Marxism argues that social classes are determined, in the last analysis, by economics, and that there has been a clear and dramatic evolution in the dominant form of economic life throughout history, from slavery to feudalism to capitalism and, in most places via eventual revolution, to socialism, when classes will 'wither away'. Marxism's economic determinism, and its apparently rigid, deterministic view of class, led to many intellectual challenges by non-Marxists, not least of all in order to provide alternative views of elites and social stratification. Probably the most famous rival theory to Marxism was provided by the celebrated German sociologist Max Weber (1856–1920). Weber argued that there were three primary modes of social stratification in modern societies – status, class and power (or politics) – which cannot be reduced into one another. In contrast to Marxism, in Weber's view class is not the 'substructure' underlying the other modes of stratification but is an independent dimension. Weber also paid attention to the often irrational nature of political leadership and loyalty, coining the term 'charisma' to describe the ability to inspire profound loyalty by force of personality found in many great leaders.

At about the same time as Weber, a group of right-wing social theorists, led by the Italians Vilfredo Pareto (1848–1923) and Gaetano Mosca (1858–1941), and the German Robert Michels (1876–1936), formulated what is known as 'elitism', the sociological theory that ruling elites and groups are present in every society and in every social institution. According to Michels there is 'an iron law of oligarchy' in any social organisation wherein control inevitably comes to a small group of insiders. To these theorists, democracy, and still more socialism, are illusions: one elite group simply replaces another via a natural 'circulation of elites' as a previous ruling group ossifies and a new one takes its place. Ideologies are merely masks for the determination of one ruling group to replace another.

This pessimistic view (often seen as laying the basis for Italian fascism) has been challenged in the past 40 years by 'pluralists', a group of academics, chiefly Americans, for whom there is, in any reasonably open society, no 'ruling class' in the older, more absolute sense, but a number of discrete interest groups which compete, and generally share, the benefits of power. In Robert A. Dahl's classic study of New Haven, Connecticut, in the 1940s and 1950s, *Who Governs?* (1961), newer Italian and Irish Catholic groups were found to share many facets of power with the older Anglo-Saxon Protestant elite, with Catholics dominant in the local government infrastructure and Protestants in the region's corporate structure.

Before examining Britain's nineteenth-century class structure in more detail, there is another important consideration to be noted in the evolution of social stratification at the time. In political terms, the nineteenth century certainly saw the extension of citizenship rights, including the right to vote, to broader and broader segments of the population – although in 1905 only about two-thirds of adult males could vote at general elections, while, of course, women remained unenfranchised in parliamentary elections. Yet this broadening may not have been paralleled by increases in equality in other areas, especially in the economic sphere. The best-known description of trends in income inequality in societies which are experiencing industrialisation like nineteenth-century Britain, was offered by Simon Kuznets, the American Nobel Prize-winning economist, in 1955. Kuznets theorised that levels of inequality during the long period of industrialisation first rose and then fell in a manner which resembled an 'inverted U'. The initial effects of industrialisation in Britain were to produce greater degrees of income inequality, followed by a move to greater equality. Most empirical evidence collected by economic historians (which is, admittedly, patchy) tends to support Kuznets's insight. Economic historians have pointed to the period around 1870–1900 as marking the zenith of income inequalities in Britain. Only since the First World War, however, have inequalities declined in a marked way.[1] In other words, the extension of citizenship rights for most of the male population as a result of the Reform Acts of 1832, 1867 and 1884, and other measures, were certainly not paralleled by increasing equality of incomes: indeed, the opposite seems to have been the case. That trends in the different components of inequality in nineteenth-century Britain may have moved in different directions at the same time makes the overall picture more difficult to describe.

By any standards, at the summit of Britain's social structure during the nineteenth century were its great landowners, who certainly remained the country's most powerful, and probably richest men until the twentieth century. In the 1870s an official government survey of the names, acreage, and landed incomes of all landowners in the United Kingdom outside of London found that just 400 peers and peeresses together owned 5.7 million out of 34.5 million acres of land in England and Wales (land in Scotland was even more unequally distributed), or over 16 per cent of all the land! Another 1288 'great landowners' (defined as non-peers owning 3000 acres or more) owned 8.5 million acres, or nearly 25 per cent of England's land. The 400 peers each owned, on average, 14 320 acres, while the 'great landowners' owned, on average, 6598 acres. At the other extreme of landownership were 703 289 cottagers (owners of less than one acre), who among them owned 151 148 acres, or one-fifth of an acre each.[2]

At the very apex of the landed class were the wealthiest landowners, mainly the great titled aristocrats, whose holdings were almost unbelievable. In the 1880s, just before the decline of the great landowners began, at least 17 landowners enjoyed an annual income from their landed rentals alone of £100 000 or more (at least £5 million in today's terms, although income tax was less than 5 per cent). The richest, the Duke of Westminster, probably received over £350 000 a year from the 476 acres he owned in central London and the 20 000 acres he owned in the north of England. The Dukes of Bedford, Buccleuch, Devonshire, Northumberland, Portland, Sutherland and Hamilton, the Marquesses of Bute and Londonderry, Earl Fitzwilliam, and the Earls of Derby, Dudley and Ancaster were nearly as rich. Many (not all) of these and other super-rich landowners were prominent among the Whig aristocracy: until the 1880s, most of Britain's very richest landowners (as opposed to those who were middling rich) were

1 It should be noted that Kuznets's research concerns only *income* inequality, not inequalities of *wealth*. Wealth inequality (the ownership of saleable commodities like housing, land, and stocks and shares, or the possession of cash savings) was and is *markedly more* unequal than income inequality.

2 These figures are somewhat misleading, as many 'cottagers' were the owners of houses or business properties of less than an acre's extent, rather than very poor farmers.

probably Whigs rather than Tories, and arguably derived their liberal values from the fact that they could afford to hold generous, progressive and tolerant opinions. Poorer landowners tended to be Conservatives. This broad distinction remained until the collectivist challenge to the great landowners as a class compelled nearly all to move into the Conservative camp.

The extraordinary wealth of the great landed aristocrats was the result of a number of separate factors which made the great British landowners unique in Europe. Since the Middle Ages, landowning in Britain had been organised on a strictly 'cash nexus' basis, with farmers paying rents to the landowners and in turn paying a money wage to their agricultural labourers. Since the Middle Ages there was no feudalism in Britain, no serfdom, and no peasants in the European sense. Instead, landownership was organised by the so-called 'triple division of land tenure' (landlords; rent-paying farmers; agricultural labourers) all of which was part and parcel of the modern cash economy. (Small independent 'yeomen' were common only in limited areas of Britain, especially in the north of England.) In Britain, primogeniture was an almost invariable rule: the eldest son inherited all of the land, and most of his father's property. Titles, including peerages, of course also passed from the father to the eldest son. Because only the eldest son of a peer or a baronet inherited the title, the other descendants of titled persons were commoners, and hence the size of the titled class in Britain remained remarkably small: in 1810 there were 292 English peers and 177 Scottish and Irish peers (a total of 469 peers altogether), although even this figure probably includes some double counting. In 1900 there were 522 British peers. There were 852 baronets in 1810 and 1072 in 1900. About 1360 knighthoods, non-hereditary, were created during the reign of Queen Victoria (1837–1901), an average of 22 per year, although many of these were themselves awarded to peers. Thus, even in 1900 no more than perhaps 2000 persons in Britain held a title of any kind. In contrast, in France on the eve of the Revolution in 1789 the size of the aristocracy has been placed by historians at between 250 000 and 400 000 (1–2 per cent of the total population) because in France, as in other continental countries, all members of the family of an aristocrat were themselves members of the aristocracy, as were their descendants. In Britain, because of primogeniture, nearly all were commoners. Because of primogeniture, younger sons, daughters, and other relatives received annuities or smaller legacies, according to the provisions of a family strict settlement agreement, but, by these strict settlements, most of the land of the great landowners was inviolate and could not be sold except in very unusual circumstances. The wealth of landowners also tended to grow over the generations by marriages between members of two families (especially where, unusually, a daughter had inherited the family's land). Most importantly, landowners were at the forefront of developing the non-agricultural resources of their estates, especially urban land and housing, mineral deposits, harbours and railways. In Britain, minerals such as coal underneath the soil belonged to the owner of the soil, whereas on the Continent it often belonged to the state. Most of the very wealthiest landowners benefited from very considerable non-agricultural assets associated with their land and, indeed, often owed their great wealth to these non-agricultural holdings. The comparatively large size of Britain's farms and of the overall acreage owned by the great landowners also produced economies of scale, and gave all participants in agricultural life a vested interest in increasing productivity through the introduction of new farming techniques and improvements. As a class, Britain's great landowners did not feel themselves to be entirely separate from businessmen, as was so often the case on the Continent. On the contrary, they often intermarried with the offspring of the richest and most prominent capitalists, especially with bankers in London and some of the wealthy who had attended a leading public school and university. (On the other hand, few new businessmen of wealth, especially those below the very wealthiest, attempted to purchase land on a vast scale.)

Britain's great landowners were thus probably becoming richer during the nineteenth century until the 1880s, often by systematically developing their non-agricultural assets. From the 1880s, however, the effects of the agricultural depression which began around 1879, and of higher taxes from the 1890s, began to undermine their economic position, especially among landowners with no non-agricultural holdings to develop. Great landowners were also predominant in the political sphere until then or even slightly later. Not only did every Cabinet contain a majority of landowners until the 1890s, but at least one-third of all MPs were themselves landowners or their close relatives until the twentieth century. Apart from Disraeli (who, in mature life, did own a country house), the first Prime Minister with no pretentions whatever to landed status was H. H. Asquith in 1908, and even he was married to the daughter of Scotland's richest businessman, Sir Charles Tennant, a man who owned nearly 4000 acres and a country house in the 1880s. Landowners were also extremely influential at the local level of county government, indeed often remaining more influential at the local level to this day.

Nevertheless, both the economic and the political fortunes of the landed aristocracy were, in the long term, almost certain to decline. Prior to the 1830s, one of the hallmarks of the landed aristocracy, and of Britain's Establishment as a whole, was that the dimensions of stratification of wealth, status and power were transmissible into one another: for instance, political office could be used to generate wealth for oneself and one's family via the patronage system of 'Old Corruption', while political office and wealth could be used to obtain a peerage or a promotion within the peerage. With the growth of the movement for 'economical reform' from the 1780s onwards, and the development of a more liberal and modern notion of civic responsibility, it gradually became impossible to amass

personal wealth (apart from one's salary) as an office-holder, or to obtain a
rank in the peerage which one did not ostensibly earn through public
services. In other words, landowners (and others) were increasingly unable
to increase their wealth in other than 'legitimate' ways, from the income of
the land and non-agricultural assets they already owned. At the same time,
as the commercial and industrial revolutions bore fruit, landowners were
increasingly outnumbered, among wealthy men, by rich businessmen and
professionals, who were, so to speak, in competition with landowners for
wealth, status and power. By 1905 there were far more wealthy and
influential businessmen than landowners. Just as the Liberal party had
ceased, by the 1880s, to be a party controlled by landowners, so the
Conservatives had, by the Edwardian period, become a party largely
dominated by businessmen.

This process, however, took much longer than one might have expected.
Until about 1880, more than one-half of all the really wealthy men in
Britain were landowners; only from about the 1860s, and definitely from
about 1880, did the number of wealthy businessmen (although not definitely the size of their fortunes) exceed the number of very rich landowners.
As a general rule, Britain's wealthiest and most successful businessmen of
the nineteenth century were to be found in finance and in commerce,
especially in the City of London and in the leading commercial ports like
Liverpool, rather than in manufacturing cities like Manchester or Birmingham or in industrial areas like South Wales. The greatest single concentration of business wealth in Britain (and probably in the world) was to be
found, not surprisingly, in London, and especially in the City of London,
the 'square mile' where Britain's leading financial and mercantile institutions were located or had their headquarters. The great international
banking dynasties, of whom the Barings and the Rothschilds were the most
renowned, probably constituted the wealthiest and most influential entrepreneurs in Britain. The Barings, with close links to the Whig aristocracy
and the Royal Family, and the Rothschilds, socially the equal of any
European monarchy, are often seen as between them deciding the economic
future of continents, the Barings being influential in the New World and the
Rothschilds in Europe and the Middle East. Like very many other City
magnates, both families were immigrants, the Barings German Lutherans
who came in the early eighteenth century and the Rothschilds German Jews
who arrived slightly later. Apart from the merchant banking elite, the City
contained a great many wealthy heads of clearing banks, stockbrokers,
insurance brokers, financiers, and merchants of every kind. While the
majority were Anglicans, many were immigrants – Jews were probably the
largest element here, but there were also many Greeks, Germans and other
continental Europeans, and Americans – or Protestant Dissenters, especially in the clearing banks, with their important Quaker influence. On the
other hand the City livery companies, which controlled the civic life and
ceremonials of the City and which often represented smaller merchants and

tradesmen, remained Anglican bastions. In the course of the nineteenth century an ever closer nexus grew up between the City and the landed aristocracy, with, by 1914, the great majority of City financial magnates having been educated at public schools and Oxbridge. That the Conservative party, especially after the 1886 split in the Liberal party over Irish Home Rule, became the normal party of the 'Establishment' was in large measure due to this increasing merger between the traditional aristocracy and the City of London. According to a now widely accepted view of British capitalism associated with Peter Cain, A. G. Hopkins and the author of this textbook, 'gentlemanly capitalism', marked by the hegemony of the City and the traditional landed aristocracy and the institutions associated with it, has dominated British capitalism since the late nineteenth century. Commercial and financial wealth was also found throughout provincial Britain, with shipowners, local bankers and merchants comprising a very large part of the entrepreneurial elite, not merely in purely commercial cities like Liverpool and Edinburgh, but also in manufacturing centres.

Britain's industrial and manufacturing elite thus comprised a much smaller component of the business class than was formerly believed to be the case. Industrialists were, however, dominant in manufacturing towns, where they formed the classical manufacturing elite we commonly imagine, heavily composed of self-made hard men, Dissenters and Evangelicals, especially in middle-sized towns in Lancashire and Yorkshire like Oldham and Bolton. Among Britain's larger towns where manufacturers comprised the bulk of the city's elite, Glasgow (engineering, coal and textiles), Newcastle upon Tyne (shipbuilding, engineering and coal), Bradford (woollens) and Belfast (shipbuilding and engineering) were probably the most important. As is well-known, in British capitalism there was traditionally a division between finance, located chiefly in London, and manufacturing, located chiefly in the north. London's banks played almost no role in financing Britain's industries while local banks in the northern cities played only a limited role. Most factories were self-financing, ploughing back their profits into investment, or receiving investment from groups of relatives or co-religionists of the founder. This, among other things, acted to deter the growth of really large manufacturing firms on the American or German models until this century. Successful factory owners and industrialists in nineteenth-century Britain tended to leave fortunes of around £100 000 or so – a substantial amount but not Midas-like wealth. There were exceptions, of course, like the founders of the Arkwright and Peel dynasties in cotton-spinning in the early nineteenth century, or the enormously wealthy Wills (tobacco) and Coats (sewing thread) dynasties a century later, but by and large manufacturers in Britain were less wealthy than either the great landowners or the great financiers. This, together with their self-made unsophistication, limited their impact on national politics, as did the fact that many entered national political life relatively late, after they had made a success of business life. On the other hand, at the local level, in industrial towns of the north and elsewhere, they often dominated local councils until the twentieth century.

Standing apart from Britain's most successful landowners was its professional elite. The professional class is somewhat difficult to define: traditionally it includes those persons who earn their livings by selling their specialised knowledge to clients who require them, receiving their earnings in the form of fees or salaries rather than in rent or profits, as do landowners and businessmen. Traditionally the older, socially prestigious professions comprised the Anglican clergy, the law (with barristers much more prestigious than solicitors), army and navy officers, perhaps some university professors, and more highly regarded physicians. The higher Anglican clergy, the Bar and Bench, the armed services, and the old universities were recognised parts of the traditional 'Establishment', with official roles in the governance of the state: 26 Anglican bishops sat in the House of Lords, the Lord Chancellor and other law officers held government positions of great importance, the old universities returned members to Parliament, the armed services were represented in a host of official roles. Many, but by no means all, of those who filled the most senior professional positions prior to the mid-nineteenth century were close relatives of the aristocracy and gentry, the Anglican clergy, for instance, traditionally being the venue for 'fools of sons' of the upper classes who could not readily be placed elsewhere. On the other hand, the linkages between the older professions and the aristocracy should not be exaggerated: many who reached the highest positions of all were, if not precisely 'self-made men' in the pure sense, at least without previous connection to the elite. Despite the considerable costs needed to enter the Bar, even some senior judges were virtually 'self-made', for example Charles Abbott, Lord Tenterden (1757–1832), Chief Justice of the King's Bench in 1818–32, who was the son of a hairdresser in Canterbury. During the eighteenth and early nineteenth centuries it had been possible for the most successful professionals, including bishops and judges, to amass simply phenomenal fortunes from the world of 'Old Corruption'. When salaries and professional fees alone became the only legitimate way of earning money as a professional, after the 1830s, top professional earnings actually declined, so that by the Edwardian period the most successful barristers in Britain like Sir Edward Carson, Rufus Isaacs, F. E. Smith and Marshall Hall probably earned no more than about £10 000 per year: far less, curiously enough, than Lords Ellenborough or Eldon could amass in previous times. Social mobility increased, too, so that, for instance, by 1900 no more than one-quarter of Anglican bishops had been born into the true upper classes, the scions of the traditional aristocracy or the new plutocracy. This broadening of the social bases of the higher professions has been concealed from many observers by the fact that (to take the case of bishops) in 1900 the majority went to a minor public school and nearly all to Oxbridge, which has wrongly been taken as evidence of elite social status instead of middle-class backgrounds, from which most demonstrably sprang.

The nineteenth century also saw the rise of the newer professions and the great expansion of many of the older professions. Even the number of Anglican clergymen rose strongly in the nineteenth century, while the number of physicians, engineers, architects, accountants, and others in the 'skilled' professions, requiring highly specialised knowledge and training, rose very sharply. Architects, for instance, rose in number (according to the Census figures) from 1486 in 1841 to 8921 in 1911, civil engineers from only 853 to 7208 and dentists from 522 to 8674 in the same period, with most, but not all, of the increase coming in the third quarter of the nineteenth century. Sociologically below the established, recognised professions were the newer 'sub-professions' like teaching, nursing and librarianship. Although normally requiring extensive training (and, in the case of nursing, dealing with matters of life and death), the 'sub-professions' enjoyed a lower social cachet and were paid far less than the older professions. The 'sub-professions' increasingly became dominated by women (except among their top administrative levels, which remained in male hands) and were, traditionally, way-stations for bright, upwardly mobile products of the working classes. As a rule, the professions in Britain evolved a fairly similar administrative infrastructure, hallmarked by the deliberate creation, to give respectability, of a professional representative body, headquartered in London, such as the Institution of Civil Engineers (founded in 1818). Each profession attempted, in particular, to regulate new entries by a universally recognised set of examinations or apprenticeship/educational procedure, to eliminate fraudulent or incompetent members threatening the legitimacy of the profession, and, above all, to regulate (and increase) fees and salaries. Professional societies also liaised with governments, Parliament and the press. By the Edwardian period the well-established professions were among the very backbones of the British upper middle classes, more important, in some respects, than the business classes. They comprised a disproportionate number of both the entrants at most public schools and the fathers of most entrants. For instance, among a random sample of 221 boys entering Winchester College in 1840, 1870 and 1895, 75 per cent undertook professional careers in adult life, while 62 per cent of the fathers of these Wykehamists were themselves professional men. Nevertheless, the influence of the professional class on the British elite structure should also not be exaggerated. Apart from barristers, professionals were underrepresented (or, indeed, unrepresented) in British Cabinets, while few, apart from naval and military commanders, very senior judges, and permanent under-secretaries in the Civil Service, ever received peerages before the First World War.

A number of broader conclusions about Britain's elites remain to be made. In general, among persons of wealth there is an inevitable drift to the political right, so that even if individual wealth-holders originally represent groups associated, for whatever reason, with the left (for instance, Nonconformist manufacturers, who were often among the leaders of early and mid-nineteenth century radicalism), they almost inevitably come, in the long term, to perceive their chief interests as lying with the political right, and normally become Tories; if they do not, their children and grandchildren almost certainly do. Something like this happened on a society-wide basis in nineteenth-century Britain. Many of the wealthy industrialists and manufacturers of the 1815–70 period who formed the backbone of the Liberal party became Conservatives, or allies of the Conservatives, by 1890. While this process was not complete until the 1918–39 period, by the time of the Boer War the Conservative party had emerged as the party of most of the wealthy and upper middle classes. There were many vehicles making for this pattern of evolution. One of the most important was the emergence of the public schools. Most of these schools drew their students overwhelmingly from the upper middle classes: only at Eton, Harrow, and one or two other schools did more than insignificant numbers of students come from aristocratic backgrounds. Yet the total number of students who attended public schools, even in the Edwardian era, was much lower than the cohort of middle- and upper-class boys whose fathers' incomes were sufficient to pay for such an education, and other factors making for class cohesion must also have been at work, for example the decline of Protestant Nonconformity among the middle classes as the strength of imperialism and its doctrines grew. Fear of socialism and mistrust of the direction of the Liberal party was also a very significant factor.

It is a cliché among historians that every age finds the middle classes rising, and the nineteenth century was obviously no exception to this truism: indeed, for many historians, the nineteenth century was the century of the middle classes, who now came into their own as the most dynamic element in society. It is, however, difficult to generalise about the middle classes: indeed, even defining them properly presents many problems. Presumably the middle classes include everyone in business or professional life below the millionaire class but above a lower income level which separates them from the working classes. However, even this is remarkably ambiguous, especially as to where the upper and lower limits and outer boundaries of the middle classes should be set. Are shopkeepers in the middle class? Farmers? Schoolteachers? At what point in wealth and status do the middle classes merge into the upper classes? Are the Barings or Rothschilds middle class or (as seems unarguable) part of the upper classes, despite the fact that they certainly remained active businessmen? Perhaps questions such as these – and there are many others – are unanswerable, although some tentative conclusions can be reached. It would appear that about 15–20 per cent of the population in mid-Victorian Britain belonged to the middle classes on an income basis, subject to fairly wide margins of error. While there are no good statistics for income distribution, from a

Table 17.1 Estimated percentage of the adult male population with an income of
£100 or more, 1859–60, in selected boroughs

London		Larger cities	
Finsbury	30.3	Birmingham	14.3
Greenwich	12.3	Bradford	11.1
Lambeth	27.8	Bristol	19.5
Marylebone	28.3	Cardiff	16.3
Southwark	12.3	Coventry	14.7
		Leeds	10.5
		Liverpool	17.3
		Manchester	15.3
		Newcastle upon Tyne	12.4
		Nottingham	11.5
		Sheffield	9.5
		Wolverhampton	9.6
Smaller boroughs (south of England)		**Smaller boroughs (north of England & Wales)**	
Brighton	23.2	Blackburn	7.9
Buckingham	30.5	Bolton	8.0
Cambridge	22.3	Chester	17.4
Cheltenham	21.0	Gateshead	10.3
Colchester	12.9	Huddersfield	14.6
Gloucester	21.6	Merthyr Tydfil	6.7
Guildford	21.2	Oldham	8.7
Maidstone	14.2	Preston	8.1
New Windsor	43.8	Swansea	15.1
Oxford	17.5	Wakefield	11.8
Reading	18.0	York	20.1

Source: W. D. Rubinstein, 'The Size and Distribution of the English Middle Classes in 1860', *Historical Research*, 61 (February 1988).

table in the Parliamentary Papers in 1860 it is possible to ascertain the percentage of the adult male population in all parliamentary boroughs with an income of £100 or more in 1859–60, and who were thus liable to pay income tax.[3]

Table 17.1 lists a typical selection of boroughs of four types (there are no comparable statistics available for Scotland or Ireland). Although there are exceptions, it will be readily seen that the percentage of men with incomes of £100 or more was generally higher in London and in the boroughs of the south of England, as well as in commercial towns like Bristol, than in industrial centres, especially the new factory towns of the north. One may point to a number of reasons for these differences. The older, genteel towns had acted as magnets for the middle classes for centuries. As we have seen, commercial wealth was more lucrative in general than manufacturing

3 In 1860 income tax was payable by anyone with an annual income of £100 or more. Very few of these taxpayers, if any, could have been employed in working-class trades. The average wage for adult males in most working class occupations was around £50–60 per year.

wealth. Most importantly, industrial towns contained vast working-class labour forces for the factories and other heavy industries. As well, they probably contained less in the way of the variety of service trades, shops, places of amusement, and so on, found in commercial towns and regional centres. Industrial towns like Bolton, Oldham and Merthyr Tydfil seemed to approach the stark Marxist division between a small class of the wealthy and the great majority of poor persons far more than other types of urban areas, especially London and the older towns. If anything, the data in this table probably understates the differences between the size of the middle classes in various types of towns, since they provide no information on women who received an income of £100 or more in their own right. Most of these women – shopkeepers, recipients of annuities and pensions, boarding-house keepers, well-to-do widows and spinsters living in their own households – almost certainly lived in greater London, genteel coastal and suburban towns, and local commercial centres, adding still further to the size of the middle classes in these types of places.

Who was in the 15–20 per cent of the British population which might be defined as, in some sense, middle class? There is no way to generalise. Perhaps the easiest way to appreciate the size and variety of this class and their growth in number is to glance at any series of nineteenth-century local directory, each of which listed thousands upon thousands of men (and women) in trade and normally above the working classes. By the late nineteenth century London directories contained literally hundreds of thousands of names, listed alphabetically, and cross-indexed by occupation and address.[4] Every conceivable category of middle-class trade and profession, from physicians to professors (i.e. teachers) of music to leather merchants to grocers, contained hundreds and in some cases thousands of names, their numbers constantly growing. Local directories for the provincial towns were very similar in scope to London's directories, and were also increasing in size at a similar rate.

Below the 15–20 per cent of the population who may be defined as 'middle class' in income terms was the lower middle class – although the two groups probably overlapped to some extent, since many shopkeepers, small clerks, self-employed artisans and so on certainly had incomes, in mid-Victorian times, of £100 or more. The lower middle class is even more difficult accurately to define than are the middle classes, and one can, at best, offer a definition by examples. The lower middle class traditionally includes smaller tradesmen and shopkeepers, especially in individual and family-owned firms, clerks and minor civil servants, certain self-employed

---

4 The compilation of these local directories on an annual basis, with each new edition containing thousands of changes and additions, and without mechanical aids of any kind, must surely be one of the most remarkable feats of nineteenth-century British civilisation. It would probably be much more difficult, and vastly more expensive, to compile comparable local directories today, despite computers: in fact, virtually no comparable directories have been published since the 1960s.

artisans and craftsmen of the traditional type, and, perhaps, the more poorly paid of the 'sub-professions' like elementary schoolteachers and nurses. It would certainly not include manual workers, even those skilled workers with incomes possibly equal to those of lower-middle-class occupations. Geographically, much of the lower middle class was probably more widely and equally distributed than the more solid part of the middle class. Small shopkeepers, publicans, self-employed artisans, and schoolteachers were found nearly everywhere (some groups possibly defined as lower-middle-class, like Nonconformist clergymen, were probably more numerous in the north of England) rather than disproportionately in London and the commercial cities. On the other hand, clerks and minor civil servants were more numerous, almost certainly, in London and the commercial towns. It is well-known that no articulate, self-defined lower-middle-class lobby emerged in nineteenth-century Britain, in contrast to parts of the Continent, especially Germany, where the *mittelstand*, especially self-employed traditional artisans, shopkeepers and minor civil servants, were long associated with political reaction (and, in the inter-war period, with fascism). It is not easy to identify any equivalent in Britain. Men of the lower middle class were in constant danger of falling into the working classes and into dire poverty, a theme which permeates many of Charles Dickens's works. They were distinguished from the working classes chiefly by status rather than by income, with little or nothing in the way of a safety net, often had large families, and frequently held middle-class pretensions and aspirations; it is indeed somewhat surprising that no lower-middle-class political lobby or movement of activists emerged. Some historians have seen the milieu of Chartism, and of the particular brand of English radicalism of the period *c.* 1830–50, as emerging largely from the 'uneasy class' of small tradesmen and the like. At the end of the nineteenth century, it is possible that the early Labour party, especially its Fabian wing, included persons from the same background. In all likelihood a higher than average share of the English lower middle classes were Nonconformists and, indeed, one of the images of nineteenth-century Methodism is as the cradle of men of this type. Including those whose incomes overlapped with the more solid part of the middle classes, probably 15 per cent or so of the British population could be counted with the lower middle classes (although – see below – this percentage probably grew in the later nineteenth century), meaning that perhaps 30 per cent of the British population could be situated above the manual working classes.

Both the lower middle class and the more solid middle class had a number of features in common. A near-permanent sense of insecurity and fear of impoverishment permeated much of the consciousness and the economic activities of both groups – stronger among the lower middle classes, since much less separated them from poverty, but strong among everyone who did not enjoy the security of wealth. For this reason, safe jobs, those with tenure and a reasonable starting salary, were the aim of much of both the middle and lower middle classes. The Civil Service, teaching, even the Anglican clergy, enjoyed a security which few jobs in the business sector could possibly offer. In business life, bankruptcy was an ever-present possibility. The search for security was one of the most potent themes in the occupational goals and strategies of the middle classes. As well, most components of the middle classes felt themselves to be citizens of a world-wide Empire: if all else failed in Britain, Sydney beckoned, or Toronto, or Auckland, or even (outside the Empire) Chicago or Buenos Aires.

Not all the economic trends in middle-class life were negative. After the mid-nineteenth century, the 'white collar' component of the workforce certainly expanded in size at a disproportionately rapid pace. The higher occupations of the upper middle classes increased significantly in numbers, while the total of newly available jobs in the lower middle classes – clerks, civil servants, teachers, minor engineers – probably expanded more rapidly still. The creation of new employment opportunities went a long way to offsetting the fears of middle-class economic failure. These fears were diminished, as well, by the typically smaller families found in many middle-class households after about 1870 and by the ever-present 'safety valve' of emigration to the Empire.

Britain's working classes were no more of an undifferentiated mass than were its middle classes. One striking way to indicate this is to review the overall statistics of occupational distribution in England and Wales. It is not possible, given the Census and other figures which exist, to ascertain in any more than a rough way how many workers there were in particular industries. The decennial censuses from 1841 onwards, however, do show the total number of males and females employed in each occupational category such as 'agricultural, horticulture, and forestry', 'mining and quarrying', 'commercial occupations', 'domestic and personal service', 'textiles', and so on. These headings, unfortunately, make no distinction between employees and workers, nor among any intermediate gradings between them, and contain innumerable ambiguities which cannot readily be resolved today (see Table 17.2). Nevertheless, one can draw some overall conclusions from these figures, taking the six census occupational categories for males in which the Victorian working classes (in the sense this term is commonly understood) are likely to be found: mining and quarrying; metal manufacturing and the manufacturing of machines, implements, vehicles, etc.; building and construction; chemicals, oil, soap, etc.; textiles; and clothing. At no time during the Victorian era did these occupational categories collectively account for more than about 40 per cent of the male workforce in England and Wales. (These occupational categories, moreover, include all employers in their fields, like factory owners, as well, probably, as many intermediate-level employees such as clerks, salesmen, foremen, etc.) The percentage of males employed in these six categories rose from about 31.5 per cent in 1841 to about 40 per cent

Table 17.2 Numbers of males employed in key industrial and manufacturing
fields, England and Wales, 1841–1901 (× 1000)

	1841	1861	1881	1901
Mining	218	457	604	931
Metals	396	747	977	1485
Building	107	593	875	1216
Textiles	525	612	554	557
Clothing	358	413	379	423
Chemicals	23	47	72	116
TOTAL	1627	2869	3461	4728
Percentage of total males in employment	31.5	39.5	39.1	40.9
Transport	196	579	870	1409
Percentage of total males in employment	3.8	8.0	9.8	12.2

throughout the rest of the nineteenth century. One might add other
working-class groups to these totals, for instance the rapidly rising number
of men in transport, many of whom were connected with the railways.
Nevertheless, it seems that the core working-class occupations of the
industrial revolution never constituted a majority among all employed
males during the nineteenth century, with the numbers in each individual
occupation smaller still: for instance, about 8.1 per cent of the male
workforce were employed as miners in 1901.

Among those not accounted for here, agriculture (the largest single
occupation until the very end of the nineteenth century), commercial
occupations, food–drink–tobacco, professionals and sub-professionals, and
domestic servants, were the largest occupational fields. Employment in key
working-class trades also, of course, varied enormously from place to
place. In small and medium-sized factory towns like Oldham and Bolton,
the class structure – as noted above – resembled the Marxist image of a
small capitalist class and a vast working class far more than in larger cities,
with their commercial, intermediate and professional strata. Coal-mining
areas were even more extreme examples of dominant working-class numbers, for these often contained, in effect, no local capitalist class at all, only
overseers and engineers acting for largely absentee mining magnates and
landowners. (It was in these areas that Labour gained its firmest and
earliest foothold.)

Just as the prevalence of the classical working class varied greatly from
place to place so did their standard of living. During the 1950s and 1960s
a well-known debate emerged among economic historians about changes in
the standards of living of the British working classes during the period of,
roughly, 1790–1850. 'Optimists' (those who argued that the standard of
living rose) were ranged against 'pessimists' (who argued the opposite). No
consensus was ever reached. The best evidence suggests that standards of
living rose somewhat during the Napoleonic War years, then stagnated

(although never actually fell) until around 1850, when they rose again, and continued to rise during the later nineteenth century. The years of wage stagnation, roughly 1815–50, coincided with the period of maximum population growth, but before the factory system and railways had become ubiquitous. By the early twentieth century working-class standards of living had certainly risen, although they were still appallingly low compared with those even several decades later, and a 'residuum' of one-third of the population continued to live in chronic poverty. The rise in living standards in the late nineteenth century was made possible by a number of factors including a slow-down in population growth, gains produced by technology and mechanisation, decreases in taxes levied upon the working classes, and the growth of a world-wide market for goods with declining barriers to trade. On the other hand, the gains in the British standard of living in the twentieth century, especially since the later 1930s, have obviously dwarfed everything seen in the nineteenth century.

Within the British working classes (as Professor Harold Perkin pointed out in his *Origins of Modern English Society*, published in 1969), there were, however, distinct gainers and losers, so that it is really rather misleading to talk of 'the working-class standard of living' in an un-differentiated way. Occupations where standards of living rose, and where incomes were among the highest earned by workers, included artisanal trades like printing, which required apprenticeships and had some trade union protection, and the most skilled components of industries which had been mechanised, such as cotton operatives with experience, engineering pattern makers, and locomotive engine drivers. Some working-class trades paid relatively less in wages but provided much greater security of tenure, especially the so-called 'uniformed working classes' like postmen and policemen. At the other end of the pay scale were workers in trades which were being bypassed and even driven out of business by mechanisation, of whom the handloom weavers were the best-known example. As well, workers in regions (like Cornwall and Cumbria) with little of an industrial base, or whose industries were shifting elsewhere, were often hard hit. At the bottom of the pay scale, however, were agricultural labourers, who were normally the worst-paid (and least well educated) of all workers, although they could often supplement their cash incomes with foodstuffs and other goods in kind. The best-paid English adult male workers probably earned between £80 and £100 (very occasionally, slightly more) per year in the late nineteenth century. A policeman or postman earned about £1 per week. Agricultural labourers probably earned around £25 per year in wages.

Members of the working classes also suffered from much else besides low wages. As a rule, earnings of adult male workers tended to peak at the age of 25–35, that is, at the age of peak physical ability, and rarely grew after the age of 40. In some physically demanding trades like coal-mining, few men older than 40 or so had the stamina to continue working. Manual workers could thus not look forward to ever-increasing seniority, as in the professions and the managerial stratum of businesses. Many trades were physically dangerous. Perhaps the worst of all was coal-mining, where dozens, even hundreds, of miners were killed every year in appalling underground accidents, while many miners lucky enough to escape a quick death underground faced a lingering one in their home villages from lung diseases. Railway accidents claimed dozens of casualties each year, with the occasional disaster involving scores of deaths, for instance at Armagh in June 1889 when 80 people were killed as overloaded passenger carriages which had been uncoupled from their engine on a steep incline ran backwards and plunged off an embankment, or at Penistone (on the moors between Manchester and Sheffield) in July 1884 when a broken locomotive axle on a speeding train led to a derailment which killed 24. One of the most dangerous industries was building construction, where even the most elementary of today's safety procedures seldom existed. For instance, scaffolding on the outside of buildings under construction was held together by rope and twine, and frequently collapsed, killing or injuring countless workmen. The use of chemicals and other substances employed in manufacturing processes was frequently unsafe: most famously, for example, the proverbial phrase 'mad as a hatter' is a reference to the use of mercury in hat manufacturing and repairing, which frequently induced insanity.

Worst of all, perhaps, were the frequent bouts of unemployment which most working men knew. Of course there was no unemployment insurance in the modern sense, and the workhouse or private charity were all that the unemployed could expect. (Similarly there was no old-age pension scheme or pay during illness.) Unemployment, broadly speaking, was of two kinds. In the factory towns of the north, the economic cycle of booms and busts meant that there would be full employment for a period of years, followed, perhaps every seven to ten years, by mass unemployment when the trade cycle was depressed. During booms, everyone in a factory town was employed; during recessions, many workers were unemployed. In London and other commercial towns, especially those with ports, this boom-and-bust cycle was much less in evidence. In London, there was chronic underemployment among those without marketable skills, with too many would-be employees chasing too few jobs. The plethora of bizarre, curious and highly unpleasant trades depicted in Henry Mayhew's famous journalistic portraits of mid-Victorian London was one outcome of this chronic poverty, as was, for instance, the daily scramble at London's docks as hundreds of hungry dockers sought employment for the day, men who had no steady or continuing work.

Realistic opportunities for upward social mobility from the working classes to the middle classes were also extremely limited. The principal method of accomplishing this, across the generations, in most of today's societies, is by means of the educational system, with at least the brightest offspring of the working classes able to secure a ticket upwards by appropriate secondary and higher education. During the nineteenth century, however, not more than one working-class boy in 50 remained in school at the age of 16 (the ratio for girls was much lower), while it is safe to say that not one working-class youth in 5000 was able to attend a university prior to the growth of the 'redbricks' at the end of the nineteenth century. A more likely way up was to found a small business and expand it, but this normally required at least some capital. In most cases it was impossible for a member of the working classes to procure venture capital of this type, unless one were able to borrow it from a relative of a slightly higher social class or from one's wealthier co-religionists.

To be sure, by the late nineteenth century there were at least some means of savings open to the working classes, especially to the skilled workers whose incomes allowed some surplus to be accumulated. In 1844 the first cooperative society was founded, the Rochdale Society of Equitable Pioneers. The so-called 'Rochdale Principles' of the early 'co-ops' – open membership, democratic control, and, most significantly, dividends paid on purchases – were extended to the nation-wide Cooperative Wholesale Society when it was founded in 1863. In 1861 the Palmerston government established the Post Office Savings Bank, allowing large numbers – chiefly skilled workers, but also many members of the lower middle classes – to bank and save their excess earnings. Workers with money to save had, first and foremost, the much more pressing spectre of saving to support themselves during bouts of unemployment and for their old age, which obviously deterred any thoughts of founding a business.

Middle-class observers of nineteenth-century Britain often referred to the working class as 'a class apart'. It has been observed that for a wealthy inhabitant of London's West End to journey a few miles into the East End slums was to visit a land as exotic as central Africa or Borneo, and few did. Apart from being crime-ridden (although not nearly as violent as America's inner cities today) and full of disease, the East End and other deprived areas were inhabited by tens of thousands of people who spoke English with a different accent and were, to the wealthy, often physically repellent. Indeed, as George Orwell pointed out in the 1930s, one important but unstated reason for class animosity was (as he put it) because 'the working classes smelled'. Workers indeed often wore the same clothes for months on end, and had little or no access to effective means of washing or laundering. Drink and drunken behaviour, signs of domestic violence, foul language and shouting, would also be unavoidable features of any venture into the slums. There was another side to this world, of course: local colour, the cleverness of the street market, and tens of thousands of people attempting to live a life as best they could under almost impossible circumstances.

As the overall standard of living rose in Britain after 1850, it was probably the case that dire poverty became less omnipresent. By the late nineteenth century, too, a working-class culture, with such institutions as the music hall and football, had emerged. Yet dire poverty virtually persisted until the First World War, as Charles Booth, Seebohm Rowntree, and many other social investigators repeatedly demonstrated. About 10 per cent of the inhabitants of London and York lived in primary poverty at the end of the nineteenth century, with about another 30 per cent living in conditions of poverty slightly less severe, figures streamlined by the press to indicate that about one-third of the British people lived in chronic poverty at this time. By the 1930s, despite two decades of mass unemployment, primary poverty had almost disappeared. Increases in overall living standards, the positive gains brought about by trade unions after the late nineteenth century, lower birth rates, and, however tentatively, an extension of social mobility via increased educational opportunities and of the mass-oriented consumer society, were all hallmarks of the inter-war years and of the rest of the twentieth century.

It thus seems clear that nineteenth-century Britain had a small inner elite which dominated political life and, to a lesser extent, economic outcomes. Yet it was arguably much more ambiguous in its nature and composition than some have argued, and constantly challenged by democracy and by social change. Its backbone remained the great landowners until the end of the nineteenth century, and changes which might reasonably have been expected to occur decades earlier were postponed or never took place at all. By the first decade of the twentieth century, however, there was an apparent consensus that Britain's traditional governing elite had increasingly failed the country. But there was no consensus regarding what should take its place.

18

Religion and the churches in British society, 1815–1905

The central social force in Britain during the nineteenth century was organised religion and the most important voluntary organisations in Britain, beyond question, were the churches. Unless these facts are appreciated, virtually nothing about nineteenth-century social and even political life will make sense and very much will seem obscure and opaque. Religious debate, that is the discussion on all aspects of organised religion, especially the present and future role of the Church of England, constituted a grossly disproportionate share of all public discussion during the nineteenth century in Britain, and especially the decades before about 1870. During this period, for every book, pamphlet or article about the alleviation of poverty, it is safe to say that there were 50 about religion; for every book, pamphlet or article which advocated more rights or a greater role in society for women, it is safe to say that there were 500 about religion (many written by women). In the 1860s the Religious Tract Society printed 33 million books and pamphlets *each year*, while the number and range of British religious periodicals possibly dwarfed all other types of magazines and periodicals. Organised religion, especially the Church of England, continued to enjoy a virtual monopoly over the conducting of *rites de passage* (baptisms, confirmations, marriage ceremonies, and funerals) throughout the nineteenth century, something which it is quite possible for us now to overlook. In 1844, for instance, a total of 132 249 marriages were conducted in England and Wales. Of these, 120 009 (90.7 per cent) took place in an Anglican church, 8795 (6.7 per cent) were held in other, non-Anglican places of worship, while only 3446 (2.6 per cent) of marriages were conducted in civil ceremonies. Even in 1901, of 259 400 marriages in England and Wales, 172 769 (66.6 per cent) were conducted in an Anglican service, 45 654 (17.6 per cent) by the rites of some other religion, and only 41 067 (15.8 per cent) in civil ceremonies. In Scotland the figures were still more striking: in 1855 (the first year for which figures exist) out of 19 680 marriages, precisely nine were conducted by civil ceremony; even in 1901, only 1952 out of 31 387 Scottish marriages (6.2 per cent) took place in a civil ceremony. Probably 99 per cent of funerals in Britain – including the tragically common funerals of children, a trauma which few families could have been spared – were religious in nature. It was thus well-nigh impossible for anyone in nineteenth-century Britain to avoid being brought into the web of religious ceremonial and practice at some stage of his or her life even if they wished to avoid it (which few did) and almost always at a crucial step in the life-cycle.

Additionally, the clergy, and especially the Anglican clergy, probably constituted the largest single profession, in terms of numbers, in Britain, certainly dwarfing the old established professions, the law and medicine, as well as new ones like engineering. Only with the rise of teaching (and nursing) as what are known as 'sub-professions' (with lower, fewer entry qualifications, and typically recruiting persons from a lower socio-economic background) did the clergy lose its pre-eminent position. One startling fact might serve to put the central place of the Anglican clergy into an appropriate perspective: in the 1840s, 73 per cent of *all* graduates of Oxford and Cambridge were ordained as Anglican clergymen. Despite the widening of middle-class occupational boundaries and the widespread 'crisis of faith', 51 per cent of graduates from Oxbridge during 1864–73 were ordained as Anglican clergymen. The Anglican clergy increased substantially in size during the nineteenth century, from about 12 000 in the 1820s to nearly 21 000 in 1871 and to a peak of 25 363 in 1901. This increase was paralleled in most of the other churches in Britain, the number of Wesleyan Methodist ministers, for example, rising from 736 in 1831 to 1675 in 1901. For young middle-class Anglican men of an intellectual cast of mind the existence of an expanding Anglican clergy came literally as a godsend, providing a virtually unique example of a profession of unques-tionably high status, whose entrants received an income (albeit often a small one) from their first moment in the field, and yet was both at the cutting-edge of contemporary intellectual debate and left ample time for cultural, literary and historical pursuits, besides the clergyman's normal service to his faith. Apart from the tiny profession of university academia (in which marriage was normally prohibited among holders of university fellowships) no other occupation provided an income from the start, security, and an intellectual life, to say nothing of the possibility, however remote, of becoming a bishop and entering the House of Lords. Almost certainly the existence of the Anglican clergy (and the clergy of other denominations) had an effect in diminishing radical discontent within an important component of the middle classes, perhaps the most talented and hence the most potentially dangerous. (Over 50 per cent of men receiving a first-class degree at Oxbridge were ordained as clergymen until the 1870s.)

In considering the role of religion in British society before the closing years of the nineteenth century, it is crucial to keep in mind that the very nature of religion as represented by the Established Churches meant something essentially very different from the nature of religion, as commonly understood in the West, today. The organised religions comprised not merely a body of ideas and speculation about personal morality, the ultimate meaning of life, survival after death, and so on – though they were all of these things, of course, in an age when most men and women profoundly *believed* in the truth of religious doctrines. Nor were they purely voluntary bodies, engaged in charitable, educational and missionary work, of a peculiar kind. Instead, and in addition, the Established Churches represented a facet of national identity, especially in England, via the Church of England, and in Scotland, via the (Presbyterian) Church of Scotland. (In Ireland, where the great majority of the people were Roman Catholics, the role of the Church of Ireland – an Episcopalian Protestant church and a close component of the Church of England – was more problematical; so, too, was the established Anglican Church in Wales, where, by the early nineteenth century, the majority were Protestant Nonconformists.) The Church of England *was* the spiritual and, indeed, in a sense the intellectual component of 'Englishness' and of the 'English nation', as was the Church of Scotland for the Scots. It embodied the spiritual and divine aspects of English national history and encapsulated its central myths and turning-points. It is very difficult to convey this today; until very recently indeed, it was often almost incomprehensible to secular historians, who regularly ignored or marginalised the role of the Church of England in the definition of English national identity. (The recent revival of our understanding of the role of the Church, and of religion generally in British society, was chiefly due to the controversial Oxford historian J. C. D. Clark, although it has been taken further by a number of other historians including Linda Colley and John Wolffe.) Several analogies might help to clarify the place of the Church of England and Scotland. If one were to ask, 'what does being a Greek person mean?' one might well suggest several superficially unrelated answers: being a citizen of Greece, speaking the Greek language, *or* being an adherent of the Greek Orthodox Church, the national church of Greece. If one were asked to 'picture in your mind some typical Greek persons', surely an image which would quickly occur to many would be a Greek Orthodox priest, familiarly robed. In the twentieth century, too, there has been a widespread debate about the nature of Jewish identity. Whereas before the nineteenth century Jews were construed by themselves almost entirely as a religion (though with a strong national element), in the twentieth century there is general agreement among most Jews that 'Jewishness' constitutes a 'Peoplehood' which is, at one and the same time, a religion, a national/ethnic identity, and a culture with its own languages, texts, a shared history and national myths.

Down to the mid-nineteenth century, the Churches of England and of Scotland were viewed by many people, especially those in the 'Establishment', in a very similar fashion, as an aspect of 'Englishness' or 'Scottishness' in no way less significant than citizenship or the ability to speak the native language. Indeed, if anything, the role of the national Church in each country was anterior and superior to other aspects of national identity, for their formation (centuries before the establishment of England and Scotland) was a divine act, with the clergy being given the power, by divine authority, to prepare their congregants for eternal life. Furthermore, to the adherents of each church, the evolution of those churches, and in particular their Protestant and reformed nature, also represented divine truth, a rejection of both the evils of the Roman Catholic Church and also of the anarchy of more extreme forms of Protestantism.

Other important aspects of English and Scottish national identity were also strongly religious in nature. It is now widely believed by historians that as well as constituting a distinct set of positive qualities and a shared history, 'Englishness' also postulated in its identity a central 'out-group' of enemies and hostile forces. The central enemy of 'Englishness' was the Roman Catholic Church and those European countries, especially Spain and France, which were primarily Catholic. Anti-Catholicism remained one of the most potent mass forces in British society throughout most of the nineteenth century. Guy Fawkes Night, for instance, is in essence an anti-Catholic celebration, commemorating the defeat of a Catholic plot to blow up Parliament.

Besides these forces of mass belief, most of the central political ceremonials in Britain were (and are) strongly religious in nature. The coronation of the Sovereign is chiefly conducted by the Archbishop of Canterbury, and is strongly religious (even mystical) in nature, while Anglican prayers and rituals were a major part of the commencement of virtually every public function. Parliament was directly imbued with Anglican ceremonials, while 26 Anglican bishops and archbishops were *ex officio* members of the House of Lords. Non-Anglican (or Presbyterian) Cabinet ministers were virtually unknown in nineteenth-century politics. Almost every commemoration of a national event or historical occasion saw the participation of Anglican clergymen and the use of Anglican prayers.

The Church of England also itself comprised an organisation of enormous size and far-reaching practical ramifications, with an infrastructure possibly surpassing in size any other body in England in the early nineteenth century. The 26 Anglican bishops and archbishops who sat (and still sit) in the House of Lords often held the balance of power on legislation. The Church of England counted no fewer than 11 883 churches and chapels in 1831, and in virtually every parish in England the local Anglican church was a prominent and central landmark. The Church of England ran many schools and was intimately connected with Oxford and Cambridge and with virtually all fee-paying schools for the upper classes. It was responsible for a considerable welfare network of almshouses and charities. The Church was itself a major English landowner and landlord. Its domain still extended to areas which were purely secular. For instance, until 1858 it held a monopoly on the probating of all wills in England and Wales (including the wills of non-Anglicans), which was not merely a far-reaching legal activity, but one with its own considerable infrastructure of ecclesiastical probate courts and lawyers. Most centrally of all, the Anglican Church remained the church of virtually the whole of the British 'Establishment', including, as mentioned, virtually all English Cabinet ministers, and virtually the whole of the British aristocracy, the great majority of senior professionals, as well as probably a majority of successful businessmen, despite the considerable numbers of the latter who were certainly Dissenters (or immigrants). All Oxbridge professors, all judges, all senior civil servants, all generals and admirals were Anglicans as a matter of course (apart from those who were members of the Church of Scotland). Virtually no persons of official influence were Protestant Dissenters.

In addition to all this, there was the fact that, to most people in Britain at the time, religion was desperately important. The Bible was regarded by most people as almost universally believed; it was literally true that one's fate in the Afterlife depended upon the teachings and powers of the Church. Few parents could have stood over the graves of their dead infants, so tragically but so commonly taken from them, without remembering this, and few people could have been seriously ill without reflecting upon how their behaviour in this world affected their status in the next. Most people believed, at least in a fitful (but, often, an overwhelmingly vivid) way, in an all-seeing, all-knowing God who observed one's every act, however private, and knew the secrets of every heart. According to virtually all Christians, God had sent His only Son, Jesus Christ, into the world to offer a way out of eternal damnation and towards eternal salvation; Christ's Church was the officially constituted guardian of this route, and thus the Church's proper constitution and functioning were supremely important.

For all of these reasons, the fate of the Church of England, including both disputes within the Church itself and the nature of its relationship both with the British state and with wider society, was centrally significant to vast numbers of English people in the first half of the nineteenth century, to an extent extremely difficult to grasp today. When Roman Catholics were politically emancipated in 1829, and, more particularly, when Parliament (controlled by Whigs and Radicals) reformed the Church of Ireland in 1833 by amalgamating many Irish bishoprics, it appeared to many leading Anglicans, including some of the best minds within the Church, that a traumatic national catastrophe had occurred. It is no exaggeration to assert that many notable intellectuals, including John Henry Newman and the young William E. Gladstone, regarded the threatened and apparently perilous state of the Church of England as more important than the 1832 Reform Act itself, and certainly far more important than the Poor Law or local government reforms. Until perhaps the 1870s, in fact, the mainstream of intellectual debate and discussion in Britain, and the chief concerns of most intellectuals and serious writers (at least as expressed in print), were religious and revolved around the nature of the national Church. Only in the last quarter of the century did a more recognisably modern notion of the role of the Church of England become general, one in which the state was essentially secular, national identity was religiously pluralistic, and the Church of England was only one religious institution among many, albeit the first among equals (or something surpassing even that). Even so, to this day the Church of England enjoys a special position in the life of the English nation which is still manifestly perceptible, especially on great and ceremonial national occasions.

Nevertheless, despite the apparent centrality of the Church of England to the English nation, there was a pervasive sense, in the early nineteenth century, that all was not well with it. So widespread was this sense of decline that the century or so before the Evangelical revival of the late eighteenth and early nineteenth centuries has almost invariably been seen as a low-point in the Church's history. The troubles of the Anglican Church were indeed manifold, but centred upon several main complaints. Probably the most glaring concerned the clergy itself: pluralism (the holding of two or more clerical livings simultaneously, often on an absentee basis) was endemic, while the parochial structure of the Church no longer reflected the population trends of industrialising England, yet could not be readily altered. Incomes in the Church varied enormously, from the princely in the case of a handful of senior bishops to penurious in the case of most junior clergy such as curates. The doctrines of belief of the Church tended to be superficial and overly optimistic, with the apparently deliberate design and apparent purpose of so much in the natural world being taken as evidence for a divine creator, a watchmaker-God, in the famous and influential theories of Archdeacon William Paley. The Church seemed almost totally disconnected from the real problems of ordinary English people, or from the political trends of the day; it was almost automatically assumed to be on the side of reaction and extreme conservatism in politics. It was widely believed by the Church's critics that as a result of all of these trends attendance at Anglican services, apart from the *rites de passage* and other special occasions, was surprisingly small and rapidly diminishing. There is simply no way of knowing whether this conclusion is true, since no comprehensive statistics for religious affiliation have ever been collected. The first and only official attempt to ascertain the number of religious believers, the 1851 Census of Religious Worship, held on 31 March 1851, found that a total of 10 419 390 persons attended any religious service on that day, of a total population in England and Wales of 17 928 000. The total of religious worshippers certainly included some double counting, as many places of worship held morning, afternoon and evening services, so that the enthusiastic attended more than one. The best reworking of these figures suggests that about one-half of the population in mid-Victorian England and Wales attended a religious service. Of these, a total of 4 940 000 attended an Anglican service, about 5 114 000 attended a

Dissenting service, and about 365 000 attended a Roman Catholic service, although multiple attendances at Dissenting services probably exceeded those at Anglican services. Even if one accepts that a great many persons who regarded themselves as devout Anglicans did not believe that frequent attendance at a church service was required of them (whereas Dissenters were more likely to enjoin frequent and regular chapel attendance), it seems perfectly clear that all was not well with the Anglican Church in mid-Victorian Britain, and indeed that its claims to being the national Church were highly questionable.

The Church of England responded to the challenges which most thoughtful persons, from the eighteenth century onwards, knew it faced, by a variety of means. Most directly, the Church attempted to put its house in order by a considerable programme of internal reformation and expansion. Legislation proposed and passed by the Whig government in 1835–36 did much to abolish pluralism, redistribute clerical incomes to reduce the disparity between rich and poor sees, and created several new bishoprics. The contentious issues of tithes and church-rates, paid by all, including non-Anglicans, was addressed (but not fully concluded until later in the century). The Church embarked on a vast programme of church building, particularly in the big cities and growing areas of the north. The size of the Anglican clergy nearly doubled in the course of the nineteenth century.

At the same time, the legal status of the Church as the national church of England, Ireland and Wales underwent considerable change. Dissenters (in 1828), Catholics (1829), Jews (1858) and atheists (1891) were admitted to Parliament, thus severing the certain linkage between the Established Church and Parliament. All public offices were, in effect, open to men of all religions by the 1870s, with the exception of some remaining restrictions on Catholics. The legal monopoly on the conducting of *rites de passage* was surrendered by the Church in 1836 in the case of the registration of births, marriages and deaths, and in 1858 in the case of the probating of wills. Oxford and Cambridge were opened to non-Anglicans in the early 1870s. By the last quarter of the nineteenth century, the Church of England remained the national Church of the English people only in a ceremonial and customary rather than in a legal way. In the meantime, and after a great deal of conflict, the Church of Ireland was disestablished by Gladstone in 1869, and Ireland became the first part of the United Kingdom without an established religion.

Within the Church of England itself, a number of distinct and mutually hostile movements arose. Much of the familiar historiography of that Church between 1750 and 1914 has been written in terms of the rise of these movements and their key leaders, some of whom continue to be household names. The rise of hostile strands within an organisation may superficially be seen as a sign of destructive weakness and discord, but, on closer inspection, precisely the opposite is true: persons – especially persons of the intellectual and moral quality of those who led the key movements within the Anglican Church – engage in fundamental conflict only on matters of fundamental importance. The strands which emerged within Anglicanism after about 1750 were evidence of its strength rather than its weakness, and of the centrality of religion to much British intellectual debate until at least the last quarter of the nineteenth century.

The first of the key movements within Anglicanism to emerge was the Evangelical movement, which is normally seen as having originated in the second quarter of the eighteenth century in such works as William Law's *Serious Call to a Devout and Holy Life* (1729) and in John Wesley's conversion to a sense of reliance upon a personal saviour in 1738. (Wesley was an Anglican vicar and only regarded his movement, Methodism, as a sect separate from the Church of England at the end of his life.) By the beginning of the nineteenth century, Evangelicalism was among the strongest forces in the Anglican Church, appealing to just those English people who felt most alienated by the superficial nature of the Anglican religion as it was commonly found.

The Evangelical movement is often seen as being hallmarked by six or seven main characteristics. Evangelicalism emphasised the intensely personal and emotional nature of religious commitment, especially through the conversion experience: religion, and still less personal salvation, could never be simply a matter of reason or habit. To Evangelicals, all human beings were *ipso facto* essentially evil and depraved, as the progeny of sinful Adam. All humans will, therefore, be damned in the world to come, with the exception of those whom God has seen fit to save. (To most Evangelicals, a personal commitment to a Christian life was a necessary but not a sufficient condition for salvation, and there was a lively difference of opinion within Evangelicalism about the questions of predestination and free will.) To Evangelicals, Jesus was the Saviour in an intensely personal sense, and belief in Him was a necessary precondition for salvation. Along with belief in Jesus went an equally strong faith in the literal truth of the Bible as God's holy book, a work to be constantly studied. Many Evangelicals seemed, in fact, to be opposed to secular learning as such, regarding it as vanity, idolatry and even sinfulness: this extended to works like the Greek and Roman classics. Evangelicalism was strongly 'Protestant' and strongly anti-Catholic: it opposed the rituals, 'superstition' and 'mummery' of the Catholic Church as the most depraved form of Christian religion and gloried in the heritage of the Reformation. Evangelicals emphasised the importance of sermons which touched the heart and of hymn-singing in church services, as well as everything which accentuated the individual commitment of Christians.

Evangelicalism became influential throughout the whole of the Anglican Church by the end of the eighteenth century, but it gained an especial historical importance from a group of adherents, closely linked with the 'Establishment', known as the 'Clapham Sect' from their residence in the south London suburb. Among this group's better-known members were the

Thornton family of bankers, Zachary Macaulay (father of the great historian Thomas B. Macaulay, first Baron Macaulay), and James Stephen (1758–1832, grandfather of Leslie Stephen and great-grandfather of Virginia Woolf). Over one hundred MPs were associated with the Evangelical movement, most famously William Wilberforce (1759–1833). Wilberforce is best-remembered for heading the long campaign (along with other Evangelicals) which led to the abolition of the slave trade in the British Empire in 1807, and to the abolition of slavery itself within the Empire in 1833.[1] This long campaign, fought against the fierce opposition of the West Indies interest in Parliament, was partially related to the spirit of reform and liberalism abroad in Britain at the time, but it must be remembered that slavery persisted in the United States for another 30 years and ended only in the course of a bloody civil war in which 600 000 men were killed. The Evangelicals also favoured the resettlement of many former West Indian slaves in West Africa, and were also responsible for the establishment of the British colony of Sierra Leone as a place of reception for many former slaves.

Regarding Britain itself, the Evangelicals were active in such areas as prison reform, but it is notable that some Evangelicals ignored urban and industrial poverty produced by Britain's economic growth. One reason for this is that most early Evangelicals were political conservatives who feared radicalism as atheistic and certain to undermine the Christian religion, whose propagation was their central concern. A good example of this world-view can be found in Hannah More (1745–1833), famous for her work on behalf of popular education and her advocacy of Sunday schools, but also the author of numerous popular tracts condemning the French Revolution and its leaders. On the other hand, and especially from the 1830s, leading Evangelical writers were certainly appalled by working-class poverty and attempted to ameliorate it. Lord Shaftesbury became renowned for his efforts on behalf of the poor. Another influential Evangelical writer was Charlotte Elizabeth Tonna (1790–1846), whose *Perils of the Nation* (1843) appealed to the upper classes and legislators to improve the lot of the poor; it strongly influenced subsequent factory acts. The paternalist, anti-*laissez-faire* strand in Conservatism which emerged strongly under Disraeli owed much to Evangelicalism.

The influence of Evangelicalism on English society was enormous. The Evangelicals are often seen as working for the same goals as many Dissenters, especially the 'New Dissent' of Methodism which had split off from Anglican Evangelicalism, and who were also profoundly influential. The 'call to seriousness' became much more common, especially among the middle classes, and the Evangelicals are sometimes known as 'the fathers of the Victorians'. This may well give undue credit to the Victorians: it may be

---

1 Slavery was legal in the British West Indies but not in Britain itself. From the mid-eighteenth century, it was established in law that any slave who set foot in the United Kingdom automatically became free.

truer to say that the Evangelicals *were* the Victorians, in the sense that they practised and proclaimed all the values and modes of behaviour that we (perhaps notoriously) associate with the Victorians. Indeed, the zenith of 'Victorianism', especially a rigorous and meticulous observation of the Sabbath and joylessness and literalness in judging both Scripture and the things of this world, probably occurred in the 1840s, when the influence of the Evangelicals was at its peak, rather than later in the Victorian age.

The Evangelicals were also chiefly responsible for the vast increase in the publication of religious works of all kinds, especially tracts, prayer-books, cheap Bibles and published sermons, and for popular religious education, centring around the Sunday schools (which were begun in Gloucester in 1780 by Robert Raikes). A rigorous observation of the Sabbath, which became an archetypal expression of 'Victorianism', was also closely associated with the Evangelicals, as was an idealisation of the home and the traditional nuclear family: the family, strongly headed by the father, was expected to be the chief venue of the inculcation of Christian values and the chief expression of Christian life. The Evangelicals are also often credited with the purification of English 'High Society' after the excesses of the eighteenth century and the Regency period: certainly the image of the high minded Whig-Liberal statesman-scholar, motivated by public *gravitas*, owes much to this movement, however much the classical education imparted to these men by the universities was looked upon with some suspicion by many Evangelicals. Certainly, too, the public display of vice and indecency, so common in aristocratic society into the 1830s, had become much less public and possibly much less common by the 1850s.

Evangelicalism was thus centrally concerned with the individual commitment and behaviour of the Christian believer and placed far greater weight on the individual believer's own faith and actions than upon the life of the Church in a corporate sense. The other great movement of challenge within the Anglican Church at this time is often seen as in many respects the opposite of Evangelicalism in its emphasis on the corporate life of that Church as a continuing, divine institution which had actually been founded by Jesus and His Apostles. This is the school within 'High Church' Anglicanism known as the Oxford Movement or as 'Tractarians' (or, sometimes, as 'Puseyites' after one of the movement's leading members). If Evangelicalism can be viewed as the 'Protestant' wing of the Anglican Church, often akin in many respects to Methodism or to other Dissenting sects, the Oxford Movement clearly represented the 'Catholic' wing of the Church of England, and indeed several of its leading members left that Church to become Roman Catholics. That the Anglican Church contained two broad and influential movements at opposite ends of the religious spectrum was the result, in part, of the highly ambiguous nature of that Church as it had evolved from the Reformation onwards, a reformed, Protestant church certainly not close to the Roman Catholic Church and often very hostile to it, yet one whose organisation, hierarchy and rituals retained a great deal of Catholicism and whose leaders stressed the unbroken continuity of Anglicanism with the pre-Reformation Christian church.

The Oxford Movement grew out of a long tradition of 'High Church' Anglicanism which had also stressed the 'Catholic' rather than the 'Protestant' features of the Church of England. This tradition emphasised the unbroken linkages of that church with the pre-Reformation church, and the divine nature of its ceremonies and services. Often, though not always, the tradition had been linked with 'Church and King' High Tory Anglicanism, stressing the duty of the Christian Englishman to obey established authority, favouring a strong monarchy established by Divine Right, and deploring radical innovations and democracy as likely to lead to the horrors of the French Revolution.

The Oxford Movement is generally seen as having emerged in 1833 as a response to the Whig government's Church Temporalities (Ireland) Bill, an attempt to reform the Church of Ireland (the established Anglican Church of Ireland, the religion of a small minority of the Irish population, most of whom were Catholics) especially by reducing by 10 the number of Church of Ireland bishops and by establishing an Ecclesiastical Commission to administer the money (estimated at £150 000) saved by the bill. This Act was deeply feared by most conservative Anglicans as opening the door to the eventual disestablishment of the Church of England and as indicative of every objectionable, radical interference with religion that was likely to eventuate from a reformed Parliament dominated by Dissenters, radicals, and followers of the Utilitarian philosophers. The activists of the Oxford Movement went further, opposing the interference of the state in the divinely-created Church of England *per se* and, indeed, the doctrines of what is known as 'Erastianism' (state control of the church). Oddly, once government power in Britain had passed from conservatives to radicals, younger 'High Church' intellectuals discarded any notion of an Established Church linked closely to the state, which all must obey, in favour of a radical position on the independence of the church which left its integrity and independence intact. For them, the Church of England was actually superior to, and historically anterior to, the British state.

The Oxford Movement derived its name from the fact that its leaders – John Henry Newman (later Cardinal Newman, 1801–90), John Keble (1792–1866), Edward Bouverie Pusey (1800–82) and Richard Hurrell Froude (1803–36) – were academics at Oxford University. In the 90 *Tracts For the Times* published by this group and its supporters between 1833 and 1841, the Oxford Movement drew repeated attention to the 'Catholic' nature of the Church of England, the continuing linkages of the Church back to the Apostles, and the divine nature of the Church and its ceremonials in a corporate sense. In politics the Oxford Movement was avowedly anti-liberal, campaigning against rationalism, atheism, Utilitarianism, and all of the Enlightenment ideas grouped together as the 'spirit of the age' of the reform period.

The Oxford Movement aroused fierce, almost irrational, hostility in many circles and mistrust and suspicion throughout much of the Anglican Church, even among some who would have been sympathetic to many of its goals. Underlying everything, the men of the Oxford Movement were seen as 'Catholics in disguise', thus awakening the barely dormant spirit of English anti-Catholicism, still one of the most powerful elements in the English national character. Newman's formal conversion to Catholicism in 1845 – he eventually became a Cardinal of the Church – did nothing to diminish these fears, nor did the reintroduction of such Catholic practices as confession, incense, and even celibate monasteries and sisterhoods by 'High Church' enthusiasts whenever they could, all practices looked upon by extreme Protestants with detestation. The perception of the Oxford Movement as Catholics in camouflage was underlain by other fears as well. Many extreme Protestants closely associated both the Catholic Church and its partisans with sexual perversion, especially with homosexuality and with bizarre sado-masochistic practices in nunneries and monasteries. Indeed, sexual fear may well have been at the base of most of the intense hostility generated by the Oxford Movement and by Roman Catholicism. It was also believed that Catholics and their partisans were deliberately untruthful and mendacious in debate, and that 'Jesuitical casuistry' was a deliberate weapon of Catholics and pro-Catholics to lure the unsuspecting to their ranks. The fears of Protestants were not palliated by several of the publications of the *Tracts For the Times*, especially Tract LXXVII by Isaac Williams, 'On Reserve in Communicating Religious Knowledge', which seemed to suggest that it was conscionable for the clergy to withhold some parts of Christian doctrine from ordinary people whenever necessary, a proposition which extreme Protestants, with their deep belief in the Bible as the revealed Word of God, found reprehensible.

While Newman and several other members of the Oxford Movement did join the Catholic Church, most remained Anglicans, heading the 'High Church' component of the Church of England which became extremely important – though still controversial – later in the century. Today, Newman (in particular) is regarded as one of the very greatest religious thinkers of the nineteenth century, and is admired by Anglicans, Catholics, and many others.

Most of the Church of England's leaders were adherents neither of Evangelicalism nor of the Oxford Movement, but of what is often known as the 'Broad Church', the Church's 'centre party' which eschewed extremes and wished the Church to be as all-embracing as possible. Some thinkers within the 'Broad Church' party, indeed, wished the Anglican Church to make its places of worship available to any Protestant form of religion, including the services of Nonconformists.

That both major social reformers like the Clapham Sect and leading intellectuals like the Oxford Movement worked within the framework of the Church of England is not coincidental: for at least the first 70 years of the nineteenth century, that church was among the most important, vital and viable institutions in England; probably indeed, the most important in terms of the number of persons whose lives it closely touched.

The late nineteenth century saw a decline in the influence of the Church of England, although it still remained central to English society. 'High' and 'Low' Church Anglicanism continued to vie with one another. The ability (or inclination) of the Anglican hierarchy to control deviant movements within the Church was curtailed by a number of judicial decisions, especially the so-called Gorham Decision of 1850, in which the Judicial Committee of the Privy Council ruled, in effect, that a clergyman could not readily be penalised for holding unorthodox views. The Gorham Decision prevented the Anglican hierarchy from ostracising dissidents within its ranks. From one viewpoint, this benefited the Church, allowing it to continue as a church of moderation and compromise which allowed many strands to flourish within it. From another viewpoint, however, it indicated that the Anglican Church, unlike the Catholic Church, lacked a clear sense of direction.

The most serious challenge to the Church's hegemony – indeed, to religion as such – was provided by science, especially by the so-called 'Higher Criticism' of the Bible and, of course, by Charles Darwin's *Origin of Species*, published in 1859. The 'Higher Criticism', derived from German sources, and widely discussed by Church intellectuals in the 1840s and 1850s, subjected the Bible to rigorous scholarship, identifying numerous inconsistencies and even obvious impossibilities in received Scripture. (For example, the first five books of the Old Testament were traditionally said to have been written by Moses, but contain a description of Moses' own death; the four gospels of the New Testament contain numerous contradictory accounts of the life of Jesus.) The 'New Criticism' shook the faith of some educated believers in the literal truth of the Bible even before Darwin. The appearance of *Origin of Species* in 1859, however, created an intellectual earthquake of the first rank; the work was probably the most influential book of the nineteenth century. Darwin not merely seemingly undermined, in a comprehensive and scientific way, the literal truth of the Bible, but presented a view of nature and man's role in nature which pointed, to many intellectuals, to a universe devoid of meaning or ethics. 'Nature red in tooth and claw' was Tennyson's famous description. If evolution consisted (in the famous phrase of Herbert Spencer) of 'the survival of the fittest', and nature's way of making progress is for the strong to destroy the weak, Christian morality itself appeared to be unscientific, not merely the Christian view of the origins of the earth and of life. British intellectuals, as those elsewhere, grappled with these doctrines as best they could. From the 1850s onwards, many intellectuals and educated persons experienced a profound 'crisis of faith', usually on reaching young adult-hood and encountering the scientific challenge to religion for the first time. The collectivist ethical doctrines which emerged in Britain in the late nineteenth century, including most strands of socialism, as well as spiritual-istic and pseudo-religious movements like Theosophy, so popular among the late Victorian middle classes, may be seen as attempts to provide meaning to life in the wake of the undermining of traditional religious faith.

During the late Victorian and Edwardian periods the Anglican Church evolved vigorous and contending 'High' and 'Low' Church wings, reflect-ing the ambiguity in the Church's heritage as both (respectively) a 'Cath-olic' and 'Protestant' church. Each wing founded organisations to further its influence, often engaging in unseemly spying and even litigation against those in the other wing who allegedly transgressed against ordained ritual. The 'High' Anglican wing, with its similarities to Catholicism, was, in particular, greatly feared by others, although it was consistently growing in influence. The Anglican Church also went through a number of significant changes during the nineteenth century, especially over the Irish Church Temporalities Act of 1833, which attempted to reform the Irish (Anglican) Church, and over Irish Church disestablishment in 1869. By the early twentieth century, the Church had reformed itself to a considerable extent, eliminating pluralism and gross inequalities in clerical incomes, and initiat-ing a measure of internal democracy by the beginnings of the Church Synod and international communion with what was, by then, a far-flung world-wide faith with the first Lambeth Conference, held in 1867. While the Church of England still remained assuredly the national and Established Church, highly visible on all public occasions, these reforms came too late to affect the growing irreligion of the majority, which, after the catastrophe of the First World War, became an even more marked feature of British life.

Nineteenth-century religious life in Scotland was dominated by the issues leading to the so-called 'Great Disruption' of 1843. Religion in Scotland was founded in Reformation Calvinism and hence derived from quite a different source than Anglicanism. It had always been more strictly ob-served than in England, and the Presbyterian Church of Scotland remained unambiguously the national Church to a much greater extent than was the case in England. Scotland had only in embryo any equivalent to the large and growing body of Dissenters south of the border.

The Presbyterian model of the Scottish Church constitution was, com-pared with the arrangement of the Anglican Church, much more demo-cratic, consisting of ministers popularly elected by heads of households, who in turn chose the higher decision-making presbyteries, synods, and the General Assembly of the Church of Scotland. Far more than England, Scotland revolved around its Church and the Church's attempt to form a 'godly community' which regulated public and private behaviour. Sabbath observation, in particular, was strongly emphasised, with the wealthy Glasgow merchant John Henderson going to the length of buying up the Edinburgh and Glasgow Railway so that he could close it down on Sundays! Dissent from the Church of Scotland had, however, existed from the eighteenth century, with the United Presbyterian Church, consisting of 3000 congregations and strong in working-class Glasgow, representing a breakaway movement within the theological framework of Presbyterianism. Between about 1820 and 1843, however, an extraordinarily severe split came within the Church of Scotland, led by Thomas Chalmers (1780–1847), a Church of Scotland minister and university professor who wanted individual churches to be independent of the central authority of the Church of Scotland, and in particular to choose their ministers without hindrance by a patron. Chalmers was a charismatic figure, who led a movement, more Evangelical than the mainstream of the Church of Scotland, which drew strong support from ministers of chapels of ease (churches built in new areas), who were not eligible to join the Church hierarchy. A long dispute with the Established Church led to the celebrated 'Disruption' of 1843, when one-third of the ministers of the Church of Scotland, led by Chalmers, walked out of the annual meeting of the General Assembly of the Church of Scotland to form the Free Church of Scotland. The new church built 700 churches and 500 schools in four years, opening its first theological college in 1850. The 1851 Census of Religious Worship found that while 351 000 people had attended Church of Scotland services, the Free Church of Scotland drew 292 000 worshippers and the United Presbyterians 159 000. The rest of the nineteenth century saw efforts at reunion, with Scotland especially notable in its support for missionary activities. While Scotland was not immune from the general tendency to increased secularisation widely evident by around 1890, it remained far more overtly religious than did England into the post-1945 era.

In England, Protestant Dissent appeared to flourish as never before during the nineteenth century. Dissent, it has been observed by historians, for the most part arrived at a coherent set of social and political attitudes and responses which set it apart from most Anglicans (and Tories) and marked it as a separate force in British politics. Between around 1830 and 1885 Nonconformity was strongly committed to individualism and to enhancing the role of the individual conscience in all aspects of public life. It opposed Anglican and aristocratic hierarchies, supported free trade, self-help as a cure for poverty, and, increasingly, temperance reform. After about 1885, the politics of Dissent became more ambiguous, with many successful Nonconformists joining the Tories, while individualism gave way to emphasising collectivism as a response for poverty and other social ills. Nonconformity scored its last, and greatest, political triumph at the 1906 general election, when, it is believed, more than 50 per cent of the MPs elected in the great Liberal landslide were Nonconformists. Thereafter its influence declined rapidly, in the wake of the First World War.

While committed to radicalism within the context of nineteenth-century British politics, Nonconformity had always had a strongly conservative (in the political sense) side as well, with John Wesley and many other radicals emphasising the absolute necessity of obedience to legitimate government, contentment with one's lot in life, and complete opposition to 'atheistic' doctrines which culminated in the French Revolution. In one of the most celebrated of historical theses, the great French historian of nineteenth-century England, Elie Halévy, claimed in 1913 that Methodism, with its strong element of political conservatism, prevented a revolution in Britain during the darkest years of the French Revolution and post-Napoleonic War periods. Other historians, too, have emphasised this side of Nonconformity, for instance the renowned radical historian E. P. Thompson, who saw in Methodist revivals the 'chiliasm of despair' which grew in strength whenever radical political agitation was suppressed and failed.[2] Whatever the truth of the matter, it cannot be denied that throughout the nineteenth century most Nonconformists felt a deep sense of being 'second-class citizens' and of being openly or subtly discriminated against by the Anglican Establishment. Even the removal of obvious disabilities suffered by Nonconformists, from gaining the right to sit in Parliament in 1828 to the abolition of church rates in 1868 to admission to Oxford or graduation from Cambridge in the 1870s, failed fully to heal this persistent sense of 'relative deprivation'. There remained, down to the First World War and perhaps beyond, a deep distrust of the Anglican Church and of much of the British 'Establishment', renewed in the late nineteenth century when pseudo-Catholic High Church Anglicanism appeared to gain the upper hand after about 1880. Dissenters were powerful at the local level, dominating many of the town councils of the new manufacturing boroughs as well as much – but certainly not all – manufacturing industry. (That there appears to be a causal connection between Protestantism and modern forms of capitalism was argued in a celebrated work, first published in 1905, by the famous German sociologist Max Weber.) The powerful and persisting sense of 'relative deprivation' kept alive a sense of separateness by many Dissenters long after the acquisition of wealth and respectability had removed any real cause for dissenting.

English Nonconformity was, of course, divided into a large number of sects of unequal size and very different constituencies. 'Old Dissent' included Baptists, Quakers, Congregationalists and Unitarians. Giving accurate membership figures for each sect is very difficult, but in 1850 the Baptists had about 175 000 members in England and Wales, rising to 346 000 in 1900. Congregationalists numbered, respectively, about

2 'Chiliasm' comprises those doctrines and beliefs concerned with the end of the world. Thompson's thesis, set out in his famous *The Making of the English Working Class* (1963), has been hotly disputed.

225 000 and 408 000 at these dates; Quakers about 15 000 and 17 500; and Unitarians perhaps 40 000 at each date. These figures are for the official membership; casual attendance at Nonconformist services was often much higher, especially before the end of the century. For instance, 1 192 000 persons attended morning, afternoon and evening Congregationalist services on 31 March 1851, the Sunday of the Census on Religious Worship, or over five times the sect's official membership. Even allowing for the fact that many persons attended two or even three services that Sunday, it seems clear that the penumbra group attracted to and influenced by a sect was often very large indeed. 'New Dissent', Methodism and its breakaway sects, numbered about 556 000 members in England and Wales in 1850 (of whom about 354 000 belonged to the mainstream Wesleyan Methodist Church), and 767 000 in 1900, yet its penumbra group of attendees was certainly far larger, with 2 630 000 attending all Methodist and Wesleyan services on Census Sunday (a figure which includes double counting), and a total of 536 000 Wesleyan Methodist Sunday school pupils in 1861 and 965 000 in 1901, perhaps one-seventh of all children aged 6–13 in England and Wales at the time. Sociologically, the old-established Quakers and Unitarians were virtual elite groups, producing grossly disproportionate numbers of intellectuals and writers, public figures and reformers, business leaders, and by the late nineteenth century, politicians, than their very small numbers warranted. These groups benefited from an emphasis placed upon, and a commitment to, education among all of their members (including women), while (as with the parallel case of the Jews) both whatever remained of prejudice against them, and their own value-systems, deterred a 'haemmorhage of talent' into the gentry and 'idle rich'. Methodists bridged the gap between the urban rich and poor, producing both many factory owners and a very large portion of the industrial working class. Newer revivalist and unorthodox sects, like the Salvation Army and the America-centred Mormons, also became a familiar part of the late Victorian scene, with the Salvation Army in particular renowned for its 'missionary' work among the poorest of the urban poor. In considering the position of Nonconformity in Victorian England, however, it is worth keeping in mind that for the most part the majority of the country, and certainly the majority of the 'Establishment' and the middle classes, remained firmly Anglican.

One exception to this was Wales. From the late eighteenth or early nineteenth century, Wales had become predominantly (though certainly not entirely) Nonconformist. By 1900 about 72 per cent of the Welsh population belonged to a Nonconformist sect (24 per cent Congregationalist, 23 per cent Calvinist Methodist, 19 per cent Baptist, 6 per cent Wesleyan), with 26 per cent Anglican, and 2 per cent belonging to other denominations, chiefly Catholics. Nonconformity became central to Welsh national identity as it emerged in the nineteenth century, especially to the nexus between religion and Wales's predominant Liberal (later Labour) political allegiance. Conversely, both Anglicanism and Toryism were much weaker there than in England. Nevertheless, Wales was not Scotland, much less Ireland: it had never, in modern times, been a separate nation with separate institutions; it lacked either a gentry or business class able to champion its interests or (until 1872) a university; it was divided geographically and linguistically, with Cardiff, recognised as its capital, remote from central and north Wales. Thus religion in Wales did not act as a catalyst for national aspirations, or even for national identity, until much later than in Scotland or Catholic Ireland. Welsh Nonconformity was, as well, divided into sects which were rivals as well as allies, and was subject, after about 1880, to the same forces of secularisation as anywhere else. Nevertheless, perhaps even more than in Scotland, strict Sabbath observation, regular chapel-going, and the drive to temperance remained a part of Welsh identity until after 1945.

The position of Roman Catholics in nineteenth-century Britain was highly ambiguous. Anti-Catholicism permeated British national culture. Elite anti-Catholicism attacked Rome, and countries under the direct influence of Rome, as duplicitous, tyrannical and permeated by medieval superstition. Popular anti-Catholicism made the Catholic Church the occa- sional target of rioting and violence, especially in areas where Irish immigrants had settled. Yet the nineteenth century also saw the Catholic Church enjoy a considerable intellectual fad among a certain sector of the upper and middle classes, especially those of a conservative bent who sought spiritual certainty and unbroken tradition, or the grandeur and majesty of Catholic ceremonials, all of which Rome certainly provided. The nineteenth century saw a steady growth in the number of Catholics in Britain, chiefly because of Irish migration to England and Scotland (which made significant areas of London's East End, and many of Lancashire's great towns, into Irish Catholic ghettos), as well as through a steady stream of conversions, of which John Henry Newman's was the most celebrated. The number of Catholics in England and Wales grew from perhaps 500 000 in the 1820s to 1.3 million by 1861 and to 1.5 million by 1900; in Scotland the increase was from only 70 000 in 1827 to 433 000 in 1900. There had always been a minority of Catholic 'Recusants' (those who did not become Protestants during the Reformation), especially in Lancashire and Sussex, and a Catholic 'cousinhood' of aristocratic, largely Recusant families, headed by the Howards (Dukes of Norfolk), Herberts (Earls of Shrewsbury), Blounts and Vavasours. Yet the mid-nineteenth century also saw perhaps the last outburst of national anti-Catholic sentiment in the old sense, when, in 1850, the Vatican re-established a Roman Catholic hier- archy in England. Fanned by some unwise remarks by Nicholas Wiseman (1802–65), the head of the Catholic Church in England (appointed Arch- bishop of Westminster in 1850), anti-Catholic sentiment in the press and among the Establishment led to the passage of the Ecclesiastical Titles Bill of 1851, officially denying the Catholic Church the right to use Anglican place names in its hierarchy (which it had already agreed not to do).[3] This Act, perhaps the only parliamentary Act of the Victorian period which worked against religious tolerance, was repealed in 1871, by which time the most vociferous anti-Catholic phase had passed, except in Northern Ireland and areas of Lancashire where 'Orange' sentiment was strong. By the late Victorian period Archbishop Henry Manning (1808–92), Wiseman's successor, played a notable public role in settling the London dock strike of 1889. Some historians have compared anti-Catholicism in Britain with anti-Semitism on the Continent, and there was indeed an underground anti-Catholic literature depicting the Vatican as the centre of a vast international conspiracy of evil, dwelling, often pornographically, on the alleged unspeakable horrors of nunneries and monasteries, and attacking Jesuits and foreign Catholic orders, which is indeed strongly reminiscent of the anti-Semitism of central Europe. The full influence of anti-Catholicism in Britain remains to be further explored by historians.

In contrast to the position of Catholics, the position of Jews in nineteenth-century Britain was relatively favourable. Anglo-Jewry was a small, low-profile community, numbering only about 25 000 in 1830 and perhaps 250 000 in 1905, following heavy immigration from Czarist Russia after the pogroms of 1881. Centred in London, and dominated by the wealthy 'Jewish cousinhood' families like the Rothschilds, Montefiores, Samuels and Sassoons who were engaged in international finance in the City of London, it attracted remarkably little hostility from the British Establishment, but was, if anything, influential and even popular. The undisputed lay leader of Anglo-Jewry for most of his remarkably long life was Sir Moses Montefiore (1784–1885), who used his very considerable influence to improve the lot of persecuted Jews overseas. Religiously, Anglo-Jewry was dominated by the mainstream Orthodox synagogues headed by the Chief Rabbi (and organised, in 1870, into the United Synagogues), which emphasised decorum, conservatism, patriotism and even mock-Anglican appearances. By the 1890s Anglo-Jewry was widely recognised as a kind of legitimate Dissenting sect, little different from any other. Benjamin Disraeli's unique position as the arch-prophet of British Conservatism did much to disarm right-wing hostility to Jews. On the other hand, British Jews were always aware that they were different from the Christian majority. Some populist anti-Semitism, of the type depicted in *Oliver Twist*, always existed; this probably became more pronounced with the migration of large numbers of impoverished, Yiddish-speaking Jews from Russia to London's East End, Manchester, Leeds and elsewhere in the late Victorian period. Yet Britain had no real tradition of anti-Semitism as either ideology or rooted social belief, and some recent historians who have

---

3 Thus, while the head of the Anglican Church is the Archbishop of Canterbury, the head of the Catholic Church was given the title of Archbishop of Westminster, a designation which did not exist in Anglican nomenclature.

claimed to identify such a tradition are distorting British reality to more closely resemble the tragic history of Jews on the Continent.

Religion fulfilled a number of other roles in nineteenth-century Britain. Religion was especially important in the life of women. By the late Victorian period (although perhaps not 50 years earlier) women probably comprised a majority of the worshippers at most church services, especially among the Anglicans. Organised religion and its services became, in fact, something of a female ghetto, but one of course entirely dominated, in its hierarchies, by men. Nevertheless, religion was the one public activity in which women could unequivocally participate, and attendance at church services and church activities became a primary mode of female social behaviour in the public sphere. Women authors of devotional material, hymns, religious tracts, and the like, were always perfectly acceptable. Catholic women (and later in the century, High Anglican women) could join female orders of nuns and *religieuses*. Except for Quakers and Unitarians, feminist women seldom emerged from an orthodox religious standpoint, and religious women in the nineteenth century were almost always conservatives. Indeed, the nexus between women and organised religion was the very backbone of traditional and ordered society.

Christianity as an established religion also sat uneasily with a persisting folk-tradition of pre-Christian quasi-religious practice, centring around witchcraft and traditional folk practices, which continued in the English countryside until the late nineteenth century. While the vicars and ministers of the orthodox religions were often seen as representing a pre-scientific, outmoded intellectual viewpoint, in rural England, and perhaps elsewhere, they sometimes had the opposite purpose and effect, bringing rational, modern learning to areas where they, and their outlook, were resented and opposed. Universal mass education, at least at the primary level, better communications, and the complete marginalistion of the unorthodox to beyond the fringes of society eliminated much of the pre-Christian element by the end of the nineteenth century, although some would argue that it continues until the present day.

19

Gender and identities

During the past 30 years the question of women's history and women's place in society has emerged from the shadows to the centre. Formerly regarded as a footnote to 'real' history, the role of women, one-half of the human race, in the evolution of all histories including modern British history, is now seen as obviously of the highest significance. Yet there are great obstacles to properly incorporating the history of women into a textbook such as this. It is a fact that no women held any significant political office of any kind in nineteenth-century Britain. There may have been some very minor and marginal exceptions to this, for example the Ladies of the Bedchamber to Queen Victoria, whose appointment aroused great controversy and who were seen as political office-holders in a party government. Above all, of course, there was Queen Victoria herself. Yet no woman figured directly in the process of high politics or of virtually any aspect of governance. This is a fact of life, and to seek exceptions is like attempting to find Catholic, Jewish or working-class Cabinet ministers in eighteenth-century Britain: they do not exist, and the historian cannot invent them. For this reason, to incorporate women into a political history of nineteenth-century Britain cannot focus on 'high politics' but on women activists and groups like the Primrose League outside of Parliament. To incorporate women into a social history of nineteenth-century Britain, although easier and more fruitful, also presents great difficulties of evidence and sources as well as the fact that most women were not in paid employment. Trends and generalisations about women's history in nineteenth-century Britain are thus less firmly based than for many male social groups.

The status of women in nineteenth-century Britain was in most perceptible ways inferior to that of men. Nevertheless, one might exaggerate this inferiority, especially when Britain is viewed in a comparative light. Such institutions as arranged marriages, child marriage, the forbidding of divorce to women, and the virtual imprisonment of widows, practised in many parts of Europe, were always unknown – and explicitly forbidden – in Britain. *A fortiori* such enormities as female infanticide, female circumcision, polygamy, *suttee*, the mandatory wearing of veils, and other practices common throughout most of the non-European world, where the status of women frequently resembled (and resembles) that of animals, were obviously unknown in Britain, and would have been greeted with universal horror. In Britain, women could not vote or hold elected office (except at the local government level from the 1870s), enter many professions like the law, or serve on juries. Most titles of nobility passed by succession only to a male heir (although women could be given titles in their own right and, very occasionally, succeed to one). Until 1882, the property of married women became, upon marriage, that of their husband. There was a general assumption in law that a woman was 'represented by' her father or husband. The procedures for divorce were different for men and women, with men having to prove adultery, women adultery plus something more heinous like deliberate cruelty. Most educational institutions catered for only one sex: obviously, in the great majority of cases, for men alone. Higher educational opportunities for women, in particular, were virtually non-existent until late in the century. While this list of women's disabilities is both oppressive and formidable, it is also, from a legal or quasi-legal sense, exhaustive: British women could do anything else, such as sue or give evidence in court, inherit or will their property, live where they wished, travel, or emigrate. There were also innumerable areas of life closed *de facto* to women by custom, but again there were areas where equality existed: for instance, men and women sat together and were treated equally in religious services (unlike Islam or Orthodox Judaism), in public transport, in theatres, as customers in shops and as consumers. Most British women were literate, and the literacy gap between men and women was relatively small and continuously narrowing. Women could write and publish books and, indeed, many of the greatest British writers of the nineteenth century were women. Women had only a handful of successful role models, but among them was Queen Victoria: succession to the British throne, though it was unequal in terms of gender, with males given preference, did not exclude women altogether, as was normal elsewhere, under the Salic Law, in continental monarchies. Several of the new, but worthy, sub-professions which emerged in nineteenth-century Britain, especially nursing and teaching, were dominated by women.

Behind everything else, however, was the widespread notion of 'separate spheres': men in gainful employment and the public sphere, women for the most part in the home. While the notion of 'separate spheres' was so ubiquitous as to be virtually pervasive, there were important and growing exceptions to it, such that it was breaking down under the weight of its incongruence with reality by 1914. The subject of paid employment for women in the Victorian and Edwardian periods shows both the reality of the notion of 'separate spheres' and also its increasing limitations. Female occupational patterns in nineteenth-century Britain were, plainly, very different from those of males. Most obviously, the majority of adult women had no occupation, while the great majority of men did. According to the Census figures, in 1841 only 25.3 per cent of females over 10 had an occupation in the workforce, compared with 76.0 per cent of males. In 1871 the percentage of women with occupations had increased to 36.0 per cent (compared with 87.5 percent of men), but in 1901 the percentage of women with an occupation had again declined slightly, to 31.6 per cent (compared with 83.7 per cent of men). It is quite possible to dispute these figures: many women who were unofficially but significantly involved with the businesses or farms of their husbands or other male relatives, are almost certainly not included as having any occupation, while the figures for male occupations probably include considerable numbers of the retired, semi-retired and unemployed. Figures for both sexes need to be considered alongside age-cohort and educational data. These figures almost certainly understate (or ignore altogether) women holding part-time jobs but chiefly occupied domestically as housewives, and women holding several part-time jobs simultaneously. Some of the occupational statistics, too, are certainly misleading: it is well-known, for example, that no Census ever included 'prostitutes' as an occupational category, although certainly many thousands of women were forced to earn their living at least in part through prostitution.

Nevertheless, the overall occupational distribution among British women in the nineteenth century certainly bore little resemblance to that for men. Women in employment tended to cluster in a handful of occupations and to be entirely absent, or virtually absent, from most others. Table 19.1 presents the overall number of occupied and unoccupied women, and the five largest occupational sectors among women in Great Britain (excluding Ireland) in 1841, 1871 and 1901.

By far the largest female occupation throughout the nineteenth century was domestic service, which accounted for more than half of all women in *any* employment in 1841, and even for 42.3 per cent of women's employment as late as 1901, at least according to the Census figures. Even if these figures are exaggerations, as some recent historians have argued (they include, for instance, live-in relatives who looked after the children of a family while the mother was at work), the types of households where women servants worked were very varied indeed, ranging from the grand country and town houses of the aristocracy to those of lower-middle-class tradesmen, and even of the skilled working class. What united virtually all female domestic servants were their extraordinarily long hours, endless bouts of drudgery, and low pay. Even if there were compensations – many servants lived in the houses where they worked, thus increasing their real wages; they were, at least, in the company of women (and men) of their own background – domestic service was surely one of the least desirable occupations imaginable. In particular (and like most women's work) there

Table 19.1 Largest women's occupations (× 1000 employees), 1841–1901

	1841		1871		1901	
Total no. unoccupied	5369	(74.7%)	6335	(64.0%)	10 247	(68.4%)
Total occupied	1815		3570		4732	
TOTAL	7184		9905		14 979	

			Largest occupations by numbers of employed women (× 1000)			
1	Domestic services	989	Domestic services	1678	Domestic services	2003
2	Textiles	358	Textiles	726	Textiles	795
3	Clothing	200	Clothing	594	Clothing	792
4	Agriculture	81	Professions, etc.	152	Professions, etc.	326
5	Professions, etc.	49	Agriculture	135	Food – Drink –Tobacco	216

was no obvious means of upward social mobility out of domestic service except by fortunate marriage.

While the number of female domestic servants continued to increase (as it did until the First World War), as a percentage of all women in gainful employment it perceptibly declined. As other, more attractive forms of women's employment opened up in the late nineteenth century, notably as shop assistants and secretaries, domestic service became even less desirable than before, especially to women with even a modicum of education. The late nineteenth century saw the 'servant problem', the alleged shortage of good, reliable women domestic servants, become a middle-class conversational cliché. As well, the introduction of some labour-saving domestic devices during the Edwardian period like primitive washing machines saw the demand for female service somewhat curtailed.

Collectively, the two women's occupational spheres of textile and clothing were growing rapidly until the later nineteenth century. Much of this activity comprised women working in textile factories in the northern factory towns. In 1871, for instance, there were 280 000 women working in cotton factories in England and Wales, 117 000 in woollen manufactories, 51 000 in silk, and 11 000 in flax. The commonness of female employment in textiles was clearly an extension of the pattern of domestic industry during the pre-industrial period. Of all the industries of the nineteenth century, women probably experienced the most satisfactory outcomes from the textile trade. Before 1860 the number of women in textiles was always just below the number of men; from about 1860, however, women outnumbered men in that trade. By 1901 there were 43 per cent more women employed in textiles than men (795 000 compared to 557 000). Wages for women were relatively high, while, remarkably, most textile activities were paid by piece-rate, the rate being the same for both men and women. In 1906 women in textiles earned, on average, 59 per cent of the average male wage, the highest percentage of any industry. Women were, however, completely excluded from officially being the overseers of mills, while a few specialist activities continued to exclude women entirely. Trade unions seldom included many women and did little to further women's interests until much later. In addition, there was a well-known pattern of women working in the textile trade from their mid-teens until, after marriage, their first child was born. Only a few would then return once their last child was born. (This pattern of course can be documented beyond the textile industry.) The effect of this was to boost the family income of young married working-class couples in Lancashire and other textile areas, but then to decrease it when it was most needed.

The clothing trade comprised such occupations as dressmakers, milliners and women tailors. Unlike factory textiles, pay for women was, generally, extremely low. Many worked in sweatshop conditions which were (unlike factories) largely unregulated by parliamentary legislation. The clothing trade was one of the classical occupations of working-class women in London, and was also entered by many Jewish immigrant women after 1880. Better off were the women who worked in bespoke ladies' dressmaking concerns, often in upmarket neighbourhoods for the rich: here there was scope for individual creativity and possibly higher rewards.

The greatest single proportionate increase in female occupational numbers came in the areas defined by the Censuses as professional in nature. Numbers of women in these increased by over 300 per cent between 1841 and 1901, from 49 000 to 216 000. Most of them were teachers or nurses, the two most significant (and characteristic) areas of female white-collar employment; librarians and the few female physicians were counted here as well. It will be seen that there were few other areas of employment where there were many women. As agricultural pursuits declined as a source of women's employment, a number of other occupations increased in size, such as process workers and others in the food–drink–tobacco trades, and workers in the printing and allied spheres, especially bookbinding, which employed 111 000 women in 1901. By the Edwardian period, women were employed at least in small numbers in virtually every trade, with the exception of the armed forces, engineering, and those professions like the law still wholly closed to females. In 1901, for instance, there were over 2000 women employed on the railways (presumably as station attendants) and 3000 in building and construction. The greatest female employment growth area of the first half of the twentieth century, of course, was as office secretaries, typists and clerks. There had already been some obvious growth here by the mid-1900s: women in 'commercial occupations', which included typists, numbered only 1000 in 1841, and 5000 in 1871, but then reached 76 000 by 1901 (and 157 000 in 1911). Women employed in 'public administration' (which included postmistresses and workhouse keepers, as well as government typists) rose from 3000 to 7000 to 29 000 in 1901. Women had worked as government typists in some London departments from the 1870s. Although their number was growing rapidly, women became virtually ubiquitous as office secretaries only in the 1930s or even later. The number of male clerks and typists continued to out-number females as late as the 1931 Census and were recorded as a minority only in the 1951 Census.

The pattern among female shop workers and shop assistants probably resembles the trends among clerical workers, although less is known as to their numbers. (The censuses failed to distinguish these categories accu-rately.) Female shop workers may be divided into the owners (or wives or daughters of owners) of shops, that is, those who managed the enterprise or had immediate and special access to the manager, and shop assistants in the pure sense. The number of female shop owners was certainly growing during the nineteenth century, as a glance through local directories at 20- or 30-year intervals will quickly reveal. Women had always run shops and businesses specialising in selling women's goods like clothing and millinery; the late nineteenth century saw the emergence of such familiar businesses as cosmetics vendors, hairdressers and toy shops. As well, the rise in the number of independent single women led to an increase in such areas as boarding houses catering especially for women and governesses. Women shop assistants (often teenage girls), on the other hand, were notoriously underpaid, overworked and overregulated by their employees.

There was, thus, a considerable broadening of the range of women's paid occupations during the later nineteenth century, even bearing in mind the many legal and customary restrictions on female employment. In a sense, this broadening closely paralleled the evolution of male employment in the same period, especially the expansion of white-collar and service occupa-tions, a trend which has marked the development of employment patterns for both sexes since the Edwardian period. Yet there were also marked differences between the sexes. There were, for instance, no notable success-ful female business entrepreneurs in nineteenth-century Britain. There were, of course, many women who were wealthy in their own right. About 10 per cent of approximately 8000 persons who left personal property at death of £100 000 or more during the nineteenth century were women (these figures are based on the probate records and exclude the capital value of land).[1] Virtually every one of the thousand or so women in this class of the very wealthy inherited her fortune from her father, husband or another male relative. So far as is known, only one woman who left £100 000 or more in the nineteenth century was directly engaged in business life, the little-known theatre proprietor Sarah Lane (*née* Borrow, 1822–99), a former singer who ran the Britannia Theatre, Hoxton, for 28 years after her husband, the previous owner, had died. Lane left £111 000 at her death.

---

1 £100 000 during the nineteenth century was worth approximately £5 million in today's money.

Only a handful of other British women achieved senior managerial positions. Mrs Rachel Beer (1858–1927), of the immensely wealthy Sassoon family (and aunt of Siegfried Sassoon, the poet), was, most astonishingly, the editor of both the *Observer* and the *Sunday Times* in the 1890s. Both papers were owned by her husband, but Rachel Beer was the working editor. At the *Observer*, her greatest scoop was to reveal that the documents which convicted Captain Dreyfus in France had been forged: one of the greatest revelations of nineteenth-century journalism. Below this level, there was a large number of reasonably successful women boardinghouse keepers and women shopkeepers, although they comprised only a fraction of the number of male counterparts. Nevertheless, the late Victorian and Edwardian periods were a time of real (albeit only very occasional) breakthroughs in occupational achievement for British women, concomitant with the emergence of the activist, intelligent 'new woman' depicted in the press at the same time. The first woman civil servant of the administrative class, Mrs Nassau Senior (the sister of Thomas Hughes, author of *Tom Brown's Schooldays*), was appointed Poor Law Inspector of the Local Government Board in January 1874. The first woman stockbroker, a Miss Bell, is known to have had an office in the City of London as early as 1890. While women physicians had performed surgery as early as 1871, the first woman admitted to the Royal College of Surgeons was Eleanor Davies-Colley in 1911; the first women dentist in Britain, Lilian Murray, qualified in 1895. At about the same time, in 1898, the first woman architect, Ethel Charles, qualified as an associate member of the Royal Institute of British Architects. Thus, by 1914 breakthroughs had been made by women into most (though certainly not all) professions.

In spite of all of this, most nineteenth-century British women were not in paid employment: most were housewives, looking after children. Nearly 88 per cent of women aged 45–49 were (or had been) married in 1871; this percentage declined somewhat by the Edwardian period, but still totalled nearly 84 per cent in 1911. Most married women were at home, looking after their children. It can easily be overlooked that one important reason why the development of a significant, powerful feminist movement was delayed in Britain (and elsewhere) was simply that most women were fully occupied as mothers and home-makers. As the age of marriage declined and the birth rate rose in the first half of the nineteenth century, women were even more fully occupied with raising children than before. The birth rate, especially among the middle classes, began to decline from the 1870s, but many couples still had, by today's standards, enormous families. Many recent feminist historians view women during those years as having lived under a double burden of exploitation: exploited as unpaid domestic workers (and bedmates) by their husbands; exploited and discriminated against in the labour force and in society as a whole. Working-class men may have faced the second of these burdens, but never the first. It is, however, unquestionable that most women certainly viewed their role in life as mothers and home-makers, accepting without questioning the notion of 'separate spheres'.

Beneath and below 'respectable' society was the Victorian sexual underworld, about which much has been written. Women who were unprotected by money or family ties were particularly vulnerable to falling into its morass; their plight was made worse by the general hostility to 'fallen women' and the great reluctance of most respectable persons openly to discuss this aspect of life. That there were enormous, almost unbelievable, numbers of prostitutes in nineteenth-century London (and in most other large cities) was remarked upon by every foreign visitor. The Haymarket near Piccadilly Circus and Waterloo Road (near Waterloo Station) south of the Thames were particularly notorious; hundreds, perhaps thousands, of prostitutes assembled there every day. The scenes of debauchery in upper-class London brothels were extraordinary, and can still shock us today. The number of prostitutes in mid-Victorian London was often estimated as high as 100 000; Friedrich Engels, obviously no partisan of bourgeois society, thought there were 40 000. One estimate, from 1838, was that there were 5000 brothels in London. In 1888, when 'Jack the Ripper' brutally murdered eight prostitutes in the Whitechapel district of the East End, the police reported that there were 62 brothels and 1200 prostitutes known to them in the single police division covering the Whitechapel district. Many girls as young as 10 were forced into prostitution by economic necessity. Many others were 'fallen women' who had been seduced and abandoned, often with illegitimate children, and ostracised by their families. Death rates among prostitutes were extraordinarily high. Many prostitutes became alcoholics. Prostitution was the product of economic necessity – few prostitutes had any other marketable skills – and was maintained by the inability of most women to rise up the economic scale. For much of the Victorian period, the scale of prostitution was bolstered by a virtual conspiracy of silence about it from respectable society, intellectuals, and, above all, the churches. For every sermon preached about the evils of prostitution, probably 500 were delivered about the evils of drink. It was widely assumed that prostitutes had brought degradation upon themselves, and deserved a minimum of sympathy. As Lord Snell (a Labour politician who was the first person of working-class origin to receive a peerage) put it:

> What of the women who had no male relatives, the young widows with children to support, and the lonely working girls? How were they to live? . . . [E]verybody knew the dangers to which they were exposed. The statesmen knew of them, the economists and the Church knew, but there was no evidence that their complacent philosophy of life was seriously disturbed.'[2]

2 Lord [Henry] Snell, *Men, Movements, and Myself* (London, 1936), p. 88.

By the late nineteenth century, some steps were taken to suppress prostitution. In 1864 the Contagious Diseases Act had been passed, regulating prostitution in the hope of diminishing venereal disease in the army and the navy (whose men made frequent use of the services of prostitutes). The Act established a system of compulsory medical examinations for what it termed 'common prostitutes' in a naval garrison or port. In the 1870s a campaign grew up, associated especially with Josephine Butler (1828–1906), to repeal the Act, on the grounds that while prostitutes could be punished (if found to be diseased, the woman could be confined to a hospital), the men to whose lusts she pandered could not be. Butler, assisted by a coalition of Evangelical Christians and early feminists, secured the repeal of the Act in 1886. She had been aided as well by the radical journalist W. T. Stead (1849–1912), editor of the *Pall Mall Gazette* newspaper, who, over several issues in 1885, published a shocking exposé of child prostitution in London, 'The Maiden Tribute of Modern Babylon', which caused one of the great journalistic uproars of the nineteenth century. In 1885, in part as a result of Stead's advocacy, brothel-keeping and the procurement of women for prostitution were made illegal. This Act had teeth in it. The number of prosecutions for brothel-keeping rose dramatically. Landlords, who were made responsible in law if they knowingly let houses for prostitution, were increasingly reluctant to rent premises to 'suspect' women. By the Edwardian period prostitution was probably less publicly visible than in mid-Victorian times, while the increase in the range of employment opportunities for women probably acted to diminish the dire economic pressures which produced prostitution.

Some feminist historians hold a notion that there was a period, prior to industrialisation, when women enjoyed more rights, and a greater degree of equality, than was subsequently the case after industrialisation began. The evidence for this viewpoint is based largely on the heavily 'gendered' nature of work and the sharp divide, in most cases, between workplace and the public sphere, dominated by men, and the home, dominated by women. According to the feminist view, this divide was at its sharpest and most comprehensive during the Victorian era. While there may be a good deal of truth to this perspective, its underlying assumption is that there was a period, before industrialisation, when women enjoyed more equality than later on. Unfortunately, there is remarkably little evidence for such a view. Restrictions, legal and customary, on what women could do were just as strong in 1700 as in 1850, if not more so, and certainly more severe in 1700 than in 1900. Most evidence for the view that the position of women in society deteriorated probably flows from the decline of domestic industry (where products like woollens and textiles were manufactured in the home) and the rise of the factory system. In domestic industry men and women worked together, often enjoying a kind of rough equality; in the factory system women were present only as subordinates.

This viewpoint also ignores the more central fact that gains in rights for women were surely part of a much larger pattern of gains for both sexes brought about by the ascendancy of liberalism and democracy. It is clearly more reasonable to view women as the last, or among the last, groups to benefit from the extension of political rights (explicitly or implicitly to males) to the middle classes and non-Anglicans in the period 1825–60 and to the working classes from 1867. The granting of rights to women in Britain presented special difficulties. There were functioning and successful societies, like the United States, where all adult males had the vote. It thus was unreasonable to maintain that universal manhood suffrage would necessarily lead to anarchy, and a crucial argument against extending the franchise to all or virtually all adult men became indefensible. However, even in 1867 there was no society anywhere which granted the vote, and other civic rights, to women, and thus no operational society to which women might point as one which had granted equal rights to women without catastrophe ensuing. In 1869 the western American state of Wyoming was the first place, anywhere, to extend the franchise to women; by the end of the nineteenth century many western American states had followed suit. New Zealand granted women the right to vote in 1893, the first self-governing British colony to do so. Granting the franchise in parliamentary elections to British women was delayed by several factors. Until 1918 not all British men had the vote. While women ratepayers could vote in British local elections from the 1870s onwards, to enfranchise them would almost certainly have advantaged the Tories (something which the Liberals, when in office, were unwilling to do), as women ratepayers would have been conservative property-owners, while to give the vote to all women was simply too vast a step for any government to take. There was no effective mass movement aimed at securing women's suffrage in Britain prior to 1903, when the Pankhursts formed the well-known Women's Social and Political Union in Manchester, moving its headquarters to London in 1906. Many women, including a surprising number of those associated with the political left, continued to oppose votes for women (as 'unfeminine') during the Edwardian period. Most of all, of course, there remained a significant majority of adult men who, down to the First World War, opposed granting the vote to women. Usually this opposition took the form of 'the ladies – God bless 'em' avowals of separate spheres, with women's sphere being the 'higher' one of the home and purity. 'We regard woman as something to admire, to reverence, to love; and while we share with her the happiness of life, we will shield her as far as possible from its harsher and sterner duties', Edward Knatchbull-Hugessen, Liberal Under-Secretary of State for the Colonies, explained in 1872. Often, too, there was a frank and open disavowal of women's intellectual fitness to exercise the vote. Henry Labouchère, a famous radical MP and editor who nevertheless strongly opposed votes or office-holding for women, stated in 1891 that 'There are certain ladies of very great intellect, no doubt they are women by accident who want to assume the position of men. Now I object to legislating for what, with all respect to the ladies, I may call freaks of nature', and in 1897 that 'Intellectually women have not the gifts which fit them for being elected. They have got a certain amount of what I might call instinct rather than reason; they are impulsive, emotional and have got absolutely no sense of proportion'. The argument against women's suffrage most often heard in the Edwardian period was that Parliament had to debate and legislate on deadly serious matters of high finance, diplomacy, the Empire, and war and peace, and women as a rule had no experience or knowledge of any of these topics. Women voters would thus either vote just as their fathers, husbands or brothers directed, or they would vote irrationally, letting the heart sway the head, and, especially, be incapable of taking the often brutal decisions necessary in political or international life, particularly military decisions. Women were 'purer' than men, and their intrusion into the dirty and vicious world of politics would corrupt them without purifying the political arena. Arguments such as these prevented women from achieving the vote in parliamentary elections in Britain until 1918. Nevertheless, they did not prevent women from achieving a range of gains in other areas, including legal rights, divorce and education, before the First World War. A fundamental change in the status of women would, however, have to wait until the closing years of that war and its immediate aftermath to be achieved. Apart from the enfranchisement of women over 30 in 1918, the Sex Disqualifications (Removal) Act of 1919 saw the obstacles to women entering the professions abolished. As a result, the first women solicitors and barristers were admitted, both in 1922. Real changes in the status of women in Britain, especially their visibility in public life, would only come after the Second World War, particularly following the impact of 'second-wave feminism' of the 1970s.

There were areas of the public sphere which women could always occupy in nineteenth-century Britain. Women were always accepted as writers, even as 'intellectuals' who were unattached to a university (as most male writers and intellectuals were similarly unattached). Wealthy and aristocratic women were the backbone of 'Society', with its perpetual social nuances and alliances that impacted strongly upon public life. Women were always welcomed in the public space of religious worship. Women's role and impact on Victorian religion in Britain has been regrettably neglected by feminist historians, with their radical biases and interests. Women probably comprised a majority of all regular worshippers in Anglican churches (although possibly not among the Dissenting chapels) in the Victorian and Edwardian period. By the late Victorian and Edwardian period women members were the lifeblood of most churches, especially in the work they did for church social, missionary and charitable societies. Women writers on religious questions were numerous and some were genuinely remarkable, like Charlotte Elizabeth Tonna, the Evangelical editor and essayist.

Several long-term gains for women's public space and the public visibility of women in nineteenth-century British society are unobtrusive and have attracted little attention from the historian. One of the most important was the development and widespread provision of single-sex public toilets. Very little is known of this topic, but it appears that the first single-sex public toilets provided by government authorities were to be found at the Great Exhibition of 1851. Large railway stations also had single-sex toilets from the 1830s. Prior to that time, anyone answering a call of nature apparently had to ask a shopkeeper to use the privies at the back of the shop. By the later nineteenth century single-sex toilets (often ornate) were to be found in all town centres, major shopping areas, public buildings and large shops. Knowledge that lavatories were widely available must certainly have made women more willing to use shopping centres beyond their local neighbourhood. Another innovation was the lift (elevator). Strange as this may seem, no buildings anywhere had lifts prior to the late 1820s, and few British buildings had lifts before the 1860s at the very earliest.[3] By the Edwardian period, however, lifts were common in larger shops like department stores and in multi-storied public buildings. Escalators were unknown in Britain before 1898, when Harrods department store installed one, and were first provided on the London underground only in 1911. Without lifts (and escalators), most women over 60, pregnant women, and those with disabilities (and many men, of course) could not have used multi-storied facilities of any kind; indeed, the latter would not have been built. Nor could the deep London tubes have been built, constructed as they were with lifts from 1890 onwards (as opposed to the 'cut-and-cover' tubes, much closer to the surface, the first of which opened in 1863). Many other technical developments and innovations also assisted women's mobility. These ranged from the mundane, such as the use of level pavements and paving stones in place of the cobblestoned streets formerly found in most British cities, to the provision of street lighting, police, and public transport. It seems clear that by, say, the 1890s most large British cities were much more inviting places for women than 50 or 60 years before, and *de facto* increased the range of opportunities open to women, especially the physically disadvantaged.

By the late Victorian period, women's mass organisations like the Primrose League and the Mother's Union existed and were recognised by men as bodies to be reckoned with. At both the elite and mass levels, in other words, women were effectively in large measure preparing for and prepared for the formal granting of equality which would come in the twentieth century.

3 The earliest powered passenger lift in the world was built in 1829 for the London Panorama at Regent's Park, containing a vast concave painting on the ceiling of the building which gave spectators a 'View of London from the Top of St Paul's'. The lift, which could carry up to 12 passengers, cost an extra 6d, and saved the visitors to this enormously popular tourist attraction an exhausting climb. The first public building in Britain to contain a lift was the six-storey Westminster Palace Hotel in London, built in 1861.

As for men, one might suppose that at a time of 'separate spheres' their role and status was the opposite of women's: complete dominance in the public and political spheres; virtually complete dominance in all forms of employment; hegemony even in the home. The bearded patriarchs who stare back at us from a thousand old Victorian daguerreotypes and paintings seem to add a visible presence to this notion of sexual separateness at its most extreme. Nevertheless, as a generalisation it needs serious qualification. To be sure, the Victorian period was the time when men were expected to exhibit all of the 'manly virtues', at their most brutal. The 'big shots' who slaughtered defenceless animals and birds from the four corners of the world in record numbers, mounting their heads or stuffing their carcasses as trophies, repel today's sensibility as little else does. No doubt too, the Victorian age was full of men who beat their wives and proved to be 'brutes' (in the phrase of the day) in the bedroom, who treated natives with murderous contempt, who fought nasty colonial wars. Yet the opposite types were to be found as well and, indeed, apart from Victorian Britain's masculinity there existed an evermore significant feminisation of the masculine values and a civilising of the barbaric. The Society for the Prevention of Cruelty to Animals was founded in 1824; through its efforts, bear- and bull-baiting were outlawed in the 1830s and cockfighting in the 1840s. It received its 'Royal' preface from Queen Victoria in 1840. By the late Victorian period, dog and cat shows – attended by large numbers of women – were taking place, and pampered pets had become increasingly common. The 'English gentleman' only really emerged in the early Victorian period, closely following the expansion of the public schools. It was John Henry Newman who defined a gentleman as 'one who never inflicts pain' and this definition was unusually perceptive in highlighting what possibly most set the English gentleman apart from his colleagues overseas. The nineteenth century, too, was the century of the rise of competitive sport in the modern sense, a legacy which might well outlive virtually everything else which that era produced. The first sport to have a mass following in Britain was horse-racing. By the early nineteenth century most of the famous races were well-established, and great jockeys and great horses known throughout the land. The funeral of a famous jockey was often the occasion for public grief. Horse-racing was also probably the first sport which, by the annual and recurrent nature of its leading events, became the vehicle by which many ordinary persons dated events in the past ('Oh aye! 1859 be the year that "Half-Caste" won the Grand National, I recall'), a pattern of memory identified by oral historians as surprisingly common. Horse races also, renownedly, saw the almost unique mixing of social classes literally from dukes to dustmen, and with dukes seeking out the demi-monde of horse-trainers and betting touts. The other main English sports either began or were transformed into a recognisably modern form in this period, the Football Association, for example, being founded in 1863. Cricket, dating from the eighteenth century or before, divided into amateur 'gentlemen' and professional 'players', a format it retained until 1962, when the distinction was withdrawn. Britain's pattern was broadly similar to that in most other Western countries, such as the United States, where baseball, played from the 1840s, became professionalised in 1869 and was formed into 'major leagues' in 1871–76; by the 1890s it was America's national sport, a powerful force at reunifying the country after the Civil War and in Americanising the immigrants.

Little of a definitive nature is known of the pre- or extramarital sexual behaviour of Victorian men. It seems reasonable to conclude that many more British males were chaste before marriage than today, especially among the middle classes, but quite possibly fewer than in the 1920–60 period in Britain. It was widely believed by social observers of the late Victorian period that virtually every normal man had frequented prostitutes from his teenage years onwards. Given the extraordinary number of prostitutes, and the fact that virtually everyone in authority ignored their existence, something like this may well be true, especially as the employment of a prostitute was much to be preferred by most Victorians to the alternatives, masturbation or homosexuality. It was also widely believed that venereal disease was rife, with (it was said) up to 10 per cent of the adult male population suffering from it. Certainly many fewer women engaged in pre-marital sex before the First World War than after: one survey, conducted in the 1950s, found that 19 per cent of women born before 1904 had engaged in pre-marital sex, compared with 39 per cent among those born in the 1914–24 period (who thus were 15 in the years 1929–39). Very large numbers of middle-class men kept mistresses, while it was reputed that virtually all men frequented prostitutes. Many affluent City men maintained their wives and families in a respectable villa in Dulwich or Sydenham, with whom they spent the weekend and holidays, but also kept full-time mistresses – in effect, a second wife – in flats in St John's Wood or Baron's Court, whom they visited during the week. This was so common as to attract virtually no attention. Male homosexuality, however, was almost universally feared and detested, although it did not become criminalised until the 1890s. While there was no break in the taboo against homosexuality until the 1960s, there was a flourishing Victorian and Edwardian homosexual underworld, feeding upon the casual homoeroticism of the public schools and Oxbridge. What was, however, utterly different from today was the virtually complete taboo on the frank discussion in print of sexual matters during the nineteenth century, except in medical circles, so that the gap between the written and spoken word in matters of sex was simply enormous. There is no reason to suppose that talk about sex did not occupy as much, or nearly as much, of the spoken language, especially among men and particularly among teenagers, as it does today. Since sex was seldom discussed in print (and, when it was, almost invariably as a sin), the amount of guilt and fear generated by sex must have been enormous, although this burden of guilt existed side-by-side with the rampant underground sexuality of the Victorian period. Naturally, too, there were millions of married couples who were happily devoted to one another and would not conceivably have engaged in extramarital sexual activity: doubtless most couples.

Victorian Britain, especially Victorian London, was the home of a large number of bachelors. In 1891 in the County of London there were 68 000 unmarried males aged 35 or more out of a total male population aged 35 or more of 523 000, or 13 per cent. Among the 12 middle-class Census districts of west and central London the percentage of bachelors was considerably higher: 17 per cent. It was highest of all in the Strand district (29 per cent), St Giles (27 per cent), Westminster (25 per cent), and the City (19 per cent). Some of these were young men such as shop assistants living on the premises and students of the Inns of Court, most of whom would eventually marry. A small but unknowable proportion were homosexuals. The majority, however, were probably confirmed bachelors who spent their idle hours at a club. Very little is known about these men, who have largely been ignored by social historians. It may be supposed that most of these bachelors had little experience of women (except, perhaps, for prostitutes) and were afraid of them: it must not be forgotten that there were few opportunities to meet respectable unmarried women. The clubs which grew up in London's West End – there were dozens by the late Victorian period – catered in part for this large group of London bachelors. There is no reason to suppose that more than a minority were homosexuals or misogynists; they must, however, have found the bachelor life at least tolerably satisfactory.

Several archetypes of male (and, occasionally, female) appeared during the Victorian period or just before; typically, these were not as well known, if at all, in the eighteenth century. The world traveller became a common figure, clearly as a result of the increasing ease of transport. When the Travellers' Club, one of the famous gentlemen's clubs in Pall Mall, opened in 1819, its main criterion for membership was that applicants had to have travelled at least 500 miles outside of Britain. The man whose career was one of effortless superiority emerged in its peculiarly English form at this time, as did the British 'Renaissance man', the great all-rounder who was remarkably good at several unrelated things; so did the phenomenally productive auto-didactical author. Sir Joseph Chitty (1828–99) is an excellent example of the man whose career is one of effortless superiority, something especially associated with Balliol College, Oxford, indeed Chitty's *alma mater*. From an eminent legal family and an Old Etonian, at Oxford Chitty obtained a first, captained the cricket eleven, rowed in the annual race, and won the Vinerian Scholarship, the most prestigious of law prizes. A QC at 46, Chitty served briefly as a Liberal MP, served as a judge for 28 years, and was appointed to the Privy Council shortly before his death. He also managed to leave £160 000, about £8 million in today's money. Late Victorian Britain produced many Joseph Chittys: he was not unique. Nor was the 'great all-rounder' uncommon, the man who was unusually gifted or productive in several fields. Howard Staunton (1810–74) was not merely the greatest chess player of his time (the standard 'Staunton design' chess pieces are named for him) but he also produced a comprehensive new annotated multi-volumed edition of Shakespeare's plays and a range of other books such as *The Great Schools of England* (1869). There were dozens of men like Staunton, including several like Bulwer-Lytton, Disraeli, Gladstone and Macaulay, who sat in Cabinets. As well there were the extraordinarily productive auto-didacts, authors whose productive labours resembled those of Hercules. Frederick Boase (1843–1916) published his six volumes of *Modern English Biography* between 1892 and (posthumously) 1921. Compiled single-handedly by Boase, the Librarian of the Law Society, they include remarkably lucid biographies of 20 000 notable British people in literally every walk of life who died between 1850 and 1901; only a small minority are listed in any other published source. John Bateman (1839–1910) corrected and collated the hundreds of thousands of entries in the official *Return of Owners of Land* of 1872–75 by writing to every notable landowner in Britain; Bateman's resultant compilation, *The Great Landowners of Great Britain and Ireland* (1883), remains one of the most valuable of all sources available to the social historian. There were talented women of this type as well, for example Jane Marcet (*née* Haldimand, 1769–1858), the daughter of a Swiss merchant and married to a physician in London, who wrote a two-volume introduction to chemistry in 1806 which had gone into 16 editions by 1853, a five-volume introductory work on economics (1824), a similar guide to the sciences (1819) which appeared in its 14th edition by 1872, and, as well, a 'Game of Grammar' (1842) and 15 books for children! It is difficult to imagine anyone of this type today: paradoxically, as experts and specialists have become ubiquitous, and as mechanical and computer-based aids to 'information technology' have multiplied, the heroic but irreplaceable broad generalist has almost vanished.

Late Victorian Britain did, however, conform to the stereotype of sexual division and patriarchy in some respects. That time was, for instance, the apogee of exclusively male social clubs and fraternal societies, like the Freemasons and the Oddfellows, with their enormous memberships. Too little attention has been directed at these bodies, although the social historian must be very careful to separate fact from fiction, especially in the case of the unfairly maligned Freemasons. Such bodies appear to have been extraordinarily popular and influential among the middle and lower middle classes of London and the provincial cities, where they doubtless served as conduits of influence and what would now be termed 'networking'. But they also did much good charitable work, and it is not self-evident that their loss of popularity in the twentieth century has been entirely for the best.

Conclusion: stability and change

Despite everything that occurred in nineteenth-century Britain, it is quite possible to identify a great many continuities which persisted between 1815 and 1905. Most clearly, the formal structure and symbolism of Britain's government was virtually identical in 1905 to what it had been 90 years before (and, indeed, remained fairly similar until the close of the twentieth century). The monarchy, the two Houses of Parliament, Cabinet government, the Established Church, the titled aristocracy, the common law, and many other fundamental British institutions appeared not to have changed in any formal sense during the nineteenth century. Even if this identity of forms concealed great changes – as, in many cases, it obviously did – the continuities were often real enough, as well as creating a deliberate impression of timelessness and conservatism rather than of innovation.

Much in Britain's social and economic history during this period also demonstrated continuity rather than change. Britain's class system, although greatly altered by the industrial revolution and its effects, was at least broadly similar in the beginning of the twentieth century to what it had been 80 years previously. The City of London still stood at the centre of the British economy, sharply divided in function from the industrial north. To a considerable extent, in 1905 the state played no greater a role in British society than it had immediately following the Napoleonic Wars.

It goes without saying that nearly everything about these continuities is also illusory, and that, while the forms may indeed have remained, virtually everything else changed. It is obviously impossible to examine all of these changes, but a number should certainly be mentioned. The nature of the British political nation changed, incorporating the middle classes and, by the end of the century, a component of the working classes, as part of the broad group which influenced public policy. By 1905, no religious or ethnic group was formally excluded from governance, although women and most of the working classes still remained tangential to the political process. Britain became an urban society, with a working class increasingly self-conscious, comprising perhaps 70 per cent of the population. Britain's population expanded enormously, with its major cities growing at a still faster rate. By 1905, Britain's Empire had become central to Britain's future, although the main goals of British foreign policy, especially the maintenance of the balance of power in Europe, remained much the same as they had done 80 years previously.

What best explains the existence, side-by-side, of continuity and great change in British society is, perhaps, the very partial and incomplete nature of fundamental political change in nineteenth-century Britain, with the structures of society, especially its formal structures, being largely resistant to dramatic alteration. Because the 'political nation', the active leaders of the political community, were for the most part strictly limited to the middle and upper classes (and normally to the aristocracy and well-off), fundamental political change was likely to be thwarted, except on the rarest of occasions when the governing elite had badly mismanaged the nation's affairs. Even in 1905 (and indeed in 1914) it was probably impossible realistically to visualise a Labour-dominated Parliament for generations, if ever; indeed, without the trauma of the First World War it is entirely possible that the Liberals would have continued as the majority left-of-centre party, with Labour playing only a marginal role. Britain never truly became a political democracy during the nineteenth century, while realistic opportunities for upward social mobility from the working class to the middle class remained exceedingly limited. Britain, in other words, did not become America, even if it was very different from France or Germany.

The greatest irony of all is that the one institution which, in 1905, seemed most central to Britain's future and most likely to be permanent, the Empire, proved to be the most fragile and ephemeral. To most well-informed observers in the Edwardian period, the twentieth century seemed certain to be the era of great empires, with only the largest powers having any chance of maintaining national supremacy or, indeed, national existence. With the largest Empire of all, Britain seemed to be at least a contender to continue as an unquestionably major power, whatever difficulties it faced, and most Britons viewed both the new white Dominions like Canada and Australia, and the tropical colonies with their unlimited natural resources and potential, with the most sanguine of hopes. Few could have seen how unimportant the Empire would have proved to be for Britain in the twentieth century, nor how easily and perhaps painlessly the links with the Empire were to be broken.

On the other hand, it is fair to say that all elements in British politics underestimated the role of the state in twentieth-century Britain, and misunderstood the shape which state intervention was to take. On the left, socialists imagined that the state would, probably benignly, come to own the means of production; on the right, tariff reform nationalists imagined a neo-Bismarckian state whose aims were to further imperialism and social reform. Yet few envisioned the relatively liberal Welfare State which evolved after 1905, nor the possibilities of limited state ownership combined with an essentially capitalistic economy. No one as yet viewed the role of the state as furthering full employment and maximum demand in the Keynesian sense. No one thought that Britain could lose its Empire but retain an important, albeit decreasing, role as a military power. No one foresaw that universal adult suffrage would have so little effect on the fundamental nature of society. No one, in other words, foresaw the themes which came to dominate twentieth-century British politics until a new set of bearings and assumptions emerged in the century's last 20 years.

Bibliography

Introduction

The standard works remain the Oxford English History volumes: Steven Watson, *The Reign of George III, 1760–1815* (Oxford, 1960); Sir Llewellyn Woodward, *The Age of Reform, 1815–1870* (Oxford, 1962); and R. C. K. Ensor, *England, 1870–1914* (Oxford, 1936). These are to be gradually superseded by the New Oxford English History volumes. The first to cover the 1815–1905 period is K. Theodore Hoppen, *The Mid-Victorian Generation, 1846–1886* (Oxford, 1998). Elie Halévy's *A History of the English People in the Nineteenth Century* (6 volumes, London, 1924) probably still remains without equal, especially the celebrated first volume, *England in 1815*. There are an intimidating number of textbooks, only some of which can be noted here. R. K. Webb's *Modern England: From the 18th Century to the Present* (New York, 1969) continues to stand out. Two constant companions for the serious student should be Chris Cook and Brendan Keith, *British Historical Facts, 1830–1900* (London, 1975), although it is badly in need of a revised and corrected edition, and B. R. Mitchell and Phyllis Deane, *Abstract of British Historical Statistics* (Cambridge, 1971).

On social history, there are also now innumerable works. The three-volume work edited by F. M. L. Thompson, *The Cambridge Social History of Britain, 1750–1950* (3 volumes, Cambridge, 1990) gives a good, if selective and partial overview. Adrian Wilson, ed., *Rethinking Social History: English Society 1570–1920 and Its Interpretation* (Manchester, 1993) contains essays, often highly tendentious, showing the directions in which some social historians are going. Students who do not understand a particular term, custom or institution should not be ashamed to use a work like Bamber Gascoigne's *Encyclopedia of Britain* (London, 1993), which is remarkably useful.

The following are a list of some important works in British political and social history during the period 1815–1905. There are innumerable others. Only a few articles have been listed. Students might wish routinely to look at recent issues of such journals as the *English History Review*, the *Historical Journal*, and the *Economic History Review* (which covers social history) for important new articles and reviews of recent books. Many of the books listed below are relevant, of course, under more than one heading. Biographical studies still rather favour Whig and Liberal over Tory figures, although this is changing. Nevertheless, there is still no comprehensive biography of the third Marquess of Salisbury, nor of many other important Tory leaders, for instance Lord Eldon and Sir Stafford Northcote.

The place of publication is London unless otherwise stated.

Political history

General and parties

Paul Adelman, *Victorian Radicalism: The Middle Class Experience* (1984).

John Belchem, *Class, Party, and the Political System in Britain, 1867–1914* (Oxford, 1990).

Michael Bentley and John Stevenson, eds, *High and Low Politics in Modern Britain* (Oxford, 1983).

Michael Bentley, *The Climax of Liberal Politics: Liberalism in Theory and Practice, 1868–1918* (1987).

Robert Blake, *The Conservative Party From Peel to Thatcher* (1985).

Alan Bullock and Maurice Shock, eds, *The Liberal Tradition From Fox to Keynes* (1956).

Ivor Bulmer-Thomas, *The Growth of the British Party System* (2 volumes, 1965).

Lord Butler, ed., *The Conservatives* (1977).

B. Coleman, *Conservatism and the Conservative Party in Nineteenth Century Britain* (1989).

Richard W. Davis, *Political Change and Continuity, 1760–1885: A Buckinghamshire Study* (Newton Abbot, 1972).

Brendan Evans, *From Salisbury to Major: Continuity and Change in Conservative Politics* (Manchester, 1996).

Brian Harrison, *The Transformation of British Politics, 1860–1995* (Oxford, 1996).

Robert Rhodes James, *The British Revolution: British Politics, 1880–1939* (1978).

T. A. Jenkins, *The Liberal Ascendancy, 1830–1886* (1994).

T. A. Jenkins, *Parliament, Party, and Politics in Victorian Britain* (Manchester, 1996).

Michael Kinnear, *The British Voter: An Atlas and Survey Since 1885* (1969).

Trevor O. Lloyd, *The British Empire, 1558–1995* (Oxford, 1996).

Simon Maccoby, ed., *English Radicalism* (5 volumes, 1935–61).

Jonathan Parry, *The Rise and Fall of Liberal Government in Victorian Britain* (New Haven, 1993).

Henry Pelling, *The Social Geography of British Elections, 1885–1910* (1967).

Martin Pugh, *The Making of Modern British Politics, 1867–1939* (Oxford, 1982).

Robert Robson, ed., *Ideas and Institutions of Victorian Britain* (1967).

G. R. Searle, *Corruption in British Politics, 1865–1930* (Oxford, 1987).

Anthony Seldon, ed., *How Tory Governments Fall: The Tory Party in Power Since 1783* (1996).

E. A. Smith, *The House of Lords in British Politics and Society, 1815–1911* (1992).

Donald Southgate, *The Passing of the Whigs, 1832–1886* (1962).

J. A. Thomas, *The House of Commons, 1822–1901: A Study of its Economic and Functional Character* (Cardiff, 1939).

R. J. White, *The Conservative Tradition* (1964).

Regency period, c. 1815–25

J. C. D. Clark, *English Society, 1688–1832* (Cambridge, 1985).

J. C. D. Clark, *Revolution and Rebellion* (Cambridge, 1986).

John W. Derry, *Castlereagh* (1976).

Norman Gash, *Lord Liverpool* (1984).

Brian Hill, *The Early Parties and Politics in Britain, 1688–1832* (1996).

Boyd Hilton, *Cash, Corn, and Commerce* (1977).

Wendy Hinde, *George Canning* (1973).

Gerrit P. Judd, *Members of Parliament, 1734–1832* (New Haven, 1972).

Elizabeth Longford, *Wellington: Pillar of the State* (1972).

Austin Mitchell, *The Whigs in Opposition, 1815–30* (Oxford, 1967).

L. G. Mitchell, *Holland House* (1980).

Frank O'Gorman, *The Evolution of the British Two-Party System, 1760–1832* (1982).

Frank O'Gorman, *Voters, Patrons and Parties: The Unreformed Electorate of Hanoverian England, 1734–1832* (1989).

J. A. Phillips, *Electoral Behaviour in Unreformed England* (Princeton, 1982).

Philip Ziegler, *Addington* (1965).

The mid-Victorian age, 1840–65

Olive Anderson, *A Liberal State at War* (1967).

David Cecil, *Melbourne* (1965).

Muriel Chamberlain, *Lord Aberdeen* (1983).

J. B. Connacher, *The Aberdeen Coalition, 1852–55* (Cambridge, 1968).

J. B. Connacher, *The Peelites and the Party System, 1846–1852* (Newton Abbot, 1972).

Norman Gash, *Peel and the Conservative Party* (1929).

Norman Gash, *Sir Robert Peel* (1972).

Norman Gash, *Politics in the Age of Peel* (Brighton, 1977).

Wendy Hinde, *Richard Cobden: A Victorian Outsider* (New Haven, 1987).

Anthony Howe, *Free Trade and Liberal England, 1846–1946* (Oxford, 1997).

Peter Mandler, *Aristocratic Government in the Age of Reform: Whigs and Liberals, 1830–1852* (Oxford, 1990).

Norman McCord, *The Anti-Corn Law League* (1958).

Donald Read, *Peel and the Victorians* (1987).

Jasper Ridley, *Lord Palmerston* (1970).

Keith Robbins, *John Bright* (1979).

G. R. Searle, *Entrepreneurial Politics in Mid-Victorian Britain* (Oxford, 1993).

Richard Shannon, *Gladstone: Volume I, 1809–65* (1982).

Donald Southgate, *The Most English Minister* (1966).

E. D. Steele, *Palmerston and Liberalism, 1855–1865* (Cambridge, 1991).

Robert Stewart, *The Politics of Protection: Lord Derby and the Protectionist Party, 1842–1852* (Cambridge, 1971).

Robert Stewart, *The Foundation of the Conservative Party, 1830–1867* (1978).

J. R. Vincent, *The Formation of the Liberal Party, 1857–1868* (Brighton, 1976).

The age of reform, 1825–40

Kenneth Bourne, *Palmerston: The Early Years, 1784–1841* (1982).

Richard Brent, *Liberal Anglican Politics: Whiggery, Religion and Reform, 1830–1841* (Oxford, 1987).

Michael Brock, *The Great Reform Act* (1973).

John Cannon, *Parliamentary Reform, 1640–1832* (Cambridge, 1973).

Norman Gash, *Reaction and Reconstruction in English Politics, 1832–52* (Oxford, 1965).

Ursula Henriques, *Religious Toleration in England, 1787–1833* (1961).

L. G. Mitchell, *Lord Melbourne, 1779–1848* (Oxford, 1997).

Ian Newbould, *Whiggery and Reform, 1830–41: The Politics of Government* (Stanford, 1990).

George Rudé, *The Crowd in History, 1730–1848* (1964).

Charles Seymour, *Electoral Reform in England and Wales* (1915; reprinted 1970) – covers the 1832, 1867 and 1884 Acts.

E. A. Smith, *Earl Grey, 1764–1845* (Oxford, 1990).

William Thomas, *The Philosophic Radicals* (Oxford, 1979).

G. M. Trevelyan, *Lord Grey of the Reform Bill* (1920).

E. A. Wasson, *Whig Renaissance: Lord Althorp and the Whig Party, 1782–1845* (New York, 1987).

Philip Ziegler, *Melbourne* (1976).

The age of Disraeli and Gladstone, 1865–90

Eugenio F. Biagini, *Liberty, Retrenchment and Reform: Popular Politics in the Age of Gladstone, 1860–1880* (Cambridge, 1992).

Robert Blake, *Disraeli* (1966).

A. B. Cooke, and J. R. Vincent, *The Governing Passion* (Brighton, 1974).

Maurice Cowling, *1867: Disraeli, Gladstone and Revolution* (Cambridge, 1967).

D. A. Hamer, *Liberal Politics in the Age of Gladstone and Rosebery* (Oxford, 1972).

H. J. Hanham, *Elections and Party Management: Politics in the Time of Disraeli and Gladstone* (Brighton, 1978).

Roy Jenkins, *Gladstone* (1995).

T. A. Jenkins, *Gladstone, Whiggery and the Liberal Party, 1874–86* (Oxford, 1988).

Bruce L. Kinzer, ed., *The Gladstonian Turn of Mind* (Toronto, 1985).

W. C. Lubenow, *Parliamentary Politics and the Home Rule Crisis: The House of Commons in 1886* (Oxford, 1988).

Philip Magnus, *Gladstone: A Biography* (1963).

H. C. G. Matthew, *Gladstone, 1809–1898* (1997).

W. F. Moneypenny and G. E. Buckle, *The Life of Benjamin Disraeli* (6 volumes, 1929).

J. P. Parry, *Democracy and Religion: Gladstone and the Liberal Party, 1867–1875* (Cambridge, 1986).

Richard Shannon, *Gladstone and the Bulgarian Agitation, 1876* (Brighton, 1975).

Richard Shannon, *The Age of Disraeli, 1868–1881: The Rise of Tory Democracy* (1992).

F. B. Smith, *The Making of the Second Reform Bill* (1966).

Paul Smith, *Disraelian Conservatism and Social Reform* (1967).

John Vincent, *Disraeli* (Oxford, 1992).

Michael Winstanley, *Gladstone and the Liberal Party* (1990).

The late Victorian period, 1890–1905

Robert Blake and H. Cecil, eds, *Salisbury: The Man and His Politics* (Basingstoke, 1987).

Neal Blewitt, 'The Franchise in the United Kingdom, 1885–1918', *Past and Present* 32 (1965).

Viscount Chilston, *W. H. Smith* (1965).

P. F. Clarke, *Lancashire and the New Liberalism* (Cambridge, 1971).

Frank Coetzee, *For Party or Country? Nationalism and the Dilemmas of Popular Conservatism in Edwardian England* (New York, 1990).

J. P. Cornford, 'The Transformation of Late Victorian Conservatism', *Victorian Studies* 6 (1963).

Roy Douglas, *Land, People and Politics: A History of the Land Question in the United Kingdom, 1878–1952* (1976).

H. V. Emy, *Liberals, Radicals, and Social Politics, 1892–1914* (Cambridge, 1973).

Matthew Fforde, *Conservatism and Collectivism, 1886–1914* (Edinburgh, 1990).

R. F. Foster, *Lord Randolph Churchill: A Political Life* (Oxford, 1981).

Peter Fraser, *Joseph Chamberlain: Radicalism and Empire* (1966).

A. L. Friedberg, *The Weary Titan* (Princeton, 1988).

E. H. H. Green, *The Crisis of Conservatism: The Politics, Economics and Ideology of the British Conservative Party, 1880–1914* (1995).

D. A. Hamer, *John Morley: Intellectual in Politics* (Oxford, 1968).

Brian Harrison, *Separate Spheres: The Opposition to Women's Suffrage in Britain* (1978).

Robert Rhodes James, *Lord Randolph Churchill* (1960).

Robert Rhodes James, *Rosebery* (1963).

Richard Jay, *Joseph Chamberlain: A Political Study* (Oxford, 1981).

Andrew Jones, *The Politics of Reform, 1884* (Cambridge, 1972).

Peter Marsh, *The Discipline of Popular Government: Lord Salisbury's Domestic Statecraft, 1881–1902* (1978).

Peter Marsh, *Joseph Chamberlain: Entrepreneur in Politics* (New Haven, 1994).

H. C. G. Matthew, *The Liberal Imperialists* (Oxford, 1973).

A. N. McBriar, *Fabian Socialism and English Politics, 1884–1918* (Cambridge, 1962).

R. Moore, *The Emergence of the Labour Party* (1978).

Michael Pinto-Duchinsky, ed., *The Political Thought of Lord Salisbury* (1968).

David Powell, *The Edwardian Crisis: Britain, 1901–1914* (1996).

Martin Pugh, *The Tories and the People, 1880–1935* (Oxford, 1985).

John Ramsden, *The Age of Balfour and Baldwin, 1902–1940* (1978).

G. R. Searle, *The Liberal Party: Triumph and Disintegration, 1886–1929* (1992).
Bernard Semmel, *Imperialism and Social Reform* (New York, 1960).
Thomas J. Spinner, *George Joachim Goschen* (1973).
Peter Stansky, *Ambitions and Strategies: The Struggle for the Leadership of the Liberal Party in the 1890s* (Oxford, 1964).
Alan Sykes, *Tariff Reform in British Politics* (Oxford, 1979).
John Wilson, *C. B.: A Life of Sir Henry Campbell-Bannerman* (1973).
Kenneth Young, *Arthur James Balfour* (1963).

Scotland, Wales, Ireland

D. G. Boyce, *The Irish Question and British Politics, 1868–1986* (1988).
Patrick Buckland, *Irish Unionism 2: Ulster Unionism and the Origins of Northern Ireland, 1886–1922* (Dublin, 1973).
Linda Colley, *Britons, 1707–1837: Forging the Nation* (1992).
R. F. Foster, *Modern Ireland, 1600–1972* (1988).
J. L. Hammond, *Gladstone and the Irish Nation* (1964).
T. W. Heyck, *The Dimensions of British Radicalism: The Case of Ireland, 1874–1895* (Urbana, Ill. 1974).
K. T. Hoppen, *Elections, Politics, and Society in Ireland, 1832–1885* (Oxford, 1984).
I. G. C. Hutchison, *A Political History of Scotland, 1832–1924* (Edinburgh, 1986).
James Loughlin, *Gladstone, Home Rule, and the Ulster Question, 1882–1893* (Dublin, 1986).
F. S. L. Lyons, *Ireland Since the Famine* (1973).
Kenneth O. Morgan, *Wales in British Politics, 1868–1922* (Cardiff, 1980).
Kenneth O. Morgan, *Wales 1880–1980* (Oxford, 1982).
Alan O'Day, *Parnell and the First Home Rule Episode, 1884–7* (Dublin, 1986).
E. D. Steele, *Irish Land and British Politics* (Cambridge, 1974).

Social history

Demography and urbanisation

Michael Anderson, *Approaches to the History of the Western Family, 1500–1914* (1980).
W. A. Armstrong, ed., *Population, Economy and Society in Pre-Industrial England* (Oxford, 1972).
J. A. Banks, *Prosperity and Parenthood* (1954).

Theo Barker and Michael Drake, eds, *Population and Society in Britain, 1850–1980* (1982).

M. J. Daunton, *Progress and Poverty: An Economic and Social History of Britain, 1700–1850* (Oxford, 1995).

M. W. Flinn, *British Population Growth, 1700–1850* (1970).

D. V. Glass and D. E. C. Eversley, eds, *Population in History: Essays in Historical Demography* (1965).

Peter Laslett, *The World We Have Lost* (1965; revised edition 1983).

Ranald C. Michie, 'London and the Process of Economic Growth Since 1750', *The London Journal* 22 (1997).

Rosalind Mitchison, *British Population Change Since 1860* (1977).

P. Scholliers, ed., *Real Wages in Nineteenth and Twentieth Century Europe: Historical and Comparative Perspectives* (Oxford, 1989).

Jeffrey G. Williamson, *Did British Capitalism Breed Inequality?* (Cambridge, 1985).

Jeffrey G. Williamson, *Coping With City Growth During the British Industrial Revolution* (Cambridge, 1990).

Robert Woods, *The Population of Britain in the Nineteenth Century* (1986).

E. A. Wrigley, 'A Simple Model of London's Importance in Changing English Society and Economy, 1650–1750', *Past and Present* 37 (1967).

E. A. Wrigley, and R. S. Schofield, *The Population History of England, 1541–1871: A Reconstruction* (1981).

Religion

David Bebbington, *The Nonconformist Conscience: Chapel and Politics, 1879–1914* (1982).

David Bebbington, *Evangelicalism in Modern Britain: A History from the 1730s to the 1980s* (1989).

Susan Budd, *Varieties of Unbelief: Atheists and Agnostics in English Society, 1850–1960* (1977).

Edward Carpenter, *Cantuar: The Archbishops in Their Office* (1971).

Owen Chadwick, *The Victorian Church, 1829–1901* (2 volumes, 1966 and 1970).

G. Kitson Clark, *Churchmen and the Condition of England 1832–85* (1973).

William Gibson, *Church, State, and Society, 1760–1850* (1994).

A. D. Gilbert, *Religion and Society in Industrial England: Church, Chapel, and Social Change, 1740–1914* (1976).

Sheridan Gilley and W. J. Sheils, eds, *A History of Religion in Britain: Practice and Belief From Pre-Roman Times to the Present* (Oxford, 1994).

Alan Haig, *The Victorian Clergy* (1984).

David Hempton, *Religion and Political Culture in Britain and Ireland: From the Glorious Revolution to the Decline of Empire* (Cambridge, 1996).

Boyd Hilton, *The Age of Atonement: The Influence of Evangelicalism on Social and Economic Thought, 1795–1865* (Oxford, 1988).

Kenneth Hylson-Smith, *Evangelicals in the Church of England 1734–1984* (Edinburgh, 1988).

Kenneth Hylson-Smith, *The Churches in England From Elizabeth I to Elizabeth II: Volume II, 1689–1833* (1997).

G. I. T. Machin, *Politics and the Churches in Great Britain, 1832–68* (Oxford, 1977).

G. I. T. Machin, *Politics and the Churches in Great Britain, 1869–1921* (Oxford, 1987).

Hugh McLeod, *Religion and Society in England, 1850–1914* (1996).

Edward Norman, *Church and Society in England 1770–1970* (1973).

Edward Norman, *The English Catholic Church in the Nineteenth Century* (1984).

Gerald Parsons, ed., *Religion in Victorian Britain* (4 volumes, Manchester, 1988).

W. D. Rubinstein, *A History of the Jews in the English-Speaking World: Great Britain* (1996).

R. A. Soloway, *Prelates and People: Ecclesiastical Social Thought in England, 1783–1852* (1969).

Michael R. Watts, *The Dissenters: Volume II, The Expansion of Evangelical Nonconformity* (Oxford, 1995).

Social class and elites

Perry Anderson, *English Questions* (1992).

R. D. Anderson, *Universities and Elites in Britain Since 1800* (1992).

T. W. Bamford, *The Rise of the Public Schools* (1967).

J. V. Beckett, *The Aristocracy in England, 1660–1914* (Oxford, 1986).

John Benson, *The Working Class in Britain, 1850–1939* (1989).

K. D. Brown, *The English Labour Movement, 1700–1951* (1982).

P. J. Cain and A. G. Hopkins, *British Imperialism* (2 volumes, 1993).

David Cannadine, *The Decline and Fall of the British Aristocracy* (New Haven, 1990).

Youssef Cassis, *City Bankers, 1890–1914* (Cambridge, 1994).

Geoffrey Crossick, ed., *The Lower Middle Classes in Britain, 1870–1914* (1977).

Leora Davidoff and Christine Hall, *Family Fortunes: Men and Women of the English Middle Class, 1780–1850* (1987).

John Foster, *Class Struggle and the Industrial Revolution: Early Industrial Capitalism in Three English Towns* (1974).

Anthony Howe, *The Cotton Masters, 1830–1860* (1984).

Patrick Joyce, *Work, Society, and Politics* (1980).

David Kynaston, *The City of London* (2 volumes, 1992 and 1995).

A. E. Musson, *British Trade Unions, 1800–1875* (1972).

Harold Perkin, *The Origins of Modern English Society, 1780–1880* (1969).

Harold Perkin, *The Rise of Professional Society: England Since 1880* (1989).

R. E. Pumphrey, 'The Introduction of Industrialists into the British Peerage', *American Historical Review 65* (1959–60).

Alistair J. Reid, *Social Classes and Social Relations in Britain, 1850–1914* (1992).

W. D. Rubinstein, *Men of Property: The Very Wealthy in Britain Since the Industrial Revolution* (1981).

W. D. Rubinstein, *Elites and the Wealthy in Modern British History* (Brighton, 1987).

John Scott, *The Upper Classes: Property and Privilege in Britain* (1982).

E. P. Thompson, *The Making of the English Working Class* (1963).

F. M. L. Thompson, *English Landed Society in the Nineteenth Century* (1963).

Richard Trainor, *Black Country Elites* (Oxford, 1993).

Martin J. Wiener, *English Culture and the Decline of the Industrial Spirit, 1850–1980* (1981).

D. G. Wright, *Popular Radicalism: The Working-Class Experience, 1780–1880* (1988).

Gender and identities

Lucy Bland, *Banishing the Beast: English Feminism and Sexual Morality, 1885–1914* (1995).

Barbara Caine, *English Feminism, 1780–1980* (Oxford, 1997).

Carl Chinn, *Poverty Amidst Prosperity: The Urban Poor in England, 1834–1914* (Manchester, 1995).

Carol Dyhouse, *No Distinction of Sex? Women in British Universities, 1870–1939* (1995).

Cate Haste, *Rules of Desire: Sex in Britain, World War I to the Present* (1992).

Jean Hawkes, *The London Journal of Flora Tristan, 1842 or The Aristocracy and the Working Class of England* (1982).

Patricia Hollis, *Women in Public: The English Women's Movement, 1850–1900* (1979).

Richard Holt, *Sport and the British: A Modern History* (1989).

Ronald Hyman, *Empire and Sexuality: The British Experience* (Manchester, 1990).

Pat Jalland, *Women, Marriage, and Politics, 1860–1914* (Oxford, 1986).

Pat Jalland, *Death in the Victorian Family* (Oxford, 1996).

Angela John, ed., *Unequal Opportunities: Women's Employment in England, 1800–1918* (1986).

Penny Kane, *Victorian Families in Fact and Fiction* (1995).

Jane Lewis, *Women in England 1870–1950: Sexual Divisions and Social Change* (Hemel Hempstead, 1984).

Linda Mahood, *Policing Gender, Class, and Family: Britain, 1850–1945* (1995).

Steven Marcus, *The Other Victorians: A Study of Sexuality and Pornography in Mid-Nineteenth Century England* (New York, 1964).

Michael Mason, *The Making of Victorian Sexual Attitudes* (Oxford, 1994).

Michael Mason, *The Making of Victorian Sexuality* (Oxford, 1995).

Paul McHugh, *Prostitution and Victorian Social Reform* (Brighton, 1977).

Ronald Pearsall, *The Worm in the Bud: The World of Victorian Sexuality* (1969).

Roy Porter, and Lesley Hall, *The Facts of Life: The Creation of Sexual Knowledge in Britain, 1650–1950* (New Haven, 1995).

Frank K. Prochaska, *Women and Philanthropy in Nineteenth Century England* (Oxford, 1980).

Jane Purvis, *Hard Lessons: The Lives and Education of Working-Class Women in Nineteenth-Century England* (1989).

Jane Purvis, ed., *Women's History: Britain, 1850–1945, An Introduction* (1995).

Elizabeth Roberts, *Women's Work, 1840–1940* (1988).

Sheila Rowbotham, *Hidden From History: 300 Years of Women's Oppression and the Fight Against It* (London, 1973).

David Rubinstein, *Before the Suffragettes: Women's Emancipation in the 1890s* (Brighton, 1988).

Martha Vicinus, *Independent Women: Work and Community For Single Women, 1850–1920* (Chicago, 1985).

Judith R. Walkowitz, *Prostitution and Victorian Society: Women, Class, and the State* (Cambridge, 1980).

Judith R. Walkowitz, *City of Dreadful Delight: Narratives of Sexual Danger in Late Victorian London* (1994).

Index